POLIS AND IMPERIUM
Studies in Honour of
Edward Togo Salmon

POLIS AND IMPERIUM
Studies in Honour of
Edward Togo Salmon

Messecar Professor of History
McMaster University
Hamilton, Canada

Edited by J. A. S. Evans

HAKKERT / TORONTO / 1974

Book design by Anya Humphrey

International Standard Book Number 0-88866-526-1
Library of Congress Catalogue Card Number 74-80411

Printed and bound in The United States of America

A. M. Hakkert Ltd., 554 Spadina Crescent, Toronto, Canada M5S 2J9

Table of Contents

POLIS AND IMPERIUM
Studies in Honour of
Edward Togo Salmon

Edward Togo Salmon

Bibliography of Books and Articles
Written by Edward Togo Salmon

I. Books and Monographs

A History of the Roman World from 30 B.C. to A.D. 138.
London, Methuen; New York, Barnes and Noble. First
ed. 1944; second ed. 1950; third ed. 1957; fourth ed.
1959; fifth repr. 1963; fifth ed. 1966; sixth ed. 1968;
hard cover and paperback.

Samnium and the Samnites, Cambridge University Press;
Toronto, Macmillan, 1967.

Roman Colonization under the Republic. London, Thames
and Hudson, 1969.

The Nemesis of Imperialism. Whidden Lecture, McMaster
University, Oxford University Press, 1974.

The End of Roman Imperialism. Australian Humanities
Research Council: Paper 4, 1961.

Augustus the Patrician. Todd Memorial Lecture No. 8,
Sydney, 1972.

The Romanization of Italy. London, Thames and Hudson
(forthcoming).

II. Articles

"The Pax Caudina," *JRS* 19, 1928, pp. 12-18.
"Historical Elements in the Story of Coriolanus," *CQ* 24,
1930, pp. 96-101.

"Pindar, *Nemea* 3.50-52," *Classical Weekly* 24, 1931, p. 143.

"Historians of the Early Republic," *Proceedings of the Ontario Educational Assoc.*, 70, 1931, pp. 188-97.

"Subordinate Clauses in Oratio Obliqua," *CR* 45, 1931, p. 173.

"The Battle of Ausculum," *PBSR* 12, 1933, pp. 45-51.

"The Last Latin Colony," *CQ* 27, 1933, pp. 30-35.

"Concerning *Hic* and *Ille*," *Classical Weekly* 28, 1934, p. 64.

"Rome's Wars: 284–282 B.C.," *CP* 30, 1935, pp. 22-31.

"Ovid, *Tristia* 1.11.15," *CR* 49, 1935, p. 128.

"Catiline, Crassus and Caesar," *AJP* 56, 1935, pp. 302-16.

"Roman Colonization, 218-133 B.C.," *JRS* 26, 1936, pp. 47-67.

"Trajan's Conquest of Dacia," *TAPA* 67, 1936, pp. 83-105.

"Concerning the *Second Sallustian Suasoria*," *CP* 32, 1937, pp. 72-74.

"The Latin Colonies at Vitellia and Circeii," *CQ* 31, 1937, pp. 111-13.

"Roumanian and Latin," *CJ* 33, 1937, pp. 69-78.

"The Fourth Eclogue Once More," *CP* 34, 1939, pp. 66-68.

"Caesar and the Consulship for 49 B.C.," *CJ* 34, 1939, pp. 388-95.

"A Note on Capua," *Classical Weekly* 37, 1943, p. 62.

"The Belated Spartan Occupation of Decelea," *Classical Review* 60, 1946, pp. 13-14.

"The Political Views of Horace," *Phoenix* 1 (2), 1946, pp. 7-14.

"Horace's Ninth Satire," *Studies in Honour of Gilbert Norwood*, ed. M. E. White, Toronto, 1952, pp. 184-93.

"Rome and the Latins," *Phoenix* 7, 1953, pp. 93-104 and 123-35.

"Roman Exapnsion and Roman Colonization in Italy," *Phoenix* 9, 1955, pp. 63-75. Reprinted in Bobbs-Merrill series in European History, 1967.

"The Evolution of Augustus' Principate," *Historia* 5, 1956, pp. 456-78. Reprinted in Bobbs-Merrill series in European History, 1967.

"The Resumption of Hostilities after the Caudine Forks,"

TAPA 87, 1956, pp. 98-108.

"Hannibal's March on Rome," *Phoenix* 11, 1957, pp. 153-63.

"Sulmo Mihi Patria Est," *Ovidiana; recherches sur Ovide, publiée à l'occasion du bimillénaire de la naissance du poète*, ed. N. I. Herescu, Paris, 1958, pp. 3-20.

"Samnite and Roman Cumae," *Vergilian Digest* 4, 1958, pp. 10-15.

"The Roman Army and the Disintegration of the Roman Empire," *Transactions of The Royal Society of Canada*, 52, 1958, pp. 43-57.

"Notes on the Social War," *TAPA* 89, 1958, pp. 159-84.

"The Strategy of the Second Punic War," *G&R* 7, 1960, pp. 131-42. Reprinted in Bobbs-Merrill series in European History, 1967.

"The Beginnings of the Latin World," *Canadian Historical Association. Historical Papers*, 1960, pp. 33-43.

"Obituary of C. W. New," *Proceedings of The Royal Society of Canada*, 55, 1961, pp. 145-46.

"State Support in Matters Cultural: The Canadian Experiment," *Meanjin Quarterly*, Melbourne, Australia, 21, 1962, pp. 488-91.

"The Cause of the Social War," *Phoenix* 16, 1962, pp. 107-19 (reprinted, abridged, *Iris* 47, 1961, pp. 5-6).

"The Coloniae Maritimae," *Athenaeum* n.s. 41, 1963, pp. 1-38.

"Colonial Foundations during the Second Samnite War," *CP* 58, 1963, pp. 235-38.

"The Roman Army and the Roman Empire," *The Fall of Rome. Can it be Explained?* ed. M. Chambers, New York, 1963, pp. 37-46.

"Sulla redux," *Athenaeum* 42, 1964, pp. 60-79.

"Obituary of G. P. Gilmour," *Proceedings of The Royal Society of Canada* 58, 1964, pp. 97-102.

"Obituary of C. H. Stearn," *Phoenix* 21, 1967, p. 236.

"The Resurgence of the Roman Patricians ca. 100 B.C.," *REL* 47 bis, 1969, pp. 321-39.

"Discussion on the Period 130-80 B.C.," *Dialoghi di Archeologia* 4/5, 1970, pp. 365 f., 371 f., 417 f.

Foreword to M. Jacobelli, *La Valle di Comino*. Rome, Bulzoni, 1971.

"M. Tullius Cicero, Romanus an Italicus anceps," *Cicero and Virgil: Studies in Honour of Harold Hunt*, ed. J. R. C. Martyn. Amsterdam, Hakkert, 1972.

In addition, from 1949 through 1972, Professor Salmon wrote hundreds of articles on historical Italian topography, Roman Republican history, Roman Republican personalities, and the history of the Roman Empire in *Oxford Classical Dictionary*, first ed. 1949, and second enlarged ed. 1970; *Collier's Encyclopedia*; *Grolier Encyclopedia Universal*; *Encyclopaedia Britannica* (1974 ed., vol. 15, pp. 1106-19), s.v., "Rome, History of: Period 4: The Early Roman Empire (31 B.C. to A.D. 192)"; *Princeton Dictionary of Classical Archaeology* (forthcoming).

III. Reviews

T. Ashby, *The Roman Campagna in Classical Times*, JRS 18, 1928, pp. 112-13.

C. Buscaroli, *Virgilio: Il libro di Didone*, CP 30, 1935, pp. 184-85.

H. H. Scullard, *A History of the Roman World from 753 to 146 B.C.*, JRS 26, 1936, pp. 95-97.

H. E. Butler, *The Fourth Book of Virgil's Aeneid*, CP 32, 1937, p. 293.

C. Daicoviciu, *La Transylvanie dans l'antiquité*, CW 32, 1939, p. 129.

T. Simenschy, *Gramatica Limbii Latine; Povestea lui Nola; Toxaris*, CW 33, 1939, p. 67.

A. Dobo, *Inscriptiones extra fines Pannoniae Daciaeque repertae*, CW 35, 1941, pp. 27-28.

L. A. A. Jouai, *De Magistraat Ausonius*, AJP 62, 1941, pp. 248-49.

M. Ghyka, *A Documented Chronology of Roumanian History from Pre-historic Times to the Present Day*, CW 37, 1943, p. 67.

A. Alföldi, *Zu den Schicksalen Siebenbürgens im Altertum*, *CW* 40, 1946, pp. 55-56.

M. Grant, *From Imperium to Auctoritas*, *Phoenix* 2, 1948, pp. 56-60.

M. L. W. Laistner, *The Greater Roman Historians*, *Phoenix* 4, 1950, pp. 73-74.

J. A. Maurer, *A Commentary on C. Suetonii Tranquilli vita C. Caligulae Caesaris, chapters 1-21*, *CP* 46, 1951, pp. 195-96.

M. Grant, *Roman Anniversary Issues*, *Phoenix* 5, 1951, pp. 119-21.

M. A. Levi, *Nerone e i suoi tempi*, *CP* 47, 1952, pp. 55-56.

W. F. Jashemski, *The Origins and History of the Proconsular and the Propraetorian Imperium to 27 B.C.*, *CP* 47, 1952, pp. 269-70.

H. R. W. Smith, *Problems Historical and Numismatic in the Reign of Augustus*, *Phoenix* 8, 1954, p. 119.

M. Rambaud, *L'art de la déformation historique dans les Commentaires de César*, *A JP* 76, 1955, pp. 201-3.

J. A. Crook, *Consilium Principis*, *Phoenix* 11, 1957, pp. 39-42.

G. W. L. Nicholson, *The Canadians in Italy, 1943-1945*, *Canadian Historical Review* 38, 1957, p. 64.

D. Daube, *Forms of Roman Legislation*, *Phoenix* 11, 1957, pp. 134-35.

A. J. and V. Toynbee, *The War and the Neutrals*, *International Journal* 12, 1957, pp. 316-17.

F. W. Walbank, *A Historical Commentary on Polybius*, Volume I. *A JP* 79, 1958, pp. 191-94.

J. Zennari, *I vercelli dei Celti nella Valle Padana e l'invasione cimbrica della Venezia*, *Phoenix* 12, 1958, pp. 85-87.

T. Kleberg, *Hôtels, Restaurants et Cabarets dans l'antiquité romaine*, *JRS* 48, 1958, pp. 198-99.

A. J. Zurcher, *The Struggle to Unite Europe, 1940-1958*, *International Journal* 14, 1959, pp. 63-64.

E. B. Haas, *The Uniting of Europe*, *International Journal* 14, 1959, p. 64.

R. Syme, *Colonial Elites*, *Waterloo Review* 2, 1959, p. 77.

H. H. Schmitt, *Rom und Rhodos, Geschichte ihrer politischen Beziehungen seit der ersten Berührung bis zum Aufgehen des Inselstaates im römischen Weltreich*, *AJP* 80, 1959, pp. 217-18.

R. E. Smith, *Service in the Post-Marian Roman Army*, Phoenix 13, 1959, pp. 215-16.

E. Badian, *Foreign Clientelae (264-70 B.C.)*, *Phoenix* 14, 1960, pp. 50-55.

R. M. Haywood, *The Myth of Rome's Fall*, *AJP* 81, 1960, pp. 215-17.

M. Hammond, *Antonine Monarchy*, *AHR* 66, 1960, pp. 113-14.

F. E. Adcock, *Roman Political Ideas and Practice*, *JRS* 50, 1960, pp. 248-49.

D. R. Dudley, *The Civilization of Rome*, *CW* 54, 1960, p. 190.

N. G. L. Hammond, *A History of Greece to 322 B.C.*, *Canadian Historical Review* 42, 1961, pp. 76-77.

G. C. Susini, *Ricerche sulla Battaglia del Trasimeno*, *Phoenix* 15, 1961, pp. 239-42.

L. R. Taylor, *The Voting Districts of the Roman Republic*, *AJP* 83, 1962, pp. 191-93.

D. C. Earl, *The Political Thought of Sallust*, *CP* 58, 1963, pp. 124-25.

T. F. Carney, *A Biography of Caius Marius*, *Phoenix* 17, 1963, pp. 231-32.

J. Suolahti, *The Roman Censors*, *Phoenix* 18, 1964, pp. 336-37.

F. Cassola, *I gruppi politici romani nel III secolo a.C.*, *AJP* 86, 1965, pp. 197-201.

E. Badian, *Studies in Greek and Roman History*, *Phoenix* 19, 1965, pp. 94-95.

P. Romanelli et al., *Studi Annibalici; Atti del Convegno svoltosi a Cortona, Tuoro sul Trasimeno, Perugia, Ottobre, 1961*, *Phoenix* 20, 1966, pp. 183-84.

F. Millar, *A Study of Cassius Dio*, *Phoenix* 20, 1966, p. 186.

G. C. Susini, *Il Lapicida Romano*, *Phoenix* 21, 1967, pp. 153-54.

A. J. Toynbee, *Hannibal's Legacy*, Vols. I and II, *AJP* 88, 1967, pp. 461-65.

R. MacMullen, *Enemies of the Roman Order*, *AHR* 72, 1967, pp. 939-40.

H. H. Scullard, *The Etruscan Cities and Rome*, *Phoenix* 22, 1968, pp. 83-85.

D. C. Earl, *The Moral and Political Tradition of Rome*, *CW* 61, 1968, p. 252.

L. R. Taylor, *Roman Voting Assemblies*, *AJP* 89, 1968, pp. 237-38.

M. A. Wes, *Das Ende des Kaisertums im Westen des römischen Reichs*, *Phoenix* 22, 1968, pp. 279-80.

R. M. Haywood, *Ancient Rome*, *AJP* 90, 1969, pp. 376-77.

W. Dahlheim, *Struktur und Entwicklung des römischen Völkerrechts im 3. und 2. Jahrhundert v. Chr.*, *CW* 74, 1970, pp. 27-28.

M. Sordi, *Roma e I Sanniti nel IV secolo a.C.*, *Phoenix* 24, 1970, pp. 278-79.

M. Sordi, *Roma e I Sanniti nel IV secolo a.C.*, *Gnomon* 43, 1970, pp. 184-87.

R. Vulpe, I. Barnea, *Romanii la Dunărea de Jos*, *AHR* 76, 1971, p. 1139.

L. Rossi, *Trajan's Column and the Dacian Wars*, *Vergilius* 17, 1971, p. 52.

J. H. D'Arms, *Romans on the Bay of Naples*, *Journal of Interdisciplinary History* 2, 1971, pp. 321-24.

J. Heurgon, *Capone Préromaine* (1970 reissue), *Gnomon* 45, 1973, pp. 628-30.

McMaster University   *A. G. McKay*

Some Notes on Trade and Traders
in Roman Spain[1]

The western provinces of the Roman Empire have left us a considerably smaller body of evidence than the eastern ones regarding the names and activities of producers and traders, and the goods they produced or transferred; but I believe, with Wilson,[2] that in the west, where an abundance of raw materials was available, the traders and business men, Greeks, Carthaginians and Italians, many of them South Italians of Greek or Oscan origin, were as active and as numerous as those that Hatzfeld found in the East. But the evidence consists of rather general literary passages, a few inscriptions, and materials that were long without honor, stamps on metal ingots or broken pottery, and inscriptions painted or scratched on these, and the shapes that revealed their origin. In this paper I shall turn particularly to Roman Spain, to only a few of the materials produced, and the almost anonymous mass of men who handled them.

From the prehistoric period Spain had ranked as an El Dorado because of the richness and variety of the metals, precious and otherwise, from its mines, and soon also for its fisheries and the fertility of the great river valleys. The *Laudes Hispaniae*, however much they need to be tempered by consideration of periods and regions, make this abundantly clear.[3] Strabo remarks, "Up to the present moment, in fact, neither gold nor silver, nor yet copper, or iron, has been found anywhere in the world in the natural state either in such quantity, or of such good quality," and similarly, the elder Pliny: "Nearly the whole of Spain is covered with mines of lead, iron, copper, silver, and gold. Nearer Spain has *lapis specularis* and Baetica has cinnabar too."[4] Although Strabo depended in part on Polybius and Posidonius, the fame of Spain was contemporary, while Pliny could add to his authorities his own experience in Spain in the Flavian period. Indeed, the desire to exploit the gold and iron mines of the north may have been an important factor in Augustus' decision to complete the conquest.

Our interest, however, is less in the fact of almost continous production, but rather in how these products were controlled and brought to their ultimate users. The silver and lead mines near Carthago Nova were exploited by the Carthaginians, and must have been taken over by Scipio and included in the regime organized by Cato in 195 (in fact, there still were Roman public properties there in 63 B.C.). They, and other mines, probably contributed to the large amounts of silver given to the treasury as booty by earlier governors of Spain. Whether they were worked directly or through intermediaries, it seems significant that the listings of booty cease about 179,[5] and in Polybius' time the mines were leased to equestrian companies. As many as 40,000 men, most of them probably slaves, were put into workings there that yielded 25,000 denarii a day for the treasury.[6] On this basis Blazquez suggests a capital investment of 180 million HS (120 million for labor and 60 million for equipment), an annual return of 36,500,000 HS and a net of 12,750,000.[7] We may suppose that other mines such as those of Castulo gave similar returns. The famous passage of Diodorus (5.34-38) shows how a multitude of Italians ($\pi\lambda\tilde{\eta}\theta$o$\varsigma$ Ἰταλῶν) gained wealth while imposing incredible hardships on the miners. In Pliny's time the mines were still in production when the primacy was passing to those in the southwest and the north, and were only a part of many that had maintained the coinage of the cities, provided materials for the masses of jewelry, decorations and plate found in

Spanish treasures, and fed the needs of commerce.[8] In 49, Varro could exact 20,000 pounds of silver from private persons,[9] intimidated Roman citizens of Farther Spain, and we have notices also of huge silver plates on a monumental scale, such as the 500 pound dish, possessed by Claudius' slave, Rotundus, dispensator of Nearer Spain.[10] Even primitive communities in the north had the practice of cutting pieces of beaten silver and using them as money.[11] In Strabo's time the silver mines had passed into private possession (3.2.10), and in the early Empire they passed, like the rest, into imperial possession. Similarly, the gold mines, important in most parts of the peninsula and particularly so in the north and west where Pliny (*NH* 33.78) reports a yield of 20,000 pounds a year, became state property. Large sums were needed to build the aqueducts, reservoirs and other equipment traceable in quite inaccessible places today, and considerable resources were mobilized,[12] but there is little to tell how the product became available. Perhaps, as at Vipasca, the mines were leased on shares to concessionaires. If the treasury had first claim, gold workers and jewellers did acquire gold for their work.

We are better informed about the cinnabar mines of Sisapo, which according to Vitruvius (7.9.4) superseded those of Asia Minor. *Socii* mentioned by Cicero, appear in a Capuan inscription of the early Empire.[13] "It is exported," Pliny remarks, "from hardly anywhere else in Spain, the most famous mine for the revenues of the Roman people being that of Sisapo in Baetica (Almaden), no item being more carefully safeguarded. It is not allowed to smelt and refine the ore on the spot, but as much as 2000 pounds per annum is delivered to Rome in the crude state under seal, and is purified in Rome. The price in selling it is fixed by law at 70 HS the pound to prevent it from going beyond limit. But it is adulterated in many ways, a source of *praeda* to the *societas*."[14] Here is a government concession to a mining company, limited production, and the product, though not guarded in quality as one might wish, was marketed at a fixed price.

As to copper, in which Spain excelled, our literary sources refer mainly to eastern and southern Spain, which were exploited chiefly during the republic and the early Empire. Strabo mentions yields up to one quarter of the ore, and Pliny gives the primacy to *aes Marianum, quod et Cordubense dicitur*, which almost certainly derived its name from Sextus Marius, whose mines of gold and copper (if the text of Tacitus is rightly supplemented) Tiberius confiscated when he put Marius to death.[15] Honors for a Flavian freedman *procurator montis Mariani* given by the *confectores aeris* at Hispalis attest the working of the product, and a *procurator massae Marian(ae)* at Ostia its export there.[16] Some at least went to the mint, as Pliny implies. The primacy, however, passed to the mines of copper, silver and lead in the southwestern part of the peninsula. Here the famous laws of Vipasca (Aljustrel)[17] give us evidence of the systematic grant of contracts to small concessionaires as individuals or consortia with half the yield, as in Cyprus, going to the fiscus, while both mining operations and provision of amenities for the community were administered by the procurator. Literary sources are replaced by the vast heaps of scoriae, estimated at 18 to 20 million tons at Riotinto, 6 to 7 million at Tharsis, and up to 5 million in southern Portugal. Surprisingly, since the chief modern product is copper, about three-quarters come from silver and lead mines, and one-quarter from copper. The date is confirmed by finds of coins, local and imperial, lamps and pottery, local and imported (mostly from Italy), and other objects very largely dating from the second century. In fact, a graph of the discoveries of coins about Huelva, an outlet for these mines, shows a steep rise in the second century, a catastrophic decline in the third, and another, smaller, rise in the fourth.[18] The laws of Vipasca appear to date from the period of greatest exploitation.

Passing over iron, of which there was a rich production, especially in Cantabria,[19] we may turn to evidence about lead[20] which yields more information about distribution in trade. Lead ores, found usually in connection with silver, were massively exploited under the Republic and the early Empire. Besides the important mines near Carthago Nova, Pliny[21] mentions others in Baetica which may have been developed a little later, such as the Samariense which was leased for 200,000 d. a year, was idle a while, and was later leased for 255,000, and the Antonianum, leased first for 100,000, and later for 400,000 (if we can depend on Pliny's text). Similarly, the ancient mine of Diogenes[22] (galena, antimony, silver) in the Alcudia valley on the northern slope of the Sierra Morena had a first phase of exploitation by a settled population which ended about the mid-first century B.C. Iberian and Roman coins of south and north, amphorae and Campanian pottery show the import of goods from outside. The second phase, dating from the first and early second centuries, is marked by imperial ceramics, Arretine, Gallo-Roman and Hispanic. These and other such workings along the mountains required some form of administration. Lead seals at El Centenillo, halfway between Diogenes and Castulo, bearing the letters S.C., suggest, since coins of Castulo are numerous, that a *societas* based on Castulo, despite the distance, had charge there during the Republic.[23] Such *societates* are well-known near Carthago Nova.[24] It is striking that there was a great decrease in activity of these mines in the late first century, when the easily worked lead mines of Britain[25] became available, and some revival in the late Empire when supplies from Britain failed.

Reverting to the late Republic and the lead from mines near Cartagena, we may note two recent articles that supplement our knowledge of the distribution of lead ingots. The first is a study of lead ingots retrieved from the harbor of Cartagena and the sea off Cape Palos and now in the Museum of Cartagena and the Naval Museum of Madrid, and the other a study of the distribution of ingots, some of them part of this same group, stamped with the names of L. Planius and other members of his family.[26] The stamps on these ingots yield the names of several originally Italian families, mostly Campanian and Oscan, who exploited the mines of argentiferous lead in the late second and early first centuries B.C.[27] It seems certain that these were among the private persons who according to Strabo (3.2.10) gained possession of the mines. Several of these family names appear on coins and inscriptions of Carthago Nova,[28] and one, C. Aquinus Mela, probably a descendant of M. Aquinus, and C. Aquinus M.f., is named on coins as II vir Quinquennalis. The lettering, the spelling and the semi-cylindrical shape of the ingots combine to show that they date from the late second century B.C. and a limit is set in the early imperial period by ingots of a new form, the frustum of a pyramid, stamped IMP. CAES on the side.[29] The stamps of L. Planius and L. Planius L.f. Russinus reveal a large trading area. Besides their place of origin, they are found at Cianciano in Sicily, in Picenum, and six of them, along with others of Spanish type, were in the famous wreck off the Tunisian coast at Mahdia which was loaded with sculpture from Athens.[30] Hence it was thought that this was lead from Laurium. However, a recent analysis of the lead isotopic composition of one of the ingots clearly showed that it could not have come from Laurium. The other evidence strongly points to Spain and yields a date contemporary with the major exploitation of the eastern Spanish mines.[31] How they came to be in that wreck is still an unanswered question.

Strabo and Pliny attest the quantity and quality of the pickled fish from the Spanish fisheries and its allied industry, the manufacture of garum,[32] for which Spain had long been famous. Archaeological discoveries document their claims. Besides the Moroccan coast where the shoals of tunny come first, remains of establishments have been found all about the Spanish coast from southern Portugal to Cartagena and Ibiza. Some have been excavated recently, particularly the ones at Bolonia (Baelo) near Gibraltar, and at Setúbal in Portugal.[33] The products were exported to Rome, Gaul and Africa, Carthago Nova being important for both fisheries and exports. It is named on an amphora at Pompeii. A *negotians salsarius*, an officer of the *corpus negotiantium Malacitanorum*, appears in Rome, while Aelian tells a tall story of an octopus that broke open the amphorae of a cargo of salt fish belonging to Spanish merchants at Puteoli. Amphorae with remains of fish still identifiable have been found in wrecks at Anthéon and Île de Levant off the coast of Provence.[34]

Recent investigations by Ponsich and Tarradell also have shown how widespread was the manufacture of *garum* or *liquamen* in connection with the salting of fish. Literary evidence indicates an origin in the East and production also in the West from early Greek and Punic times. The archaeological evidence documents an active manufacture and distribution in Mauretania and Spain from Augustus to the late Empire as the pottery shows, though divided into two periods by the crisis of the third century, with smaller and more local industries thereafter. Smaller vats of water-proofed concrete in the salting establishments reveal where garum was prepared by the autolysis of fish entrails and other scraps packed in salt to prevent putrefaction, and ripened in the sun or often concentrated over a furnace.[35] In demand as a condiment and a medicine, it appears frequently in the recipes of Apicius, and was widely in popular use in different grades at different prices. The grades probably depended on the variety of fish.[36] At Cartagena it was the *scomber* which produced the grade most highly prized.[37] The wide extent of the trade is easily attested: characteristic amphorae at Pompeii inscribed *G(ari) flos* or *liq(uamen) gari, f(los) scombr(i)*, others at Rome, and some in Provence although *muria* was manufactured there, at Rauraca where *garum Hispanum* and *muria Hispana* are mentioned, in the Rhine-land and along the *Limes* where supplies for the armies included *garum*.[38]

What then of *garum sociorum*? "Today," writes Pliny, "the most popular garum is made from the *scomber* in the fisheries of Carthago Spartaria — it is called *garum sociorum* — 1,000 sesterces being exchanged for about 12 congii" (about 12 pints). Somewhat biliously, Seneca too mentions *illud sociorum garum, pretiosam malorum piscium saniem*. Amphorae inscribed *garum sociorum* are found at Pompeii and elsewhere, and it remained popular into the late Empire. It was a prized gift to that gourmet Ausonius.[39] Piganiol and Étienne[40] both associate the term *sociorum*, not with the general word "allies" found in most translations, but with the analogy of the mining companies, and Étienne, noting that salt, a necessary ingredient, was regularly produced from the public lease of salt pans and salt mines to concessionaires, holds that this too was the status of the company at Carthago Nova. Their discovery was that the *scomber* made the best garum. Even so, lapse of time may have made the term merely a designation for an excellent grade. What Ausonius received came as a present from his former pupil in Barcino, and followed one of olive oil.

Of the many agricultural products for which Baetica was famous, the most renowned was olive oil. It was known perhaps in the time of Cicero, giving additional point to his joke (*Arch.* 26) about the "oily" accent of the poets of Corduba. According to Strabo (3.2.6) it was exported "not only in large quantities but of the best quality," and Pliny (*NH* 15.8) ranks it second only to that of Venafrum and equal to that of Istria. Well known and widely distributed Baetican stamps have been found at Pompeii and Stabiae,[41] thus dating before A.D. 79 (oil to Pompeii, coal to Newcastle, as Tchernia remarks) a sign that even then Spanish oil was beginning to inundate the western markets. But most of the evidence refers to the second and third centuries and consists of broken pieces of amphorae of the type (Dressel 20) used for oil in southern Spain. These form a major part of Monte Testaccio in Rome and are found distributed over almost all the west from North Africa to Britain.[42]

Besides the find spots and some inscriptions on stone, the evidence for the production and distribution of olive oil derives from inscriptions, stamped, painted or scratched on the amphorae themselves. There are several kinds: first, a potter's stamp impressed before firing, usually on the handle; second, painted inscriptions on the body of the amphora, consisting regularly (when sherds are found whole or corresponding pieces can be joined) of a number on one line, a name on a second, and another, larger, number on a third. These are shown to be the weight of the amphora when empty, the name of the shipper, and the weight when full.

Third, a series of more cryptic marks, names and numbers, ending with a consular date, is painted near the second and often aslant near the handle. One example is reconstructed and interpreted as follows: "Received; Hispalis; value 20 sesterces; weight 215 lbs.; estate of Capito; export tax, 2 asses; date A.D. 179," but at times the name of the checking clerk seems included.[43] Each of these items, when frequently repeated, contributes to our knowledge of the trade in Baetican oil.

First, the stamps. Surface surveys by Bonsor and Clark-Maxwell of the valleys of the Baetis and its tributary, the Singilis, from Cordova to Seville, between 1889 and 1901 brought to light at their places of origin large numbers of the amphora stamps which are found in Monte Testaccio in Rome and other localities in the west and discovered many of the numerous kilns where they had been fired. It appears that the kilns and their potters served producing estates, now of one proprietor, perhaps of several adjacent proprietors, the pottery owners often being proprietors themselves, and were conveniently placed near points of lading for river traffic to the seaports.[44] Three examples out of hundreds must suffice.[45]

The stamp M.I.M. (M. Iulius Mopsus?) was at home, along with many others and kilns nearby, at Arva (Peña de la Sal) where there was either a customs station or a river port, or both, according to the interpretation given to P.ARVA on widely distributed stamps also found there. The stamp M.I.M appears on oil amphorae at Pompeii, several in Rome, and according to Tchernia's list turns up at thirty-one locations in Mauretania, Gallia Narbonensis and Gallia Comata, Raetia, Germany and Britain. These stamps appear to date from the mid-first century into the second, with greatest activity from A.D. 60-80.[46] The stamps of C. Antonius Quietus, also found in Pompeii, are frequent in Rome, elsewhere in central Italy and in all the western provinces. Callender's count of ninety examples from forty-eight sites has recently been extended in central France by Thévenot to Autun and the region of Bourges. Callender estimates a chronological range from A.D. 70 to 120.[47] The stamps of L. Iunius Melissus and his family

are the most frequent and the most widely distributed of all.
On three, perhaps four, sites the name is associated with F
(figlino?) Scimniano, which a painted inscription from Monte
Testaccio dates to A.D. 161. Bonsor found one of their
establishments along with Scimnianus and eight others at Las
Delicias on the right bank of the Singilis near Astigi (Ecija), a
customs and distribution center from which many amphorae
came to Rome. This firm apparently ranged from Hispalis
past Astigi purchasing amphorae and their contents and was
active in the second and third centuries.[48]

In the painted inscriptions interest centers on the names
in the second line on the body of the amphora. These were
proved to be shippers who purchased the oil in Spain and
brought it to Rome where amphorae of indubitably Spanish
origin were found bearing the names of shipmen prominent
in Narbo, Sextus Fadius Secundus and P. Olitius
Apollonius.[49] But these Gallic shippers had no monopoly. It
may suffice to mention D. D. Caeciliorum found at Pompeii,
on Monte Testaccio, and elsewhere in Rome. The D. D.
Caecilii Hospitalis et Materni on amphorae of A.D. 154 were
later members of the firm, and were honored at Astigi with a
statue and inscription. Here is an example of a family of
traders in Baetica who continued almost a century.[50]

Other examples are collected in T. Frank (1) (n. 43), but
one may note the additional evidence, recently cited by
Thévenot from Autun and Saint Satur near Bourges, for the
Aelii Optati, oil dealers of the mid-second century, whose
stamps have been found at El Judio, their place of origin
between Axati and Arva, who are represented by an epitaph
at Celti, and by stamps and painted inscriptions on amphorae
in Rome.[51]

The inscriptions on the amphorae name many places in
southern Spain. Some reveal places of origin, and names of
estates and their owners appear. Many, particularly the
painted ones, mark customs offices at distribution points
where the oil was bought, valued for customs dues, and
carried off for transfer or sale by private shippers. The
centers most frequently named are Corduba, Astigi and
Hispalis. Ilipa, at the upper limit of navigation by sea going

vessels, also had a customs station.[52]

Tenney Frank's view that this production of oil during the late Republic and the first two centuries of the Empire came from private estates, was checked only for the collection of customs dues (these dues were still farmed until late in the second century), and was bought and shipped in vessels owned by private entrepreneurs has won the assent of Callender and De Laet.[53] What then were the relations with the central government in view of the emperor's need to control supplies adequate for the city of Rome and the armies? So far as we know, the extra supplies, apart from the tributes in kind, were bought from private producers, and the carriage, both of tributes and extras, was in the hands of the *navicularii*. Encouragement consisted in giving them rewards and privileges.[54] An example in the reign of Marcus Aurelius suggests that imperial control was on the way, though exercised for emergency purposes and at a relatively low level. Sextus Iulius Possessor, an *eques* from Mactar in Africa Proconsularis, is found between A.D. 161 and 169 at Hispalis as an assistant to the *praefectus annonae* to survey the stocks of Spanish and African oil, to arrange for the transport of *solamina* (according to Pflaum, supplementary provisions other than grain) and to see to the payment of the cost of transport (*vectura*) to the *navicularii*. Pflaum suggests that his appointment came at a moment of special concern for supplies in Rome, perhaps the time of the triumphs after the Parthian war.[55]

Shortly after the victory of Septimius Severus over Clodius Albinus and the huge confiscations which ensued, large numbers of amphorae begin to bear the inscription FISCI RATIONIS PATRIMONII PROVINCIAE BAETICAE or PROVINCIAE TARRACONENSIS.[56] Two factors may be noted: first, the extensive confiscations of land, much of it in Spain, from the estates of his opponents; and second, his institution of free distribution of oil in Rome. The oil from Spain was most available in quantity and quality, as Africa was primarily a grain province and its oil, though considerable in amount, was considered inferior. Moreover, Leptis, a major producer, received *ius Italicum*, and freedom from taxes.[57] The inscriptions quoted above, painted on the amphorae at the point where the names of the shippers once appeared, suggest, as Frank and Étienne have said, that Septimius organized under the *patrimonium* a public shipping fleet intended to meet the new demand (as Commodus had once done in an emergency for grain from Alexandria).[58] These inscriptions dominate the later finds in Monte Testaccio, the marks certifying customs payments disappear, since these were now largely treasury goods from imperial lands incorporated in the *ratio privata*.[59] Stamps with such formulae as AUGGGNNN also show that many of the amphorae were owned by the emperors, and that along with the estates they often took over *figlinae* up and down the valley from Corduba to Ilipa.[60] The importance of the product remained as great as ever but a large share of the production and distribution came into imperial hands and a larger proportion was probably diverted to Rome.

This is far from exhausting the list of Spanish products in trade: olives, wine, grain, honey, pitch, kermes and esparto grass for cables may be added. Nor is it more than a beginning to mention the Campanian Ware, the sigillata from Italy and Gaul that is found along with the native product, or the lamps, mostly imported from Italy and Africa, that aid in dating the workings of the mines.[61] But the concentration here on such products as lead, salt fish and garum, olive oil and the amphorae that carried it, may give some impression of their importance, their mode of distribution and the changing system that governed it.

University of North Carolina   *T. Robert S. Broughton*

NOTES

1. For previous discussions of the trade of Roman Spain, see L. C. West, *Imperial Roman Spain. The Objects of Trade*, Oxford, 1929; J. J. Van Nostrand, in Tenney Frank, *Economic Survey of Ancient Rome* (hereafter *ESAR*) III, Baltimore, 1937; the relevant chapters in M. P. Charlesworth, *Trade Routes and Commerce in the Roman Empire*, Cambridge, 1924, and R. Menéndez Pidal, *Historia de España*, II *España Romana*, esp. pp. 317-62, by M. Torres, 2nd ed. Madrid, 1955. C. H. V. Sutherland, *The Romans in Spain*, London, 1939, remains a useful book. See also A. García y Bellido, "Las 'mercatores,' 'negotiatores' y 'publicani' como vehiculos de romanización en la España preimperial," *Hispania* 26, 1966, pp. 497-512.

2. A. S. N. Wilson, *Emigration in the Republican Age of Rome*, Manchester, 1966, pp. 3 ff.; cf. J. Hatzfeld, *Les trafiquants Italiens dans l'Orient Hellénique*, Paris, 1919.

3. Note Scipio's booty from Carthago Nova in 209, Liv. 26.47. On the *Laudes Hispaniae*, besides Strabo and Pliny, note Mela 2.86; Iustin 44; Isidor Sev. 14.28-20; C. Fernandez Chicarro, *Laudes Hispaniae*, Madrid, 1948, (not available to me).

4. Strabo 3.2.8, cf. 3.3.5, 3.2.9: not Hades but Pluto lives underground in Spain. Pliny *NH* 3.30; cf. 4.112, on the north, where Pliny reports a yield of 20,000 lbs of gold a year (*NH* 33.73, cf. 76 ff.).

5. Cic. *Leg. Agr.* 1.5; 2.51. See T. Frank, *ESAR* I, pp. 127 ff., pp. 154 ff.

6. Polybius 34.9, in Strabo 3.2.10.

7. J. Blazquez Martínez, "Exportación y importación en Hispania a final de la republica Romana y durante el gobierno de Augusto, y sus consecuencias," *Anuario de Historia Economica y Social*, 1, 1958, pp. 37-84, esp. pp. 45-46.

8. E.g. Baebelo near Castulo, Plin. *NH* 33.96. On coinage of cities, see in general A. Vives y Escudero, *La moneda hispánica* I-IV, Madrid, 1924; Sutherland (n. 1), pp. 100 ff. and Plates. On Spanish treasures, see Blazquez (n. 7), pp. 46 ff.

9. Caes. *BC* 2.18.

10. Plin. *NH* 33.145.

11. Strabo 3.3.7.

12. See O. Davies, *Roman Mines in Europe*, Oxford, 1935, pp. 99-105; T. Rickard, "The Mining of Roman Spain," *JRS* 18, 1928, pp.

129-43; and now especially, P. R. Lewis and G. D. B. Jones, "Roman Gold Mining in North-West Spain," *JRS* 60, 1970, pp. 169-85, on Las Medullas and other mines.

13. Cic. *Phil.* 2.48; *CIL* X.3964 = *ILS* 1875: Epaphra I socioru I Sisapo[n]es[ium] I vilico.

14. Plin. *NH* 33.118-19; cf. Iustin. 44.1.6; Pausan. 8.39.6.

15. Strabo 3.2.3; Plin. *NH* 34.4; Tac. *Ann.* 6.19. See H. Sandars, "The Linares Bas-Relief and Roman Mining Operations in Baetica," *Archaeologia* 59, 1904, p. 315. On production of copper, see Blazquez (n. 7), p. 48. O. Davies (n. 12), p. 114, n. 5, dates the *mons Marianus* to the fourth century B.C. on the basis of *IG* II², 1675, but this refers to copper from Marion in Cyprus.

16. *CIL* II.1179 = *ILS* 1591; *CIL* XIV, 52 = *ILS* 1592, 3527.

17. See Alvaro d'Ors Perez-Peix, *Epigrafía Jurídica de la España Romana*, Madrid, 1953, pp. 71-134, and the translation of the laws in *ESAR* III, pp. 167-71.

18. O. Davies (n. 12), pp. 114 ff. and maps III a-e; Jose M. Luzón Nogue and Antonio Blanco Freijeiro, "Mineros antiquos españoles," *A Esp Arq* 39, 1966, pp. 73-88; and on the lamps, Luzón, "Lucernas mineras de Riotinto," *A Esp Arq* 40, 1967, pp. 138-50. The graph is on p. 76 fig. 1, in Luzón and Freijeiro (above). A copper ingot from these mines, weighing 95 1/2 Kgm., was found in a wreck (Planier 4) near Marseilles (F. Benoît, *Gallia* 20, 1962, pp. 154 ff.), inscribed as follows: M(etallum) P(ublicum) nomi(ne) I Primuli (et) Silonis I CCXCVII I Pro(curator) Col(oniae) Ono I bensis, or, perhaps, in line 1, Imp(eratoris). Here are the names of the contractors, the weight, the procurator in charge of the mining region near Onoba, one of the ports for Riotinto mines. On Colonia, see A. d'Ors (n. 17) p. 117 and *Studia et Documenta Historia et Iuris* 32, 1966, p. 485 f.

19. Plin. *NH* 34.149, a mountain of iron; cf. Davies (n. 12) p. 98 f.

20. Used widely for pipes, tubing, vessels and in sheets, Plin. *NH* 34.164, or mingled with copper to make the dark Capuan bronzes (*NH* 34.95).

21. Plin. *NH* 34.165; cf. Davies (n. 12), p. 115.

22. Cl. Domergue, "La mine antique de Diogénes (Province de Ciudad Real)," *Mélanges de la Casa de Velazquez* 3, 1967, pp. 28-81; cf. Davies (n. 12), p. 115; Rickard (n. 12), pp. 139-43; Van Nostrand (n. 1), pp. 139-40, pp. 158-61.

23. Domergue (n. 22), pp. 28-81, on these phases, the coins and other material, and El Centenillo. A bronze bucket there also bears the letters S.C.

24. SOCIET. // MONT. ARGENT. // ILVCRO at Coto Fortuna near Lorca, *A Epig* 1907, no. 135; SOCIET. ARGENT. // FOD. MONT. ILVCRO // GALENA, on an ingot found in the Tiber, *ILS* 8708, dated to early first century by Domergue (n. 22), pp. 62-63. See H. de Villefosse, *RA* 9, 1907, pp. 63-68, and H. Jecquier, pp. 58-62. On galena, see Plin. *NH* 33.95; 34.159 and 173.

25. On lead mines in Britain, see Plin. *NH* 34.164; Davies (n. 12), pp. 148 ff.; I. A. Richmond, *Roman Britain*, Pelican A.315, pp. 149-54; S. Frere, *Britannia*, Cambridge, Mass., 1967, pp. 283-86.

26. Cl. Domergue, *A Esp Arq.* 39, 1966, pp. 41-72 (hereafter Domergue 1), and "Les Planii et leur activité industrielle en Espagne sous la République," *Mélanges de la Casa de Velazquez* 1, 1965, pp. 9-25 (Domergue 2).

27. Names such as M. Aquinus, C. Aquinus M.f., P. Nona P.f. Nuc(erinus?), C. Messius, C. Fiduus and S. Lucretius (both on the same stamp), L. Planius Russinus, and M. Rai(us) Rufus. For other names, see Domergue 1 (n. 26) and *ESAR* III, 140. M. P. Roscius M.f. Maic. appears to be one of the earlier ones (*ILS* 8706). The combination of S. and T. Lucretius appears on an ingot of Klingenthal (now in the Basel Museum, *CIL* XIII, 10026, 26 = *ILS* 8707). See also *Eph. Epig.* 8.254, 1 and 2; 9.428.3.

28. E.g., on Lucretius, freedwomen, *CIL* II, 3477, 3478; on C. Aquinus Mela, see Vives y Escudero (n. 8), 4.34, no. 5 and Pl. 30, no. 5. Planius may be an earlier member of the family of M. Planius Heres of Cales, in Spain in 45 B.C. when Cicero pleaded his case with Dolabella (*Fam.* 9.13).

29. Domergue 1 (n. 26).

30. Domergue 2 (n. 26). See also M. Ponsich, "Le trafic de plomb dans le détroit de Gibraltar," *Mélanges Piganiol*, Paris, 1966, pp. 1271-79, almost entirely on mines on the African side.

31. Domergue 2 (n. 26). On the date of the sculpture, see W. Fuchs, *Der Schiffsfund von Mahdia*, Tübingen, 1963, pp. 11 f. Perhaps they remained in the ship from an earlier voyage. Similar ingots from a wreck on the strait of Bonifacio have the same chemical composition as those from Cartagena, F. Benoît, *Gallia* 16, 1958, p. 539, no. 16. I wish to thank C. C. Patterson and D. M. Settle, California Institute of Technology, for their kindness in permitting me to include information about the analysis of lead isotopic composition, a personal communication from an unpublished manuscript.

32. Strabo 3.2.6; 3.4.2; 3.4.6; cf. 3.2.7; Plin. *NH* 9.49 on *vivaria*; 9.92 on works at Carteia, attacked by a giant cuttle fish with a head as

big as a ninety gallon cask!; and references below. On the tunny on coins of cities of southern Spain from early times, see R. Étienne, "A propos du 'garum sociorum,'" *Latomus* 29, 1970, pp. 302 f.

33. M. Ponsich and M. Tarradell, *Garum et industries antiques de salaison dans la Mediterranée*, Paris, 1965, Bibl. Hautes Études Hisp. 36. On Baelo, see also notices of excavations in *Mélanges de la Casa de Velazquez* 3, 1967, pp. 507-10; 4, 1969, pp. 393-99, and, earlier, P. Paris, *et al. Fouilles de Belo* 1917-21, Bordeaux-Paris, 1923-26. Cl. Domergue (cited by R. Étienne, (n. 32), pp. 301 f.) connects the first Roman establishment there with the salt fish industry. On Setúbal see P. MacKendrick, *The Iberian Stones Speak*, New York, 1969, p. 210, fig. 8.24.

34. Strabo 3.4.6. The guild of *piscatores et propolae* at Carthago Nova (*CIL* II, 5929 = *ILS* 3624) probably consisted of local fishermen. On their organization at Parium, see *Hellenica* 9, pp. 81 ff., 10, pp. 272 ff. CARTH at Pompeii, *CIL* IV.2648c. Malaca, *CIL* VI.9677 = *ILS* 7278. Puteoli, Aelian *Hist. Anim.* 13.6. Wrecks: F. Benoît, "Relations commerciales entre le monde ibéropunique et la Midi de la Gaule archaique à l'époque romaine," *REA* 58, 1961, pp. 328-29, cf. *Gallia* 14, 1956, pp. 23-24, no. 10, and 16, 1958, pp. 5-39, no. 1. On a wreck, found near Punta de las Entinas, carrying a cargo of salt fish from Baetica to Rome or Gaul and shown by amphora forms to date from the late first century, see R. P. Guasch, *Pyrenae* 4, 1968, pp. 135-41 (not available to me, reported in *APh* 1969, p. 441).

35. Ponsich and Tarradell (n. 33) especially pp. 85 ff. See *RE* s.v. on the history, manufacture and uses of garum. P. Grimal and Th. Monod, "Sur la veritable nature du 'garum,'" *REA* 54, 1952, pp. 27-38, describe the process more fully, find that it is still prepared in Turkey as *garon*, and that a national condiment in Vietnam, *Nuoc-nam*, made from certain fishes and brine, resembles it. The latter has invaded the region of Fort Bragg in North Carolina where it is used as a sauce "whose legendary odor Mr. Tri (the restauranteur) cuts with lemon, sugar, and garlic powder." (*N.Y. Times*, Oct. 7, 1971).

36. In Diocletian's Edict on Maximum Prices there are two grades, one of 16 d. the sextarius and one of 12, not high prices as honey was 20 d.

37. Plin. *NH* 31.92, *exquisiti liquoris genus*. The island of Scombraria lay near Carthago Nova, Strabo 3.4.6.

38. Pompeii, *CIL* IV, p. 173 ff., p. 635 ff. and esp. 5659; *ILS* 8599 a-d. Rome, *CIL* XV, 2, p. 657, nos. 4529-4806; cf. Hor. *Sat.* 2.8.46. Augst, see A. Grenier *Manuel d'archéologie gallo-romaine* 2.2,

pp. 616-20 on these and other amphorae. On the inferior product of Antipolis, Martial 13.103; Plin. *NH* 31.94-95. On shapes and sizes of amphorae, see Dressel, *CIL* XV, p. 491 ff. and Pl. 2; Grenier (above) pp. 633 ff.; M. H. Callender, *Roman Amphorae with an Index of Stamps*, Oxford, 1965, pp. 4 ff. and p. 281.

39. Plin. *NH* 31.94 (LCL); Seneca, *Ep. Mor.* 95.25; Manilius 5.672; Martial 13.102; Pompeii, see n. 38; Ausonius *Epist.* 25 (18.25 in LCL). See R. Étienne, "Ausone et l'Espagne," *Mélanges Carcopino*, Paris, 1966, pp. 319-32, esp. pp. 322-25 on sea food and pp. 324-25 on *garum sociorum*.

40. A. Piganiol in the foreword to Ponsich and Tarradell (n. 33), and Étienne (n. 32). On fishing rights as a *portorium* see S. J. DeLaet, *Portorium*, Bruges, 1949, p. 335, n. 1, and on Tyras and Istria, pp. 206-9. Publicans in *salinae*, see Cic. *Leg. Man.* 16 in Asia, and in Sardinia, *CIL* I²2226 = *ILLRP* 41.

41. A. Tchernia, "Amphores et marques d'amphores de Bétique à Pompeii et à Stabies," *MEFR* 76, 1964, pp. 419-49.

42. It is agreed that while wine amphorae appear, the type that predominates in the center and upper parts of Monte Testaccio (the lower, earlier levels have not been investigated) is Dressel 20, which was regularly the container for Spanish oil. See Dressel, *CIL* XV, p. 491 f., pp. 560 ff., on Monte Testaccio and other find spots in Rome; Callender (n. 38), p. 4 ff. See J. Aubin, "Der Rheinhandel in römischer Zeit," *BJ* 130, 1925, pp. 1-27; E. Thévenot, "L'importation des produits espagnoles chez les Éduens et les Lingons," *RAE* I, 1950, pp. 65-75; (2) Les amphores du Musée de Sens," *RAE* 4, 1953, pp. 50-60; (3) "Les amphores de provenance espagnoles importées dans le department du Cher," *RACE* 3, 1964, pp. 203-16; A. Grenier, *ESAR* III, pp. 580 ff.

43. See Grenier (n. 38), pp. 608-43; T. Frank, (1) "Notes on Roman Commerce," *JRS* 27, 1937, pp. 72-79; (2) "On the Export Tax of Spanish Harbors," *AJPh* 57, 1936, pp. 89-90; and *CIL* XV, 4366, on which this reconstruction is based. For an example of the painted inscription on the body of the amphora, see *CIL* XV, 3699b: XXCVIIIS I C. Antoni Bal(bi) I CCX . . .

44. W. G. Clark-Maxwell, "The Roman Towns in the Valley of the Baetis between Cordova and Seville," *Archaeological Journal* 56, 1899, pp. 345-305; G. E. Bonsor, "Los pueblos antiquos del Guadalquivir y las alfererías romanas," *Rev. de archivos, bibliotecas y museos* 5, 1901, pp. 827-57 (the finds of both these are included in *Eph. Epig.* 9, pp. 158 ff., no. 424); G. E. Bonsor, (2) *The Archaeological Expedition*

along the Guadalquivir 1889-1901 (Hispanic Notes and Monographs, New York, 1931); J. F. La Peña, "Alfares y marcas de anforas del valle medio del Guadalquivir," *A Esp Arq*. 40, 1967, pp. 129-37.

45. Callender (n. 38) lists 1812 stamps with notes on forms, origins and distribution. He seems not to have made full use of Bonsor (2) (n. 44).

46. Callender (n. 38) pp. 73-74, no. 130; Bonsor (2) (n.44) 32; Tchernia (n. 41) pp. 422-24 and P.I.I. Note that in northern Italy, Noricum and Pannonia Istrian production held its own. See A. Degrassi, *Scritti vari di antichità* II, Rome, 1962, pp. 951-72.

47. Callender (n. 38) pp. 90-91, no. 243 and p. 321, fig. 25; Thévenot (3) (n. 42) pp. 206-10, no. 2; Tchernia (n. 41) lists 49 find spots, including Canana (Alcolea del Rio), Arva (Peña de la Sal), and Alcotrista near Astigi (Ecija) pp. 425-29, and Pl.II.

48. Callender (n. 38) pp. 158-60, no. 879. On F. (or FIG) Scimniano, see *RE* s.v. Scimnianus; Bonsor (2) (n. 44) pp. 14-15; Callender (n. 38) pp. 243-44, no. 1579.

49. H. de Villefosse, "Deux armateurs narbonais," *Mém. Soc. Nat. Antiquaires de France* 64, 1914, 153-80, corrected to prove Spanish, not Gallic, origin of the products by Grenier (note 38) pp. 612-18 and T. Frank (1) (n. 43) pp. 72-79.

50. *CIL* IV, 9480; 15.3773-81; Tchernia (n. 41) pp. 434-39; *CIL* II, 1474 (at Astigi).

51. E. Thévenot, "Una familia de negociantes en aceite establecida en la Baetica en el siglo II: Los Aelii Optati," *A Esp Arq*. 25, 1952, pp. 225-31; cf. Bonsor (2) (n. 44) p. 28 and Pl. XXXV; *CIL* XV, 2685 a-d, 3060 a-d, and 3694 (painted); *CIL* XIII, 10002, 83 (Autun); *CIL* II, 2329 (Celti); Thévenot (3) (n. 42) pp. 213-15, no. 6. Note also a knight, *diffusor olearius ex Baetica* in Rome, *CIL* VI, 29722 = *ILS* 7490; a humbler *mercator olei Hispani ex provincia Baetica*, *CIL* VI, 1933 = *ILS* 7499; a knight, patron at Rome of the *negotiatores olearii ex Baetica*, *CIL* VI, 1625b = *ILS* 1340; and a *diffusor olearius* at Astigi, *CIL* II, 1481.

52. See DeLaet (n. 40) pp. 286-91, who lists Illiberis (Granada), Ilipa (Alcalá del Rio), Astigi (Ecija), Corduba (Cordova), Hispalis (Seville), Malaca (Malaga) and Portus (Gades), which Callender however interprets as store house (n. 38; p. 214, no. 1370). A *dispensator portus Ilipensis*, *CIL* II, 1085 = *ILS* 1406.

53. T. Frank (1) (n. 43) pp. 72-79; *ESAR* V, pp. 82-83; Callender (n. 38) pp. 49-50; DeLaet (n. 40) p. 292; cf. also R. Étienne, "Les amphores du Testaccio au IIIe siècle," *MEFR* 61, 1949, pp. 151-81.

54. E.g. those granted by Claudius, T. Frank, *ESAR* V, pp. 268 ff.
55. *CIL* II, 1180 = *ILS* 1408; H. G. Pflaum, *Les carrières procuratoriennes sous la haut empire romain*, Paris, 1960-61, pp. 504-7, no. 185. Note that he became *proc. Augg. ad ripam Baetis* and was honored by the *scapharii Hispalenses* for *innocentia* and *iustitia*.
56. *CIL* XV, 4097-4141; T. Frank, *ESAR* V, pp. 81-82, and SHA *V. Sev.* 18.3, on distribution of oil; cf. 23.2, and *V. Alex.* 22.2.
57. Iuv. *Sat.* 5.86-91; Plin. *NH* 15.8, and cf. on oil of Leptis, R. Haywood, *CPh* 36, 1941, pp. 246-56. On the *ius Italicum* of Leptis, *Dig.* 50.15.8.11, and see Étienne (n. 53) p. 162.
58. T. Frank, *ESAR* V, pp. 81-82, and especially R. Étienne (n. 53) pp. 151-81. On Commodus see SHA, *V. Comm.* 17.7.
59. The statements of Frank and Étienne may be modified slightly by Nesselhauf's recent discovery that the *ratio privata* existed under Antoninus Pius, "Patrimonium und res privata der römischen Kaisers," *Hist. Aug. Colloquium, Antiquitas* 4, Bonn, 1963, pp. 75-94. It was probably expanded and reorganized under Severus (A. R. Birley, *Septimius Severus. A Biography*, London, 1970, p. 200).
60. *CIL* 15.2558 ff.; Callender (n. 38) pp. 267 ff., imperial stamps, p. 267, nos. 1808 ff., and see his discussion at p. 77 f. on no. 160.
61. Strabo 3.2.6; Plin. *NH* 14.41 and 71; Martial 13.118, cf. 7.5.3; Van Nostrand, *ESAR* III, pp. 177-78. On objects of trade see West (n. 1) *passim*; imports from Italy, Frank *ESAR* V, p. 292; Blazquez (n. 7) pp. 78-79. The stamps listed by A. Balil, "Marcas de ceramistas en lucernas romanas halladas en España," *A Esp Arq.* 41, 1968, pp. 158-78, are almost entirely Italian or African in origin. On the *sigillata* ware see H. Comfort, "Roman Ceramics in Spain: An Exploratory Visit," *A Esp Arq* 34, 1961, pp. 3-17, and works cited there.

Addendum

Since the submission of this article there have come to my attention further studies which contribute to our knowledge of the trade in olive oil from Baetica. Professor E. L. Will's recent collection of amphora stamps of Dressel's type 20 (unpublished), which she has kindly made available to me, contains a considerable number of well known Baetican stamps from Egypt, Corinth, Athens and the Athenian Agora. The recent book by Miguel Beltrán Lloris, *Las anforas romanas en España*, Zaragoza, 1970, though perhaps more concerned with forms and their development, expands and completes Callender's material, but still, like him, takes no account of evidence for export of Baetican oil to the eastern provinces. See now also the important review of Beltrán's book by A. J. Parker, *International Journal of Nautical Archaeology and Underwater Exploration* 1, 1972, pp. 225-29.

Solon's Archonship:
The Epigraphic Evidence

First, I must express my satisfaction for the opportunity of contributing to a volume published in honour of E. T. Salmon, a scholar who over the years has added such distinction to Classical learning in Canada.

My contribution is a small one. It adds nothing that is hitherto unknown; rather, it applies with new emphasis the knowledge gained from a fairly recent discovery in the conviction that an old chronological problem may now be deemed solved once and for all.

The old chronological problem is the date of Solon's archonship at Athens. I take Molly Miller's interesting article entitled "Solon's Coinage" as a place of departure and I quote her conclusions:[1] "The purely historical case for the initiation of the Athenian coinage by Solon may therefore be said to be complete, if not indeed overwhelming. In relation to the evidence of the actual coins however, it cannot be accepted if the date of Solon's archonship was 594/3. The two bodies of evidence can only be brought together if the true date of the archonship was 573/2."

In 1939 B. D. Meritt published[2] a small fragment of inscribed Pentelic marble that had been found in the Agora and that he identified as part of a list of Athenian archons set up in the city about 425 B.C. The identification was accepted almost universally.[3] It became unassailable when D. W.

Bradeen in 1960 brilliantly recognised three small pieces, little more than chips, on the shelves of the Stoa of Attalos as parts of the same list.[4] I give his fragment *a* without restoration:

$$[\, \ldots \,]\backslash[\, \text{---} \,]$$
$$[\, .. \,]\phi\sigma\epsilon\lambda o\overset{.}{[}\, \text{---} \,]$$
$$[\, .. \,]\lambda\epsilon\kappa\lambda\epsilon[\, \text{---} \,]$$
$$[\, \ldots \,]o\mu\beta[\, \text{---} \,]$$

The restoration of line 2 as [Κύ]φσελο[ς], the only known Athenian of this name and father of the elder Miltiades (founder of the Athenian colony in the Thracian Chersonnese),[5] I take as unquestionable. If we consider line 4 in isolation, a number of names fit the surviving letters. Only one, however, is attested for the first half of the sixth century and he, Philombrotos, is said by Plutarch to have held the archonship before Solon.[6]

To assist in placing Kypselos in his generation, I excerpt from the stemma of the Philaids and Kimonids:

```
Kypselos Korinthios
         |
     daughter = Athenian
              |
    Kypselos Athenaios = wife = Stesagoras
                     |         |
          Miltiades I   Kimon Koalemos
                             |
                 ┌───────────┴───────────┐
            Stesagoras          Miltiades II
                                Archon 524/3
```

Bradeen argues persuasively that Miltiades II, archon in 524/3, must have been born no later than 554; that his father, Kimon Koalemos, half-brother of Miltiades I by a common mother, was born no later than 584; that Kypselos, therefore, husband of the mother and father of Miltiades I, was dead by 585 B.C.[7]

We now seek a place for Kypselos and his associates of the four-lined fragment in the list of Athenian archons known before 585.[8] As we move backwards, the first vacancy appears in the 590s.[9] Now the early date for Solon's archonship is 594/3 and we know that Philombrotos was archon in the preceding year. It cannot be coincidence that [φιλ]όμβ[ροτος] fits line 4 of our fragment. He must therefore belong in 595/4, the year before Solon, and [Κύ]φσελο[ς] now falls neatly into the year 597/6. Kypselos, then, was born no later than 627/6 B.C.

I have mentioned (n.7) certain assumptions in the argument. Cumulatively, the reconstruction is utterly convincing. I therefore print the restored fragment as follows:[10]

$$[\dots]\backslash [\text{- - -}]$$
$$[Κύ]φσελο[ς]$$
$$[Τε]λεκλε[\text{- - -}]$$
$$[Φιλ]όμβ[ροτος]$$
$$[Σόλον]$$

As Bradeen has already noted,[11] this small fragment, which was found in 1935 and lay on the shelves for twenty-five years, virtually proves that the list of archons inscribed about 425 began with Kreon (682/1) rather than with Solon; and that the Philaidai were Eupatrids.

In addition, the fragment strongly supports the "high" chronology rather than the "low" for the Korinthian Kypselids.[12]

My own primary aim here concerns the chronology of Solon's career. His archonship must be firmly assigned to 594/3 B.C., without qualms, and the lower date, some twenty years later, must be remorselessly abandoned.

University of British Columbia   *Malcolm F. McGregor*

NOTES

1. *Arethusa* 4, 1971, pp. 25-47, especially pp. 45-46.
2. *Hesperia* 8, 1939, pp. 59-65.
3. J. W. Alexander's doubts, *CJ* 54, 1958-1959, pp. 307-14, were allayed by W. E. Thompson, *CJ* 55, 1959-1960, pp. 217-20, and

C. W. J. Eliot and M. F. McGregor, *Phoenix* 14, 1960, pp. 27-35.

4. *Hesperia* 32, 1963, pp. 187-208, with Plates 58 and 59. It is Bradeen's creative work that I am using, with his approval.

5. Johannes Kirchner, *Prosopographia Attica*, Berlin, 1901-1903, I no. 8951 (Kypselos), II nos. 10209 (Miltiades I) and 10212 (Miltiades II with a stemma).

6. *Solon* 14.2: ἠρέθη δὲ ἄρχων μετὰ Φιλόμβροτον. The context makes it quite clear that Solon and Philombrotos were archons in successive years.

7. The inherent assumptions seem to me secure: (1) that the archonship was not held before the age of 30; (2) that the Athenian male tended not to marry before the age of 30 (note that Miltiades II was the second son of Kimon); (3) that Stesagoras was the second husband, *i.e.*, he married the widow of Kypselos. Bradeen deals effectively with these points, pp. 195-96.

8. The basic study is by T. J. Cadoux, "The Athenian Archons from Kreon to Hypsichides," *JHS* 68, 1948, pp. 70-123: I use his table (pp. 120-23).

9. See Cadoux's notes on these years (*supra*, n.8), pp. 92-99.

10. I remove Bradeen's question-mark from line 4 and I add [Σόλον].

11. Pp. 196-197.

12. See Bradeen, p. 194 n.31.

Vegetius and His Proposed
Reforms of the Army

At the beginnings and again the ends of the various manuscripts of the *Epitoma Rei Militaris* the author's name is given as Flavius Vegetius Renatus and he is referred to as a *vir illustris*, a member of the minor nobility. In some manuscripts he is also given the higher rank of Comes, sometimes specified as *comes sacrum* (*sacrarum*), a treasury official, and sometimes *comes Constantinopolitanus*. Nothing else is known about his life except what a reader can gather from his one known book.[1] He seems to have read widely and not only in the field of military science but there is no evidence in his work that he had ever had any practical experience as a soldier.

The date of his work and the name of the emperor for whom he wrote his book have been much disputed. He refers to the Emperor Gratian by name (1.20) as some time dead. This puts the date of the work after A.D. 383. Similarly in a postscript a certain Flavius Eutropius says he emended the text in the consulship of Valentinian Augustus for the seventh time and of Abienus. That was the year 450. Of the emperors between these two dates, Valentinian II (died 392) Theodosius the Great (died 395) Honorius in the west (died 425) and Arcadius in the east (died 408), Theodosius II in the east (died 450) and Valentinian III in the west (died 455) are all possible candidates for Vegetius's "*imperator invicte.*"

Because some inferior manuscripts actually contain a dedication to Theodosius, because there are flattering references to the triumphs and victories of the unknown emperor and because Vegetius nowhere mentions the disaster of Rome's fall in 410, many scholars have conjectured that the author's patron was the great Theodosius. Since 1876, however, when the German scholar Seeck[2] turned his mind to the problem most commentators have agreed that the emperor referred to was Valentinian III. To begin with, we can discard the eastern emperors since this Latin work was obviously not directed to a ruler of a Greek-speaking world. Moreover certain more concrete considerations are important. The emperor was young (3, 26 *fin.*), had founded many cities (4 *prol.*) and had a fleet on the Danube (4 *fin.*) all of which suit Valentinian but not Theodosius. Furthermore, it would seem somewhat presumptuous to address a military text book to an emperor who had already proved himself a consummate general. We should, of course, pay no attention to the flattery, however ill-deserved, as evidence against even the most disastrously weak ruler; this was all too sickeningly a part of the late Roman literature. (If one could doubt this, a glance at the sycophantic panegyrics of Claudian, directed to the hapless Honorius in the very midst of the terrible disasters afflicting the Roman west in the early years of the fifth century, should be convincing.) In any case, there is at least one veiled allusion to the disasters preceding 425 when Vegetius seems to comfort his patron with the assertion that ultimate victory often follows lost battles (3, 25 *fin.*). One minor piece of evidence has strangely been ignored. Vegetius twice mentioned the Huns, once as having supplied useful cavalry lessons to the Romans (1.20) and once as desiring to emulate the unknown emperor's skill and grace in horsemanship (3.26 *fin.*). Now the Huns were a virtually unknown tribe before the fifth century, there being only some seven or eight references to them before 405, and they were no real threat to the empire until the accession of Attila in 433 or so. References to a very dangerous enemy would be more likely at this later period than under Theodosius I.

Let us assume, then, that Vegetius was writing in the second quarter of the fifth century and probably nearer 435 than 425. What was the military background of this period?

After the disasters of the third century Diocletian and Constantine between them had completely reorganized the government, and particularly the army, to restore internal unity to the empire and give it security from outside threats. We know a great deal about the changes in military organization from various laws collected in the Theodosian Code, from the *Notitia Dignitatum* and particularly from the excellent history of Ammianus Marcellinus. We can gather further details from lesser historians like Zosimus or fragments of historical writings but Ammianus will always remain our best and most valuable source because, apart from everything else, he himself was a soldier under Julian and speaks from first hand experience.

There are many detailed studies of the new organization[3] and the following is of necessity the briefest of summaries. The army was divided into two main types of troops. There were, as always, the garrison troops on the frontiers still organized into legions of infantry and *vexillationes* of cavalry reinforced by auxiliary cohorts and cavalry *alae*. Here we find preserved even down to the sixth century old republican forms and old names of officers.[4] These so-called *limitanei* or *riparienses* were looked down on as an inferior branch of the service and their strength was progressively reduced. Contrary to the common view, however, these troops in the fourth century were not so far immobilized as to become a sort of local militia settled on frontier farms, and when we do begin to hear of this situation the *limitanei* were of very small consequence, the bulk of them having been transformed into elements of the field armies.[5] The command of the frontier forces was exercised by officers of the rank of *comes* or *dux* who were responsible directly to the emperor for the defence of specified geographic regions.

However, reliance on these troops steadily lessened and the new field armies steadily increased in size and strength. The term *comitatenses* originally applied to the troops under the direct command of the emperor, but as time passed and more and more of these troops were recruited, élite corps came into being, grew and gave birth to corps still more carefully selected. Thus we have the *legiones palatini*, the *scholae* and the *candidati* in the order of their formation and in rising order of prestige and of closeness to the actual person of the ruler. At the other end of the scale we find troops transferred from the *limitanei* into the field forces and called *pseudo-comitatenses*. As time passed the distinction between *comitatenses* and *limitanei* became blurred and there was a recurring tendency, especially in the fifth century, to disperse the field armies on local garrison duties, thus contributing to the degeneracy of the later Roman armies. It was not so much that these armies were smaller but that they were used less effectively for defence in the fifth than in the fourth century.

The system of command in the field armies also differed from that in the garrison troops. In accordance with the principal of division of powers whereby civil officials had had all military power taken from them, the field forces also were divided into cavalry and infantry units each commanded by different officers, and also into regional commands. In the East there were five army groups commanded by *magistri peditum* and *magistri equitum*; occasionally the responsibilities of these men were combined in the offices of five *magistri utriusque militiae* (or *magistri militum*) and their subordinate *vicarii*. In the West there was greater centralization of command under one *magister peditum in praesenti* and his subordinate *magister equitum*, and this supreme commander seems to have had the right to use the frontier troops if they were needed. In both areas subordinate commands were given to *duces* or *comites*.

The composition of the armies had also undergone a profound change during the fourth century. The trend was steadily towards the use of men from the less civilized parts of the empire, from Illyricum and Isauria (in Asia Minor), and from beyond the frontiers. Under Constantine especially very many German tribesmen were enrolled in the Roman army, but we also hear of Irish, Scottish, Sarmatian and Armenian soldiers in large numbers.[6] So far had this trend gone even in, or perhaps especially in, the highest ranking of the imperial bodyguards, that it is not unjust to talk of a general barbarization of the armies. These men were mostly volunteers but some were prisoners of war impressed into the army (*dediticii*) and some were settlers on Roman territory who by terms of the peace treaty by which they obtained their land, had to serve a term in the army. In most units the native and foreign elements were mixed and the officers were generally, though by no means always, Romans. Though on the surface this seems to be a dangerous state of affairs at a time when the chief threats were coming from German areas to the north, nevertheless these foreigners seem generally to have been loyal[7] and to have benefitted from their contact with Roman civilization. They would obviously all have to learn at least some rudimentary Latin.

Quite distinct from these troops in the Roman army were the *foederati*, native troops serving with their own native chieftains under various treaty arrangements with the Roman government. These units served on all frontiers and at times even in the field forces. Often they were settled on their own treaty lands and were not subject to Roman military discipline, command or government. The individuals looked only to their own chief for pay which was given to him in block sums by the Romans.

It is not surprising that the loyalty of these *foederati* was far from perfect, as the constant revolts of the native chieftains bear witness. The revolt of the Visigoths which ended in the disastrous battle of Adrianople (378) is only one example of this, and Vegetius (2.2) is not the only man aware both of the dangers of reliance on what he calls the *auxilia* and yet of their importance to imperial defence. It is doubtful whether in the time of Marcellinus in the mid-fourth century "the *foederati* were the most important part of the army";[8] more likely it was only under Theodosius I (378-95) that the barbarians became the dominant element,[9] but this was the culmination of a long-standing trend and penetrated all aspects of the army. This barbarization eventually "affected the size of troop units, formations of attack, war cries, armour with corps of specialists in one type of weapon or another; it affected army slang, army worship."[10]

The importance of these auxiliaries is made evident by the very considerable difficulties that the government apparently had in filling the ranks of its own armies. There are frequent laws regulating recruitment and trying to stop evasion of service, but in spite of them the size of the legions, for instance, steadily declined from the old ideal of six thousand to no more than one thousand.[11] And yet all the evidence shows that the forced drafts were still a severe strain on the rural population, both on its manpower and economic resources. Nevertheless Vegetius begs his emperor to reverse the trend towards the use of *foederati*, explaining in detail why reliance on the *foederati* was dangerous (2.2) and the reasons for the decline in the old legion (2.3). Among the latter he lists neglect on the part of the government, favoritism in the distribution of rewards and the harder discipline in the legions as compared to the auxiliaries. We can doubt whether, even if these abuses had been corrected, any ruler of the fifth century could have cured the overall manpower shortage and resistance to military service which was at the root of Rome's recruitment problems. "If the government felt obliged to rely more and more upon non-Roman elements in order to provide for the defence of the Empire, this can hardly have resulted from any other cause than the increasing lack of available reserves among the Romans themselves."[12]

Apart from the development of the field armies, the increasing Germanization of the Roman armies and the increased reliance being put on the untrustworthy *foederati*, there was one other major change in the military from the middle of the fourth century onward. It is not too strong a word to call the gradual replacement of the heavy armed footsoldier by light armed troops and cavalry a real revolution in military science. To some extent this change may have been due to Persian influence, as, for instance, in the case of the *cataphracti* (heavy armed cavalry) and *clibanarii* (heavy armed infantry) but generally the innovations came from the North. In the writings of Ammianus we can already see the strong Germanic element in the army even in positions of command; a glance through his pages shows us imperial generals with the very un-Roman names of Agila, Merobandes, Vadomar, Fullofaudes, Malarich and so on. But also quite obviously the infantry branch still predominates over the cavalry, as for example, in Julian's victory over the Germans at Strasbourg in 357. By the time of the *Notitia Dignitatum* (about 435) we find, in contrast, that the proportion of cavalry to infantry has risen from about 1:10 to 1:3; we hear of *cunei*, *alae* and *vexillationes* in all branches of both the *comitatenses*, *palatini* and *limitanei*.

Without a doubt Oman is right in making the battle of Adrianople the turning point. This proved to be the first time that a foreign tribe established its right to permanent settlement within the empire by force of arms, and the very magnitude of the Visigothic victory and the death in the battle of a Roman emperor made an impression on contemporary minds so strong that they were forced to an acknowledgement of the weaknesses of their traditional army. The most obvious factor in the battle was the large-scale use by the Germans of heavy cavalry, their own as well as that of their allies, the Huns and Alans. As far back as Caesar's day the Germans had been famous for this branch of service, but for centuries the well-disciplined legions had, with only minor set-backs, successfully held them at bay. But now the legions, all too obviously lax in discipline, untrained and undermanned, were no longer a match for their Germanic adversaries. The Roman infantry no longer had its old superiority over the enemy infantry, and battles came to be decided by the cavalry of which the Germans and their allies had far greater and more experienced forces. The change, of course, could be excused on the ground of the need to pursue the marauders and raiding parties from across the frontier, but it was made easier by the fact of the Roman

army containing a heavy concentration of Germanic tribesmen already in the ranks.

Theodosius learned the lesson of Adrianople, a victory of
heavy Germanic cavalry over infantry, and not only undertook a more thorough Germanization of the armies but a
reorientation of them towards the cavalry. These policies,
combined with the defeats they had suffered, contributed to
the demoralization of the old legionaries.

With the emphasis now placed on the cavalry in place of
the heavy infantry the role of the infantry itself had to be
re-examined. They became, in effect, light-armed skirmishers
to back up the cavalry, almost a complete reversal of the
roles that cavalry and infantry had played for many
centuries. To claim, as Vegetius does (1.20), that under
Gratian the infantry discarded their heavy armour out of
sheer negligence and sloth and lack of discipline is nonsense.
No doubt the change from heavy to light-armed troops was
beginning under Gratian but the bulk of the infantry still
wore armour at the battle of Adrianople.[13] After this date it
is obvious from all military writings, including that of
Vegetius, that the emphasis was on missile weapons, the
primary arm of the light infantry. Vegetius has noticed this
trend but assigned to the change too early a date and
completely false reasons. At a somewhat later date we can
see, for example at the battle of Châlons (451), that the use
of archers, both mounted and on foot, had become widely
adopted in the Roman armies; this was possibly due to the
influence of the Huns or the ancient Persian practice.

This in very brief summary was the situation of the
Roman army in Vegetius' time. It remains, equally briefly, to
summarize the military events immediately preceding the
period in which Vegetius was writing.

After the battle of Adrianople Theodosius for a time
restored order on the frontiers, though he had to allow the
Visigoths to settle permanently within the empire under their
own leaders. Under his weak sons, Honorius in the West and
Arcadius in the East, the Roman army lost almost all
semblance of discipline. For a while the great Germanic

magister militum, Stilicho, successfully held the Danube frontier against inroads of the Vandals and Alans, but even he could not hold the upper Rhine frontier when, in 406, a vast horde of Vandals, Alans, Suevi and Burgundians broke through. The Vandals at first settled in Spain along with the Alans and Suevi but in 429, under Gaiseric, moved on to set up their independent kingdom in North Africa; the Burgundians after some years of warfare settled in the land to which they gave their name. Further north the Rhine frontier was also breached by the Franks, and with he withdrawal of troops from Britain to meet these threats the wild Saxon sea raiders gained a foothold in that province from which, some four decades later, they forced the empire to retire for ever. While Stilicho was trying as well as he was able to meet all these manifold threats he could not at the same time prevent Alaric and the Visigoths from rebelling against imperial authority and devastating the Balkan peninsula. When, however, the Goths attempted to invade Italy, Stilicho held them in check for a time partly by military force and partly by bribery. In 408 Stilicho was accused of treason and put to death, and, with the only general capable of resisting him out of the way, Alaric again attacked Italy. Rome was captured in 410, a catastrophe so shocking to the men of the time that St. Augustine could hold out only the consolation of the City of God.

Now most of Gaul, Spain and North Africa was under the *de facto* control of the various Germanic tribesmen and their kings and the weak western government cowering behind the marshes of Ravenna could do very little about restoring the old frontiers. The best that can be said of the western empire was that the armies under the strong leadership of Aetius lost no more territory to barbarian invaders. In the more populous and richer Eastern Empire no frontiers were breached permanently, though the Danubian lands in particular suffered heavily, if sporadically, from Gothic and Hunish raiders. This then was the rather chaotic picture of events at the period when Vegetius undertook to instruct the government on how the army should be organized, how battles might be won and how cities saved from sack. Never was such advice more needed and seldom can such useless advice have been proferred in a crisis.

In the all too evident collapse of imperial military power two possible solutions could be suggested. The anonymous author of the *De Rebus Bellicis* offers the first solution, improvement in military equipment – the sort of solution that most readily occurs to modern generals as, for instance, Hitler and his V1 and V2 weapons. That some lip service was paid to this solution is indicated by Ammianus' praise of Valentinian I as a *novorum inventor armorum* but it was not a solution widely adopted.[14] The other solution is the return to a proved system; in Vegetius' argument this is a restoration of the type of army with which Rome had conquered and for centuries controlled the Mediterranean world. The great flaw in this kind of solution is that the army could not be treated in isolation from its social context; and social and economic conditions existing in the fifth century bore no similarity to conditions of the late republic or early empire. To illustrate this in detail is far beyond the scope of this paper but as examples of the differences might be mentioned the unwillingness of provincials in the later period to serve in the army, the loss of military qualities in large segments of the population due to the long *pax Romana*, the fragmentation of loyalties which found many corps more devoted to their general and their particular province than to the empire or its ruler, and the recruitment of less civilized populations to the growing exclusion of the old peasant soldiers.

Vegetius makes it quite clear in many places that he is only writing an epitome or summary of previous writings on matters military. He names some but certainly not all of his sources (1.8; 2.3) – the lost military text books of Cato the Elder, Cornelius Celsus and Paternus, the extant work of Frontinus and the constitutions of Augustus, Trajan and Hadrian. He also quotes Sallust twice (1.4; 1.9) and it has been conjectured that he also used Hyginus. It is also certain that there is a close relationship between his work and the small work by a certain Modestus that goes under the name of *De Vocabulis Rei Militaris*.[15] This last work may have been dedicated to the emperor Tacitus, giving a date of about 275, but there is no real internal or external evidence which would prevent it being dated much later. In any case it seems to precede Vegetius' work. It contains some fifty definitions occasionally useful for understanding some points in Vegetius, but what is striking is that almost the whole of it, some 358 lines, is repeated, in most cases repeated almost verbatim, in Vegetius. This work in passages running from a few lines in length to whole paragraphs is the source of much of books 2 and 3, three passages of book 1 but of nothing in book 4. It is to be observed that we should not hold Vegetius wholly to blame for some of his most trite maxims; he can only be accused of uncritically copying them.

There is no reason to suppose that Vegetius has given us a complete list of his sources; indeed he ather vaguely mentions other sources *quae dispersa sunt* — but his sources stated or inferred are of only passing interest here.[16] What matters is that he made almost no use of personal observation; he was a studious worker in the library rather than an acute observer of his own day. Anything derived from times at least two centuries removed from his own was to be preferred to any contemporary usage. For this reason we find him consistently describing the ideal (only to be found in the services of Rome's greatest age) in place of the actual. Oman gives Vegetius very much the benefit of the doubt when he says that the author was not "wholly destitute of any insight into the meaning of the change in military science" which had taken place during the previous century.[17]

The Epitoma covers almost the whole range of military activity and thought, from the selection of recruits (he has to quote Homer (1.5) to indicate that strong men make better soldiers than men who are merely tall!), the process of enlistment, basic training (including swimming), arms drill, the kinds of troops, the lay-out of a camp and marching. All this is in book 1; book 2 describes the differences between legionaries and auxiliaries, the organization of the legion, its officers, non-commissioned officers and specialists, the cavalry (one paragraph only), the importance of records and pay, promotion, military music, machines and tools (though later, 4.22, he admits that the use of missile-throwing machines was declining). In book 3 we have discussions on health services, commissariat problems, prescriptions on how to prevent mutiny, conduct marches in the presence of the enemy and avoid ambushes, how to cross rivers and make and fortify a camp. A long section deals with tactics on the battle field, how to raise morale, and prepare for an engagement and more particularly with the exact orders of battle in various situations (again cavalry being dismissed in a single paragraph, 16), with the use of chariots and elephants (!), and with what one should do if defeated. The book ends with a long collection of military maxims of quite paralyzing triteness. "Valour is superior to numbers"; "A general who has confidence in his cavalry should choose ground suitable for cavalry"; "A general who does not prepare ahead of time, grain and other necessaries, can be conquered without a fight." Of course, maxims have always been a part of the intellectual equipment of the military mind and Vegetius thinks he is only preserving the essence of the military wisdom of the past. But what is striking here is the banality of a great deal of his collected sayings. There is, however, one of his maxims that has the independent backing of a practical soldier of nearly his own period. He says that "the radiance of arms carries the greatest terror to the foe" (2.14). In this he is backed several times by the factual observations of Ammianus.[18]

The fourth book deals with two separate problems,[19] with the defence of cities and with naval affairs. Regarding the former, we have discussions of static defence works (walls, ditches, entrances) and active defence by machines and weapons of various kinds, as well as a long list of what supplies are needed to withstand a siege. Far more attention is given here to defence than to the means by which fortified cities may be captured; for almost every offensive weapon or tactic described, more space is devoted to the means of countering it. This emphasis on defence is surely a reflection of the difficulties Rome was facing in Vegetius' day, the raison d'être of his book, and would tend to corroborate the late date (c.435) herein assigned to it. The chapters on naval affairs, interest in them reflecting the piratical raids of Vandals at this time, cover the names of officers, the construction of warships, the importance of weather sense, tides, geography, weapons and tactics. We are here informed that the sea is calm unless the wind blows (38)!

The whole book only runs to about 150 short pages or 29,000 words. It is understandable that, even if Vegetius had had another sort of mind, the large range of subjects he touches on could only be dealt with in the most superficial way. It is somewhat surprising, therefore, to notice the widespread popularity his book has had over the centuries. In his introduction to the Teubner text, Lang notices more than one hundred and fifty manuscripts dating all the way from the seventh to the fourteenth and fifteenth centuries. The London Museum catalogue lists twenty-two printings of the text from the first in 1473 to modern times; it was printed five times before 1500; it was translated into English, French and Bulgarian before the invention of printing and printed translations in German (as early as 1474), French and English appeared before 1500. The English version was by Caxton in 1489. This popularity raises, for the modern critic, the question, "Why?"

There have been, it would seem, two reasons for Vegetius' wide circulation, its value to the military historian as the only general description of all aspects of military science to have come down to us from antiquity and its use as a text book for practicing soldiers. In the late Middle Ages and at the Renaissance efforts were being made to reduce many aspects of life to a system and to give them what, I suppose, we would call a "scientific basis." This accounts very largely for the turning back to the great intellectual efforts of antiquity as to an age in all ways superior in its knowledge and judgment, and for the renewed interest in scientific works of ancient Greeks and Romans in all fields. It was in keeping with this spirit to try to produce an intellectually satisfying *ars militaris*; but there was very little in the way of military treatises to be found in ancient writings. When one considers the emphasis given in ancient historians to military matters and warfare, and when one remembers that the greatest successes claimed by Rome were those achieved by her army, it is rather surprising to find such a dearth of military manuals and treatises. Of those that were written most disappeared in he course of centuries, and the *Epitoma* of Vegetius became the sole surviving example of a general military manual which later ages could use. Of course the sources he names are respectably orthodox and authoritative, in reputation at least, and it was, therefore, easy to accept his work as a classically pure standard text book. Even if this had not been the case the seekers after ancient doctrine had no one else to turn to.

Thus we hear that in the time of Charlemagne a copy of the Epitoma was considered a necessity for his commanders. Henry II of England and his more famous son Richard Coeur de Lion carried the book wherever they went on their campaigns. Even earlier Foulques the Black, Count of Anjou, held Vegetius as his favorite author. Montecuculi, the Italian conqueror of the Turks at St. Gothard (1609-1680), says in his memoirs that a man can believe himself a great Captain when he has read the precepts of Vegetius. And as late as 1770 the Austrian Field Marshal, Prince de Ligne, called the *Epitoma* a golden book and its author god-inspired.[20]

It certainly does not, however, speak well for the military mind down the ages that generals had to get their common sense out of Vegetius' work be it ever so respectably classical. In an age when cavalry was dominant a leader could find little practical advice in the *Epitoma* except that fodder supplies are desirable. In an age of gunpowder all his remarks about more ancient weapons were out of date. Therefore, presumably, what these generals derived from Vegetius was only the generalized advice, hallowed by its antiquity, that to a lay mind seems self-evident. Apparently to a soldier's mind it seems desirable to have authority, and especially ancient authority, for believing that the point of a sword penetrates a body more easily than the side (1.12), that the health of the army is important (3.2), that famine more often destroys an army than the enemy does (3.3), that night affords the best chances to surprise the enemy (3.8), that cavalry should be used on level ground (2.1), that in using a sword the right foot is advanced (1.20) and so on. At least one piece of advice still followed is that the first exercise recruits should be taught is marching. "For nothing is more to be watched both on the march and in the battle line than that all soldiers keep their ranks" (1.9). Like the laws of the Medes and the Persians the military mentality changeth not.

The other reason for Vegetius' popularity in the past is more respectable, if rather debatable; it is his value to military historians. Since he is quite frankly excerpting ancient authorities and making no original proposals of his own, and since most of his sources are no longer extant, he has to be used willy-nilly by those who would understand Roman armies. His value and reliability as a recorder has been much discussed.[21] The one great drawback to his work, though, is obvious to the most casual reader, and that is his complete lack of any sense of chronology. Arms, formations, names of officers and soldiers, tactics and technology are drawn in a completely heterogeneous mixture from all ages of Rome, from the earliest days down to the second century or later. There is no attempt to indicate any kind of evolution in Roman military arts, but all his ideas are assigned to some nebulous golden age of the far past. For this reason any use of Vegetius by a military historian has to be very cautious. When he describes a legionary's armour or a *ballista* or the fortifications of a camp only diligent comparisons with Caesar or Livy or Frontinus can indicate to what age this description applies.

Even though he is only an epitomist he cannot help but refer occasionally to his own day. This usually is only to point a contrast between the sad state of the present and the glorious past. He is, after all, describing an ideal state of affairs, what changes should be made, not those that could be, nor the actual present. However if a close examination is made of the work some hints of contemporaneous life peep through the hazy idealism. So far as is known Vegetius' work has not been systematically looked at from this point of view before and to do so is therefore, perhaps, worthwhile.

One thing that soon becomes obvious is that military terminology had changed over the centuries between Vegetius' sources and his own day. He is constantly using terms found, no doubt, in the books he used, and then having to give modern equivalents. Did he get even these from Modestus' book instead of from practicing soldiers? Thus we hear, for instance, that a *primus hastatus* and a centurion are now respectively *ducenarius* and *centenarius* (2.8), that the old light-armed *ferentarii* are now called *exculcatores* (2.15), that the old inspectors of the camp guard have had their name shortened from *circumitores* to *circitores* and the term had become one of rank rather than of function (3.8), and that the old missile throwing "scorpions" have become *manuballistae* (4.22). As a mark of the Germanization of the army the Roman war cry (*clamor*) is now called *barritus* (3.18), a word used in Tacitus (*Germ.* 3) and even Ammianus (16.12.43; 26.7.17) specifically to describe a barbaric German war cry. Similarly the word *drungus* (3.16) for a detachment of troops is of undoubtedly foreign origin. There are many more of these references to changed terminology, inserted, of course, to make the old texts intelligible to a fifth-century reader. Sometimes he himself is confused in his terminology. Talking about the old *pilum* (1.20) he says "this type of weapon is now rare among us but the barbarians use it widely and call it a *bebra*." This, he makes clear, is a missile weapon but a few lines later he uses the same word *pilum* of a thrusting spear, and elsewhere (2.15) says that the old *pilum* "is now called a *spiculum*" as if it were still in use. Furthermore, the old meaning of *testudo*, a formation of locked shields, has changed to indicate a shelter for a battering ram (4.14). There is, on the other hand, no confusion of meaning in the term *plumbata* or *mattiobarbulus* to indicate a weighted javelin (1.17; 3.14; 4.21), even though elsewhere the term seems to indicate lead balls on a thong.[22] The reference to the office of praetorian prefect as an "honorable and sought after end of a military career" (2.21) is again harking back to what had been, since the official of that name in Vegetius' day was, of course, a purely civil official.

Vegetius' chief criticisms, implied or stated, of the Roman armies of his day continually revolve around two points, the inferiority of the recruits and the lack of training which they are given. As was mentioned above the frequency of laws which dealt with recruiting shows all too clearly the difficulty that the armies had in obtaining good men. So when Vegetius complains (1.7) about the poor quality of the men drafted into the army he is certainly on firm ground. Some of the reasons he gives for this state of affairs are also probably valid. They are the preferences on the part of the more decent men for civil employment and the graft prevalent among the recruiting officers to induce them to take from the large estates only men whom the landowners have found useless. But what one is to make of the negligence caused by the "long peace" existing in his own day, I cannot say, unless this is just another rather silly piece of flattery. In any case references to this utterly mythical long peace and its debilitating effects occur elsewhere in other connections (1.8; 1.28). The possibility seems strong that the reference to the "long peace" is simply the commonplace, referring to the *pax Romana*, which Vegetius found in his first or second century sources and transferred, however inappropriately, to his own day.

Of even more disastrous effect in Vegetius' mind is the falling off in the training given to recruits. The training in horsemanship is now avoided (1.18), the ancient arms and armour have been abandoned through laziness (1.20), and arms drill is only "partly" still observed; "The art of fortifying a camp is now quite dead;" the Persians carry sandbags to build ramparts and other barbarians form wagon laagers at night, ideas they learnt from us. "Are we afraid that we cannot learn what others learnt from us?" (1.21; 3.10). This is a continuously recurring theme and one that seems well founded in the facts of the period. Even when he makes no direct criticism of current practice, his constant reiteration of "the custom of our ancestors," "the usage of former times" and so on, imply that these old ideas have fallen into limbo. When, for example, he recalls that "the ancient custom was constant, and confirmed by the orders of Augustus and Hadrian, that three times a month cavalry and infantry should be led on route marches," (1.27) he implies that this practice was, regrettably, no longer kept up in his day.

Changes in the arms, armour and types of troops are noticed also, and usually with regret. He implies the increasing use of cutting as opposed to thrusting swords (1.12), and seems to shove back into the past the variety of large and small swords (*spathae* and *semispathae*) which he found in his day (2.15). In the same passage where, using past tenses, he seems to be describing the arms of the far past he refers to the undoubtedly more recently introduced *plumbata*. These weighted javelins seem, according to Vegetius (1.17), only to have come into prominent use under Diocletian and Maximian who honoured two Illyrian legions so armed with the titles of Jovian and Herculean. Five of these *plumbata* or *mattiobarbuli* were carried by each soldier in his shield so that "the heavy-armed troops seem to fill the function of archers," and strike at greather range than *missibilia* (whatever that means).[23] He refers to the disappearance of several kinds of missile-throwing devices (4.22) though in other places he describes their importance. He notices the greatly increased use of archers and slingers (1.15) though he does not realize, when he quotes Cato and the practice of Scipio Aemilianus in this connection, that in those early days light-armed troops were distinctly secondary to the legionary in honour and importance. As we have seen he particularly notices the increase in light-armed troops after the time of Gratian, since when, he hints, they have become the *principale auxilium*, but he assigns the wrong reason for the change. He deplores the wider use of foreign troops (1.28; 2.2): "it is cheaper to train one's own men in arms than to hire foreigners for pay." With regard to cavalry he specifically states that infantry are superior because they can act anywhere, can perform a wider range of duties and are cheaper (2.1). The Roman cavalry in his day was inferior to that of the enemy and apparently had often to be bolstered by intermingling light-armed troops (*velites* 3.16), but it had recently been improved in skill even though nothing could be found out from books about how to use or train it (3.26 *fin*). This improvement has come from the example of Goths, Alans and Huns (1.20). In a long description (3.20) of the seven recognized battle formations the primary force is always the heavy infantry as in the past and the light-armed troops and cavalry are still only auxiliaries, skirmishers and defenders of the flanks. How blind Vegetius was to the military revolution and realities of his time is indicated by this quotation (3.23): "Heavy-armed cavalry on account of the defensive armour that they wear are safe from wounds, but because of the encumbrance and weight of their armour are easily captured and, often subject to snares, are better against scattered infantry than against cavalry in a fight. Nevertheless when, either placed before the legions or mingled in with the legionaries, they fight at close quarters, that is hand to hand, they often break the enemy's battle line." It was these *cataphracti* that since Adrianople had been masters of all battle fields!

Throughout the epitome there is an air of despair at the contemporary scene in spite of the flattery accorded the *invicte imperator*. The purpose of Vegetius is to reform the inefficient armies, but only rarely does he hint at the underlying defects in the system. Thus he only once refers to the empire's money difficulties. "Skill can effect anything if sufficient funds are not denied" (2.18). He occasionally mentions the rampant corruption of the bureaucracy and the incredible complexity of the system of paying soldiers. He finds it necessary to recommend that food be supplied to soldiers on campaign *per capita*, as used to be done, not *per dignitates* (3.3), and his emphasis on a sufficiency of supplies clearly shows that there were times when they were not available. This sort of situation, combined with the decline in training and discipline, must account for the need he feels to discuss how to avoid or repress a mutiny (3.4). (He does not suggest any redress of grievances but only more severe discipline!). There is, as was said, a constant attitude of defence and of caution; "Attack only with superior forces," "Join battle only when strategems and ambushes fail" and so on (3.9). It is a dispiriting picture of his own day that seeps out of the nostalgic maxims of Vegetius, and an undoubtedly accurate one. His solution for the military problems facing Rome, however, and his real explanations of the causes of the army's decay are so superficial as to be virtually meaningless.

It is interesting, by way of comparison, briefly to notice another writer of about this same period. This is the unknown author of a short pamphlet known as *de rebus bellicis*, who seems to have composed his work about A.D. 366-75.[24] The illustrations that have come down to us with the work are probably based on originals done by or for the author. That this writer clearly understood, far better than Vegetius did, the underlying causes of the army's sad state is revealed by his beginning his treatise with a discussion of monetary and fiscal policy. He asserts that rash *largitiones* by the rulers are causing the decline of imperial power (1.1; 2.4-5), and with great originality (compared with other writers of the age) explains the problems in terms solely of the economic and social conditions. Like Salvian (*de gub. Dei*, 5, pp. 15 ff.), who wrote some fifty years later, he argues that the military disasters suffered at the hands of the barbarians arose because of the social and administrative inequities of the Empire, and that these must be righted before the enemy can be defeated. The donatives in gold dating from Constantine's reign have caused inflation (2) and so great hardship for the poor,[25] and consequent disaffection. He, therefore, advises against a continuation of this dissipation of public funds. Similarly there has been corruption in the mints leading to debasement in the value of coins; this too must be stopped and new reliable types of coins minted. Since the author's viewpoint is that of the curiale class it is not so surprising to find him advocating curbs on the corrupt provincial officials, governors and revenue officers.[26] Like Vegetius he particularly mentions the supplying of inferior recruits through fraud (4). It follows that if the civil and fiscal offices are reformed the state will save money, but he realizes that it is the vast expenditures on the army which have upset the whole taxation system (5). He offers two solutions to this problem: first, reduce the numbers of higher paid officers and settle discharged veterans on land as tax-payers as opposed to the *limitanei* who held tax-free lands; and second, replace manpower by the use of military machines.[27]

Most of the rest of the work is devoted to elaborate descriptions of new military equipment, various kinds of *ballistae*, shields, arms, chariots, body armour, a portable bridge and even a heavy warship driven by means of oxen turning flanged paddlewheels. If many of these ideas are, or were, impracticable and never taken up, nevertheless, the author is to be praised as having had, so far as is known, the only original mind of his age directed towards military problems. Where Vegetius sought solutions only in a return to past methods and ignored contemporary, changed circumstances, the Anonymous is concerned with innovations and improvements in the social organization and the technology of his day. However, the most striking difference in temperament in the two authors lies in the defensive attitudes of Vegetius and the spirit of attack in the Anonymous. Most of the latter's new devices are offensive weapons; "nations must be attacked by diverse new machines," (6) and the chariots are primarily of advantage in pursuing a fleeing enemy (18). This attitude might seem to us more admirable, but it was as unrealistic in the circumstances of the late fourth or early fifth as was that of the reactionary and timid Vegetius.

McGill University   *C. D. Gordon*

NOTES

1. A certain Publius Vegetius Renatus whose work on veterinary science, *Mulomedicina*, is preserved, may or may not be identified with Flavius. There is little evidence either way, though L. Bieler, *History of Roman Literature*, New York, 1966, p. 192, for instance, assumes the two works to be by the same man.

2. "Die Zeit des Vegetius" *Hermes* 2, 1876, pp. 61-83.

3. E.g. A. H. M. Jones, *The Later Roman Empire*, II, Oxford, 1964, pp. 284-602.

4. E.g. in Egypt we find *primicerius* and Augustales, Flaviales, etc. cf. Vegetius 2.7 and Jones, n. 158.

5. Jones, *The Later Roman Empire*, II, pp. 649-51; cf. *Cod. Theod.* 7.15.2 (423) and *Theod.* 2 Nov. 24, 4 (443).

6. E. T. Salmon, "The Roman Army and the Disintegration of the Roman Empire," *Trans. of the Royal Society of Canada*, Series III, Section II, 52, 1956, pp. 43-57 (reprinted by Chambers, *The Fall of Rome*, New York, 1963, pp. 37-46) has argued that when, after the Antonine Constitution of 212, citizenship ceased to be the great reward for military service among the provincials such service became less attractive and forced the government to supplement volunteers with drafted recruits and foreigners.

7. Ammianus mentions only four cases of careless talk or treason on the part of German troops, 14.10.8; 16.12.2; 31.10.3; 29.4.7.

8. C. Oman, *The History of the Art of War* — The Middle Ages, London, 1898, p. 17.

9. H. Grosse, *Römische Militärgeschichte von Gallienus bis zum Beginn der byzantinischen Themenverfassung*, Berlin, 1920, pp. 259-65; and cf. Jordanes, *De rebus Gothicis*, 28.

10. Ramsay MacMullen, "Some Pictures in Ammianus Marcellinus," *The Art Bulletin* 46, 1964, p. 446.

11. Vegetius (I.17) speaks of two legions under Diocletian which had six thousand men each as if that was an exception worth recording.

12. A. E. R. Boak, *Manpower Shortage and the Fall of the Roman Empire in the West*, Ann Arbor, 1955, p. 97. Boak's thesis has been questioned by M. I. FInley in a review in *JRS* 48, 1958, pp. 156-64 and largely reprinted in Chambers, *The Fall of Rome*, pp. 29-36. Even if we agree with Finley in his hesitancy in accepting a population decline there was certainly a shortage of manpower available within the empire for military service. The endless laws needed to assure recruitment can

only indicate government difficulties in this field.

13. Ammianus 31.13.3 and 7 (*armorum gravantibus sarcinis*) and cf. Anonymous, *De Rebus Bellicis*, 9.1; 15.1 and 4. The date of this latter treatise has been set by E. A. Thompson, *A Roman Reformer and Inventor*, Oxford, 1952, p. 2, probably between 366 and 375, though others date it as late as 395.

14. For *de rebus bellicis* cf. n. 13. For Valentinian, Amm. 30.9.4 cp. Pseudo-Aurelius Victor *Epit.* 45.6 *nova arma meditari*.

15. The text and French translation is to be found in *Ammien Marcellin, Jornandes, Frontin, Vegece, Modestus*, edited by de M. Nisard, Paris, 1869. The only other Modestus known in antiquity was Quintus Julius Modestus, a *magistrianus* or *agens in rebus* who wrote about the Emperor Anthemius during the reign of Leo. John Malalas 14.374.17 (Bonn) records that his book came into the hands of Ricimer. There is no way of telling whether this is the author of the *De Vocabulis*; but it is certainly possible that the man could have excerpted Vegetius to make a short military manual for new non-Latin-speaking recruits. On the other hand Vegetius could have made use of such a manual for his own work. Such evidence as there is indicates that the author of the *De Vocabulis* is not the same as Quintus Julius and that he wrote before Vegetius.

16. On Vegetius' sources cf. M. Schanz, "Zu den Quellen des Vegetius," *Hermes* 16, 1881, pp. 137-46, and more recently D. Schenk, *Flavius Vegetius Renatus, Die Quellen der Epitoma Rei Militaris*, Nürnberg, 1963, reprinted from *Klio* 22, 1930. Apart from the sources he names he certainly used Frontinus very widely for Bk. 4, and for 1.2, regarding the effects of climate on people, cf. Vitruvius 6.1; Pliny *NH* 3.14 and Diodorus Sic. 3.12; for the value of country boys in an army cf. Pliny, *NH* 18.5.

17. C. Oman, *Art of War*, p. 18.

18. 18.2.17; 21.13.15; 27.2.6; 27.5.3; 28.5.3; 29.5.15; 31.10.9. Cf. also Ramsay Macmullen, *Some Pictures*, p. 441.

19. Some texts split the book and call the chapters from 31 on Book 5.

20. These details I take from the Introduction by Brig. Gen. T. R. Phillips to the translation of Vegetius, *The Military Institutions of the Romans*, Harrisburg, 1944. He obviously considers these users of Vegetius sensible men and rather hints that the old author can still teach military leaders much!

21. C. Lang, in the Teubner text of Vegetius, Leipsig, 1885, xiii f., discusses this problem with references.

22. *Cod. Theod.* 9.35.2. Here it is an instrument of punishment. The Anonymous *de rebus bellicis*, 10, agrees with Vegetius.

23. In 2.23 he speaks of *missibilia vel plumbatas* as if the two were almost interchangeable terms.

24. The best edition, with commentary and translation, is by E. A. Thompson, *A Roman Reformer and Inventor*, Oxford, 1952. For the date cf. n. 13.

25. Cf. Eusebius *VC* 3.1; 54; *Laud. Const.* 7.13; 8; 9.6; Julian *Or.* 7, 228b.

26. The latter, the *exactores*, were curbed in 386 in *Cod. Theod.* 12.6.20.

27. Discussion in Thompson, *Roman Reformer*, p. 49.

Synchronisms in Polybius, Books 4 and 5[1]

I

Polybius devotes books 3 to 5 to Olympiad 140 (220-216 B.C.), and in these he organises his narrative differently from elsewhere in the *Histories*. There, events in the various theatres, viz. Italy, Sicily, Spain, Africa, Greece and Macedonia, Asia, and Egypt,[2] are dealt with year by year, in that order;[3] but, he explains,[4] it was only at the conference of Naupactus (217) that the affairs of Greece, Italy and Africa first came together, and shortly afterwards that those of the Aegean and Asia Minor were involved. Consequently, in Ol. 140, instead of proceeding year by year, and theatre by theatre within each year, Polybius devotes long sections to the Hannibalic War, the Social War, and the Fourth Syrian War, neglecting the separate Olympiad years. To help the reader he introduces eight synchronisms,[5] listing events which allegedly occurred about the same time. In 5.31.3-5 he explains why. "I am confident," he writes, "that I shall effectively prevent my readers from going astray about dates, if I indicate ... at what times in this Olympiad, and contemporaneously with what events in Greece each episode elsewhere began and ended. So that my narrative may be easy to follow and lucid, I think it most essential for this Olympiad not to interweave the histories of the various countries, but to keep them as separate and distinct as possible until, upon reaching the next and subsequent

Olympiads, I can begin to narrate the events of each year which occurred at the same time."

This is the only passage where Polybius explains why he introduces these eight synchronisms;[6] his frequent discussions of his chronological methods do not mention them at all.[7] Recently, however, it has been argued that they form an important part of Polybius' structural machinery and have a significance not previously discerned. Pédech describes Polybius' procedure as follows:[8] "He has divided the Olympic year into two equal semesters. It would be tempting to put the points of transition at the equinoxes. But this division would have no raison d'être in a system resting, not on the tropical year, but on a luni-solar calendar. Moreover, it is contrary to the usage of the ancients, who determined the seasons not by tropical signs, but by the signs of the zodiac. Consequently the six-monthly periods instituted by Polybius for Ol.140 have slightly variable dimensions, of which the appended table[9] indicates the limits." Pédech asserts that Polybius treats all events occurring within such a six-monthly period as synchronous. It is this hypothesis that I wish to examine.

II

Polybius' first synchronism is at 4.28.1. Philip V's departure from Macedonia — it is convenient to call this the "primary event" of the synchronism — took place, he says, at the time that Hannibal, having subdued all Spain south of the Ebro, was setting out against Saguntum (ἐποιεῖτο τὴν ὁρμὴν ἐπὶ τὴν Ζακανθαίων πόλιν). The Aetolians had just elected Scopas general (27.1), and the decree passed by the Greek Symmachy was in the first year of Ol.140; clearly it is late September, 220.[10] What is the meaning of ἐποιεῖτο τὴν ὁρμήν? According to 3.16.7-17.1 Aemilius Paulus was sent to operate in Illyria ὑπὸ τὴν ὡραίαν, "just before the campaigning season" of 219, and Hannibal advanced on Saguntum (ποιούμενος τὴν πορείαν ἐπὶ τὴν Ζάκανθαν). Polybius implies (both here and in 4.37.4) that these two events occurred simultaneously. Hence the siege of Saguntum began in spring 219. The common phrase ποιεῖσθαι τὴν ὁρμήν usually means "to set out," often against someone. That is the natural meaning here. It would imply, however, that the siege of Saguntum began in autumn 220 and (since it lasted eight months)[11] ended by late spring, 219. This is Schnabel's date,[12] and more recently Werner's,[13] who thinks Roman propaganda put the siege later so as to relate it more closely to the Hannibalic War. But the remaining evidence strongly favours putting the siege in 219, and late April/early May[14] seems a likely date; it could be a little later to allow flooded Spanish rivers to subside, but hardly earlier.

Consequently, either Polybius is mistaken in connecting Hannibal's attack on Saguntum with events of autumn 220 (as well as with those of spring 219) or else ἐποιεῖτο τὴν ὁρμήν (4.28.1) bears some other meaning. In my Commentary[15] I took the former view, suggesting that "Polybius has been led to make a false synchronism by his desire to insert the didactic observations contained in 4.28.2-6"; more recently, however, Eucken[16] has argued that ὁρμή here means "Unternehmen, Anschlag," i.e. "under-taking, plan." This would save Polybius from the charge of careless writing; but in the only other passage which Eucken quotes to support his view (9.31.2), παρώξυνε ... ὁρμήν means "he aroused their hostility," which clearly furnishes no parallel.

Polybius' reference to Hannibal as master of all Spain south of the Ebro echoes 3.14.9,[17] where he explains that after Hannibal's campaign of 220 "none of the peoples within the river Ebro dared lightly to face the Carthaginians, except the Saguntines." Hannibal held off from Saguntum for reasons of policy, but the Saguntines foreseeing the danger informed the Romans, and Roman envoys sent to Hannibal διεμαρτύροντο Ζακανθαίων ἀπέχεσθαι.[18] Polybius, then, believed Hannibal's hostility towards Saguntum to have become acute by autumn 220, and it is tempting to translate ἐποιεῖτο τὴν ὁρμὴν ἐπὶ τὴν Ζακανθαίων πόλιν (4.28.1) as "he directed his hostile intentions against Saguntum." This

involves an unusual meaning for a common phrase; but it is
clearly possible, and avoids assuming that Polybius was
careless at a point where chronological clarity was important.

Pédech would save Polybius' credit differently, with the
aid of his six-monthly periods. Hannibal, he argues, set out
against Saguntum "at the soonest at the end of winter
220/19," and so in the half-Olympiad year running allegedly
from 26 July, 220, to 13 February, 219. Unfortunately the
validity of these Julian calendar equivalents is far from being
established. The Julian date of the Olympic games cannot be
determined within a month. Ancient sources say only that it
was in high summer and at full moon.[19] Moreover, even if
Olympiad 140 proved to have begun on 26 July, 220, an
event occurring ὑπὸ τὴν ὡραίαν, i.e. at the earliest in April,
219, could hardly fall within a half Olympiad year ending 13
February, 219. Thus Polybius' first synchronism is not
satisfactorily explained by Pédech's theory.

In the second (4.37.1-7) the "primary event," to which
the rest are related, is the moment when Aratus' year as
Achaean general for 220/19 was ending and his son was
about to succeed him. Scopas was now half-way through his
year of office, since at that time the Aetolian elections were
held just after the autumn equinox and the Achaean about
the rising of the Pleiades, i.e. late May.[20] Since Polybius here
draws no distinction between election and entry into office,
presumably no substantial period was involved or else he
considered the interval negligible for his purpose. In fact he
makes the younger Aratus assume office τῆς θερείας
ἐνισταμένης, but ends his year at the rising of the Pleiades
(5.1.1). The primary event may therefore be dated as late
May, 219.

At this time (Polybius refers back specifically to
3.16.7-17.1) Hannibal was opening the siege of Saguntum
(ἐνεχείρει ... πολιορκεῖν), the Romans were dispatching
Aemilius Paulus to Illyria, Antiochus was about to invade
Coele Syria (after Theodotus' surrender of Ptolemais and
Tyre)[21] and Ptolemy was preparing to resist,[22] Lycurgus of

Sparta was besieging the Athenaeum,[23] the Achaeans were collecting mercenaries,[24] and Philip was moving from Macedonia.[25] (The Rhodian war on Byzantium which opened κατὰ ... τοὺς αὐτοὺς χρόνους (37.8) seems to be a new episode loosely linked to what precedes, and not part of the synchronism;[26] see below, p. 64).

Having made the siege of Saguntum begin in the previous half Olympiad year, ending 13 February, Pédech has to attach a different meaning to ἐνεχείρει ... πολιορκεῖν. Polybius often uses πολιορκία and πολιορκεῖν to mean "taking by storm" rather than "besieging."[27] Following Schnabel, Pédech gives πολιορκεῖν this meaning here.[28] But the cross-reference to 3.16.7-17.1 shows that Polybius here refers to the siege, not to the final assault. Moreover, there would still be chronological problems. The siege of Saguntum lasted eight months.[29] From 3.15.13-16.1 it is clear that when the Romans decided to send Aemilius Paulus to Illyria, they had not yet heard of Hannibal's attack on Saguntum. Aemilius and Hannibal both set out simultaneously (3.16.7-17.1). Pédech, however, having dated the assault on Saguntum before 12 August (when his six-monthly period ends), cannot date its fall later than September; equally he has to make the beginning of the siege coincide with Aemilius' departure for Illyria (which cannot precede his entry upon the consulship for 219). On the assumption that the Roman year coincided with Julian reckoning at this time, and that the consular year began on the Ides of March,[30] he therefore concludes: "If Aemilius Paulus set out about 1 March (since he entered office on the Ides of March, he could not set out earlier), Hannibal did not march against Saguntum before February, and he did not capture it before September." This seems to confuse the Ides and the Kalends. Aemilius Paulus could not leave before 15 (not 1) March; consequently Hannibal set out against Saguntum in mid-March, not February. Pédech dates the march on Saguntum to February so as to include it within the six-monthly period ending on 13 February. This is hardly reconcilable with

Polybius' statement that Hannibal left New Carthage and
Aemilius set out for Illyria ὑπὸ τὴν ὡραίαν (3.16.7).
Furthermore,[31] it is not certain that the consuls of 219
entered office on 15 March. This was so for 217 and
Mommsen[32] put the change from 1 May in 222. But it could
have occurred in 218, thus invalidating Pédech's calculations
for 219 based on 15 March (or 1 March). Nor is it possible[33]
to determine which years at this time were intercalary, nor
how closely the Roman and the Julian years coincided.
Probability is against the Romans' having sent their forces
across the Adriatic in March; still less will Hannibal have left
New Carthage in February. The rivers would be swollen and
neither month is ὑπὸ τὴν ὡραίαν. But on Pédech's scheme
the siege of Saguntum must start at the *beginning* of
February and its *fall* occur at the end of September — about
six weeks after the assault began. These assumptions seem
fragile.

Other events in the synchronism provide problems for
Pédech's theory. The Pithom stele[34] dates the agreement
made after the battle of Raphia to October, 127, two years
and two months after the Ptolemaic generals defected. This
brings one to August, 219, and the warlike preparations
mentioned follow that date. Only the tightest reckoning,
therefore, can bring them within the six-monthly period
ending 12 August, 219. Lycurgus' attack on the Athenaeum
cannot be independently dated; and, as I have indicated, the
Rhodian-Byzantine war is not strictly part of the synchronism. Pédech[35] argues that it is, but that assumption is not
without difficulty. According to 4.48.1-3, once Rhodes had
declared war, the Byzantines sent envoys to Attalus and
Achaeus requesting help. Achaeus had recently (προσφάτως)
assumed the royal title; and 5.57.5 indicates that this was in
summer, 220. Since the Rhodians sent ships to Crete before
winter 220/19, their war with Byzantium was probably over
by then;[36] Schmitt[37] has argued convincingly that the number
of events to be fitted in before winter suggests that Achaeus
took the royal title in early summer, 220.[38] Consequently,
the Rhodian-Byzantine War cannot have broken out within

the period 14 February – 12 August, 219, as Pédech's theory requires.

III

The "primary event" of Polybius' third synchronism (4.66.7-67.1) is Philip's dispatch of Macedonian troops home for the fruit-harvest (ὀπώρα), hence August/September, 219.[39] Philip spent the rest of the summer in Thessaly.[40] Three other events followed: a) Aemilius Paulus' return from Illyria and triumph; b) Hannibal's dismissal of his army to winter quarters after taking Saguntum; c) the Roman dispatch of envoys to Carthage to demand the surrender of Hannibal, following the news of the fall of Saguntum, and Roman war-preparations after the consular elections for 218. Immediately afterwards Polybius states that the first year of Olympiad 140 was drawing to a close and Dorimachus was elected general in Aetolia. This remark is an embarrassment if one supposes the synchronism to be closely related to the first half of Ol.140.2; Pédech therefore argues[41] that it is not part of the synchronism, but serves only "to take up the thread of Greek history which Polybius was anticipating." This seems unlikely.[42] If the synchronisms are to help the reader, Dorimachus' election is an obvious point of orientation, like that of Scopas (autumn, 220),[43] of the younger Aratus (spring, 219),[44] and of Eperatus (spring, 218).[45] To exclude it from the synchronism of 4.66.8-10 seems arbitrary, especially as it is one of the few events here mentioned with a close chronological relationship to the return home of the Macedonian troops.

The date of neither Aemilius' return from Illyria nor his triumph is known for certain; 3.19.12, ληγούσης ἤδη τῆς θερείας, furnishes a *terminus post quem*[46] but the triumph may have been later. It is not recorded in the *Fasti*, but even after the beginning of the consular year changed from 1 May to 15 March, February, the intercalary month, and early March remained the favourite months for triumphing. Aemilius' triumph was probably not celebrated before December, 219.[47] In view of ληγούσης . . θερείας Pédech puts it in

October;[48] and Werner,[49] closely equating it with the ὀπώρας συγκομιδή in Macedonia (which he takes to be the corn harvest) puts it in August. The latter certainly, the former probably, is too early.

Pédech assumes that the synchronism of 4.66.7-67.1 mentions events occurring between 13 August, 219 and 7 February, 218. He argues[50] that the Ides of March, 217, fell shortly after the eclipse mentioned by Livy (22.1.4-9), and identifiable with that of 11 February; hence if 218 was intercalary, the Ides of March 218 may have fallen a little after 1 February (Julian), and so in time for the consuls of 218 to assume office within the six-monthly period ending 7 February, 218. Unfortunately, as mentioned above,[51] it cannot be determined which years were intercalary at this time.

The fall of Saguntum creates no problems; this and Hannibal's winter quarters, eight months after the first attack (3.17.9), fall in late December, 219 or early January, 218. But the date of the Roman embassy to Carthage is controversial. If the names of the envoys in Livy are genuine, and M. Livius and L. Aemilius are, as seems likely, the consuls of 219,[52] they cannot have left Rome before 15 March, 218 (if the consular year began then).[53] Summing up, it is difficult to accommodate all the events of this synchronism within the period 13 August, 219 to 7 February, 218. Read without preconceptions, 4.66.7-67.1 gives the impression of being at the end of the campaigning season of 219 and of the first year of the Olympiad (which Polybius usually interprets as running on to the end of the campaigning period);[54] but Polybius then goes on to mention other later events only loosely connected and occurring in later months — the fall of Saguntum, news of this at Rome, Hannibal's winter quarters, and the Roman elections and embassy to Carthage. Pédech rightly underlines the long period covered by these events, which form no strict synchronism at all: but whether his own explanation is valid is another matter.

IV

Book 5 opens with a "primary event," the end of the younger Aratus' *strategia* and Eperatus' succession; Dorimachus was still Aetolian general (his election having been mentioned in the previous synchronism).[55] The date is the rising of the Pleiades, hence towards the end of May 218.[56] Three other events are contemporaneous (5.1.1-4). Hannibal, ἀρχομένης τῆς θερείας, having set out from New Carthage and crossed the Ebro, was beginning his journey to Italy; the Romans were sending the consuls to Africa and Spain; and Antiochus and Ptolemy were beginning to make war on each other. The first of these fits Pédech's scheme. The words ἀρχομένης τῆς θερείας clearly refers to the date when Hannibal set off northwards after crossing the Ebro.[57] In my *Commentary*,[58] assuming that he could not be on the Alpine pass after the third week in September, I calculated that he left New Carthage about the end of April, implying an Ebro crossing in May. This could be described as "the beginning of summer," for in 4.37.3 the same time of the year is ἤδη τῆς θερείας ἐνισταμένης. But Proctor, in the most recent study of Hannibal's march,[59] makes Hannibal leave Emporiae in mid-September, to reach the Rhone at the end of September and the Po valley in mid-November. These dates fit Polybius' statement[60] that Hannibal was on the pass at the setting of the Pleiades (early November). Whether a crossing so late in the year was feasible is problematical. Either date, however, allows the Ebro crossing to fall within the six months ending on 2 August, 218.

According to 3.41.2 the consuls were sent to Spain and Sicily ἐπὶ τὴν ὡραίαν,[61] presumably "in the campaigning season," a vague phrase. Scipio coincided with Hannibal at the Rhone crossing, and if Hannibal reached the Po valley at the end of September, he must have crossed the Rhone towards the end of August: hence Scipio left Rome a little before mid-August.[62] Whether his colleague left earlier is unknown; Polybius suggests that they left simultaneously. This hardly fits into Pédech's six-monthly period ending 2

August, 218; and if Proctor's dates are right, the coincidence at the Rhone was at the end of September, creating an even greater discrepancy. Pédech's explanation of his scheme at this point is unsatisfactory. "If Hannibal arrived in Italy towards the setting of the Pleiades (end of October)," he writes,[63] "he set out at the end of April." The consuls were sent to their provinces later, since the passage of the Ebro was then already known at Rome; and Pédech uses Asconius' dating for the foundation of Placentia as *pridie kal. Iun.*[64] to date the consuls' departure about that time. But this will not do, for it rests on an unusual Julian equivalent (Oct. 20/24) for the morning setting of the Pleiades, normally dated to early November,[65] and it treats this as the date of Hannibal's arrival in the Po valley, although according to Polybius this is when Hannibal was on the pass, a week earlier. Pédech also makes the fifteen days spent crossing the Alps additional to the five months Polybius allows for the journey from New Carthage to the Po valley, though clearly they are included. Finally, if Hannibal, setting out at the end of April, reached the Po valley at the end of October, his journey took not five, but six months. Given the usual dating for the setting of the Pleiades, however, Hannibal must have started out, not at the end of April, but at the end of May or even in early June, with obvious repercussions on the date of Scipio's arrival at the Rhone and so on that of his departure from Rome.

The consuls then seem to have left Rome well into summer 218, and after 2 August, when Pédech's six-monthly period terminates. In 3.41.2 Polybius is not apparently conscious of Scipio's late departure, and in 5.1.1-4 there is no difficulty if he is merely indicating the parallel actions of Hannibal and the Romans in the campaigning season of 218. But on Pédech's hypothesis the dates established create serious problems. In 5.68.1 Polybius confirms that the preparations of Aetolia and Ptolemy were in spring (συνῆπτε . . . τὰ τῆς ἐαρινῆς ὥρας);[66] this causes no difficulties.

V

The synchronism at the end of summer, 218 (5.29.5-8) is quickly dealt with. The "primary event" is Philip's dismissal of his troops and their dispatch through Thessaly; simultaneously Hannibal was encamped opposite the Romans in the Po valley. Antiochus having seized most of Coele Syria went into winter quarters, and Lycurgus of Sparta escaped to Aetolia. Hannibal's presence in the Po valley has already been discussed.[67] Antiochus' winter quarters cannot be dated more closely than the end of the campaigning season;[68] and Lycurgus' flight is not mentioned elsewhere. Polybius here omits to mention the Aetolian elections; but in the next chapter he refers to the Achaean demoralisation which ended with Aratus' election as general the following year (30.7, τῆς θερείας ἐναρχομένης). Thus he keeps the readers in touch with the chronology of the confederations; the slight irregularity in the form of reference matters less if the synchronisms are not held to constitute a highly formal system.

The next synchronism also shows some irregularity since the date proper (at 5.105.3) is anticipated with a subsidiary synchronism (5.101.3), in which Philip's siege of Phthiotic Thebes coincides with the battle of Trasimene. The reason is clear. It was the news of Trasimene that led Philip to summon the conference to Naupactus, at which the events of Greece, Italy and Africa first began to be intertwined. Polybius is therefore concerned to establish the relative chronology, even if this involves introducing a subsidiary synchronism. In 5.105.3 he says that "all these events – Trasimene, Raphia, and the treaty of the Achaeans and Philip with the Aetolians – took place in the third year of Ol.140." From then on – and precisely from the conference at Naupactus – events of the *oecumene* began to be interconnected. This conference thus constitutes the "primary event" (it is in fact the only Greek event mentioned) and the purpose of the synchronisms was to indicate "at what times in this Olympiad and contemporaneously with what events in Greece each episode elsewhere began and ended."[69]

Trasimene was probably fought in June 217: Ovid (*Fasti*, 6.767-8) dates it 21 June and Philip heard of it at Argos at the Nemean games in July. Uncertainty about the Julian equivalents would however permit a few weeks' error either way.[70] The Pithom stele[71] shows Ptolemy setting out for Coele Syria on 13 June (1 Pachons), and Polybius[72] confirms the statement there that Raphia was fought ten days later, on 22 June (10 Pachons). The conference of Naupactus must have been round about August, and the "lateness" of this synchronism is due to the importance of that conference in Polybius' scheme.

VI

The autumn synchronism of 217 follows shortly afterwards (5.108.9-10). Its "primary event" is typical: Philip, after campaigning in Dassaretia, sent his troops into winter quarters. Hannibal was going into winter quarters at Gerunium; and the Romans appointed Varro and Aemilius Paulus consuls (two events also closely linked at 3.105.11-106.1). The final synchronism (5.109.4-6) has for its "primary event" Philip's setting out round Malea with his fleet, ἀρχομένης τῆς θερείας. His arrival near Cephallenia and Leucas coincided with Antiochus' crossing of Taurus;[73] and Pédech argues[74] reasonably that the reference to the Roman fleet off Lilybaeum and (at 5.110.10) to the imminence of Cannae provides a correlation with Italian events, while Prusias' crushing of the Gauls κατὰ τούτους τοὺς χρόνους (5.111.1-7) fills out the synchronism with a reference to Asia. Antiochus' crossing of Taurus cannot be dated more closely than spring, 216,[75] and Philip will have sailed as soon as the weather allowed. The fleet at Lilybaeum creates a problem. According to 3.106.7 the consuls of 216 were to effect the recall τοῦ παραχειμάζοντος ἐν τῷ Λιλυβαίῳ στόλου. Pédech[76] would apply παραχειμάζειν to the whole period of naval seasonal inactivity, observing that "the fleet could still worry Philip in May"; but Thiel has argued[77] from Livy that Otacilius had 50 ships at Lilybaeum independent of Servilius' squadron and if that were so, it could have been these that alarmed Philip in 216.

VII

It remains to consider how far Pédech's theory explains the synchronisms and how far it is consonant with their function in the *Histories*. The following considerations seem to me to weigh against it:

i) Polybius nowhere suggests that his synchronisms are closely linked with Olympiad years, still less half years. In the whole of books 3 to 5 only twelve passages mention Olympiads or Olympiad years. Of these, five (3.1.1, 3.118.10; 4.1.3; 5.30.8; 5.111.9) simply refer to Ol.140; one (4.14.9)[78] mentions the point in Greek events at which that Olympiad began; two (3.16.7; 4.26.1) date Aemilius' expedition to Illyria and the symmachic decree launching the Social War in the first year of Ol.140; one (4.67.1) mentions that that year was drawing to a close; two (4.28.5; 5.105.3) stress that συμπλοκή of the various theatres in the third year of the Olympiad; finally 5.31.3-5 is the discussion already mentioned of the special use of synchronisms for this Olympiad. Nowhere is there any reference to half Olympiad years.

ii) To render his system plausible Pédech must demonstrate that every date in every synchronism fits his half year periods. Many do, some are dubious, and two do not. These are Hannibal's ὁρμή on Saguntum which, if taken literally, cannot be before 13 February 219, and Scipio's departure for Spain, which cannot be before 2 August, 219.

iii) Polybius indicates (4.28.2 ff.) that the synchronisms are intended to orientate the reader on the chronological relationship of events occurring in theatres not yet organically connected. But a system treating as simultaneous events which can be as much as six months apart, simply because they fall within an arbitrarily defined "half Olympiad year" — a wholly artificial concept — could only confuse a reader.

iv) Not only are such "half Olympiad years" unhelpful to the reader (who is never even told of their existence), but one can hardly conceive how Polybius could determine their beginning and end or assign events to them. An Olympiad was the period between two celebrations of the games; but how could anyone determine at what point in the intermediate summers year one became year two, etc.? Pédech claims[79] that Polybius used a luni-solar *octaeteris* – an eight-year cycle covering two Olympiads – and divided up the Olympiad years by lunar months; it is on this basis that he assigns Julian dates to his six-month periods. The *octaeteris* is known from Geminus and elsewhere; but it is highly unlikely that any Greek state actually used it,[80] and there is no evidence suggesting that Polybius took any account of it. For how could events, perhaps dated to a Roman month (which might or might not be part of an intercalated year) be equated with anything so elusive as a "half Olympiad year"? Faced with a narrative based, for example, on summer campaigns and winter quarters, how could any historian divide it up into such sub-divisions of the Olympiad? As I hope to have shown, the Julian equivalents are quite uncertain in view of the unknown variables.

Pédech has done well to draw attention to these synchronisms, and to the fact that there are two for each year. But that, I suggest, is not because Olympiad years have been neatly bisected, but because Polybius is describing campaigns on various unconnected fronts which usually began in spring, or thereabouts, and ended in autumn, or thereabouts. Hence, as he says,[81] he tries to provide a clear chronology for this Olympiad by indicating the beginning and end of various actions and putting them into relation with what was happening in Greece at the same time. Of the eight "primary events," five refer to Philip V entering or leaving winter quarters,[82] two are the entry of Achaean generals into office,[83] and one is the Peace of Naupactus;[84] other synchronised events include four references to the election of Aetolian generals.[85] This suggests that Polybius has used a simple method of relating events elsewhere to those most familiar to his primarily Greek (and even Achaean) readers. The basic narrative is the Social War in mainland Greece. The important thing is clarity — knowing which year one is in — since events are not being described theatre by theatre within each Olympiad year, as they would be later. There is nothing esoteric about it: the mechanism largely exploits a convenient coincidence — that at this time Achaean generals took office in spring and Aetolian in autumn.

VIII

One difficulty remains: undoubtedly many of the events mentioned are only approximately contemporary. But that is perhaps not serious. If the purpose of the synchronisms is in general[86] to mark the beginning and end of campaigning seasons and to ensure that the reader is in the right year, it does not matter overmuch if for instance Antiochus' invasion of Coele Syria after August 219 is correlated with Hannibal's siege of Saguntum in April-May of that year, or if Hannibal's entry into winter quarters after the fall of Saguntum, probably in January 218, was related to the return home of Macedonian troops the previous August-September. The point is that that synchronism marks the end of operations for the year we call 219. In fact, as far as we can tell, serious discrepancies are rare. I have already discussed the problem of Hannibal's ὀρμή against Saguntum. There is the stretching of the events of late 219 to include Hannibal's winter quarters, the election of next year's consuls and the sending of Roman envoys to declare war on Carthage; there is the dispatch of the consuls of 218 to their provinces as late as August. And that is all. None of these is likely to confuse the reader, especially in view of the many other chronological indications interspersed in the narrative.

Partly because his public was primarily Greek and partly of course because the events of the Illyrian War and the Hannibalic War down to Cannae had already been described in book 3, the synchronisms had to be pegged to Greek events. For mainland Greeks the movement of Macedonian troops and the familiar electoral arrangements of the two confederacies provided the basis for a very simple, rough and ready, pragmatic device for orientating Polybius' readers in this exceptional Olympiad.

The University of Liverpool   *Frank W. Walbank*

NOTES

1. This paper owes a great deal to many friends and colleagues who discussed it with me at a seminar held in the State University of New York at Buffalo in October 1970. They included several from McMaster University, but Togo Salmon could not be among them, as he was directing the *Centro universitario per studi classici* in Rome. It is therefore an especial pleasure to submit the results to him now as a token of a friendship lasting over many years. (References without the author's name are to Polybius.)

2. See my *Historical commentary on Polybius*, Oxford, 1957-67, II, p. 1.

3. Exceptions: 14.12.1-6, 32.11.2-4.

4. 5.105.3.

5. See the appended table, pp. 78-80.

6. P. Pédech, *La Méthode historique de Polybe*, Paris, 1964, p. 467, argues that there is a reference to the synchronisms in 39.8.6; but this passage describes Polybius' programme for his *Histories* generally, and the arranging of events in different theatres in each Olympiad year, not the synchronisms of books 4-5.

7. E.g. 14.12; 15.24a; 28.16.10; 32.11.2-4.

8. *Méthode*, p. 472.

9. I have indicated Pédech's divisions in my table on p. 000.

10. On the date of the Aetolian elections cf. 4.37.2; above, p. 62 n. 20.

11. Cf. 3.17.9; see G. V. Sumner, *Proc. Afr. Class. Ass.* 9, 1966, p. 7 n. 15.

12. P. Schnabel, *Klio* 20, 1926, pp. 113 ff.

13. R. Werner, *Der Beginn der römischen Republik*, Munich, 1963, pp. 54 ff.

14. Sumner, *Proc. Afr. Class. Ass.*, 1966, p. 5.

15. *Commentary* I, p. 328 (on 3.17).

16. H. C. Eucken, *Probleme der Vorgeschichte des zweiten punischen Krieges*, Diss. Freiburg, 1968, p. 106.

17. Cf. Sumner, *Proc. Afr. Class. Ass.* 9, 1966, p. 7.

18. 3.15.5.

19. See R. Sealey, *CR* 10, 1960, pp. 185-86; the implications for Pédech's theory are underlined by R. M. Errington, *JRS* 57, 1967, p. 99.

20. Cf. my *Commentary* I, p. 258 (on 2.55.5). I made this 22 May, but Werner, *Röm. Rep.*, p. 47 n. 5. has elaborate calculations pointing to 28 May; cf. Sumner, *Proc. Afr. Class. Ass.*, 9, 1966, p. 6.

21. 5.40.1 ff.

22. 5.63 ff.

23. 4.60.3.

24. 4.60.4.

25. 4.57.1.

26. Cf. 4.56.1 for a similar lead into the war between Mithridates and Sinope.

27. See my *Commentary* II, p. 120 (on 9.3.2); K.-E. Petzold, *Studien zur Methode des Polybios and zu ihrer historischen Auswertung*, Munich, 1969, p. 132 n. 1.

28. Schnabel, *Klio* 20, 1926, p. 114; Pédech, *Méthode*, p. 468.

29. See above, n. 11.

30. Pédech, *Méthode*, p. 469 n. 216.

31. See R. M. Errington, *Latomus* 29, 1970, pp. 54-55.

32. T. Mommsen, *Römische Chronologie bis auf Cäsar*[2], Berlin, 1859, p. 102; *Römisches Staatsrecht*, Leipzig, 1888, I, p. 599.

33. A. K. Michels, *The Calendar of the Roman Republic*, Princeton, 1967, pp. 167 f.

34. See my *Commentary* I, pp. 611-13 (on 5.83).

35. *Méthode*, p. 469.

36. 4.53.1; cf. B. Niese, *Geschichte der griechischen und makedonischen Staaten*, Gotha, 1893-1903, III, p. 383 n. 5.

37. H. H. Schmitt, *Untersuchungen zur Geschichte Antiochos des Grossen und seiner Zeit*, Wiesbaden, 1964, p. 114.

38. Not in autumn (as in my *Commentary* I, p. 502 (on 4.48.12)).

39. Cf. Pédech, *Méthode*, p. 458 n. 154.

40. 4.66.7, τὸ λοιπὸν μέρος τοῦ θέρους (hardly a technical term, as Pédech, *loc. cit.* asserts).

41. *Méthode*, p. 469.

42. Cf. Eucken, *Probleme*, p. 105 n. 3.

43. 4.28.1.

44. 4.37.1.

45. 5.1.1.

46. See my *Commentary* I, pp. 331-32 (on 3.20.1), rejecting Schnabel's view, *Klio* 20, 1926, p. 114, that this passage implies that Aemilius triumphed after news of the fall of Saguntum reached Rome.

47. Cf. Sumner, *Proc. Afr. Class. Ass.* 9, 1966, pp. 9-10.

48. *Méthode*, p. 469.

49. *Röm. Rep.*, p. 52.

50. *Méthode*, p. 469.

51. See p. 64 n. 33.

52. Livy 21.18.1; M. Gelzer, *Kleine Schriften* III, Wiesbaden, 1964, p. 211, thinks the names untrustworthy, and Sumner, *Proc. Afr. Class. Ass.* 9, 1966, p. 24 n. 63, questions the presence of the consuls of 219 on this embassy.

53. See above, p. 64 n. 31. Sumner, *Proc. Afr. Class. Ass.* 9, 1966, p. 11, argues that news of the fall of Saguntum reached Rome in January or February and that the embassy was not sent until the new consuls had taken office — on 3/4 March (Julian) on his calculation; leaving on 5 March (Julian) it would deliver the ultimatum c. 15 March (Julian). This is feasible, but hypothetical; cf. Errington, *Latomus* 29, 1970, pp. 54 ff.

54. See my *Commentary* I, pp. 36-37.

55. 4.67.1.

56. See above, n. 20.

57. According to 2.34.6 Hannibal left winter quarters ὑπὸ τὴν ἐαρινὴν ὥραν.

58. *Commentary* I, p. 365 (on 3.34.6).

59. Sir Dennis Proctor, *Hannibal's March in History*, Oxford, 1971, pp. 13-75.

60. 3.54.1.

61. ὑπό edd., until Büttner-Wobst restored the MSS reading.

62. See the calculations in my *Commentary* I, p. 377 (on 3.41.2).

63. *Méthode*, p. 470.

64. Ascon. *in Pis.* 3; this passage is suspect evidence, however, since *Iun.* is Madvig's emendation of the MS *Ian.*

65. 10 Nov. (Euctemon and Callippus), 11 Nov. (Hipparchus), 14 Nov. (Eudoxus), 20-24 Oct. (Aelius, Clodius Tuscus and Columella); cf. Pédech, *Méthode,* p. 450 and p. 470 n. 219.

66. On this phrase see Pédech, *Méthode*, p. 464.

67. Above, pp. 67-68.

68. 5.71.12.

69. 5.31.3; see above, p. 59.

70. See Errington, *Latomus* 29, 1970, p. 55.

71. See above, n. 34.

72. 5.80.3 πεμπταῖος; 82.1 πένθ᾽ ἡμέρας.

73. Cf. 5.107.4.

74. *Méthode*, pp. 471-72.

75. O. Leuze, *Hermes* 58, 1923, p. 188 n. 1.

76. *Méthode*, p. 472 n. 229.

77. J. H. Thiel, *Studies on the History of Roman Sea-power in Republican Times*, Amsterdam, 1946, pp. 57-58; cf. pp. 46 ff.

78. Unless this strange sentence is a gloss inserted in the text; see my *Commentary* I, p. 462 (on 4.14.9).

79. *Méthode*, pp. 456-61.

80. E. J. Bickerman, *Chronology of the Ancient World*, London, 1968, p. 29; M. P. Nilsson, *RE* "Oktaeteris," cols. 2387-92.

81. 5.31.3-5; see above, p. 59.

82. 4.27.9-10, 66.7, 5.29.5, 108.9, 109.4.

83. 4.37.1, 5.1.1.

84. 5.105.3.

85. 4.27.1, 37.2, 67.1, 5.1.2.

86. The synchronism with the Peace of Naupactus performs a slightly different function; for this marked the beginning of the συμπλοκή of events in different parts of the *oecumene*. See above, p. 59, n. 4.

Synchronisms in Polybius 4 and 5

SYNCHRO-NISMS	REFERENCES	EVENTS: 'PRIMARY EVENTS' ITALICIZED	DATES	PÉDECH'S 'SIX-MONTH' PERIODS
I	4.27.1 – 28.1	(1) Scopas' election in Aetolia	Late Sept. 220	(01.140.1 – I)
		Philip's return to Macedon	Autumn 220	26 July 220 – 13 Feb. 219
		(3) Hannibal ἐποιεῖτο τὴν ὁρμὴν on Saguntum	April/May 219(?) [error?] more probably autumn 220	
II	4.37.1 – 7	(1) *Aratus Jr. succeeds his father as Achaean general*	Late May 219	(01.140.1 – II)
		(2) Scopas half way through his year of office	"	
		(3) Hannibal ἐνεχείρει ... πολιορκεῖν Saguntum	April/May 219 (?)	14 Feb. – 12 Aug. 219
		(4) L. Aemilius sent to Illyria	April/May 219 (?)	
		(5) Antiochus about to invade Coele-Syria and Ptolemy to resist him	After Aug. 219	
		(6) Lycurgus besieging Athenaeum	?	
		(7) Achaeans gathering mercenaries	? (May?)	
		(8) Philip moving from Macedonia	Spring 219	
	[4.37.8]	(9) Rhodian war on Byzantium	Summer 220]	

III	4.66.7 – 67.1	(1) Philip sends his troops home for fruit harvest and goest to spend the rest of the summer at *Larisa*	Aug./Sept. 219	
		(2) Aemilius Paullus returns from Illyria and triumphs	end of summer 219	(01.140.2 – I)
		(3) Hannibal, after fall of Saguntum, goes into winter quarters	? Dec. 219/Jan. 218 ?	13 Aug. 219 – 7 Feb. 218
		(4) Romans send envoys to Carthage and, having elected coss. for 218, prepare for war	? after 15 March 218	
		(5) Olympiad year 140.1 was ending	? aut. 219	
		(6) Dorimachus became Aetolian general	late Sept. 219	
IV	5.1.1 – 4	(1) *Eperatus succeeds Aratus as Achaean general*	Late May 218	
		(2) Dorimachus still Aetolian general	"	(01.140.2 – II)
		(3) Hannibal begins his journey to Italy	May 218 (?) (or later)	8 Feb. – 2 Aug. 218
		(4) Consuls setting off for Africa and Spain	mid-Aug. 218 (?) or later	
		(5) Antiochus and Ptolemy beginning their war	Spring 218	

V	5.29.5 – 8	(1) *Philip sends his troops home for the winter*	Autumn 218 (?)	(01.140.3 – I)
		(2) Hannibal and Romans encamped in Po Valley	Oct. (or Nov.) 218	3 Aug. 218 – 11 Feb. 217
		(3) Antiochus' winter quarters	Autumn 218 (?)	
		(4) Lycurgus escaped to Aetolia	?	
VI	[5.101.3]	Philip's siege of Phthiotic Thebes contemporary with Trasimene	June 217 (?)]	(01.140.3 – II)
	5.105.3	(1) *Peace of Naupactus*	Aug. 217	12 Feb. – 20 Aug. 217
		(2) Trasimene	June 217?	
		(3) Raphia	June 22, 217	
VII	5.108.9 – 10	(1) *Philip sends his troops into winter quarters*	end of campaigning season 217	(01.140.4 – I)
		(2) Hannibal winters at Gerunium	"	
		(3) Romans appoint Varro and Aemilius coss. for 216	?	21 Aug. 217 – 14 Feb. 216
VIII	5.109.4 – 6	(1) *Philip sails round Malea to Cephallenia ἀρχομένης τῆς θερείας*	'early summer' 216	(01.140.4 – II)
		(2) Antiochus crosses Taurus against Achaeus	"	15 Feb. – 10 Aug. 216
		(3) Roman fleet at Lilybaeum	"	
	[5.111.1]	(4) Prusias destroys the Galatians	?]	

Hippias and the Athenian Archon List

My concern in this discussion will be with the first fragment of the Athenian archon list found in the Agora and published by Meritt in 1939.[1] Since Bradeen's identification of other fragments,[2] it is now numbered (c) by Meiggs and Lewis in their recent selection of Greek inscriptions.[3] Fragment (c) is the most interesting historically of the four fragments now known because it contains six names that can be restored with reasonable certainty, and because it belongs to the years immediately after the death of Peisistratos and therefore throws light on the use of the archonship by the Peisistratids mentioned by Thucydides at 6.54.6: "In other respects the city observed without interference the laws previously in force,[4] except in so far as they (the Peisistratids) saw to it that one of themselves was always in the archonships." (τὰ δὲ ἄλλα αὐτὴ ἡ πόλις τοῖς πρὶν κειμενοῖς νομοῖς ἐχρῆτο, πλὴν καθ᾽ ὅσον αἰεί τινα ἐπεμέλοντο σφῶν αὐτῶν ἐν ταῖς ἀρχαῖς εἶναι). The phrase πλὴν καθ᾽ ὅσον κ.τ.λ. indicates that the Peisistratids made one change in the existing laws and that it had to do with the method of choosing the archons. Dover suggests that the change was substitution of nomination for election in order to secure the "right" men in the archonships.[5] Such a change would have secured the desired result but would have been a violent departure from any pretence of abiding by "the laws previously in force." Since

81

the archonship was the most prestigious political office, nomination without election would have been an open exercise of tyrannical power and bound to give offence. Moreover, Herodotus (1.59.6) and Aristotle (*A.P.*14.3, 16.2) as well as Thucydides emphasize that Peisistratos was careful to observe constitutional forms. He more probably made a change that would seem to be a mere simplification of the procedure but would prove equally effective for his purposes, the substitution of straight election for the double process of *klerosis ek prokriton* instituted by Solon (*A.P.* 8.1). Elections continued to be held, the "right" people were nominated, and the appearance of normal constitutional procedure was observed. As Aristotle says: διώκει ... τὰ περὶ τὴν πόλιν μετρίως καὶ μᾶλλον πολιτικῶς ἢ τυραννικῶς (*A.P.* 16.2). This use of simple election continued throughout the tyranny and afterwards until 487/6 when a double process was re-introduced, selection by lot from candidates previously elected by the demesmen. Aristotle at the end of his description of it adds: τότε μετὰ τὴν τυραννίδα πρῶτον· οἱ δὲ πρότεροι πάντες ἦσαν αἱρετοί (*A.P.* 22.5).[6] This double process in which lot was made the more important element is contrasted with the elections that had prevailed from the tyranny until that year.

The meanings of the two elements of the next phrase in Thucydides call for some comment. "One of themselves" (τινα ... σφῶν αὐτῶν) from the evidence of the archon list must be taken to go beyond relatives and to include those prominent men who had been persuaded to co-operate with the régime, political friends and even former enemies who had been conciliated and were willing to accept office. The words ἐν ταῖς ἀρχαῖς, as Dover points out, need not refer only to the eponymous archonship, and probably included all nine archons.[7] The nine archons became members of the Areopagus for life at the end of their term of office, and the tyrant policy seems to have been to use them to ensure loyal annual recruitment for the council that remained a powerful body with important judicial functions until the legislation of Ephialtes. Only when Thucydides uses technical formulation, τὴν ἐνιαύσιον Ἀθηναίοις ἀρχήν, as he does in the next sentence for the archonship of the younger Peisistratos, can it be certain that he is referring to the eponymous archonship.[8]

The list itself of Fragment (c) contains six names which I quote in the format used by Meiggs and Lewis:

[Ὀν]ετο[ρίδες]	527/6)
[h]ιππία[ς]	(526/5)
[Κ]λεισθέν[ες]	525/4)
[Μ]ιλτιάδες	524/3)
[Κ]αλλιάδες	(523/2)
[. . 5 . . .]στρατ[ος]	(522/1)

The dates assigned depend upon the date given by Dionysios of Halikarnassos (A.R. 7.3.1) for the archonship of Miltiades in Olympiad 64 (524/3-521/0). Dionysios does not specify the first year of Ol. 64, i.e. 524/3, but Cadoux points out that his usual practice makes this the most reasonable assumption. The only alternative he allows is Ol. 64.2, i.e. 523/2, and if that were accepted all six names would have to come down a year.[9] There are two reasons, in addition to the most cogent reason already given, Dionysios' practice, for not moving the whole block downwards one year. The first is epigraphical: the name Philoneos is one of the few names that would fit above the first line of the fragment. If Miltiades was archon in 524/3 and [Ὀν]ετο[ρίδες] in 527/6, the name in the line directly above must have been Φιλονεος, the archon of the year of Peisistratos' death (A.P.17.1). No traces are preserved of this line but the space above the T of ΕΤΟ seems too wide for most letters except omicron or theta to have been inscribed there. The first omicron of Philoneos would come above the tau of Onetorides. The second reason is historical. Hippias' name is second on the list, and it is generally agreed that its presence shows that he held the archonship as soon as possible after his father's death to inaugurate his tyranny. Bringing down the block of names by a year would require explanation of an improbable two-year delay between his father's death and his archonship. For these reasons the dates given above are accepted, so far as I know, by all commentators.

This brings us to the first name on the list. The restoration Onetorides is chosen by Meiggs and Lewis in preference to Onetor, the alternative restoration of Meritt, because the former name occurs as a *kalos*-name on vases of painters working in the 540s, while the name Onetor appears only at the end of the century.[10] The question immediately arises: why Onetorides rather than Hippias, if the inference made above is correct that Hippias wanted to be archon as soon as possible after his father's death? The natural explanation is that Peisistratos had died late in the archon-year 528/7 after the election or at least the public nomination of Onetorides for 527/6 had taken place. There could be no question of annulling the nomination or election without violating the constitutional proprieties and therefore Onetorides did hold office in 527/6 and Hippias had to wait until the next year. This time for the death of Peisistratos in the latter half of the archon-year 528/7 involves, however, the dates of the three famous Olympic victories of Kimon, father of Miltiades II, and the date of the murder of Kimon by the Peisistratidai after Peisistratos' death. Herodotus (6.103) tells the story: Kimon in exile won a first victory with his team of mares; after his second victory he had it announced in Peisistratos' name and was allowed to return to his estates in Attica under promise of immunity; when he won a third time with the same team he was killed secretly by Peisistratos' sons, Peisistratos being no longer alive. Herodotus at 6.39.1 had already said that Miltiades II was sent by the Peisistratidai in a trireme to the Chersonese to take over the government on the death of his brother Stesagoras, and added that they showed the younger Miltiades great favour in Athens, "as if indeed they had not been privy to the death of his father Kimon."

Kimon's three victories with the same mares must be consecutive — otherwise the mares would be too old by the third victory. Wade-Gery dated them at the Olympic games of 536, 532, and 528, and saw the murder of Kimon as part of "the crisis of the succession" when Kimon's glory from a third victory would have been dangerous. He placed the death of Peisistratos "at the time of, or at least very soon after, the third win."[11] Since the Olympic games occur in early August within a few weeks of the beginning of the Athenian archon-year, the death of Peisistratos would have taken place very early in 528/7 and well before the time for election of archons for the next year, 527/6. Unless archons were elected and announced almost a year in advance, it is difficult to see why Hippias could not have been nominated and elected to the archonship of 527/6 rather than Onetorides. Such a departure from the normal times of election is improbable, since Peisistratos was scrupulous about maintaining at least the outward formalities of constitutional procedure. Onetorides' name as archon for 527/6 is, therefore, a serious objection to placing the death of Peisistratos at the time of, or soon after, the Olympic games of 528/7.

The later dates for Kimon's three consecutive victories are 532, 528, 524.[12] Kimon on these dates returned to Athens in August of 528, after ceding his second victory to Peisistratos who died later in the same year. Wade-Gery (p. 157) calls it "more or less a deathbed reconciliation," but although Peisistratos was an old man there is no reason to think that he anticipated almost immediate death. Reconciliation with former adversaries was probably a policy he had been following as opportunity offered during the later years of his tyranny when he felt secure in his position. He had been firmly installed as tyrant since 546 B.C., and had proved himself as a beneficent and popular ruler, exercising power with moderation and wisdom. Thucydides (6.54.5) and Aristotle (A.P. 16) give him high praise for these qualities, and the anecdotes told about him show the affectionate admiration he had won from the Athenian people. He could afford to be conciliatory and generous even to the nobles who had opposed him in the beginning. The names of Kleisthenes for 525/4 and Miltiades for 524/3 in the archon list are usually interpreted as a policy of reconciliation inaugurated by Hippias when he succeeded to the tyranny.

The policy is more appropriate to the later years of Peisistratos. Herodotus provides the example of Kimon who, by having his second victory proclaimed in Peisistratos' name, made a public gesture of respect and deference which was magnanimously accepted. His case shows that there had been no confiscation of estates, so that the return of exiles presented no difficulties. As for the Alkmeonidai, Kleisthenes' name as archon in 525/4 is evidence for the return of the family, but not for the time of the return. There is no evidence for the length of time they, or for that matter any other families, remained in exile after the Battle of Pallene. The probabilities are that they gradually returned when it was clear from Peisistratos' attitude that reprisals would not be taken and that it was safe to do so. In other words, the policy of conciliation and of disarming opposition by inducing former opponents to accept public office should be assigned not to Hippias but to Peisistratos' later years. There is no need to postulate "a crisis of the succession," as Wade-Gery does, since Hippias followed this aspect of his father's policy about the archonship. Onetorides had been elected before his father's death and was archon in 527/6, Kleisthenes of the Alkmeonidai in 525/4, and the Kimonid Miltiades II in 524/3.

The archonship of Kleisthenes has occasioned surprise chiefly because Herodotus (6.123) had stressed the family's uncompromising opposition to the tyranny and had said that they were in exile throughout the whole period. The second statement is in all probability an inference from the first; and for the first, that the Alkmeonidai were the enemies of the tyranny *par excellence*, Herodotus had the best of evidence in that they were mainly responsible for bringing the tyranny to an end in 511/10 (6.123.2). Moreover, when he moved in Athenian political circles in the mid-fifth century, collaboration with, or even acquiescence in, the tyranny were matters of family history to be disavowed. In fact relations between the Alkmeonidai and the Peisistratidai were by no means invariably hostile. It is sufficient only to recall the alliance between Megakles of the Coast and Peisistratos for his second return and the marriage alliance then contracted. True, the family (or some members of it, if Ἀλκμεωνίδεω is read at Hdt. 1.64.3) had gone into exile after the victory at Pallene, but that was prudent precaution since it was the breach between the families that had driven Peisistratos into his ten-year exile and he might still harbour resentment on his return. Kleisthenes' archonship raises legitimate doubts that the differences between the families were at all stages of the tyranny irreconcilable.

The archonship of the younger Miltiades in 524/3 has occasioned less surprise. His maternal half-uncle, Miltiades I, had as oikistes led an official colony of Athenian citizens to the Chersonese. He was still there and alive, and Stesagoras, the younger Miltiades' older brother, was with him to take over on his death since he was childless. The Philaid family to which Miltiades I belonged had ancient connections with Brauron, Peisistratos' home, and Miltiades I was certainly acting in accordance with Peisistratid policy in holding the important Chersonese area.[13] Herodotus (6.35.3), as in the Alkmeonid case, suggests hostility: that Miltiades accepted the invitation of the Dolonkoi because of dislike of Peisistratos and desire to be away from the hateful tyrant régime. The jealousy and irritation were no doubt real enough, and both were happier when Miltiades removed himself to the Chersonese where his ambitions could have free rein and he could contribute to Athenian policy without being irked by the constant reminder of the greater power of Peisistratos. Davies accepts from Herodotus hostility between Miltiades I and later the Kimonids and Peisistratos: "In the 540s and later the family most obviously at loggerheads with the regime was not the Alkmeonidai but the Kimonids."[14] This is an exaggeration: the inevitable tension between two ambitious families with long-standing connections, one in power and the other resenting its predominance, did not prevent a collaboration beneficial to both.

The archonship of 524/3 for his younger nephew, who had probably just reached the age of thirty,[15] was therefore an appropriate honour for the Kimonid branch of the family, especially since the father Kimon had four years before been reconciled with Peisistratos. Shortly after he took office, Kimon won a third victory, a feat remarkable enough to arouse popular enthusiasm for the family. But he was not wise enough to proclaim Hippias as victor this time.[16] Hippias became alarmed at the unexpected turn of events, the son as eponymous archon and the father Olympic victor for the third time, and had Kimon secretly murdered as he returned from dining in the Prytaneion, a privilege enjoyed by Olympic victors. Wade-Gery considered this reading of events "a tangled story," too "melodramatic" to be probable — the father murdered as he returned from the archon's (his son) table![17] But Hippias was less sure of his position than his father; the most dangerous rivals were families close to the throne and the Kimonids were riding high. His latent jealousy and fear flared up and he arranged the murder, after which, to prevent suspicion, he allowed Miltiades to bury his father and the mares with conspicuous pomp, and continued outwardly to treat him well in Athens. Some eight or nine years later he was glad to send him away to succeed Stesagoras who had been killed by the local chieftains of the Chersonese. He may have hoped that Miltiades too would be eliminated by the troubles there.

The murder of Kimon was not the only occasion when Hippias betrayed insecurity by reacting with unnecessary violence to the threat of danger. In this first instance there is no hint of conspiracy against him by Kimon and Miltiades — had there been any reliable evidence of such Miltiades would not have been sent to so vital a spot as the Chersonese. The notorious example is the real conspiracy of 514 when his brother Hipparchos was killed. Hippias' excessive harshness thereafter drove the Alkmeonids and other noble families into exile to plot his overthrow. It was almost more serious that, badly shaken by developments at home, he turned to Persia and gave his daughter in marriage to the son of the tyrant of Lampsakos, perceiving as Thucydides (6.59.3) says, that the Lampsakenes were in high favour with Darius. This was a double betrayal: of Athens and of Miltiades. Darius had conquered Thrace and it seemed that his next move would be into Greece; Hippias had made clear that he would cooperate with Persia. Lampsakos was the traditional enemy of the Chersonese; Hippias had deserted Miltiades and sacrificed him and the Chersonese for the sake of the marriage alliance. In this later crisis, his errors of judgement were unwise and in the outcome, fatal.

These events, however, lie outside the scope of the archon list. Hippias' own name in the second place in the fragment and that of his son the younger Peisistratos at the end are significant for his attitude and policy.[18] The presence of the name Hippias has given rise to little comment other than that the new tyrant would wish to hold the archonship as soon as possible after his father's death. It is not impossible that this is an unknown Hippias, but since neither in the literary evidence, dedications, kalos-names, nor any other sources is any Hippias except the tyrant mentioned in this period or for a century afterwards, it would be begging the question to take this easy solution. Granted then that it is the tyrant, why did he hold the archonship so late in his life as the mid-fifties and only after his father's death? This is the more surprising when we accept the last name five years later as his son. It appears that Hippias himself did what Thucydides said was the policy of the tyranny and had his son hold the archonship as soon as he was old enough, about thirty. Why had Peisistratos not done the same? After Pallene it might be thought that he would be anxious to strengthen and legitimize his position, and what better way than to have as archon his eldest son, then in his mid-thirties?[19]

There is no evidence that Peisistratos himself was ever eponymous archon. It is inferred from his command of Athenian forces at the capture of Nisaia that he was polemarch and therefore a member of the Areopagus for the rest of his life (Hdt. 1.59.4). Again there is no evidence that any of his three legitimate sons was archon during his lifetime, but this is an *argumentum e silentio* of little value, since Cadoux knows the name of only one archon between 546/5 and 528/7.[20] Without the name Hippias on our list the natural inference would be that some or all three sons had held archonships during these blank years, and that Thucydides selected to illustrate his remark about the policy of the tyranny the younger Peisistratos because he wished to mention the two monuments dedicated in his archonship. In other words, Thucydides' silence about archonships held by other members of the family can be readily explained, and the lack of names for the period 546-528 leaves plenty of room for the sons to have held office earlier.

If that is the case, how should Hippias' name in 526/5 be interpreted? The explanation must be that it is a second ceremonial eponymous archonship to inaugurate his tyranny, analogous to the practice of the early Roman principate. But a second eponymous archonship in Athens, unlike repeated consulships in Rome, is unprecedented. Moreover, Herodotus, Thucydides and Aristotle emphasize the constitutional character of the Peisistratid tyranny, and a second archonship would be decidedly unconstitutional. The assumption of an earlier archonship in the blank years held by Hippias is sufficiently improbable that other possibilities should be explored. If Hippias had not been archon in his father's lifetime, it can be assumed that the younger sons had not been preferred before him, and none of them had held office. It would seem therefore that Peisistratos had regarded the archonship as the most obvious reward he could give his followers, especially the nobles who might in this way be induced to support him publicly, and that he saw no reason to waste it on his sons. Like many able and dominating fathers, he took his sons' support for granted, kept the reins of power in his own hands, and gave them little public voice in determining policy and scant share of conspicuous honours. It may have been his deliberate policy to avoid any suggestion of "a ruling family." Whether Hippias resented his exclusion from the archonship by his father we have no means of knowing, but we do know from the archon list that he hastened to hold it at the earliest opportunity after his father's death and arranged for his eldest son to hold it as soon as he was of age, two actions that suggest that he was exploiting the dynastic possibilities of the office. The prestige of his son's archonship was enhanced by the inauguration of the cult of the Twelve Gods with its altar in the Agora, and the dedication of the altar of the Pythian Apollo on the Ilissos. The inscription on the altar of the Pythian Apollo began: μνῆμα τοδ᾽ ἧς ἀρχῆς Πεισίστρατος Ἱππίου υἱός (Thuc.6.54.7). The emphasis on the tyrant family was explicit enough to make clear that Hippias intended to rule more openly and to assure the hereditary claims of his family. His reason for doing so may be connected with the incident of Kimon and Miltiades II two years before, the son in the archonship and the father an Olympic victor for the third time. Another family might conceive dynastic ambitions, and he hastens to strengthen his own position by bringing into the highest office and dedicating in his name two conspicuous monuments an heir apparent.

Peisistratos' policy had been more considerate of the tender susceptibilities of the noble families and Hippias' change could not have failed to be offensive to many Athenians. Even his brother Hipparchos' interest in arts and letters came to smack of semi-royal patronage, and it was his arrogant assumption that what he wanted, he should have, that brought to a head in 514 the growing irritation with the régime (Thuc. 6.54-59; Arist. A.P. 18). The quarrel began as a personal one, but was no less dangerous for that. It is notorious that Greek tyrannies rarely lasted beyond the second generation, partly because fathers do not always breed sons as wise in the ways of power as themselves – a serious reason since the strength of a tyranny resides not in any office but in the personality of the tyrant, and partly because, the more successful it is, the more likely that by the second generation the grievances that were its raison d'être have been removed and resentment increases. The troubles that beset Hippias were in part internal opposition inevitable in the second generation, in part external complications vis-à-vis Persia over which he had no control, but some were of his own making. The dynastic use of the archonship with its open display of hereditary power was one of them.

Fragment (c) of the archon list is historical evidence of the utmost value: the names of the six archons immediately after the death of Peisistratos, four of them political figures about whose later careers there is substantial evidence, and two of the four members of the tyrant family. It is a bare list of names, inviting speculation about the circumstances and meaning of their election. The foregoing discussion may have seemed unduly speculative, but only by exploring the possibilities suggested by the incomplete evidence we possess for this period can the names throw light on the critical first years of Hippias' tyranny.

Trinity College, Toronto   *Mary E. White*

NOTES

1. B. D. Meritt, *Hesperia* 8, 1939, pp. 59-65.

2. D. W. Bradeen, "The Fifth-Century Archon List," *Hesperia* 32, 1963, pp. 187-208. His discovery of three new fragments has removed doubt that all the pieces belong to an inscribing of the archon list; see p. 187, n.2 for references to the controversy provoked by the discovery of the first fragment.

3. R. Meiggs and D. M. Lewis, *A Selection of Greek Historical Inscriptions to the End of the Fifth Century B.C.*, Oxford, 1969, No. 6, pp. 9-12, abbreviated hereafter *SGHI*.

4. Dover so translates this phrase to bring out the predicative force of αὐτή; A. W. Gomme, A. Andrewes and K. J. Dover, *A Historical Commentary on Thucydides* IV, Oxford, 1970, *ad loc.* p. 330.

5. *Commentary* IV, p. 331.

6. This is not the place to argue the vexed question of the Solonian introduction of *klerosis ek prokriton*, which I accept. For the arguments in favour see H. T. Wade-Gery, *Essays in Greek History*, Oxford, 1958, pp. 110-115; against C. Hignett, *A History of the Athenian Constitution*, Oxford, 1952, Appendix XIV, pp. 321-326. Hignett (173), in order to maintain his view that *klerosis ek prokriton* was not introduced by Solon, says that the "natural interpretation" of πρότεροι in *A.P.* 22.5 is that all the earlier archons from the beginning of the magistracy had been elected. πρότεροι, however, should be taken

with the immediately preceding phrase τότε μετὰ τὴν τυραννίδα πρῶτον, and then refers to all the archons since the beginning of the tyranny. Hignett suggests that μετὰ τὴν τυραννίδα is an insertion by the author of the *A.P.* into material he took from the Atthis and should be removed, as possibly also τότε πρῶτον. He says: "As the author of the *Athenaion Politeia* believed this method of appointment was introduced by Solon, he was driven to the hypothesis that it had lapsed under the tyranny" (173). My position is that it had been introduced by Solon, was changed by the tyranny to simple election, and continued until 487/6 when lot came in.

7. *Commentary*, pp. 330-31. Dover suggests that when the eponymous archonship was not held by a relative, there may still have been a relative ἐν ταῖς ἀρχαῖς as polemarch or archon basileus. The supply of relatives would scarcely have permitted this annually for the thirty-six years of the tyranny. So far as Peisistratos himself was concerned, it will be argued later that he was careful not to put even his sons in official positions. σφῶν αυτῶν therefore seems to mean not primarily relatives, but to be deliberately vague – any who would be "their men."

8. For two other variations of the technical formula see Thuc. 1.93.3 and 2.2.1; both refer explicitly to the eponymous archonship, *pace* C. W. Fornara, "Themistocles' Archonship," *Historia* 20, 1971, pp. 534-40 on 1.93.3.

9. T. J. Cadoux, "The Athenian Archons from Kreon to Hypsichides," *JHS* 68, 1948, p. 110, n. 216.

10. Meiggs and Lewis, *SGHI* 11; cf. J. K. Davies, *Athenian Propertied Families*, Oxford, 1971, p. 421, who notes that an Onetor (I in his numbering) appears as dedicator of a statue c.500, and Onetor II as a *kalos*-name in the 470's.

11. *Essays*, pp. 155-70. There are unsolved difficulties in this tale of Kimon's murder, not the least being when, by whom, and why the information leaked out that it was murder and not simply a street brawl in which Kimon was set upon by thugs and killed.

12. They are so placed by, e.g., J. Kirchner, *Prosopographia Attica*, Berlin, 1901-3, No. 8426, H. Berve, *Miltiades, Hermes*, Einzelschr. 2, 1937, p. 40, and N.G.L. Hammond, "The Philaids and the Chersonese," *CQ* n.s. 6, 1956, p. 117, n. 4.

13. Plut. *Sol.* 10.2. It is inferred from the Kleisthenic deme-name Philaidai for Brauron that the family originated there. But Miltiades I obviously did not live near Brauron when the Dolonkoi passed his house on the way from Delphi (Hdt. 6.35). It is probable that his house

was in what became the city deme of Lakiadai and passed ultimately by inheritance to his half-nephew Miltiades II who was registered in that deme when the Kleisthenic reforms were implemented. See Plut. *Kim.* 10.2 and *IG I²* 295.8 for Lakiadai as the deme of his son Kimon. Cf. D. M. Lewis, "Cleisthenes and Attica," *Historia* 12, 1963, p. 25.

14. *Athenian Propertied Families*, p. 300.

15. Wade-Gery, *Essays*, pp. 167-168; Davies, *Athenian Propertied Families*, p. 301. N. G. L. Hammond, *CQ* n.s. 6, 1956, pp. 113-21 inserts another Miltiades between the elder and the younger but agrees that the archon of 524/3 is Kimon's son; for refutation of this additional Miltiades see D. W. Bradeen, *Hesperia* 32, 1963, pp. 206-208.

16. Plut. *Kim.* 4, says that his nickname was κοάλε μος, "Simpleton."

17. *Essays*, pp. 157-58; his dating of the murder to 528/7 led him to refer Herodotus' remark in 6.39.2 (that the Peisistratids treated Miltiades well in spite of their complicity in the murder) both to his advancement to the archonship and his dispatch to the Chersonese. But it should be observed that ch. 39 is concerned only with his dispatch to the Chersonese.

18. The fifth name Kalliades is found in several families and it is not possible to identify either the individual or the family, so no comment is possible. See Meiggs and Lewis, *SGHI* 12, and Davies, *Athenian Propertied Families*, pp. 253 ff. for Kallias names.

I accept the restoration of the sixth name as Peisistratos, son of Hippias. Thucydides 6.54.6-7 cites him as the example of the eponymous archonship held by one of the family, and mentions his two dedications, the altar of the Twelve Gods, and the altar of the Pythian Apollo. The evidence for the altar of the Twelve Gods agrees with the 522/1 date; M. Crosby, "Altar of the Twelve Gods," *Hesperia*, Suppl. 8, 1949, pp. 97-103. The Plataians when they came to request an alliance with Athens in 519, sat there as suppliants (Hdt. 6.108.4 and for the date Thuc. 3.68.5). The elegance of the lettering of the inscription on the altar of the Pythian Apollo led to doubts that it could be as early as 522/1, but see now for defence of the date Dover, *Commentary* IV, pp. 331-32 and Meiggs and Lewis, *SGHI* No. 11, pp. 19-20.

19. If the younger Peisistratos held the archonship at the usual age of 30 in 522/1, he was born in 552/1. If his father was 30 when he was born, Hippias himself was born about 582; he would be 36 in 546, and 56 in 526. The marriage or marriages of Hippias present some difficulties. Kleidemos (*FGrH* 323 F 15) says that Peisistratos arranged marriages for his two sons after the second coup d'état, i.e. by 556 at

the latest, and Hippias married the daughter of Charmos. But Thucydides (6.55.1), says that Hippias' wife and mother of his children was Myrrhine, daughter of Kallias, son of Hyperochides. Were there two marriages, or one, and if only one, which of our authorities has given the wrong name? I prefer the less difficult solution, that there were two marriages (so also Dover, *Commentary* IV, pp. 333-34). Hippias married the daughter of Charmos, the polemarch, c. 557 or 556, even though he was rather younger than the usual age of thirty for marriage, only 25 or 26 if born in 582. There were political reasons for an early marriage, since Peisistratos needed the support of the polemarch. The first wife died very soon, in childbirth or of some illness, and Hippias married a second time, Myrrhine daughter of Kallias. The evidence favours this solution. First, Hipparchos, son of Charmos, the archon of 496/5 and the first Athenian to be ostracized in 488/7 is described as συγγενής of the tyrants, in this case a marriage connexion (*A.P.* 22.4). Secondly, Thucydides could draw upon local Athenian family traditions and is unlikely to be wrong about the name and pedigree of the wife of Hippias who was mother of his children. The name and pedigree came from family traditions and not from the stele adikias which he quotes for male members of the family. Only the nemes of Peisistratos, his sons, and Hippias' sons were I believe on the stele, an official record of their condemnation, and therefore the male line.

Hippias' birth c. 582 has been doubted because it would make him 92 at Marathon. It cannot, however, be brought down more than a few years, and that only by lowering his age at marriage much beyond the normal practice and/or having his son Peisistratos hold the archonship earlier than 30. There is little gained by making him 86 or 87 at Marathon, rather than 92. By any calculation he was a very old man, and this is not incredible. A man who survived the perils of childhood, military age, and middle life was physically tough and could live into the nineties as well as the late eighties. Davies, *Athenian Propertied Families*, p. 446, says that 570 is the latest possible date for Hippias' birth, and sees the difficulties of early marriage for Hippias, and the age of the younger Peisistratos in 522/1. But he has not worked out quite how great the difficulties are, and 570 is too late. I shall discuss more fully elsewhere his entry about Hippias' marriage (450) and the entry about the relationship with Hipparchos, son of Charmos (pp. 451-52).

20. Cadoux, "Athenian Archons," *JHS* 68, 1948, p. 109.

Quelques Remarques sur les Comparaisons dans les Histoires de Polybe

Le style de Polybe a été au cours des siècles jugé de façon un peu trop rapide et sommaire par les critiques littéraires et les historiens de la littérature grecque. Ceux-ci se sont en effet appliqués jusqu'ici au jeu assez facile de monter en épingle ses graves défauts au point de négliger presque complètement la critique de ses qualités. Car il en possède de solides qu'on a à peine soulignées. On généralise ou simplifie, me semble-t-il, un peu trop les choses en affirmant, par exemple, qu'il est "un médiocre écrivain"[1] ou en trouvant son "style franchement mauvais."[2] A dire vrai, le style de Polybe est loin d'être uniforme, étant donné que la rédaction de son immense ouvrage a demandé nombre d'années. Sans doute est-il, dans l'ensemble, inférieur au point de vue de l'expression à Hérodote, à Thucydide et à Xénophon; il rompt avec la tradition artistique et littéraire de ses grands prédécesseurs des Ve et IVe siècles. Peut-être a-t-il souffert d'avoir été trop souvent rapproché de Tite-Live, bien que ce dernier l'ait imité de près et même traduit sans toujours le reconnaître; tant il est naturel à l'écrivain de se croire grandi d'une coudée, qui feint de ne rien devoir à ses devanciers. Cette façon de procéder, d'ailleurs aussi chère à Polybe[3] qu'à Tite-Live, semble être de bonne guerre puisqu'elle s'est perpétuée jusqu'à nos jours. En tout cas, de tous les grands écrivains grecs, Polybe est encore celui qui perd le moins à être lu en traduction,[4] c'est-à-dire sous la plume d'un traducteur exact, précis, consciencieux et féru de lettres.

Cet historien rigoureux et méthodique, cet esprit froid, lucide et positif, qui a créé l'histoire pragmatique, sérieuse, utile et universelle, qui a précisé et élargi la méthode de l'histoire politique de Thucydide, exprimé des vues si profondes, voire géniales sur l'évolution des institutions et la mentalité des peuples, regardé la géographie comme le support fondamental de l'histoire, cet écrivain possède à un haut degré deux grandes qualités: la clarté et le sens de la composition. Ainsi sa narration de la marche d'Hannibal, d'Espagne en Italie, ses multiples récits de bataille et de sièges de ville — Myles, Ecnome, Drépane, Iles Egates, Lilybée, Cannes, Carthage, Syracuse, Tarente etc. — sont d'une netteté supérieure et comparent favorablement au point de vue dramatique avec les meilleurs de Thucydide ou de Xénophon, voire de Tite-Live ou de Tacite. On peut en dire autant de ses discours, dont le total s'élève à trente-sept.[5] Remarquable aussi est son sens de la composition. Polybe sait expliquer les événements avec précision, comme il sait marquer avec exactitude l'enchaînement des faits. Il conduit ses dissertations de main de maître grâce à la vigueur de son esprit et à son souci de voir clair au fond des choses.[6]

Mais il gâche ses hautes qualités par la démangeaison qu'il éprouve de disserter, de commenter, de moraliser, de juger, de donner des leçons, comme un professeur, d'enseigner la politique et l'art militaire, sans compter qu'il parle sans cesse de lui-même et de sa méthode. Il ne donne pas l'impression d'écrire, mais de réfléchir tout haut, de parler à haute voix, de dicter à de certaines heures comme en marchant, à tel point il déborde d'énergie et semble manquer de temps pour se relire. Ces digressions d'ordre moral, militaire et politique ont pour effet d'interrompre presque continuellement la marche de l'exposé et finissent par donner sur les nerfs du lecteur; Polybe nous rappelle trop souvent qu'il revient à son sujet et nous fait penser ainsi à Hérodote et à Xénophon, qui multiplient également les parenthèses et les réflexions du même genre. Fait paradoxal, en agissant de la sorte, Polybe croit bien écrire; il se donne même beaucoup de mal pour bien écrire. Conscient de sa valeur et de son originalité, fier de sa mémoire qui me paraît avoir été aussi prodigieuse que sa faculté d'observation, quelque peu prétentieux même et vaniteux, il brûle d'être lu et apprécié à tout prix des maîtres de rhétorique aussi bien que du public cultivé; il évite avec grand soin l'hiatus comme s'il voulait être le nouvel Isocrate de son siècle. Mais il est loin d'être un artiste en prose. Son vocabulaire est assez banal et limité. Il répète les mêmes mots jusqu'à nous en donner la nausée. Quant à ses phrases, elles sont ordinairement longues et compliquées.[7]

Tout cela dit, il est un aspect de son style, qu'on a jusqu'ici négligé de considérer et qui révèle sa tournure d'esprit aussi bien que ses idées favorites, c'est l'emploi qu'il fait des comparaisons dans ses *Histoires*. Nous nous proposons d'en faire un relevé complet, d'en souligner la nature, la variété et l'objet, de montrer la façon dont elles sont amenées et la place qu'elles occupent, espérant ainsi projeter quelque éclairage sur l'historien et le style historique.

I

J'ai relevé une centaine de comparaisons[8] dans ce qui nous reste des *Histoires* de Polybe. Elles figurent en plus grand nombre tout particulièrement dans les livres 1, 3, 6, 10, 11, et 12. Polybe les introduit habituellement par καθάπερ ou ὥσπερ; il lui arrive aussi d'employer ὡς, ὡσανεί, οἷον, ὅμοιον, ὁμοίως, παραπλῆσιον, παραπλησίως, τὸν αὐτὸν τρόπον. Les unes sont courtes, denses, ramassées, comme chez Théognis, les autres sont développées, soutenues, parfois même plus longues que celles d'Homère ou d'Eschyle. Certaines rapprochent hardiment l'homme de l'animal; d'autres comparent un groupe d'animaux à un autre. Quelques-unes reviennent à plusieurs reprises sous la plume de l'auteur; la plupart cependant sont uniques. Tantôt elles sont si familières qu'on dirait des proverbes, tantôt elles sont vives, pittoresques, voire hautes en couleur. Les unes sont insérées dans des harangues de généraux ou des discours d'ambassa-

deurs; les autres font partie d'une digression, d'une disserta-
tion morale, d'une réflexion personnelle, ordinairement
consécutive à un portrait ou à un récit de bataille; il en est
aussi qui sont rapportées textuellement, comme celles de
Caton, avec un évident plaisir par Polybe. Elles sont
empruntées à la guerre, à la marine et aux sports, à
l'agriculture, à l'eau et au feu, aux arts, aux lettres et aux
sciences.

Commençons par considérer celles qui ont pour objet
Polybe lui-même — à tout seigneur tout honneur: il parle si
souvent de lui-même dans ses *Histoires*, — Timée, les
historiens et l'histoire en général.

Polybe (6.58), qui vient de décrire en détail la constitution de la république romaine, désire terminer son exposé et
l'illustrer même par un fait qui fasse ressortir la vigueur de
cette constitution, ce par quoi il espère ressembler à un
artiste habile qui donne par un chef-d'oeuvre une preuve de
son adresse:

Τῶν δὲ συναπτόντων μερῶν τῆς ἱστορίας τοῖς καιροῖς, ἀφ' ὧν
παρεξέβημεν, παραλαβόντες ἐπὶ βραχὺ μιᾶς πράξεως ποιησόμεθα
κεφαλαιώδη μνήμην, ἵνα μὴ τῷ λόγῳ μόνον ἀλλὰ καὶ τοῖς
πράγμασιν, ὥσπερ ἀγαθοῦ τεχνίτου δεῖγμα τῶν ἔργων ἕν τι
προενεγκάμενοι . . .

Polybe (33.21) éprouve aussi par moment le besoin de
s'arrêter, par crainte d'écrire des songes ou de donner dans la
fable et de se conduire ainsi comme un berger qui trairait une
chèvre en tenant un crible au-dessous:

Ἀλλὰ γὰρ ὀκνῶ μή ποτ' εἰς τὸ περιφερόμενον ἐμπεσὼν λάθω,
πότερο ὁ τὸν τράγον ἀμέλγων ἀφρονέστερος ἢ ὁ τὸ κόσκινον
ὑπέχων· δοκῶ γὰρ δὴ κἀγὼ πρὸς ὁμολογουμένην ψευδολογίαν
ἀκριβολογούμενος καὶ τὸν ἐπιμετροῦντα λόγον εἰσφέρων
παραπλήσιόν τι ποιεῖν.

Polybe (35.6.4), naturellement désireux de voir les bannis
d'Achaïe, ses compatriotes, rentrer dans leur patrie et y
revêtir les dignités dont ils jouissaient avant leur exil, se
rendit un jour au sénat à Rome pour y sonder Caton sur

l'affaire. Ce dernier, qui avait des lettres et ne manquait pas d'esprit, lui répondit en riant qu'il ressemblait à Ulysse qui, une fois sorti de l'antre du Cyclope, aimerait y retourner pour y reprendre son chapeau et sa ceinture:

ὁ δὲ μειδιάσας ἔφη τὸν Πολύβιον, ὥσπερ τὸν Ὀδυσσέα, βούλεσθαι πάλιν εἰς τὸ τοῦ Κύκλωπος σπήλαιον εἰσελθεῖν, τὸ πιλίον ἐκεῖ καὶ τὴν ζώνην ἐπιλελησμένον.

En quatre passages du livre 12,[9] Polybe critique Timée de Tauroménion (Sicile) et sa méthode historique. Il s'en prend d'abord à ses erreurs. De même qu'il suffit d'une seule goutte d'eau d'un récipient pour en connaître le contenu, ainsi il suffit de relever une erreur ou deux dans un livre pour nous rendre méfiant quant aux dires de son auteur:

Καθάπερ γὰρ ἐκ τῶν παροιμιῶν ἱκανὸν εἶναι φασι σταλαγμὸν ἕνα τοῦ μεγίστου τεύχους εἰς τὸ γνῶναι τὸ πᾶν ἔγχυμα, τὸν αὐτὸν τρόπον καὶ περὶ τῶν ὑποκειμένων χρὴ διαλαμβάνειν.

Polybe (12.25a.5) en veut aussi à la façon dont Timée compose ses discours; loin de rapporter exactement ce qui a été dit, comme le fait si judicieusement Polybe, il parle sur un sujet donné comme un professeur dans une école de rhétorique pour faire valoir son talent:

οὐ γὰρ τὰ ῥηθέντα γέγραφεν, οὐδ᾽ ὡς ἐρρήθη κατ᾽ ἀλήθειαν, ἀλλὰ προθέμενος ὡς δεῖ ῥηθῆναι, πάντας ἐξαριθμεῖται τοὺς ῥηθέντας λόγους καὶ τὰ παρεπόμενα τοῖς πράγμασιν οὕτως, ὡσανεί τις ἐν διατριβῇ πρὸς ὑπόθεσιν ἐπιχειροίη, ὥσπερ ἀπόδειξιν τῆς ἑαυτοῦ δυνάμεως ποιούμενος, ἀλλ᾽ οὐκ ἐξήγησιν τῶν κατ᾽ ἀλήθειαν εἰρημένων.

Timée, pour avoir vécu cinquante ans sans interruption à Athènes, sans aucune expérience de la réalité, de la guerre et de la politique, effleure la vérité comme un peintre qui prend pour modèle un mannequin empaillé: il lui manque l'expression de la vie, parce qu'il est trop livresque et se fonde uniquement sur la maîtrise des documents (12.25h.2-3):

κἂν ποτε δὲ τῆς ἀληθείας ἐπιψαύσῃ, παραπλήσιός ἐστι τοῖς ζωγράφοις τοῖς ἀπὸ τῶν ἀνασεσαγμένων θυλάκων ποιουμένοις τὰς ὑπογραφάς· καὶ γὰρ ἐπ' ἐκείνων ἡ μὲν ἐκτὸς ἐνίοτε γραμμὴ σῴζεται, τὸ δὲ τῆς ἐμφάσεως καὶ τῆς ἐναργείας τῶν ἀληθινῶν ζῴων ἄπεστιν, ὅπερ ἴδιον ὑπάρχει τῆς ζωγραφικῆς τέχνης. Τὸ δ' αὐτὸ συμβαίνει καὶ περὶ Τίμαιον καὶ καθόλου τοὺς ἀπὸ ταύτης τῆς βιβλιακῆς ἕξεως ὁρμωμένους.

D'autre part, Timée est bien naïf de croire qu'il pourra écrire comme il faut l'histoire moderne en se modelant sur l'histoire ancienne; pour écrire l'histoire de l'époque moderne, qui repose sur une réalité proche de lui, l'historien doit être versé dans la politique et l'art militaire; autrement il serait comme un artiste, qui croirait être un bon peintre pour avoir observé les oeuvres des peintres anciens (12.25e.7):

τό γε μὴν ἀπ' αὐτῆς ταύτης τῆς δυνάμεως ὁρμηθέντα πεπεῖσθαι γράφειν τὰς ἐπιγνομένας πράξεις καλῶς, ὃ πέπεισται Τίμαιος, τελέως εὔηθες καὶ παραπλήσιον ὡς ἂν εἴ τις τὰ τῶν ἀρχαίων ζωγράφων ἔργα θεασάμενος ἱκανὸς οἴοιτο ζωγράφος εἶναι καὶ προστάτης τῆς τέχνης.

Pour Polybe, l'histoire n'est utile que si elle exprime la vérité; l'utilité y va de pair avec la vérité. Faute de quoi, l'histoire ressemble à un animal privé de la vie; il ne sert absolument à rien. Cette image favorite de Polybe revient à deux reprises aux livres 1 (1.14-16) et 12 (12.12.3) en des termes presque identiques:

α) ὥσπερ γὰρ ζῷον τῶν ὄψεων ἀφαιρεθεισῶν ἀχρειοῦται τὸ ὅλον, οὕτως ἐξ ἱστορίας ἀναιρεθείσης τῆς ἀληθείας τὸ καταλειπόμενον αὐτῆς ἀνωφελὲς γίνεται διήγημα. (1.7)

β) καθάπερ ἐμφύχου σώματος τῶν ὄψεων ἐξαιρεθεισῶν ἀρχειοῦται τὸ ὅλον, οὕτως ἐξ ἱστορίας ἐὰν ἄρῃς τὴν ἀλήθειαν, τὸ καταλειπόμενον αὐτῆς ἀνωφελὲς γίνεται διήγημα. (12.3)

La vérité doit être le guide par excellence des ouvrages historiques. Le véritable historien rapporte exactement ce qui est arrivé et ce qui a été dit; loin de lui l'idée de vouloir impressionner ses lecteurs par des descriptions exagérées, sensationnelles, ou de faire comme les poètes tragiques qui imaginent ce que les caractères ont probablement dit;

l'histoire et la tragédie n'ont certes pas le même fin (2.56.10):

> δεῖ τοιγαροῦν οὐκ ἐπιπλήττειν τὸν συγγραφέα τερατευόμενον διὰ τῆς ἱστορίας τοὺς ἐντυγχάνοντας οὐδὲ τοὺς ἐνδεχομένους λόγους ζητεῖν καὶ τὰ παρεπόμενα τοῖς ὑποκειμένοις ἐξαριθμεῖσθαι, καθάπερ οἱ τραγῳδιογράφοι, τῶν δὲ πραχθέντων καὶ ῥηθέντων κατ᾽ ἀλήθειαν αὐτῶν μνημονεύειν πάμπαν, (κ) ἄν πάνυ μέτρια τυγχάνωσιν ὄντα.

Que Polybe n'ait pas toujours respecté cet excellent principe, est l'évidence même; il est relativement facile de relever chez lui des descriptions et des narrations qui sentent l'école de rhétorique et visent à la sensation; il n'a pas toujours su se garder du principal défaut de style de son époque: la boursouflure ou l'exagération. Quoi qu'il en soit, il revient au livre suivant (3.48.8) à son image favorite des poètes tragiques quand il fait la critique de quelques historiens qui ont décrit avec beaucoup d'exagération le passage des Alpes par Hannibal; comme les poètes tragiques, ils choisissent des sujets extraordinaires et emploient des dieux ou des demi-dieux pour la catastrophe de leurs pièces:

> ἐξ ὧν εἰκότως ἐμπίπτουσιν εἰς τὸ παραπλήσιον τοῖς τραγῳδιογράφοις· καὶ γὰρ ἐκείνοις πᾶσιν αἱ καταστροφαὶ τῶν δραμάτων προσδέονται θεοῦ καὶ μηχανῆς διὰ τὸ τὰς πρώτας ὑποθέσεις ψευδεῖς καὶ παραλόγους λαμβάνειν, τούς τε συγγραφέας ἀνάγκη τὸ παραπλήσιον πάσχειν καὶ ποιεῖν ἥρωάς τε καὶ θεοὺς ἐπιφαινομένους, ἐπειδὰν τὰς ἀρχὰς ἀπιθάνους καὶ ψευδεῖς ὑποστήσωνται.

Pas plus que les poètes tragiques, le véritable historien ne doit imiter ces peintres de fresques murales qui tracent les faits sur les murailles des villes à mesure qu'ils arrivent et se vantent ensuite d'embrasser tout ce qui s'est passé tant chez les Grecs que chez les Barbares; loin de procéder comme ces artistes, il doit plutôt expliquer les faits et montrer les relations entre ces derniers (5.33.5): ...

> ...ἔνιοι τῶν πραγματευομένων οὐδ᾽ ἐφ᾽ ὅσον οἱ κατὰ καιροὺς ἐν ταῖς χρονογραφίαις ὑπομνηματιζόμενοι πολιτικῶς εἰς τοὺς τοίχους, οὐδ᾽ ἐπὶ τοσοῦτο μνησθέντες, πάσας φασὶ τὰς κατὰ τὴν

Ἑλλάδα καὶ βάρβαρον περιειληφέναι πράξεις.

Il doit aussi éviter de se perdre en des détails et de s'arrêter à tout propos sur tout ce qui lui paraît étranger ou singulier; procède-t-il ainsi, il ressemble fort à ces gourmets qui, mettant la main à tous les plats, ne savourent aucun mets à loisir et nuisent ainsi à leur santé au lieu de l'entretenir et de la fortifier. De même, ceux qui aiment seulement l'histoire remplie de faits extraordinaires et dépourvue d'un thème principal ne peuvent goûter l'histoire comme elle mérite de l'être (3.57.10):

εἰ δέ τινες πάντως ἐπιζητοῦσι κατὰ τόπον καὶ κατὰ μέρος τῶν τοιούτων ἀκούειν, ἴσως ἀγνοοῦσι παραπλήσιόν τι πάσχοντες τοῖς λίχνοις τῶν δειπνητῶν. Καὶ γὰρ ἐκεῖνοι πάντων ἀπογευόμενοι τῶν παρακειμένων οὔτε κατὰ τὸ παρὸν οὐδενὸς ἀληθινῶς ἀπολαύουσι τῶν βρωμάτων οὔτ᾽ εἰς τὸ μέλλον ὠφέλλιμον ἐξ αὐτῶν τὴν ἀνάδοσιν καὶ τροφὴν κομίζονται, πᾶν δέ τοὐναντίον· οἵ τε περὶ τὴν ἀνάγνωσιν τὸ παραπλήσιον ποιοῦντες οὔτε τῆς παραυτίκα διαγωγῆς ἀληθινῶς οὔτε τῆς εἰς τὸ μέλλον ὠφελείας στοχάζονται δεόντως.

Polybe revient souvent sur l'idée qu'il est absolument impossible d'écrire l'histoire moderne en restant enfermé dans son cabinet de travail. Il faut que l'historien joigne la pratique à la théorie, c'est-à-dire ait une connaissance directe des lieux et des hommes, des institutions et des peuples, de la guerre et de la politique. A quoi sert-il, par exemple, d'avoir une connaissance profonde de la théorie médicale si l'on est impuissant devant un malade? La médecine et l'histoire ont plusieurs points de comparaison. C'est une image favorite de Polybe.[10] Les médecins versés dans la partie théorique de la médecine sont comme les pilotes qui dirigent un navire d'après un livre:

... ὅταν ἐπὶ τὴν ἀλήθειαν ἀπαγαγὼν ἄρρωστον ἐγχειρίσῃς, τοσοῦτον ἀπέχοντες εὑρίσκονται τῆς χρείας ὅσον καὶ οἱ μηδ᾽ ἀνεγνωκότες ἁπλῶς ἰατρικὸν ὑπόμνημα· ·... εἰσὶ γὰρ ἀληθῶς ὅμοιοι τοῖς ἐκ βιβλίου κυβερνῶσιν.

Du reste, du temps de Polybe, beaucoup d'écrivains se

lançaient dans la science historique, comme d'autres en
médecine, en raison de sa vénérable réputation, sans
préparation dans un cas comme dans l'autre, de sorte que
beaucoup d'auteurs, comme de vils apothicaires assoiffés de
popularité, débitent tout ce qu'ils jugent opportun pour
gagner leur vie:

παραπλησίως (δ') ἐφίενται μὲν ταύτης πολλοὶ διὰ τὴν
προγεγενημένην περὶ αὐτῆς δόξαν, προσφέρονται δὲ πρὸς τὴν
ἐπιβολὴν οἱ μὲν πλεῖστοι τῶν γραφόντων ἁπλῶς δίκαιον οὐδὲν
πλὴν εὐχέρειαν καὶ τόλμαν καὶ ῥᾳδιουργίαν, παραπλήσιον τοῖς
φαρμακοπώλαις δοξοκοποῦντες καὶ πρὸς χάριν βλέποντες ἀεὶ τὰ
πρὸς τοὺς καιροὺς ἕνεκα τοῦ πορίζειν τὸν βίον διὰ τούτων.

Ajoutons que ces historiens mal préparés, en formant des
projets au-dessus de leurs forces (39.1.8), sont comme ces
athlètes qui, après avoir donné leur nom pour les combats de
lutte ou de pugilat, déclareraient à l'auditoire ce mot spirituel
de Caton: "Messieurs, je vous demande pardon si je ne puis
endurer ni la fatigue ni les plaies."

Καὶ παραπλησίως ἄχρηστον ὡσανεί τις εἰς τοὺς γυμνικοὺς
ἀγῶνας ἀπογραψάμενος πυγμὴν ἢ παγκράτιον, παρελθὼν εἰς τὸ
στάδιον, ὅτε δέοι μάχεσθαι, παραιτοῖτο τοὺς θεωμένους
συγγνώμην ἔχειν, ἐὰν μὴ δύνηται μήτε τὸν πόνον ὑπομένειν μήτε
τὰς πληγάς. Δῆλον γὰρ ὡς εἰκὸς γέλωτα τὸν τοιοῦτον ὀφλεῖν καὶ
τὴν δίκην ἐκ χειρὸς λαμβάνειν· ὅπερ ἔδει καὶ τοὺς τοιούτους
ἱστοριογράφους, ἵνα μὴ κατετόλμων τοῦ καλῶς ἔχοντος.

II

Les personnages historiques suivants sont aussi l'objet de
comparaison dans les *Histoires* de Polybe: Antiochus
Epiphane, Aristocratès, Cléomène, Dioeus, Hamilcar Barca,
Hannibal, Nabis, Persée et Eumène, Philippe V, Prusias,
Scipion et Timoléon. Commençons par "les trois grands" de
Carthage: Hamilcar Barca, Hannibal et Hasdrubal.

Hamilcar Barca, campé devant Palerme (247-44), et le
commandant du camp romain se livrent des combats
nombreux et variés comme deux pugilistes de valeur égale qui

se disputent une couronne (l.57 .1-2):

> Καθάπερ γὰρ ἐπὶ τῶν διαφερόντων πυκτῶν καὶ ταῖς γενναιότησι
> καὶ ταῖς εὐεξίαις, ὅταν εἰς τὸν ὑπὲρ αὐτοῦ τοῦ στεφάνου
> συγκαταστάντες καιρὸν διαμάχωνται πληγὴν ἐπὶ πληγῇ τιθέντες
> ἀδιαπαύστως, λόγον μὲν ἢ πρόνοιαν ἔχειν ὑπὲρ ἑκάστης ἐπιβολῆς
> καὶ πληγῆς οὔτε τοῖς ἀγωνιζομένοις οὔτε τοῖς θεωμένοις ἐστὶ
> δυνατόν, ἐκ δὲ τῆς καθόλου τῶν ἀνδρῶν ἐνεργείας καὶ τῆς
> ἑκατέρου φιλοτιμίας ἔστι καὶ τῆς ἐμπειρίας αὐτῶν καὶ τῆς
> δυνάμεως πρὸς δὲ καὶ τῆς εὐψυχίας ἱκανὴν ἔννοιαν λαβεῖν, οὕτως
> δὲ καὶ περὶ τῶν νῦν λεγομένων στρατηγῶν.

A Eryx, les deux puissances en présence finirent, comme deux lutteurs insensibles èt invincibles, par remporter chacune une couronne sacrée (1.58.7):

> τέλος οὐχ ὡς Φάβιός φησιν, ἐξαδυνατοῦντες καὶ περικακοῦντες,
> ἀλλ ὡς ἄν ἀπαθεῖς καὶ ἀήττητοί τινες ἄνδρες ἱερὸν ἐποιήσαντο
> στέφανον.

Les deux puissances en présence se livraient un combat dśespéré comme font des coqs de race (1.58.7-8):

> Τὰ μὲν οὖν περὶ τὸν Ἔρυκα καὶ τὰς πεζικὰς δυνάμεις τοιαύτην
> ἔσχε διάθεσιν, τὰ δὲ πολιτεύματα ἦν ἀμφοτέρων παραπλήσια τοῖς
> ψυχομαχοῦσι τῶν εὐγενῶν ὀρνίθων...

Et l'auteur de développer la comparaison avec autant de plaisir que de connaissance de la matière, les combats de coqs étant un sport favori des Grecs.

Hamilcar, lors du défilé de la hache, se conduisit comme un habile joueur en isolant et en encerclant les mercenaires de Mâtho et de Spendius, de sorte qu'il put en tuer un grand nombre au cours d'opérations secondaires (1.84.7):

> Πολλοὺς μὲν γὰρ αὐτῶν ἐν ταῖς κατὰ μέρος χρείαις
> ἀποτεμνόμενος καὶ συγκλείων ὥσπερ ἀγαθὸς πεττευτὴς ἀμαχεὶ
> διέφθειρε.

Technicien de métier, il ne laissait rien au hasard ou à l'improvisation. Hannibal (9.19.3), son fils, avait été formé à bonne école. Ainsi, pendant les seize années qu'il combattit les Romains, réussit-il, comme un bon capitaine de navire, à tenir ses troupes sous son ferme commandement:

συνέχων ὑφ᾿ αὑτόν, ὥσπερ ἀγαθὸς κυβερνήτης.

Quant à Hasdrubal, son frère, il se présenta un jour à une conférence avec les Romains en véritable acteur de premier rôle dans une tragédie. Comme il était démesurément gros et replet, le public aurait pu aisément le prendre, non pas pour un général ou pour le gouverneur de Carthage, mais plutôt pour un homme qui vit dans un marché comme les boeufs qu'on y engraisse. Polybe (38.8.6-7) prend un évident plaisir à le présenter ainsi et à l'écraser sous son mépris:

ὁ δὲ πάλιν ἐξεπορεύετο μετὰ μεγάλης ἀξίας ἐν τῇ πορφυρίδι καὶ τῇ πανοπλίᾳ βάδην, ὥστε τοὺς ἐν ταῖς τραγῳδίαις τυράννους πολύ τι προσοφείλειν. ἦν μὲν οὖν καὶ φύσει σάρκινος, τότε δὲ καὶ κοιλίαν εἰλήφει καὶ τῷ χρώματι παρὰ φύσιν ἐπικεκαυμένος ἦν, ὥστε δοκεῖν ἐν πανηγύρει που διαιτᾶσθαι παραπλησίως τοῖς σιτευτοῖς βουσῶ ...

   Par contraste, Scipion Emilien, qui lui faisait face à Carthage, promenait ses regards un peu comme un roi et était aussi ardent, infatigable même, qu'un lévrier de race à la chasse (31.29.7):

γενομένης δὲ μεγάλης ἐνθουσιάσεως περὶ τοῦτο τὸ μέρος, ὡς κατά τε τὴν ἡλικίαν ἀκμαίως ἔχοντος αὐτοῦ καὶ κατὰ φύσιν οἰκείως διακειμένου, καθάπερ εὐγενοῦς σκύλακος, ἐπίμονον αὐτοῦ συνέβη γενέσθαι τὴν περὶ τὰς κυνηγεσίας ὁρμήν.

Polybe rapproche aussi de l'animal Philippe V de Macédoine,[11] dont les défauts, comme ceux des chevaux se faisant vieux, augmentaient à mesure qu'il avançait en âge:

τὰ δὲ κακὰ προβαίνοντι κατὰ τὴν ἡλικίαν ἐπιγενέσθαι, καθάπερ ἐνίοις ἐπιγένεται γηράσκουσι τῶν ἵππων.

Bien plus, une fois rendu au pays des Bargyliens, il y vécut comme un loup affamé, pillant les uns, arrachant aux autres par force de quoi nourrir son armée qui souffrait (16.24.4-5):

ἐξ ὧν ἐδυσχρηστεῖτο μὲν ὑπερβαλλόντως, ἠναγκάζετο δὲ κατὰ τὸ παρὸν ἐπιμένων αὐτοῦ, τὸ δὴ λεγόμενον, λύκου βίον ζῆν.

Persée, son fils,[12] qui était trop bien connu pour son avarice et ses folles dépenses, en vint un jour à un accommodement avec Eumène de Crète, pour qui les appâts, les promesses et les ruses n'avaient point de secret. Le combat entre les deux, au dire de Polybe, dut être ridicule; en tout cas l'historien le considère comme un spectacle de gymnase ou de palestre; Persée hésitait à remettre les quinze talents promis, brûlant, tel un médecin charlatan, de tenir les arrhes plutôt que d'atteindre un paiement, tandis qu'Eumène rivalisait d'ardeur pour toucher la somme et mettre fin à la guerre; on eût dit deux vaillants athlètes de force égale luttant pour la couronne sacrée:

ὁ δ' Εὐμένης σπουδάζων, καθάπερ οἱ μοχθηροὶ τῶν ἰατρῶν, περὶ τὸ πρόδομα μᾶλλον ἤ περὶ τὸν μισθὸν τέλος ἀπέστη τῆς ἐπιβολῆς, ἀδυνατήσας καταγωνίσασθαι τῇ σφετέρᾳ πανουργίᾳ τὴν τοῦ Περσέως μικρολογίαν καὶ δὴ τῷ τοιούτῳ τρόπῳ ποιήσαντας ἱερὸν τὸν στέφανον τῆς φιλαργυρίας διελύθησαν ἐπ᾽ ἴσης, καθάπερ ἀγαθοὶ παλαισταί.

Antiochus Epiphane de Syrie (26.1.5) aimait fréquenter les boutiques de l'agora *incognito* ou encore s'y promener revêtu de la toge comme un démarque ou comme un agoranome, donnant la main à ceux-ci, embrassant ceux-là:

πολλάκις δὲ καὶ τὴν βασιλικὴν ἀποθέμενος ἐσθῆτα τήβενναν ἀναλαβὼν περιῄει κατὰ τὴν ἀγορὰν ἀρχαιρεσιάζων καὶ τοὺς μὲν δεξιούμενος, τοὺς δὲ καὶ περιπτύσσων παρεκάλει φέρειν αὐτῷ τὴν ψῆφον, ποτὲ μὲν ὡς ἀγορανόμος γένηται, ποτὲ δὲ καὶ ὡς δήμαρχος.

Aristocratès, préteur de Rhodes, fut choisi général pour son air noble et sa taille avantageuse (33.4). Mais les Rhodiens eurent tôt fait de se repentir de leur geste, car il se mit à agir avec précipitation et se révéla tout autre à l'épreuve comme une fausse monnaie dans le creuset:

ἐλθὼν γὰρ εἰς τὰς πράξεις ὥσπερ εἰς πῦρ, καθάπερ τὰ κίβδηλα τῶν νομισμάτων, ἀλλοῖος ἐφάνη. Τοῦτο δ' ἐγένετο δῆλον ἐπ' αὐτῶν τῶν ἔργων.

Dioeus, préteur des Achéens, désirait rentrer dans sa

patrie comme un homme dépourvu de toute expérience de la natation qui, après s'être jeté à la mer sans réfléchir, penserait ensuite aux moyens de gagner la terre (38.16.12):

Καὶ ἐβουλεύετο περὶ τῆς εἰς οἶκον ἀνακομιδῆς, ὅμοιων ποιῶν ὡς εἴ τις ἄπειρος ὑπάρχων τοῦ νεῖν καὶ μέλλων αὐτὸν ῥίπτειν εἰς τὸ πέλαγος περὶ μὲν τοῦ ῥῖψαι μὴ βουλεύοιτο, ῥίψας δὲ διανοοῖτο περὶ τοῦ πῶς ἂν ἐκνήξαιτο πρὸς τὴν γῆν.

Nabis, tyran de Lacédémone, tenait sa puissance pour un asile sacré et considérait Sparte comme un repaire de scélérats (16.13.2):

ὁμοίως δὲ καὶ τίνα τρόπον ἀναδείξας, τὴν ἑαυτοῦ δύναμιν οἷον ἄσυλον ἱερὸν τοῖς ἢ δι' ἀσέβειαν ἢ πονηρίαν φεύγουσι τὰς ἑαυτῶν πατρίδας ἤθροισε πλῆθος ἀνθρώπων ἀνοσίων εἰς τὴν Σπάρτην, ἐν τοῖς πρὸ τούτων δεδηλώκαμεν.

Prusias,[13] roi de Bithynie, fut pris un jour d'un tel accès de colère et de folie que, non content de renverser les temples et d'en dépouiller les images des dieux, il tomba à genoux et se mit, habillé comme une femme, à adorer la statue d'Esculape, qu'il prit ensuite sur ses épaules et emporta chez lui:

προσκυνοῦντα καὶ λιπαροῦντα τὰς τραπέζας καὶ τοὺς βωμοὺς ἐξάλλως, ὅπερ ὁ Προυσίας εἴθιστο ποιεῖν γονυπετῶν καὶ γυναικιζόμενος.

Timoléon (12.23.7), que Timée mettait au-dessus des dieux, se comparaît aux héros les plus éclatants et se tenait pour le modèle achevé du citoyen et de l'homme d'Etat, bien qu'il n'eût accompli rien de grandiose. Timoléon n'était jamais sorti de Corinthe, sa ville natale, sauf une fois pour acquérir de la gloire à Syracuse, en Sicile, dans une île comme dans une saucière à vinaigre:

πεφιλοδοξηκὼς ἐν αὐτῇ Σικελίᾳ, καθάπερ ἐν ὀξυβάφῳ.

III

Polybe emploie aussi des comparaisons pour caractériser des peuples, des groupes de gens, des foules, des villes, des lieux.

Les Achéens[14] se sentaient comme emportés par un torrent impétueux à tel point leur chef Dioeus débordait de fureur et de témérité. Les uns se livraient aux Romains à l'envi comme des gens coupables de s'être opposés à eux, les autres, tels des suppliants, avouaient avoir violé les traités:

λοιπόν, οἷον ὑπὸ χειμάρρου τινὸς λάβρου προωθούμενοι καὶ φερόμενοι μετὰ βίας, ἐπηκολούθουν τῇ τοῦ προεστᾶτος ἀγνοίᾳ καὶ παρακοπῇ ... οἱ μὲν ἦγον ἐκδώσοντες ἀλλήλους τοῖς πολεμίοις ὡς ἀλλοτρίους γεγονότας Ῥωμαίων ... οἱ δὲ μεθ᾽ ἱκετηρίας ἀπήντων, ὁμολογοῦντες παρεσπονδηκέναι καὶ πυνθανόμενοι τί δεῖ πάσχειν.

Pour Philopoemen, les Achéens, en s'empressant comme des prisonniers de guerre de faire toutes les volontés des Romains, ne diffèrent guère des gens de Sicile et de Capoue qui furent toujours des esclaves (24.13.4):

Ἐὰν δ᾽ αὐτοὶ καταγνόντες τῶν ἰδίων δικαίων αὐτόθεν εὐθέως καθάπερ οἱ δοριάλωτοι πρὸς πᾶν τὸ κελευόμενον ἑτοίμους ἡμᾶς αὐτοὺς παρασκευάζωμεν, τί διοίσει τὸ τῶν Ἀχαιῶν ἔθνος Σικελιωτῶν καὶ Καπυανῶν τῶν ὁμολογουμένως καὶ πάλαι δουλευόντων;

Les Athéniens, eux, sont si changeants, mobiles, indisciplinés, donc difficiles à gouverner, qu'ils sont comme des vaisseaux sans capitaines (6.44.2-4):

ἀεὶ γάρ ποτε τὸν τῶν Ἀθηναίων δῆμον παραπλήσιον εἶναι συμβαίνει τοῖς ἀδεσπότοις σκάφεσι.

Et Polybe de poursuivre l'image nautique en une quinzaine de lignes:

ὅ δὴ καὶ τῇ τῶν Ἀθηναίων πολιτείᾳ πλεονάκις ἤδη συμβέβηκε.

C'est aussi à eux-mêmes, et non à la Fortune ou à leurs voisins, que doivent s'en prendre les Cianiens (15.21.5) pour les grandes calamités dans lesquelles ils sont tombés; ils sont comme des brutes incapables du moindre soupçon. Philippe n'éprouva donc pas beaucoup de difficulté à s'emparer de la ville des Cianiens:

εἰς ταύτας οἷον ἐθελοντὴν ἐνέπεσον τὰς ἀτυχίας, εἰς ἃς οὐκ οἶδ᾿ ὅπως πάντες ἄνθρωποι προφανῶς ἐμπίπτοντες οὐ δύνανται λῆξαι τῆς ἀνοίας, ἀλλ᾿ οὐδὲ βραχὺ διαπιστῆσαι (ῥᾴδιον), καθάπερ ἔνια τῶν ἀλόγων ζῴων ...

Les habitants de Péra ne se conduisent guère mieux (30.24). Comme des esclaves tirés inopinément de leurs fers, ils ne savent trop que faire de leur délivrance. Tant il est vrai que tout a une fin, même la souffrance. Mais ils sont si peu habitués à l'usage de la liberté qu'ils s'agitent sans cesse et se croient même tenus de faire des choses extraordinaires.

Ὅμοιοι γὰρ ἦσαν οἱ τὴν Περαίαν κατοικοῦντες τοῖς οἰκέταις τοῖς ἐκτῶν δεσμῶν ἀνελπίστως λελυμένοις, οἵτινες ἀπιστοῦντες τοῖς παροῦσι μείζω μὲν διαβαίνουσι τῆς κατὰ φύσιν κινήσεως, οὐ δοκοῦσι δὲ γινώσκεσθαι παρὰ τοῖς ἀπαντῶσιν οὐδὲ συνορᾶσθαι διότι λέλυνται σαφῶς, ἐὰν μή τι παράλογον ποιῶσι καὶ τῶν ἄλλων ἐξηλλαγμένον.

Polybe (36.17.8), observant le dépeuplement des villes de Grèce par suite de la lâcheté, de la paresse et des débauches des hommes qui refusent de se marier ou d'avoir de nombreux enfants, voit les maisons désertes et les villes, semblables aux ruches des abeilles, dénuées de force:

ὅτε γὰρ ἑνὸς ὄντος ἢ δυεῖν, τούτων τὸν μὲν πόλεμος, τὸν δὲ νόσος ἐνστᾶσα παρείλετο, δῆλον ὡς ἀνάγκη καταλείπεσθαι τὰς οἰκήσεις ἐρήμους, καὶ καθάπερ ἐπὶ τῶν μελιττῶν τὰ σμήνη, τὸν αὐτὸν τρόπον κατὰ βραχὺ καὶ τὰς πόλεις ἀπορουμένας ἀδυνατεῖν.

L'image de la multitude, comparée à la mer, revient à plusieurs reprises sous la plume de Polybe.[15] Elle est toujours développée. Ainsi Scipion, dans son discours où il parle de la sédition qui avait éclaté parmi ses soldats (11.29.10-11), reconnaît que la foule est susceptible des mêmes agitations que la mer:

καθάπερ γὰρ κἀκείνης ἡ μὲν ἰδία φύσις ἐστὶν ἀβλαβὴς τοῖς
χρωμένοις καὶ στάσιμος, ὅταν δ᾽ εἰς αὐτὴν ἐμπέσῃ τὰ πνεύματα
βίᾳ, τοιαύτη φαίνεται τοῖς χρωμένοις οἷοί τινες ἂν ὦσιν οἱ
κυκλοῦντες αὐτὴν ἄνεμοι, τὸν αὐτὸν τρόπον καὶ τὸ πλῆθος ἀεὶ καὶ
φαίνεται καὶ γίνεται πρὸς τοὺς χρωμένους οἵους ἂν ἔχῃ
προστάτας καὶ συμβούλους.

Parlant de la situation politique dans les états de la Grèce,
Polybe y constate que la multitude, calme et tranquille
comme la mer jusqu'au jour où des vents impétueux viennent
à fondre sur ses eaux, peut être aussi terrible et formidable
que l'océan agité, comme cela était arrivé en Italie
(21.31.10-11):

καὶ γὰρ ἐκείνην κατὰ μὲν τὴν αὐτῆς φύσιν ἀεί ποτ᾽ εἶναι γαληνὴν
καὶ καθεστηκυῖαν καὶ συλλήβδην τοιαύτην ὥστε μηδέποτ᾽ ἂν
ἐνοχλῆσαι μηδένα τῶν προσπελαζόντων αὐτῇ καὶ χρωμένων·
ἐπειδὰν δ᾽ ἐμπεσόντες εἰς αὐτὴν ἄνεμοι βίαιοι ταράξωσι καὶ παρὰ
φύσιν ἀναγκάσωσι κινεῖσθαι, τότε μηθὲν ἔτι δεινότερον εἶναι μηδὲ
φοβερώτερον θαλάττης· ὃ καὶ νῦν τοῖς κατὰ τὴν Αἰτωλίαν
συμπεσεῖν.

Toujours en Etolie (l'animosité de Polybe contre cet Etat est
évidente), écrit Polybe (30.11.6), personne n'agissait selon le
bon sens et la raison, à tel point la population était troublée
comme une mer agitée par la tempête:

διόπερ ἦν ἀκρισίας καὶ παρανομίας καὶ φόνου πλήρη τὰ κατὰ
τὴν Αἰτωλίαν, καὶ τῶν πραττομένων παρ᾽ αὐτοῖς ἐκ λογισμοῦ μὲν
καὶ προθέσεως οὐδὲν ἐπετελεῖτο, πάντα δ᾽ εἰκῇ καὶ φύρδην
ἐπράττετο, καθαπερεὶ λαίλαπός τινος ἐκπεπτωκυίας εἰς αὐτούς.

Outre la foule et la ville, il est un autre groupe humain
qui fait l'objet d'une comparaison favorite chez Polybe: ce
sont les commandants. Pour avoir été lui-même commandant
de cavalerie et stratège, pour avoir vécu en la compagnie de
grands généraux, l'historien de la république romaine ne
manque jamais l'occasion de faire des réflexions sur le
commandement militaire. Ainsi le commandant d'une armée
est fort important, puisque tous les espoirs des soldats
reposent sur lui. Vient-il à tomber, sa disparition, comme
celle d'un pilote de vaisseau, est une ruine complète

(10.33.5); même la victoire en pareil cas n'est d'aucune utilité:

> πταίσαντος δέ, καθάπερ ἐν νηὶ τοῦ κυβερνήτου, κἂν (τὸ νικᾶν) ἡ τύχη τοῖς πολλοῖς παραδιδῷ κρατεῖν τῶν ἐχθρῶν, οὐδὲν ὄφελος γίνεται διὰ τὸ πάσας ἐξηρτῆθαι τὰς ἐλπίδας ἑκάστοις ἐκ τῶν ἡγουμένων.

Dans un autre passage (3.81.11), il compare également un commandant d'armée à un pilote de vaisseau; ôtez ce dernier de son poste de commande, le bateau ne manquera pas de tomber peu après aux mains de l'ennemi; le même sort arrivera à une armée, si l'on surprend son général par ruse ou par artifice:

> καθάπερ γὰρ νεὼς ἐὰν ἀφέλῃ τις τὸν κυβερνήτην, τὸ ὅλον αὐτανδρὶ σκάφος ὑποχείριον γίνεται τοῖς ἐχθροῖς, τὸν αὐτὸν τρόπον ἐὰν τὸν προεστῶτα (πόλεμον) δυνάμεως χειρώσηταί τις κατὰ τὰς ἐπιβολὰς καὶ συλλογισμούς, αὐτανδρὶ γίνεται πολλάκις κρατεῖν τῶν ἀντιταττομένων.

Il en est des généraux comme des bêtes sauvages (10.41.7); celles-ci révèlent leur courage et leur force dans la chasse, quand elles sont de tous côtés exposées au péril:

> καθάπερ (γὰρ) ἐν ταῖς κυνηγεσίαις τὰ ζῷα τότε δίαδηλα γίνεται κατὰ τὴν ἀλκὴν καὶ τὴν δύναμιν, ὅταν τὸ δεινὸν αὐτὰ περιστῇ πανταχόθεν, τὸν ἀυτὸν τρόπον συμβαίνει καὶ ἐπὶ τῶν ἡγουμενων.

Et Polybe de citer Philippe en exemple. Du reste, de part et d'autre, c'est la victoire de l'esprit ou de la ruse autant que de la force. De même que dans un combat singulier, il faut un peu de recul pour saisir la partie découverte ou vulnérable de son adversaire, de même le général d'armée doit essayer de découvrir, dans le caractère de son adversaire, le penchant par où le surprendre le plus facilement (3.81.2):

> καθάπερ γὰρ ἐπὶ τῶν κατ' ἄνδρα καὶ ζυγὸν ἀγωνισμάτων δεῖ τὸν μέλλοντα νικᾶν συνθεωρεῖν πῶς δυνατὸν ἐφικέσθαι τοῦ σκοποῦ καὶ τί γυμνὸν ἢ ποιὸν ἔξοπλον μέρος φαίνεται τῶν ἀνταγωνιστῶν, οὕτως χρὴ καὶ τοὺς ὑπὲρ τῶν ὅλων προεστῶτας σκοπεῖν οὐχ ὅπου τι τοῦ σώματος γυμνόν, ἀλλὰ ποῦ τῆς ψυχῆς εὐχείρωτόν τι παραφαίνεται τοῦ τῶν ἐναντίων ἡγεμόνος ...

Qu'il s'agisse du corps ou de l'esprit, il faut un peu de distance pour prendre une vue d'ensemble, pour saisir l'essentiel, le point capital. Ainsi les adultes devraient-ils se conduire.

A deux reprises Polybe rapproche les adultes des enfants. Après avoir décrit Byzance en détail et fait des observations sur le Pont-Euxin (4.42.7), il justifie les réflexions sans doute exactes, du moins le croyait-il, pour mettre les lecteurs en garde contre les prodiges rapportés par les voyageurs qui courent les mers et pour les empêcher d'écouter comme des enfants sans expérience tout ce que l'on débite sur les courants:

ἔτι δὲ μᾶλλον εἰρῆσθω καὶ τῆς τῶν πλοϊζομένων ψευδολογίας καὶ τερατείας χάρω, ἵνα μὴ παντὶ τῷ λεγομένῳ προσκεχηνέναι παιδικῶς ἀναγκαζώμεθα διὰ τὴν ἀπειρίαν . . .

Les Etoliens, que Polybe n'aimait guère, croyaient se jouer du jeune roi Philippe comme d'un enfant, mais à vrai dire ce sont eux qui se conduisaient comme des enfants dans toutes leurs entreprises (5.29.2):

ἐλπίσαντες γὰρ ὡς παιδίῳ νηπίῳ χρήσασθαι τῷ Φιλίππῳ διά τε τὴν ἡλικίαν καὶ τὴν ἀπειρίαν, τὸν μὲν Φίλιππον εὗρον τέλειον ἄνδρα καὶ κατὰ τὰς ἐπιβολὰς καὶ κατὰ τὰς πράξεις, αὐτοὶ δ' ἐφάνησαν εὐκαταφρόνητοι καὶ παιδαριώδεις ἔν τε τοῖς κατὰ μέρος καὶ καθόλου πράγμασιν.

Il arrive aussi aux hommes de se conduire comme les autres animaux. Dans un passage resté célèbre du Livre VI où Polybe traite des diverses sortes de gouvernements et des origines de la monarchie (6.5.6-7), il montre que des hommes nouveaux se lèvent, comme d'une semence, au lendemain d'un déluge ou d'une autre calamité et se rassemblent, comme font les autres animaux. Puis, de même que parmi les autres animaux nous voyons les plus forts dominer, ainsi font les hommes sous la conduite des plus forts:

ὅταν ἐκ τῶν περιλειφθέντων οἶον εἰ σπερμάτων αὖθις αὐξηθῇ σὺν χρόνῳ πλῆθος ἀνθρώπων, τότε δήπου, καθάπερ ἐπὶ τῶν ἄλλων ζῴων, καὶ ἐπὶ τούτων συναθροιζομένων . . . ἀνάγκη τὸν τῇ

σωματικῇ καὶ τῇ ψυχικῇ τόλμῃ διαφέροντα, τοῦτον ἡγεῖσθαι καὶ
κρατεῖν, καθαπερ καὶ ἐπὶ τῶν ἄλλων γενῶν ἀδοξοποιήτων ζῴων
θεωρούμενον τοῦτο χρὴ φύσεως ἔργον ἀληθινώτατον νομίζειν
παρ᾽ οἷς ὁμολογουμένως τοὺς ἰσχυροτάτους ὁρῶμεν ἡγουμένους,
λέγω δὲ ταύρους, κάπρους, ἀλεκτρυόνας, τὰ τοιούτοις
παραπλήσια.

Bien plus, les hommes, au plus fort des grandes calamités, ne
savent mettre un frein à leur volonté insensée, encore moins
se défier d'eux-mêmes comme font les autres animaux
(15.21.5-6):

εἰς ταύτας οἷον ἐθελοντὴν ἐνέπεσον τὰς ἀτυχίας, εἰς ἃς οὐκ οἶδ᾽
ὅπως πάντες ἄνθρωποι προφανῶς ἐμπίπτοντες οὐ δύνανται λῆξαι
τῆς ἀνοίας, ἀλλ᾽ οὐδὲ βραχὺ διαπιστῆσαι (ῥᾴδιον), καθάπερ ἔνια
τῶν ἀλόγων ζῴων.

Dans la bataille de Raphie (5.84.3-4), mettant aux prises
les armées respectives d'Antiochus et de Ptolomée, Polybe
nous fait assister à un combat d'éléphants. Un romancier
n'aurait pas mieux fait pour agrémenter son récit. Les
éléphants fondent les uns sur les autres et se poussent
mutuellement de toutes leurs forces sans changer de position,
se prenant par les dents et se perçant à coups de dents,
comme font les taureaux avec leurs cornes:

ὅταν δ᾽ ἅπαξ ἐγκλῖναν πλάγιον λάβῃ, τιτρώσκει τοῖς ὀδοῦσι,
καθάπερ οἱ ταῦροι τοῖς κέρασι.

Au dire de Polybe, parlant des pays d'Ibérie et de Lusitanie
(34.8), il y aurait dans les profondeurs de la mer des chênes à
glands, dont les thons seraient friands; de là à dire que les
thons sont comme des cochons de terre, il n'y a qu'un pas:

φησιν ὅτι βάλανοι εἰσι κατὰ βάθος ἐν τῇ αὐθότι θαλάττῃ
πεφυτευμέναι, ὧν τὸν καρπὸν σιτουμένους τοὺς θύννους
πιαίνεσθαι. διόπερ οὐκ ἂν ἁμάρτοι τις λέγων ὗς εἶναι θαλαττίους
τοὺς θύννους.

IV

On s'attend tout naturellement à relever sous la plume de Polybe des comparaisons ayant pour objet la constitution, l'armée, la guerre, la paix et la diplomatie. Autant de thèmes qui lui étaient aussi familiers que la cavalerie et la géographie. Il a exprimé plus d'une vue profonde sur la constitution de Rome. Mais c'est peut-être sous la forme de la comparaison suivante, à la fois concrète et développée, qu'il a exprimé une loi générale que les historiens subséquents ont reprise à l'envi. Il s'agit des germes de mort que renferme chaque forme particulière de gouvernement (6.10.3-4). De même, des substances comme le fer avec la rouille et le bois avec les vers portent en elles les principes de leur destruction:

καθάπερ γὰρ σιδήρῳ μὲν ἰός, ξύλοις δὲ θρῖπες καὶ τερηδόνες σύμφυεῖς εἰσι λῦμαι, δι᾽ ὧν, κἂν πάσας τὰς ἔξωθεν διαφύγωσι βλάβας, ὑπ᾽ αὐτῶν φθείρονται τῶν συγγενομένων, τὸν αὐτὸν τρόπον καὶ τῶν πολιτειῶν συγγεννᾶται κατὰ φύσιν ἑκάστῃ καὶ παρέπεταί τις κακία, βασιλείᾳ μὲν ὁ μοναρχικὸς λεγόμενος τρόπος, ἀριστοκρατίᾳ δ᾽ ὁ τῆς ὀλιγαρχίας, δημοκρατίᾳ δ᾽ ὁ θηριώδης καὶ χειροκρατικός.

Quant à la république de Platon, on doit l'exclure de toute discussion sur la préférence, étant donné qu'elle n'a jamais été appliquée quelque part, de même que dans les combats des athlètes on n'admet pas ceux qui manquent de préparation ou qui n'y sont pas reçus (6.47.8):

ὥσπερ γὰρ οὐδὲ τῶν τεχνιτῶν ἢ τῶν ἀθλητῶν τούς γε μὴ νενεμημένους ἢ σεσωμασκηκότας παρίεμεν εἰς τοὺς ἀθλητικοὺς ἀγῶνας, οὕτως οὐδὲ ταύτην χρὴ παρεισαγαγεῖν εἰς τὴν τῶν πρωτείων ἅμιλλαν ἐὰν μὴ πρότερον ἐπιδείξηταί τι τῶν ἑαυτῆς ἔργων ἀληθινῶς.

La comparer, comme on l'a fait jusqu'ici, à celle de Rome, de Lacédémone ou de Carthage, ce serait comparer une statue humaine avec des êtres vivants et animés (6.47.9):

ὡς ἂν εἰ τῶν ἀγαλμάτων τις ἕν προθέμενος τοῦτο συγκρίνοι τοῖς ζῶσι καὶ πεπνυμένοις ἀνδράσι.

Pour Polybe, on doit regarder une constitution de la même manière qu'on considère les vertus et les vices des particuliers (6.2.5-6):

καθάπερ (γὰρ) οἱ κατ' ἰδίαν ὑπὲρ τῶν φαύλων ἢ τῶν σπουδαίων ἀνδρῶν ποιούμενοι τὰς διαλήψεις, ἐπειδὰν ἀληθῶς πρόθωνται δοκιμάζειν, οὐκ ἐκ τῆς ἀπεριστάτου ῥαστώνης κατὰ τὸν βίον ποιοῦνται τὰς ἐπισκέψεις, ἀλλ' ἐκ τῶν ἐν ταῖς ἀτυχίαις περιπετειῶν καὶ τῶν ἐν ταῖς ἐπιτυχίαις κατορθωμάτων, μόνον νομίζοντες εἶναι ταύτην ἀνδρὸς τελείου βάσανον τὸ τὰς ὁλοσχερεῖς μεταβολὰς τῆς τύχης μεγαλοψύχως δύνασθαι καὶ γενναίως ὑποφέρειν, τὸν αὐτὸν τρόπον χρὴ θεωρεῖν καὶ πολιτείαν . . .

On doit prendre pour point d'observation cette partie de l'existence composée tour à tour de succès et de revers ou comprenant les révolutions de la fortune endurées avec constance et courage. Une constitution doit s'apprécier de la même façon que les hommes.

Les lois et les moeurs sont les deux principes de toute république (6.47.3-5). Si un Etat et les citoyens sont justes, les lois et les moeurs seront justes; si des particuliers sont avaricieux et l'Etat commet des actions injustes, c'est que les lois y sont mauvaises et les moeurs, déréglées:

ὥσπερ οὖν, ὅταν τοὺς ἐθισμοὺς καὶ νόμους κατίδωμεν παρά τισι σπουδαίους ὑπάρχοντας, θαρροῦντες ἀποφαινόμεθα καὶ τοὺς ἄνδρας ἐκ τούτων ἔσεσθαι καὶ τὴν τούτων πολιτείαν σπουδαίαν, οὕτως, ὅταν τοὺς τε κατ' ἰδίαν βίους τινῶν πλεονεκτικοὺς τάς τε κοινὰς πράξεις ἀδίκους θεωρήσαμεν, δῆλον ὡς εἰκὸς λέγειν καὶ τοὺς νόμους καὶ τὰ κατὰ μέρος ἤθη καὶ τὴν ὅλην πολιτείαν αὐτῶν εἶναι φαύλην.

La bataille de Mantinée, au cours de laquelle Machanidas fut défait et tué, inspire à Polybe une réflexion juste et profonde sur le rôle respectif des soldats républicains, des sujets d'un tyran et des mercenaires à la solde du plus offrant (11.13.6):

ὥσπερ γὰρ ἐπ' ἐκείνων οἷς μὲν ὑπὲρ ἐλευθερίας ἐστιν, οἷς δ' ὑπὲρ δουλείας ὁ κίνδυνος, οὕτως ἐπὶ τῶν μισθοφόρων οἷς μὲν ὑπὲρ

ὁμολογουμένης ἐπανορθώσεως, (οἷς δ᾽) ὑπὲρ προδήλου βλάβης
γίνεται φιλοτιμία . . .

Pour ce qui est de l'armée elle-même, avec chaque homme
placé exactement au bon endroit, elle est aussi forte ou solide
qu'une construction où chaque brique est posée avec soin
(10.24.7). Ainsi l'exprime Démétrios de Phalère dans un
discours:

καθάπερ ἐν οἰκοδομίαις, ἐὰν κατὰ μίαν πλίνθον θῇς καὶ καθ᾽ ἕνα
δόμον ἐπιμελείας τύχῃ τὸ παρατεθέν, οὕτως ἐν στρατοπέδῳ τὸ
κατ᾽ ἄνδρα καὶ κατὰ λόχον ἀκριβωθὲν ὅλην ποιεῖ τὴν δύναμιν
ἰσχυράν.

D'ailleurs, le camp romain était comme une ville, formant
une figure carrée, aussi bien par le partage des terres que par
le tracé des rues (6.31.10); chacun sait exactement dans
quelle rue et dans quel endroit de cette rue il doit loger
(61.41.10):

Τούτων δ᾽ οὕτως ἐχόντων τὸ μὲν σύμπαν σχῆμα γίνεται τῆς
στρατοπεδείας τετράγωνον ἰσόπλευρον, τὰ δὲ κατὰ μέρος ἤδη τῆς
τε ῥυμοτομίας ἐν αὐτῇ καὶ τῆς ἄλλης οἰκονομίας πόλει
παραπλησίαν ἔχει τὴν διάθεσιν . . . λοιπὸν ἑκάστου σαφῶς
γινώσκοντος ἐν ποίᾳ ῥύμῃ καὶ ποίῳ τόπῳ τῆς ῥύμης σκηνοῖ διὰ τὸ
πάντας ἀεὶ τὸν αὐτὸν ἐπέχειν τῆς στρατοπεδείας, γίνεταί τι
παραπλήσιον, οἷον ὅταν εἰς πόλιν εἰσίῃ στρατόπεδον ἐγχώριον . . .

Dans une harangue faite aux Etoliens sur leur guerre avec
Philippe (11.4.4), l'ambassadeur compare la guerre à un
incendie, dont on n'est pas toujours maître d'arrêter les
funestes effets, l'embrasement gagnant du terrain à mesure
que le vent active le feu:

καθάπερ γὰρ ἐπὶ τοῦ πυρός, ὅταν ὑφάνῃ τις ἅπαξ τὴν ὕλην,
οὐκέτι τὸ λοιπὸν ἐπὶ τῇ τούτου προαιρέσει γίνεται τὸ συμβαῖνον,
ἀλλ᾽ ᾗ ποτ᾽ ἂν τύχῃ λαμβάνει τὴν νομήν, τὸ πλεῖον τοῖς ἀνέμοις
κυβερνώμενον καὶ τῇ τῆς ὑποκειμένης ὕλης διαφθορᾷ, καὶ
πολλάκις ἐπ᾽ αὐτὸν τὸν ἐμπρήσαντα πρῶτον ὥρμησε
παραλόγως, τὸν αὐτὸν τρόπον (καὶ) ὁ πόλεμος ὑπό τινων ὅταν
ἅπαξ ἐκκαυθῇ, τοτὲ μὲν αὐτοὺς τούτους πρώτους ἀπόλλυσι, τοτὲ
δὲ φέρεται φθείρων ἀδίκως πᾶν τὸ παραπεσόν, αἰεὶ

καινοποιούμενος καὶ προσφυσώμενος, ὥσπερ ὑπ᾽ ἀνέμων, ὑπὸ τῆς τῶν πλησιαζόντων ἀγνοίας.

Ce langage disert et fleuri à la Polonius convient à un ambassadeur formé à bonne école.

Le feu est une image favorite de Polybe. Il l'emploie encore à deux reprises pour caractériser la révolte.[16] La révolte contre Persée de Macédoine éclata comme un feu dès longtemps caché:

ὅτι τῆς κατὰ τὴν ἱππομαχίαν φήμης μετὰ τὴν νίκην τῶν Μακεδόνων εἰς τὴν Ἑλλάδα διαγγελθείσης ἐξέλαμψε καθαπερεὶ πῦρ ἡ τῶν πολλῶν πρὸς τὸν Περσέα διάθεσις, τὸν πρὸ τούτου χρόνον ἐπικρυπτομένων τῶν πλείστων.

Et la révolte, une fois commencée, de se répandre comme un feu sauvage:

οὔσης δὲ τῆς μὲν ὁρμῆς πάλαι προχείρου τῆς τῶν πολλῶν, προσδεομένης δὲ τοῦ προκαλεσομένου μόνον καὶ τολμήσοντος, ἅμα τῷ λαβεῖν ἀρχὴν τὸ πρᾶγμα ταχέως οἷον εἰ πῦρ ἐξέλαμψεν.

Cette image est aussi conventionnelle que celle qui compare la guerre à la maladie, la santé à la paix (12.26.6).

Scipion, après avoir réprimé une sédition qui s'était élevée parmi ses soldats, compare dans une harangue l'attitude de ces derniers à celle d'un fils qui irait jusqu'à enlever la vie à son père sous prétexte que ce dernier l'aurait trompé dans un compte à régler ensemble (11.28.8):

ἔστι γὰρ παραπλήσιον ὡς ἂν εἴ τις ὑπὸ γονέως ἰδίου φάσκων εἰς ἀργυρίου λόγον ἀδικεῖσθαι παρείη μετὰ τῶν ὅπλων, ἀποκτενῶν τοῦτον παρ᾽ οὗ τὸ ζῆν αὐτὸς ἔλαβε.

On ne doit point, cependant, être surpris de ce qui est arrivé à Scipion, car s'il est relativement facile de se protéger contre les maladies du corps qui viennent de l'extérieur comme le chaud ou le froid, il n'est certes pas facile de se garder contre celles qui s'engendrent dans le corps même (11.25.2-7); il en va de même d'une armée ou d'une république, des maux, comme une émeute et une faction, pouvant s'y produire secrètement:

καθάπερ (γὰρ) ἐπὶ τῶν σωμάτων τὰς μὲν ἐκτὸς αἰτίας τοῦ
βλάπτειν, λέγω δ' οἷον ψύχους, καύματος, κόπου, τραυμάτων, καὶ
πρὶν γίνεσθαι φυλάξασθαι δυνατὸν καὶ γενομέναις εὐμαρὲς
βοηθῆσαι, τὰ δ' ἐξ αὐτῶν τῶν σωμάτων γινόμενα φύματα καὶ
νόσους δυστυχερὲς μὲν προϊδέσθαι, δυσχερὲς δὲ γενομένοις
βοηθεῖν, τὸν αὐτὸν δὴ τρόπον καὶ περὶ πολιτείας καὶ περὶ
στρατοπέδων διαληπτέον.

Cette image des plaies du corps et de l'âme, de l'extérieur
et de l'intérieur, on la trouve aussi dans la description de la
révolte des mercenaires (1.81.5-11), aussi développée dans un
cas comme dans l'autre. Elle révèle, non seulement l'attitude
déterminée de l'historien en face du phénomène social de la
révolte, mais aussi l'influence des idées de Platon sur le
rapprochement entre les maladies du corps et celles de l'âme;
cette longue digression est peut-être aussi un écho de la
révolte achéenne de 146[17]:

Διόπερ εἰς ταῦτα βλέπων οὐκ ἄν τις εἰπεῖν ὀκνήσειεν ὡς οὐ μόνον
τὰ σώματα τῶν ἀνθρώπων καί τινα τῶν ἐν αὐτοῖς γεννωμένων
ἑλκῶν καὶ φυμάτων ἀποθηριοῦσθαι συμβαίνει καὶ τελέως
ἀβοήθητα γίνεσθαι, πολὺ δὲ μάλιστα τὰς ψυχάς. Ἐπί τε γὰρ τῶν
ἑλκῶν, ἐὰν μὲν θεραπείαν τοῖς τοιούτοις προσάγῃ τις, ὑπ' αὐτῆς
ἐνίοτε ταύτης ἐθεριζόμενα θᾶττον ποιεῖται τὴν νομήν, ἐὰν δὲ
πάλιν ἀφῇ, κατὰ τὴν ἐξ αὐτῶν φύσιν φθείροντα τὸ συνεχὲς οὐκ
ἴσχει παῦλαν, ἕως ἂν ἀφανίσῃ τὸ ὑποκείμενον. Ταῖς τε ψυχαῖς
παραπλησίως τοιαῦται πολλάκις ἐπιφύονται μελανίαι καὶ
σηπεδόνες ὥστε μηδὲν ἀσεβέστερον ἀνθρώπου μηδ' ὠμότερον
ἀποτελεῖσθαι τῶν ζῴων . . .

La harangue de Chléneas, Etolien, contre les rois de
Macédoine, une fois terminée, Lysiscus, ambassadeur des
Acarnaniens, prit la parole à son tour et déclara au début sans
ambages (9.32.4):

ὥσπερ δὲ καὶ κατὰ τοὺς κινδύνους διὰ τὴν ὑπερχογὴν καὶ τὸ
μέγεθος τῆς Μακεδόνων δυνάμεως ἐμπεριέχεσθαι συμβαίνει τὴν
ἡμετέραν ἀσφάλειαν ἐν ταῖς ἐκείνων ἀρεταῖς, οὕτως καὶ κατὰ
τοὺς πρεσβευτικοὺς ἀγῶνας ἐμπεριέχεται τὸ τῶν Ἀκαρνάνων
συμφέρον ἐν τοῖς Μακεδόνων δικαίοις.

Les Acarnaniens, dans les luttes diplomatiques, ne tenaient

pas à séparer leurs intérêts des droits des Macédoniens, tout comme en guerre les Macédoniens, en raison de leur courage et de la supériorité de leur puissance, garantissaient la sécurité des Acarnaniens. Lysiscus est aussi franc un peu plus loin dans sa harangue quand il laisse entendre ce que vont faire les Etoliens (9.37.9); toute ville en danger qui invite dans ses murs une garnison plus forte que sa propre défense doit se soumettre à la nouvelle autorité:

ὥσπερ γὰρ οἱ κατὰ τὰς πολεμικὰς περιστάσεις βαρυτέρας ἐπαγόμενοι φυλακὰς εἰς τὰς πόλεις τῆς αὐτῶν δυνάμεως χάριν τῆς ἀσφαλείας ἅμα τὸν ἀπὸ τῶν ἐχθρῶν ἀπωθοῦντας φόβον καὶ ποιοῦσιν ὑποχειρίους σφᾶς αὐτοὺς παῖς τῶν φίλων ἐξουσίαις, τὸν αὐτὸν τρόπον καὶ νῦν Αἰτωλοὶ διανοοῦνται.

V

Polybe qui a beaucoup voyagé et possède de vastes connaissances géographiques, éprouve un évident plaisir de professeur à établir des comparaisons et à faire montre ainsi de son savoir. Dans sa description d'Abydos et de Sestos (16.29.6-7), par exemple, il rappelle un souvenir qui fera mieux comprendre la position de ces deux villes, de sorte que le lecteur les connaîtra mieux que s'il était sur les lieux; il est impossible d'aller de la Méditerranée à la Propontide et au Pont-Euxin sans passer entre Abydos et Sestos, pas plus qu'il n'est possible de passer de l'Atlantique à la Méditerranée sans franchir les colonnes d'Hercule:

καθάπερ γὰρ οὐδ' ἐκ τοῦ παρὰ μέν τισιν Ὠκεανοῦ προσαγορευομένου, παρὰ δέ τισιν Ἀτλαντικοῦ πελάγους · δυνατὸν εἰς τὴν καθ' ἡμᾶς θάλατταν εἰσπλεῦσαι μὴ οὐχὶ διὰ τοῦ καθ' Ἡρακλέους στήλας περαιωθέντα στόματος, οὕτως οὐδ' ἐκ τῆς καθ' ἡμᾶς εἰς τὸν Προποντίδα καὶ τὸν Πόντον ἀφικέσθαι μὴ οὐχὶ διὰ τοῦ μεταξὺ Σηστοῦ καὶ Ἀβύδου διαστήματος ποιησάμενον τὸν εἴσπλουν.

Scopas, général et législateur des Etoliens (13.2.2), après avoir été dépouillé de toutes ses dignités, s'exila à Alexandrie dans l'espoir d'y soulager sa misère et satisfaire son avarice.

Pareille conduite inspire à Polybe, qui n'aimait guère les Etoliens, une comparaison amusante avec l'hydropisie. Scopas ignorait — on ne peut tout savoir — qu'un hydropique ne peut étancher sa soif avant qu'un médecin ait guéri sa maladie; la soif de posséder, aussi insatiable, ne peut être extirpée sans qu'on fasse disparaître d'une façon ou de l'autre le vice de l'âme qui le produit:

> οὐκ εἰδὼς ὅτι, καθάπερ ἐπὶ τῶν ὑδρωπικῶν οὐδέποτε ποιεῖ παῦλαν οὐδὲ κόρον τῆς ἐπιθυμίας ἡ τῶν ἔξωθεν ὑγρῶν παράθεσις, ἐὰν μὴ τὴν ἐν αὐτῷ σώματι διάθεσιν ὑγιάσῃ τις, τὸν αὐτὸν τρόπον οὐδὲ τὴν πρὸς τὸ πλεῖον ἐπιθυμίαν οἷόν τε κορέσαι μὴ οὐ τὴν ἐν τῇ ψυχῇ κακίαν λόγῳ τινὶ διορθωσάμενον.

Tout esprit avide d'instruction se plaît d'ordinaire dans l'observation des causes. C'est en effet de ce principe, comme d'une source que découlent à la fois nos desseins, nos entreprises et leur réalisation (6.2.10):

> ἐκ γὰρ ταύτης ἥπερ ἐκ πηγῆς οὐ μόνον ἀναφέρεσθαι συμβαίνει πάσας τὰς ἐπινοίας καὶ τὰς ἐπιβολὰς τῶν ἔργων, ἀλλὰ καὶ συντέλειαν λαμβάνειν.

Appius et Marcellus, qui faisaient le siège de Syracuse par mer (8.36.3-4), eurent tôt fait de constater la cause de leur défaite; les inventions du géomètre Archimède y étaient si extraordinaires et si nombreuses qu'elles détruisaient les machines de Marcellus. Ce dernier remarqua en plaisantant qu'Archimède se servait de ses vaisseaux comme de cruches pour puiser de l'eau, et trouvait ses sambuques, qu'il chassait à coups de bâton, indignes de sa présence:

> ὅμως δ' ἐπισκώπτων τὰς αὑτοῦ πράξεις ἔφη ταῖς μὲν ναυσὶν αὐτοῦ κυαθίζειν ἐκ θαλάττης Ἀρχιμήδη, τὰς δὲ σαμβύκας ῥαπιζομένας ὥσπερ ἐκσπόνδους μετ' αἰσχύνης ἐκπεπτωκέναι.

Polybe fait une observation assez juste sur les noms de lieux (3.36.3-4). Pour ceux qui sont déjà connus, il suffit de les nommer pour en rappeler le souvenir; pour ceux qu'on ne connaît pas du tout, les nommer produit le même son que celui d'un instrument quelconque. Cette digression n'est pas sans intérêt, puisque Polybe songe à inventer une méthode par laquelle on arriverait à intéresser le lecteur à des lieux inconnus, en les rapportant soit à des idées qui lui seraient déjà familières ou encore à d'autres connaissances acquises:

οἶμαι δ᾽ ἐπὶ μὲν τῶν γνωριζομένων τόπων οὐ μικρὰ μεγάλα δὲ συμβάλλεσθαι πεποίηκε πρὸς ἀνάμνησιν ἡ τῶν ὀνομάτων παράθεσις. ἐπὶ δὲ τῶν ἀγνοουμένων εἰς τέλος ὁμοίαν ἔχει τὴν δύναμιν ἡ τῶν ὀνομάτων ἐξήγησις ταῖς ἀδιανοήτοις καὶ κρουσματικαῖς λέξεσι . . .

Tout lecteur, il est vrai, ne peut être géographe et connaître personnellement tous les lieux. Mais à la lecture il faut se transporter par l'esprit dans les lieux comme en regardant c'est l'usage de tourner le regard vers l'endroit qui nous est montré (3.38.5):

καθάπερ γὰρ ἐπὶ τῆς ὁράσεως εἰθίσμεθα συνεπιστρέφειν ἀεὶ τὰ πρόσωπα πρὸς τὸ κατὰ τὴν ἔνδειξιν ὑποδεικνύμενον, οὕτως καὶ τῇ διανοίᾳ χρὴ συνδιανεύειν καὶ συρρέπειν ἐπὶ τοὺς τόπους ἀεὶ τοὺς διὰ τοῦ λόγου συνεπιδεικνυμένους.

VI

Pour Polybe, la Fortune joue un rôle important dans l'histoire et dans la vie humaine. Tantôt il la voit, comme un bon arbitre (1.58.1), qui finit par arracher les combattants, Hamilcar et les Romains, au terrain et à la joute:

οὐ μὴν ἀλλ᾽ ὥσπερ ἀγαθὸς βραβευτὴς ἡ τύχη μεταβιβάσασα παραβόλως αὐτοὺς ἐκ τοῦ προειρημένου τόπου καὶ τοῦ προϋπάρχοντος ἀθλήματος εἰς παραβολώτερον ἀγώνισμα καὶ τόπον ἐλάττω συνέκλεισεν.

Tantôt elle se joue des hommes comme de jetons qui, d'un moment à l'autre, passent de la plus petite à la plus grande valeur, au gré du calculateur (5.26.20); cela se passe ainsi surtout à la cour du roi; aujourd'hui ils sont heureux, demain ils sont dignes de pitié, au bon plaisir du prince régnant:

βραχεῖς γὰρ δὴ πάνυ καιροὶ πάντας μὲν ἀνθρώπους ʹως ἐπίπαν ὑψοῦσι καὶ πάλιν ταπεινοῦσι, μάλιστα δὲ τοὺς ἐν ταῖς βασιλείαις. ὄντως γὰρ εἰσιν οὗτοι παραπλήσιοι ταῖς ἐπὶ τῶν ἀβακίων ψήφοις· ἐκεῖναί τε γὰρ κατὰ τὴν τοῦ ψηφίζοντος βούλησιν ἄρτι χαλκοῦν

καὶ παραυτίκα τάλαντον ἰσχύουσιν, οἵ τε περὶ τὰς αὐλὰς κατὰ τὸ
τοῦ βασιλέως νεῦμα μακάριοι καὶ παρὰ πόδας ἐλεεινοὶ γίνονται.

La Fortune se manifeste ainsi tour à tour aux hommes,
comme elle se manifeste alternativement à chacun des
adversaires, tantôt à Hannibal, tantôt à Hamilcar (1.86.7):

τῆς τύχης ὥσπερ ἐπίτηδες ἐκ παραθέσεως ἀμφοτέροις ἐναλλάξ
διδούσης ἀφορμὰς εἰς ὑπερβολὴν τῆς κατ᾽ ἀλλήλων τιμωρίας.

A ce propos, Polybe se plaît à personnifier la Fortune et à la
faire monter sur un théâtre ou sur un pont mobile pour les
sièges:

τῆς τύχης ὥσπερ ἐπίτηδες ἐπὶ τὴν ἐξώστραν ἀναβιβαζούσης τὴν
ὑμετέραν ἄγνοιαν. τῆς τύχης ὥσπερ ἐπίτηδες ἀναβιβαζούσης ἐπὶ
σκηνὴν ἐν ἑνὶ καιρῷ τὰς τούτων συμφοράς (11.5.8).

Outre cette conception particulière de la Fortune, on
relève d'autres attitudes de Polybe dans les quatre autres
comparaisons de lui qu'il nous reste à présenter. Elles
résument si bien, croyons-nous du moins, la pensée de
l'historien qu'elles peuvent servir de conclusion à cet essai.
Dans la première, l'auteur avoue s'être livré à une digression
ou à une réflexion morale après avoir tracé un portrait
parallèle d'Attale et de Philippe et reconnu la supériorité de
ce dernier quant à la constance. S'il a été amené à agir ainsi,
c'est qu'il avait déjà vu des hommes qui, comme de mauvais
coureurs (16.28.9), s'étaient arrêtés en pleine carrière et
avaient abandonné la partie déjà avancée — c'était le cas
d'Attale; il en avait vu d'autres aussi qui s'étaient cramponnés
à la tâche et avaient exécuté leur dessein avec succès — tel
était le cas de Philippe en l'occurrence. On pourrait en dire
autant de Polybe qui, pour s'être arc-bouté au travail, a fini
par réaliser avec gloire son projet d'histoire universelle:

ταῦτα μὲν οὖν προήχθην εἰπεῖν διὰ τὸ τινὰς μὲν πρὸς τῷ τέρματι,
καθάπερ οἱ κακοὶ τῶν σταδιέων, ἐγκαταλιπεῖν τὰς ἑαυτῶν
προθέσεις, τινὰς δ᾽ ἐν τούτῳ μάλιστα νικᾶν τοὺς ἀντιπάλους.

Du reste, pour avoir longuement observé son milieu et
entendu bien des propos, Polybe fait sur les projets une

réflexion marquée au coin de l'expérience et de la sagesse. La plupart des projets, selon lui, sont aisés et praticables, du moins à la parole; mais en pratique, comme de la fausse monnaie soumise au feu du creuset, ils ne présentent guère de ressemblance avec le commencement de l'entreprise (29.17.2):

ὅτι πολλὰ τῶν ἐπινομάτων κατὰ μὲν τὸν λόγον φαίνεται πιθανὰ καὶ δυνατά, παραγενόμενα δ᾽ εἰς τὴν χρείαν, καθάπερ τὰ κίβδηλα τῶν νομισμάτων εἰς πῦρ, οὐκέτι ποιεῖ τἀκόλουθον ταῖς πρώταις ἐπινοίαις.

Mais tel n'est pas le cas de l'histoire de Polybe. Loin de là! Il a parfaitement raison de se rendre ce témoignage à la fin de son oeuvre (39.39.8), où il nous dit qu'il a fouillé les affaires de Rome avec soin et qu'elles sont comme les fondations d'un édifice politique à élever:

ταῦτα μὲν οὖν ἡμεῖς καταπράξαντες ἐκ τῆς Ῥώμης ἐπανήλθομεν, ὡσανεὶ κεφάλαιά τινα τῶν προπεπολιτευμένων κατειργασμένοι, χάριν ἀξίαν τῆς πρὸς Ῥωμαίους εὐνοίας.

Cet édifice, il l'a fait reposer sur la vérité pour laquelle il était extrêmement passionné. L'histoire doit être utile, et elle l'est dans la mesure où elle sert la vérité. Si l'histoire n'est pas vraie, elle est inutile; dans les ouvrages historiques, l'utilité doit aller de pair avec la vérité, qui reste la règle des règles. Polybe développe cette idée en une longue comparaison du Livre 12 (12.12.1-2):

Καθάπερ γὰρ ἐπὶ τῶν κανόνων, κἂν ἐλάττων ᾖ τῷ μήκει κἂν τῷ πλάτει ταπεινότερος, μετέχῃ δὲ τῆς τοῦ κανόνος ἰδιότητος, κανόνα φησὶ δεῖν προσαγορεύειν αὐτόν, ὅταν δὲ τῆς εὐθείας καὶ τῆς πρὸς ταύτην οἰκειότητος ἐπιδέῃ πάντα μᾶλλον δεῖν ἢ κανόνα καλεῖν, τὸν αὐτὸν τρόπον καὶ τῶν συγγραμμάτων ὅσα μὲν ἂν ἢ κατὰ τὴν λέξιν ἢ κατὰ τὸν χειρισμὸν ἢ κατ᾽ ἄλλο τι διαμαρτάνηται τῶν ἰδίων μερῶν, ἀντέχηται δὲ τῆς ἀληθείας, προσίεσθαί φησι τὸ τῆς ἱστορίας ὄνομα τὰς βίβλους, ὅταν δὲ ταύτης παραπέσῃ, μηκέτι καλεῖσθαι δεῖν ἱστορίαν.

De même qu'une règle, pour s'appeler une règle, doit avoir les propriétés de la ligne droite, de la même manière l'histoire, pour être utile, doit avoir la vérité pour règle fondamentale; les défauts de composition ou de style y sont secondaires; les ornements doivent venir en second lieu. Polybe reproche ailleurs à Zénon (16.17.9) de s'intéresser beaucoup plus à la beauté et à l'élégance du style qu'à la recherche et à l'arrangement des faits, comme se vantent aussi de le faire plusieurs autres écrivains célèbres, καθάπερ καὶ πλείους ἕτεροι τῶν ἐπιφανῶν συγγραφέων. Au rebours de ces derniers, Polybe va jusqu'à prier ses lecteurs (16.20.8-9) de le condamner sans pitié s'il a menti quelque part volontairement ou s'il a caché la vérité tout en la connaissant.

L'idéal de Polybe est aussi celui de tous les historiens vraiment dignes de ce nom, voire de tous les esprits soucieux de probité intellectuelle. Boileau l'a résumé en un vers resté célèbre:

Rien n'est beau que le vrai: le vrai seul est aimable.[18]

Faculté des Lettres, Université Laval   *Maurice Lebel*

NOTES

1. Jules Humbert et Henri Berguin dans *Histoire de la littérature grecque*, p. 365.

2. Alfred et Maurice Croiset dans *Manuel d'histoire de la littérature grecque*, p. 688.

3. Polybe ne manque jamais de critiquer ses modèles ou ses prédécesseurs, qu'ils soient historiens ou géographes, comme Dicéarque, Eratosthène, Pythéas, Théopompe, Ephore, Aristote, Callisthène, Timée, Phylarque, Aratos de Sicyone, Fabius Pictor et Philinos. Cela ne l'empêche pas de les défendre au besoin et de reconnaître même leurs mérites. Fait singulier, il feint d'ignorer Hérodote, Thucydide et Xénophon. Il ne cite jamais Hérodote, et pourtant les observations océanographiques de Polybe ne sont pas sans rapport avec celles d'Hérodote. Il mentionne Thucydide une fois seulement (L.VIII,11, 3), et pourtant, à l'instar de l'historien de la guerre du Péloponnèse, il

marque sous chaque année les événements qui y sont arrivés, sans compter que plusieurs récits de bataille ou sièges de ville de Thucydide, comme la bataille de Platées, le massacre de Mycallessos et le siège de Syracuse semblent avoir été connus de Polybe, à en juger du moins par certains rapprochements qui viennent tout naturellement à l'esprit du lecteur familier avec les oeuvres historiques de Thucydide et de Polybe. Quant à Xénophon, Polybe renvoie deux fois à lui (6.45; 10.20), et pourtant il n'ignore pas *Les Helléniques*.

4. Celle de J. A. C. Buchon (1842) n'est même pas une belle infidèle. La meilleure que je connaisse est encore, à mon avis du moins, la traduction latine de Schweighäuser (1789-95). Tout traducteur moderne se doit d'y recourir. On n'a rien fait de mieux depuis en allemand, en anglais, en français et en italien. Elle est de beaucoup supérieure à celle de Casaubon (1609).

5. On en trouve un nombre à peu près égal chez Thucydide, du moins en style direct. En revanche, les discours de Polybe en style indirect se lisent, à tel point ils sont secs, un peu comme des inscriptions, des articles de traité, des listes de catalogue, des arrêtés ministériels.

6. Fénelon, dans sa *Lettre à l'Académie* (1714), a magistralement décrit ce trait caractéristique: "Polybe est habile dans l'art de la guerre et dans la politique; mais il raisonne trop quoi qu'il raisonne très bien. Il va au delà des bornes d'un simple historien; il développe chaque événement dans sa cause; c'est une anatomie exacte. Il montre par une espèce de mécanique qu'un tel peuple doit vaincre un tel autre peuple, et qu'une telle paix faite entre Rome et Carthage ne saurait durer."

7. Par bonheur, les traducteurs les plus récents ont eu le bon goût de les couper. Magistrale est la traduction française de Paul Pédech à cet égard; elle nous fait totalement oublier le style rude et raboteux de Polybe. Celle de Denis Roussel (Coll. Pléiade, Paris, 1970) est d'un style aisé et naturel, tout en étant exacte et précise. On pourrait faire une étude des traductions françaises de Polybe, allant de Louis Maigret (1557-58) à Denis Roussel (1970). Les récentes traductions anglaises de W. R. Paton (Loeb Classical Library) et d'Evelyn S. Shuckburgh (with a new introduction by F. W. Walbank) sont aussi de haute qualité. Une étude générale des traductions de Polybe en latin, anglais, allemand, italien, français et peut-être même en d'autres langues reste à faire.

8. 1.14.6; 1.57.1-2; 1.58.1; 1.58.5; 1.58.7-8; 1.76.7; 1.81.5-11; 1.84.7; 1.86.7. 2.56.10. 3.36.4; 3.38.5; 3.48.8-10; 3.57.10; 3.81.2, 11. 4.42.7. 5.26.20; 5.29.2; 5.33.5; 5.84.3. 6.2.5-6; 6.10; 6.10.3; 6.31.10; 6.39.10; 6.41.10; 6.44.3; 6.47.3-5; 6.47.8; 6.47.9; 6.58.1. 7.7. 8.6.6;

8.27.4. 9.32.4; 9.37.9; 9.8.2-13. 10.9.1; 10.21.8; 10.24.7; 10.26.8;
10.33.5; 10.41.7. 11.4.4; 11.5.8; 11.13.6-7; 11.19.3; 11.25.2-7;
11.29.10-12. 12.12.1-2; 12.12.3; 12.14.3-4; 12.23.7; 12.25^a.1-2;
12.25^a.5; 12.25^d.6; 12.25^d.3-4; 12.25^e.7; 12.25^h.2-3; 12.26.6-7;
13.2.2; 15.6.8; 15.21.5-6; 15.29.4; 16.13; 16.17.9; 16.24.4-5; 16.28.9;
16.29.6; 18.41; 19.31.9-11; 22.22.20; 23.10.11; 24.13.4; 26.1.5; 27.9;
29.17.2; 30.24; 31.29; 32.3.15; 33.4.20; 34.2.16; 34.5.3-8; 35.6; 36.17;
38.6; 38.16.3; 38.16.6; 38.16.8; 39.1.8; 39.8.

9. 12.25^a.1-2; 12.25^a.5; 12.25^h.2-3; 12.25^e.7.

10. 12.25^d.2-5; 12.25^d.6; 12.25^e.3-4.

11. 10.26.8. Polybe, lui-même ancien commandant de cavalerie, avait un faible bien connu pour l'équitation. Il serait même mort par accident d'une chute de cheval. A l'instar de Xénophon, il aimait beaucoup les chevaux.

12. 29.8.8; 29.8.9.

13. 32.15.7. La comparaison est ici sous-entendue ou plutôt comprise dans le verbe γυκαικίζω, s'habiller comme une femme.

14. 38.16.2; 38.16.6.

15. 11.29.10-11; 21.31.9-11; 30.11.6.

16. 27.9; 15.29.4.

17. 38.9-13. Les deux passages des livres 1 et 38 présentent plus d'un point de ressemblance.

18. Boileau, *Satires. IX*. A. M. le marquis de Seignelay.

Motivazioni Economiche nell' Opposizione alla Legge Agraria di Tib. Sempronio Gracco

La presentazione della proposta agraria di Tib. Gracco e, poi, l'applicazione della legge suscitarono una larga opposizione, i cui motivi, ampiamente esposti nelle narrazioni di Appiano e di Plutarco, si lasciano, altresì, riconoscere, nei loro strascichi polemici, nella pubblicistica del I sec. a.C. e soprattutto in Cicerone. Essi corrispondono, sostanzialmente ed ovviamente in contrasto, alle ragioni poste innanzi da Tib. Gracco per sostenere la propria *rogatio agraria*. Le finalità di Gracco (e, ben inteso, dei gruppi politici dei quali era rappresentante e portavoce) erano dichiaratamente militari o, se meglio piace, imperialistici (non vi è nessun motivo per supporre che egli, ben ancorato nell'oligarchia romana dominante, avesse ideali politici e sociali molto differenti da quelli generalmente professati dai politici del suo tempo). Tib. Gracco era preoccupato dal vedere un declino delle capacità militari romane e cercava di porvi rimedio. E poichè aveva identificato le cause del declino nel venir meno della classe contadina, cercava di ricostituirla. Le sue preoccupazioni erano largamente condivise da molti altri uomini politici, pur appartenenti a differenti fazioni, che, per altro, identificavano cause diverse del fenomeno e proponevano differenti rimedi. Per esempio Scipione Emiliano, pur consapevole delle difficoltà che lo stato romano attraversava, sembra fosse prevalentemente interessato agli aspetti morali della crisi.

Anche se la rappresentazione ciceroniana di Scipione deve essere accolta con molta cautela e considerata piuttosto una idealizzazione, è certo, tuttavia, che dai frammenti dei discorsi politici di Scipione emerge un'ansietà profondamente e nobilmente sentita sul declinare della pubblica moralità, specialmente fra la gioventù nobile, e sulla corruzione del corpo civico ad opera di elementi estranei. Egli probabilmente spiegava in questo modo il venir meno della tradizionale disciplina e dei sentimenti di patriottismo, che aveva sperimentato negli eserciti al suo comando. Si può supporre che molti altri membri della *nobilitas* romana condividessero le sue vedute e, in perfetta buona fede, credessero che la proposta di Gracco aggiungesse un altro motivo di confusione e di corruzione.

Per Tib. Gracco la ricostituzione della classe dei piccoli proprietari contadini, per mezzo della distribuzione dell'agro pubblico, ricuperato dagli occupanti, aveva, quindi, uno scopo conservatore. Questo scopo è confermato chiaramente dal tenore dei suoi argomenti quando egli presentò la sua proposta agraria. Bisogna tener presente che Gracco aveva davanti a sè un compito difficile, poichè doveva nello stesso tempo dimostrare l'utilità e i vantaggi della legge tanto alle masse popolari (soprattutto a quelle rurali), quanto alla classe dei possessori e al Senato. Di qui un'indubbia differenza di tono nei suoi discorsi, secondo che erano rivolti al popolo o all'assemblea senatoria, che si lascia nettamente scorgere nelle due narrazioni di Plutarco e di Appiano: nel primo, forse perchè più interessato ai lati morali nella descrizione del suo personaggio, vi è maggior enfasi sul punto di vista sociale del problema (esposto nel discorso al popolo, che il biografo tiene presente); Appiano, riportando le argomentazioni rivolte alla classe dirigente, insiste sugli aspetti imperialistici, più importanti per la generale prospettiva di tutta la sua esposizione storica.

Queste argomentazioni sono troppo note per essere qui ripetute: è necessario però dire che alla base del pensiero di Gracco era sempre la stessa teoria: l'amor di patria ed una leale partecipazione alla sua difesa, come pure ai suoi futuri ed auspicabili ingrandimenti, erano strettamente legati alla partecipazione dei cittadini stessi alla vita dello stato ed ai vantaggi che lo stato poteva offrire: nel caso particolare lo sfruttamento dell'agro pubblico. Non si potevano domandare sacrifici a coloro che non conoscevano i vantaggi che potevano ottenere dallo stato alla cui espansione contribuivano; in altre parole, la consapevolezza di avere qualcosa da difendere rendeva i cittadini più attivi e più interessati alla vita ed alla difesa della patria. Il fondamento di questa teoria è a tal punto conservatore che lo ritroveremo più tardi fra gli argomenti impiegati dagli oligarchi nella critica all'arruolamento dei volontari proletari ad opera di Gaio Mario nel 107 a.C. E si possono agevolmente indicare precedenti greci della stessa teoria. Ma qui importa notare che, avanzata da Tib. Gracco in connessione con il ricupero dell'agro pubblico, essa poteva assumere un nuovo aspetto. Per questo motivo Gracco (richiamandosi, in definitiva, al vetusto e "catoniano" precetto del contadino-soldato) ricordava anche il problema degli schiavi, sfruttando un argomento che toccava da vicino gli interessi della classe possidente e che, in quel momento, era ben attuale a causa della guerra servile in Sicilia. E per la stessa ragione Tiberio insisteva sugli aspetti "equi" della sua proposta: i beni della comunità e, quindi, anche l'agro pubblico, dovevano essere sfruttati dalla comunità.

Si aggiunga che gli interventi dello stato nel regolare lo sfruttamento dell'agro pubblico erano pressochè l'unico mezzo che il governo romano potesse impiegare per cercare di incidere sul processo economico (la colonizzazione era pressochè finita; la politica dei lavori pubblici, malgrado autorevoli pareri contrari, non aveva, nè poteva avere il ruolo di strumento in mano allo stato per promuovere o "dirigere" l'economia: una sola eccezione in questo senso può essere ricordata per il primo tribunato di Gaio Gracco). E che un migliore, e differente, sfruttamento dell'agro pubblico potesse servire ai fini prospettati da Gracco era, a quel che sembra potersi ricavare dall'iscrizione, di tono antigraccano, di Polla, ammesso e riconosciuto anche da uomini di parte avversa. D'altro canto, la politica agraria di Gracco era, almeno a mio avviso, sostanzialmente in linea con la politica agrario-coloniaria perseguita dalla classe dirigente romana nella prima metà del II sec. a.C., con la fondamentale differenza che l'oligarchia aveva cercato, anche per evitare guai alle proprie possessioni di agro pubblico, di indirizzare quella colonizzazione verso la Gallia Cisalpina (con il che non si rimediava di sicuro alla crisi, *in loco*, della classe contadina centro-meridionale), mentre Gracco voleva attuare la stessa politica colonizzatrice nell'Italia del Centro-Sud, vale a dire sull'agro pubblico per l'appunto in possesso della nobiltà senatoria.

I ragionamenti contrari a Gracco si muovevano sulla stesso piano delle sue argomentazioni. Ovviamente da un punto di vista legale e costituzionale non si poteva mettere in discussione il superiore diritto dello stato a ricuperare, in ogni momento e nella maniera che ritenesse più opportuno, l'agro pubblico, la cui occupazione era soltanto precaria. Un problema differente, e squisitamente politico, era se un *generale* ricupero dell'agro pubblico fosse in accordo con la concezione dell'*aequitas*. Questo concetto, posto innanzi, come si è detto da Gracco a sostegno delle proprie tesi, fu sfruttato con opposte implicazioni dai suoi avversari. E' superfluo ripetere qui quanto è detto in Appiano, *Bella Civilia*, 1.39, che offre un ottimo sommario dei ragionamenti oligarchici su questo tema, dei quali un riflesso ben noto è nel passo di Cicerone, *de Officiis*, 2.81-82, che si suppone conservi, per tramite di Panezio, un'eco dei contrastanti punti di vista dell'età graccana.[1] La proposta di Tiberio era, pertanto, considerata e rappresentata come una violazione di una situazione oramai stabilita e che trovava, appunto, nel lungo tempo trascorso la propria legittimità.[2] Il ragionamento oligarchico era anche spinto più innanzi, come appare da un passo della *pro Sestio*, 103 di Cicerone, che dichiaratamente riporta una replica oligarchica a Gracco: si sosteneva che proprio con l'allontanamento dei possessori dai terreni da essi per lungo tempo occupati, oltre che suscitare elemento di discordia, si veniva a privare lo stato di soldati. L'argomento "militare" di Tiberio era così, se pur in modo piuttosto capzioso, rovesciato contro di lui.

Ancor più significative obiezioni politiche venivano mosse alla legge graccana in quanto questa rappresentava una violazione dei diritti dei Latini e degli altri Alleati Italici, le cui classi alte erano in possesso di larghe porzioni di agro pubblico, che ora, come gli occupanti romani, essi venivano a perdere (gli occupanti, romani e alleati, sotto il limite dei 500 iugeri non subivano alcun danno e saranno stati certamente non pochi). E' probabile che il diritto degli Alleati all'occupazione di agro pubblico fosse contemplato nei loro trattati con Roma. A proposito di questo problema, oltre alla chiara esposizione di Appiano, bisogna richiamare un passo del *de Re Publica* di Cicerone (2.41), che può essere considerato un generale rifiuto dell'intera politica graccana. Lelio asserisce che lo stesso mettere in discussione i fondamenti tradizionali dello stato, sia in politica interna sia in quella estera, crea le condizioni per la decadenza dello stato.

Dalle repliche oligarchiche, qui riassunte, basate, come le argomentazioni di Gracco, sugli aspetti politici e costituzionali del problema, si può facilmente comprendere come la proposta agraria graccana, in sè non rivoluzionaria, abbia acquistato quel carattere di misura che vuol sconvolgere i fondamenti dello stato con il quale essa (ed in genere ogni altra legge agraria) appare nel I sec. a.C. Più che negli interventi contro la proposta di Rullo nel 63 a.C. (quando parlando alla folla Cicerone, con impudenza senza scrupoli, non esitò ad affermare che egli non si opponeva alla legge agraria in quanto tale e lodò i Gracchi per i loro sforzi a favore delle plebe), fu nel *de officiis* (2.72-85), scritto nel 44 a.C. e con l'esperienza della legislazione cesariana alle spalle, che Cicerone contribuì a sanzionare il mito della legge agraria come misura rivoluzionaria. Con intenzionale confusione fra terre pubbliche e proprietà privata, fra legge graccana e proposte per l'abolizione dei debiti, egli fece ampiamente rivivere l'antica raffigurazione dei Gracchi come pericolosi sovvertitori dell'ordine pubblico e della società ed i loro scopi furono da lui grottescamente descritti come *aequatio bonorum*.

Fino a questo punto, e per quanto ci è tramandato, non sembrerebbe che nè dalla parte graccana nè da quella avversa siano stati prospettati chiaramente i presupposti economici della riforma agraria. Penso che tutti oggi siano sostanzialmente d'accordo nel riconoscere che la proposta di Gracco era anacronistica proprio nel suo fondamento economico-sociale. Rappresenta un differente problema il fatto che essa, invece, venisse incontro ad esigenze sentite profondamente dalle masse rurali diseredate: il persistere, ben addentro al I sec. a.C., di una ideologia graccana, spesso abilmente sfruttata dai capi politici popolari, mostra un'innegabile aderenza di quella proposta a bisogni reali e poi ancora a lungo presenti per esempio nell'esercito professionale. In realtà la piccola proprietà contadina ricostituita, se la legge di Gracco avesse avuto successo, avrebbe incontrato le stesse difficoltà a sopravvivere che avevano condotto al declino della piccola proprietà in Italia nel corso della prima metà del II sec. a.C. Era oramai impossibile modificare il movimento economico dell'agricoltura italica e ritornare, generalmente, ad un tipo di produzione familiare in un momento in cui, come già mostra almeno in parte il *de agri cultura* di Catone, l'agricoltura italica sia era avviata da decenni verso una graduale riorganizzazione con nuove forma di produzione, più rimunerative e, per dir così, "industrializzate," e che, comunque, richiedevano per svolgersi e svilupparsi delle aziende agricole di larga estensione. La specializzazione delle colture era connessa, e lo sarà ancor più in seguito, alla possibilità di importare, se non altro per Roma e per le truppe, cereali dalle province e si appoggiava, quindi, alla nuova struttura imperiale dello stato.

Nè, d'altro canto, era possibile rimuovere le cause politiche della crisi della piccola proprietà contadina, perchè questo avrebbe significato appunto abbandonare e disfare la politica imperiale, una delle ragioni principali dell'allontanamento del contadino italico dalla terra.

Orbene, io penso che si possa dire che da parte di alcuni oppositori oligarchici questa basilare obiezione fu rivolta contro la riforma agraria graccana. Di essa, a quel che so, non vi è cenno nè in Appiano, nè in Plutarco e nemmeno in altri autori direttamente concernenti l'episodio dei Gracchi, ma si ritrova in Dionigi d'Alicarnasso a proposito della proposta di legge agraria attribuita, per il 486 a.C., al console Spurio Cassio (8.68-76). Come ho già cercato di dimostrare ampiamente altrove sulla scia di studiosi precedenti,[3] l'intiera rappresentazione storica dell'episodio è senza valore. L'annalistica del I sec. a.C., seguita da Dionigi, non senza sue personali rielaborazioni, ha pensato di ricostruire un tentativo di tirannide, abbastanza naturale subito dopo la cacciata dei re, immaginando una legge agraria come mezzo per accattivarsi la plebe. Penso anche di aver indicato come l'episodio sia stato costruito, secondo il sistema della tarda annalistica, sfruttando ed adattando motivi, situazioni, atteggiamenti propri dell'episodio graccano, il modello migliore (oligarchicamente parlando) di una legge agraria intesa a fini puramente demagogici e "tirannici." In tal modo la ricostruzione di Dionigi può offrire anche spunti preziosi per la comprensione dell'episodio stesso dei Gracchi. E' stato pure rilevato[4] come in Dionigi sia stato proiettato anacronisticamente nel V sec. a.C. quel contrasto fra plebe cittadina e plebe rurale, che divenne motivo caratteristico e politicamente di grande rilievo proprio dal 133 in poi.

Nel contesto dell'episodio, sapientemente ricostruito da Dionigi, vi è un discorso attribuito ad Appio Claudio, padre del decemviro, che contiene elementi di grande valore (8.73.2-5). Di questo discorso meritano di essere ricordati alcuni punti, e su uno di essi si deve insistere particolarmente. A 73.3 Appio Claudio raccomanda che il decemvirato agrario, da istituire, ricuperi allo stato l'agro pubblico posseduto per frode e violenza; lo divida in appezzamenti delimitati da cippi iscritti; venda le parti soggette a contestazioni; affitti il rimanente per cinque anni; impieghi il ricavato per pagare le truppe e provvedere alle spese di guerre. Come ho già indicato nel mio lavoro sopra citato, io ritengo che questo passo offra la spiegazione migliore al controverso luogo di Appiano, I 122, relativo alla distribuzione al popolo del φόρος pagato dagli occupanti dell'agro pubblico, in sostituzione delle assegnazioni agrarie, secondo la legge di Sp. Thorius.[5] Più avanti nel suo discorso (73.4) Ap. Claudio presenta una sua teoria, nella quale è difficile non sentire una risposta al motivo graccano dell'equità della distribuzione delle terre pubbliche, come compartecipazione dei poveri al godimento dei beni comuni. Per Ap. Claudio proprio questa compartecipazione del popolo al reddito dell'agro pubblico realizzerà veramente il godimento comune dei beni comuni, molto meglio che non una distribuzione di piccoli lotti di terra. Il discorso a 73.5 contiene, infine, osservazioni ancor più di rilievo.

L'oratore indica la situazione di grave disagio in cui potrebbe venir a trovarsi l'eventuale assegnatario di un piccolo lotto: la presenza di vicini fastidiosi; la mancanza di mezzi per mettere a coltura il proprio terreno; la necessità di affittare la propria terra appunto ad uno dei vicini. Sembra chiaro che Ap. Claudio ipotizza casi molto probabili, nei quali gli assegnatari si trovavano in possibile contrasto con vicini ricchi, ai quali probabilmente gli appezzamenti di agro pubblico, a loro assegnati, erano stati tolti (ad ogni modo, il motivo del vicino incomodo, che insidia la proprietà del piccolo contadino, è notoriamente comune, anche se qui, in bocca oligarchica, assume un aspetto più moderato). La mancanza di mezzi nei nuovi assegnatari doveva rappresentare un grave ostacolo per ogni riforma agraria e lo rappresentò di fatto, forse al di là del previsto, anche per Tib. Gracco, che sembra abbia destinato a questo fine i tesori di Attalo (Plut. *Gracchi* 14.1; Liv., *per.* 58). La necessità di affittare gli appezzamenti agli stessi vicini, con i quali gli assegnatari potevano essere in contrasto, si chiarisce, mi pare, nel seguito del discorso, quando Claudio raffigura la grave situazione dei piccoli assegnatari, costretti a lasciare i loro campi per andare a combattere (e, quindi, ad affittarli quasi di necessità ai vicini), e per di più (in quanto cittadini *adsidui*) tenuti a effettuare dal proprio i versamenti all'erario (si deve intendere per il vitto, le vesti e le armi: Polyb., 6.39.15) pur nelle gravi ristrettezze di vita e nella difficoltà di procurarsi il denaro necessario.

E' difficile non collegare questo ragionamento assai acuto

alla stessa situazione nella quale maturò la legge militare di Gaio Gracco ricordata da Plutarco, *Gracchi*, 26.1, che vietava le trattenute sul soldo dei soldati, che, pur *adsidui*, dovevano essere poverissimi. Torno a dire che il rimedio prospettato qui da Claudio, vale a dire la distribuzione ai soldati del reddito derivante dall'affitto dell'agro pubblico, mi pare da riferirsi ad una situazione storicamente reale, che giunse ad un punto di rottura negli anni subito successivi ai Gracchi.

Se Claudio è così acuto nel cogliere l'intrinseca contraddizione della riforma agraria nel suo tentativo di ricostruire una piccola proprietà contadina aperta al rischio immediato ed inevitabile di un nuovo, rapido crollo, egli sa altrettanto bene suggerire le forme del miglior sfruttamento dell'agro pubblico stesso, in vista di un'alta redditività per lo stato. Ecco il passo a 73.5: εἰ δὲ μεγάλοι κλῆροι ποικίλας τε καὶ ἀξιολόγους ἔχοντες γεωργοῖς ἐργασίας ὑπὸ τοῦ κοινοῦ μισθοῖντο, πολλὰς οἴσουσι προσόδους.

Ap. Claudio contrappone alla distribuzione di piccoli lotti a cittadini poveri l'affitto da parte dello stato, che ne riceverà grandi redditi, di ampi appezzamenti di terreno pubblico, che offrono la possibilità di coltivazioni varie e importanti (cioè redditizie) per chi li coltiva. Questo reddito lo stato lo potrà distribuire ai soldati.

Questo passo, che, come ho detto, ritengo sia da collegare con l'esperienza della fine del II sec. a.C., è l'unica testimonianza, a mia conoscenza, che dimostri la consapevolezza, ad un tempo, del carattere anacronisticamente antieconomico della riforma agraria graccana, e delle linee direttrici lungo le quali si muoveva il rinnovamento dell'agricoltura italica nel II sec. a.C. Nuovi tipi di colture e nuove produzioni, che esigevano grandi spese di impianto, ma che promettevano larghi redditi, richiedevano strutture agrarie diverse, vale a dire aziende agricole estese, e condannavano inesorabilmente il ritorno alla piccola proprietà contadina con la sua produzione unifamiliare, esposta a tutti i rischi.

Io credo che argomenti di questo genere, se pur non ricordati dalla nostra tradizione diretta, interessata, al solito, agli aspetti politici e costituzionali del problema, devono probabilmente essere stati prospettati nelle discussioni sulla legge agraria di Tib. Gracco; e certamente essi devono avere influenzato la graduale liquidazione delle leggi graccane, che seguì nei quindici anni successivi alla morte di Gaio Gracco. Si ricordi, del resto, che lo stesso Gaio Gracco, sebbene avesse ripreso la politica agraria del fratello, organizzò la prima grande colonizzazione transmarina: un'iniziativa che non era certamente in linea con lo sforzo di Tib. Gracco di risollevare in Italia la classe contadina proletarizzata.

Il mito della piccola proprietà contadina (che, per altro, nella realtà dell'agricoltura italica è ben testimoniata ancora nel I sec. a.C.) rimase negli esempi del buon tempo antico e delle vecchie virtù romane. Ma il caso di Atilio Regolo, quale è descritto dalla tarda annalistica (Val. Max., 4.4.6), illustra bene l'oramai acquisita coscienza dell'inconciliabilità fra la diretta coltivazione del piccolo campo familiare e la politica imperiale di Roma.

Istituto di Storia Antica,   *Emilio Gabba*
Pisa, Italia

NOTES

1. In generale sul *de officiis* vede ora K. Bringmann, *Untersuchungen zum späten Cicero*, Göttingen, 1971, pp. 229-50.

2. B. Brugi, *Le dottrine giuridiche degli agrimensori romani comparate a quelle del Digesto*, Verona-Padova, 1897, p. 279 ss.

3. "Studi su Dionigi d'Alicarnasso. III. La proposta di legge agraria di Spurio Cassio," *Athenaeum* n.s. 42, 1964, pp. 29-41; vedi anche "Dionigi d'Alicarnasso sul processo di Spurio Cassio," in *La storia del diritto nel quadro delle scienze storiche (Atti del I Congresso Internazionale dell'Società Italiana di Storia del Diritto)*, Firenze, 1966, pp. 143-53.

4. A. W. Lintott, *Violence in Republican Rome*,Oxford, 1969, pp. 188-89, dove anche si ricordano di passaggio motivi del discorso di Ap. Claudio.

5. Per la datazione della legge, da porre nel contesto delle difficoltà militari suscitate dalla guerra di Numidia, vede il mio articolo "Mario e Silla," *Aufstieg und Niedergang der römischen Welt*, I, Berlin, 1972, pp. 775-76.

A Note on the Aetolian Treaty of 189 B.C.[1]

Among the peace terms imposed upon the Aetolians by the Romans in 189 B.C. was the submission of hostages. Polybius provides the fullest account of the regulations governing the selection and delivery of these hostages: δότωσαν Αἰτωλοὶ ὁμήρους τῷ στρατηγῷ τεττεράκοντα, . . ., εἰς ἔτη ἕξ, οὓς ἄν Ῥωμαῖοι προκρίνωσιν, χωρὶς στρατηγοῦ καὶ ἱππάρχου καὶ δημοσίου γραμματέως καὶ τῶν ὡμηρευκότων ἐν Ῥώμῃ. καὶ τὰ ὄμηρα καθιστάτωσαν εἰς Ῥώμην· ἐὰν δέ τις ἀποθάνῃ τῶν ὁμήρων, ἄλλον ἀντικαθιστάτωσαν.[2] The restriction prohibiting the submission of persons who had served previously as hostages in Rome suggests that 189 was not the first time that the Aetolians had rendered hostages to the Romans.[3] However, since no ancient source specifically mentions Aetolian hostages prior to 189, Täubler, followed recently by Aymard, proposed that the restriction was probably associated with procedures relating to *mutatio obsidum*[4] Since forty hostages were handed over to the consul in 189, Täubler argued that the clause instructing the Aetolians to deliver hostages to Rome must have applied to persons who were to be submitted at some later date.[5] Thus, the hostages rendered in 189 would have been subsequently restored, but excluded from groups of hostages delivered in later exchanges.

Täubler's interpretation creates several difficulties. In the first place, it presumes a monumental blunder on the part of Polybius, whose account gives absolutely no indication that *mutatio* was to be applied in the case of the Aetolian hostages.[6] Moreover, since hostages were to be furnished for only six years, it is unlikely that more than one exchange, if even that, would have been scheduled.[7] Consequently, there would have been no need to prohibit hostages from serving a second term. It therefore seems likely that the restriction regarding former hostages refers to persons submitted prior to 189. The regulation governing the delivery of hostages to Rome probably refers to the very hostages rendered in 189. These hostages were handed over to the consul for his approval, but the Aetolians were held responsible for transporting them to Italy.

Despite the silence of the sources, there are several occasions prior to 189 when the Aetolians may have surrendered hostages to the Romans. After the Romans captured Heraclea in July of 191, Phaeneas, the Aetolian strategos, sent envoys to Acilius Glabrio to discuss peace terms.[8] Glabrio granted a ten day truce and sent Valerius Flaccus to Hypata to continue the negotiations. Flaccus advised the Aetolians to surrender unconditionally. Several days later Phaeneas appeared before Glabrio and declared that the Aetolians were prepared to surrender. However, when he objected to the consul's demand for the surrender of several prominent Aetolian leaders, Glabrio commanded that chains be brought out in order to impress upon the Aetolians the real meaning of *deditio in fidem populi Romani*. Although it is clear that the Aetolians had not fully comprehended the implications of their decision to surrender, it seems likely that Flaccus would have informed them of the necessity to submit hostages in conjunction with their capitulation.[9] This much, at least, the Aetolians may have understood. If hostages were rendered by Phaeneas and his supporters, the subsequent failure of the peace talks need not have jeopardized their lives, since Glabrio may have hoped that by retaining them he could secure Phaeneas' cooperation in the future.

During August and September of 191 the Romans besieged the Aetolians at Naupactus.[10] Flamininus, concerned about the activities of Philip V, persuaded Glabrio to grant an armistice to the Aetolians and permit envoys to be sent to Rome. Hostages may have been demanded by the Romans in conjunction with this armistice. However, the Aetolians had little success at Rome. The Senate demanded that they either submit their case unconditionally to the arbitrament of Rome, or pay 1000 talents and make an offensive-defensive alliance with her. When the Aetolians tried to determine what they might expect by surrendering unconditionally, no positive reply was given, and they were ordered to leave the City immediately. If hostages had been rendered at the commencement of the armistice, they may have been released at this time, or they may have been among the forty-three Aetolians who were sent to Rome by Glabrio and detained in the Lautumiae.[11]

There is one other possible occasion prior to 189 when the Aetolians may have surrendered hostages to the Romans. In the Spring of 190 Lucius and Publius Scipio arrived in Greece and undertook further negotiations with the Aetolians.[12] However, the Romans proposed the same harsh alternatives as they had presented earlier, and the offer was refused by the full consilium of the Aetolian league. Nevertheless, the Aetolians did succeed in gaining a six-months truce in order that envoys might be sent to Rome. Although the submission of hostages would have been appropriate at this time, the subsequent treatment of the Aetolian ambassadors in Rome shows that the Romans had no intention of granting peace to the Aetolians until they had finished with Antiochus. The six-months truce ensured that the Aetolians would not hamper Roman operations in Asia, and thus it is likely that no hostages were taken.

It appears most likely that the Aetolian hostages taken by the Romans prior to 189 were submitted at Naupactus in late 191. We do not know when they were restored, but the regulation in the treaty of 189 which excluded them from serving again indicates that they had been liberated. It remains to suggest why these former hostages were deemed ineligible for a second term. Possibly the restriction was simply in accordance with a general Roman policy which sought to acquaint as many non-Italian hostages as possible with aspects of Latin culture. However, the reason for the restriction may have been political. We have suggested that the former Aetolian hostages may have come from the party of Phaeneas. From 198 until the final peace the Romans had directed their efforts for a settlement to negotiations with that party. This policy had not been very successful, since the radicals, under Thoas and Damocritus, had been extremely influential in the Aetolian assembly. Therefore the Romans, in order to secure hostages from the dominant party, instructed their consul to avoid selecting those hostages who had served before. It is noteworthy that even though the radical party continued to dominate Aetolian politics, the Romans experienced no unusual difficulties with the Aetolians for the six year period during which the hostages were detained.

University of Western Ontario   *M. James Moscovich*

NOTES

1. As Dr. Salmon's first doctoral student, I am happy to offer this essay as a small token of my gratitude for his personal assistance as well as my regard for his scholarly studies in Ancient History.

2. Polyb. 21.32.10-12; cf. Liv. 38.11.6-7.

3. An alternate reading, τῶν ὁμηρευόντων, preserved in Ms. O, although accepted as correct by Casaubon, does not seem likely in view of Liv. 38.11.7 (*quis qui ante obses fuit*).

4. E. Täubler, *Imperium Romanum*, Leipzig-Berlin, 1913, p. 71. Cf. A. Aymard, *JRS* 51, 1961, p. 140, n. 2.

5. Polybius (21.32.9) employs the same imperative, καθιστάτωσαν, in the instructions regarding the annual submission of indemnity payments.

6. Polybius' account (21.42.22) of the treaty granted by Rome to Antiochus III shows that he was well acquainted with *mutatio obsidum*.

7. The hostages submitted by Antiochus III were to be exchanged every three years (Polyb. 21.42.22). Täubler does not state what he believes would have been the frequency of exchange in the case of the Aetolian hostages.

8. Polyb. 20.9-10; cf. Liv. 36.27-29.

9. Liv. 28.34.7 indicates that the submission of hostages was an ancient and standard feature of *deditio*: *Mos vetustus erat Romanis, cum quo nec foedere nec aequis legibus iungeretur amicitia, non prius imperio in eum tamquam pacatum uti quam omnia divina humanaque dedidisset, obsides accepti, arma adempta, praesidia urbibus imposita forent.*

10. Liv. 36.34-35.

11. Liv. 37.3.8. Among the Aetolians sent to Rome by Glabrio were Damocritus and his brother, who had been captured at Heraclea. 36 of these Aetolians later marched in Glabrio's triumph in 190 B.C. (Liv. 37.46).

12. Polyb. 21.4-5; cf. Liv. 36.6-7.

The Attempt to Try Caesar

Suetonius, *DJ* 23.1 Functus consulatu Gaio Memmio Lucioque Domitio praetoribus de superioris anni actis referentibus cognitionem senatui detulit; nec illo suscipiente triduoque per inritas altercationes absumpto in prouinciam abiit. et statim quaestor eius in praeiudicium aliquot criminibus arreptus est. mox et ipse a Lucio Antistio tr. pl. postulatus appellato demum collegio optinuit, cum rei publicae causa abesset reus ne fieret.

I. *Praeiudicium*

In *CQ* 19, 1969, pp. 200-204 I analysed this passage, trying to show that the action by the tribune L. Antistius did not (as has always been thought) necessarily take place in 58, but as probably in 57 or 56, and that the tribune is quite probably not an otherwise unknown tribune of 58, but identical with a known Antistius Vetus, tribune in 56.

E. S. Gruen, in a discussion of some criminal trials of the late Republic (*Athenaeum* n.s. 49, 1971, pp. 62-67), has made an important contribution to the proper understanding of the involved story of the attack on Caesar in his absence. Unfortunately he ended by trying to restore the incident to 58 and to revive the imaginary tribune of that year. Yet his own arguments in fact add to the case I tried to make and help to make my originally tentative suggestion as certain as any such historical reconstruction can be. The matter needs renewed discussion. The points which I missed and which

Gruen's acumen and scholarship have now discovered must be worked into the context of the whole story.

But first some debris must be cleared away. Gruen allows that *mox* "need not mean 'soon'" but continues: "That it conceals a gap of two years is more difficult to accept." Before his reasons for that presumed difficulty are investigated in detail, the linguistic and contextual facts must be firmly reiterated. As far as the meaning of *mox* in Suetonius is concerned, quite superficial scrutiny suffices to establish that he can use the word for intervals even longer than two years.[1] As far as the context is concerned, this is no precise chronological narrative, and any time from 58 (not early in the year) to at least 56 is possible for this incident.[2]

What, then, is Gruen's "difficulty"? He offers only one:[3] "In that event, the *praeiudicium* arranged for Caesar's quaestor would lose much of its value or purpose." We must first ask: what precisely was the *praeiudicium*? As I pointed out, clearly the conviction of Caesar's quaestor of 59 (i.e. perhaps his *ex*-quaestor in 58, unless the same man had stayed with him *pro quaestore*), for acts carried out on the consul's instructions, would declare those instructions to be illegal, assuring (in theory!) the consul's later conviction. Gruen has doubts: it need not have been the quaestor of 59. He usefully reminds us that, in one case, a quaestor in office is known to have been prosecuted before a *quaestio*: P. Clodius in 61, overlooked both by Weinrib (*Phoenix*, 1968, pp. 35 f.) and by myself; therefore it could be Caesar's quaestor of 58. The fact is worth recalling. So is the further fact (not mentioned by Gruen) that Clodius was tried before an extraordinary *quaestio*, set up by a special law of the Roman People *ex Senatus consulto*.[4] It was free to set its own terms.

We must, in any case, look at the context and not be dazzled by abstract legal possibilities. What is at issue, in the whole of Suetonius' account of these attempts, is Caesar's consulate and its *acta*. This, surely, could hardly be made clearer. Two praetors of 58 consult the Senate *de superioris anni actis*; Caesar offers to abide by its verdict and, after three days of ineffectual debate, leaves Rome. It is now that, at once (*statim*), his quaestor is charged *in praeiudicium*; and later on (*mox*) Caesar himself is impeached by the tribune L. Antistius, clearly for those same *acta*. Throughout, the battle is over Caesar and the events of 59. It is absurd to suppose – what commonly has been supposed – that the quaestor is the quaestor of 58, totally unconnected with those events. The unique case of Clodius in 61, though it must be remembered, is not strikingly relevant to the story of the attack on Caesar. The nature of the *praeiudicium* is obvious enough. Nor is it obvious why the *praeiudicium* of the quaestor's conviction should "lose much of its value or purpose" in two years. That was not how the Roman mind worked. Demonstration seems almost superfluous; but let us point (quite at random) to a scene in Livy where, in 185 B.C., Pergamene envoys appeal to a *praeiudicium* in the Asian settlement of 188.[5]

But quite apart from this, there is a basic question that Gruen fails to ask and that is surely of some importance in the evaluation of his argument: was the prosecution of Caesar's quaestor successful? It would be difficult to maintain that it was, and no one (to my knowledge) has ever done so. The point of Suetonius' catalogue is surely that all these attempts failed. Had Caesar's quaestor of 59 been convicted on criminal charges in 58, it would have been a *cause célèbre*, and we could not have failed to hear of such a success for the enemies of the dynasts. But, of course, in the political context of 58 success is inconceivable, Pompey, for one, could not have permitted it – not to mention P. Clodius. In fact, far from its becoming a sensational case, it must have ended with a whimper – we do not even know the quaestor's name, or the prosecutor's.

The confusion lurking in the whole argument is now exposed. If the case was unsuccessful (and I expect Gruen, had he considered the point, would have agreed that it was), there was no real *praeiudicium* after all. Hence the intended *praeiudicium* acquired no "value or purpose" to lose. Hence the action taken (*mox*, not *statim*) by L. Antistius against Caesar need not have directly and immediately followed up

the action against the unknown quaestor. Suetonius is giving
us — as we have repeatedly had to say — a list of unsuccessful
attempts to attack the *acta* of 59. There is no reason why
two years cannot separate two of these incidents. The *acta* of
59 were by no means forgotten in 56: indeed, Cicero claims
that he was intending to launch a major attack on them on
the Ides of May of that very year.[6] The sole alleged difficulty
in taking *mox* to mark an interval of two years dissolves into
thin air. The attack may, as I showed, have come at any time
down to 56.

II. L. Antistius

It is a different — though related — question whether we
may identify the tribune L. Antistius (of 58, 57 or 56) who
launched the attack with the tribune of 56 Antistius Vetus.
Gruen objects, on various grounds. First, the Antistii Veteres
"show hereditary connections with Caesar" — i.e., the father
was Caesar's *praetor* in Spain, and Caesar in his turn took the
son with him as his quaestor. The story is well known.[7]
Gruen (p. 63), not for the first time, tentatively identifies
that son with the tribune Vetus and with a Caesarian officer
in 45. "The pattern is consistent," he concludes. Alas, the
officer is not. After Caesar's death he betook himself, with
his treasure chest, to the better and (at that time) stronger
cause: he joined Brutus and, with his blessing, departed for
Rome to seek high office. By 35 he was acting for Octavian
in Illyria. By 30, he had managed to become consul. I had, of
course, noted Plutarch's story and the possible identification
with the officer of 45, implying strong doubt.[8] In fact, the
officer of 45 wanted to go home and become praetor for 42;
and no quaestor of 61, of good family and favoured by
Caesar, can possibly have waited as long as this for a
praetorship.[9] The identification must be abandoned. The
pattern is less consistent than was claimed.

Next, the tribune of 56. Gruen admits that he is recorded
(Cic. *Q. fr.* 2.1.8) as strongly supporting Cicero in working
for the conviction of Clodius, in a Senate meeting of

December 57, though he plays this down[10] and claims that it "tells us nothing about relations with Caesar." Some time ago, in an interesting article, Gruen plausibly exhorted us not to regard P. Clodius Pulcher as a mere tool of others.[11] But it is surely clear that at this point the attack on Clodius was connected with a planned attack on Caesar, and that Caesar must therefore have been behind the attempt to shield Clodius. They at least had the same enemies, for what that is worth: notably the consuls of 56, Marcellinus and Philippus.[12] Antistius' colleague L. Racilius, mentioned together with him by Cicero, was a friend of Milo,[13] whose opposition to the *regnum* of the dynasts is well known. If the identification of Caesar's quaestor Antistius Vetus with the tribune of 56 is natural, indeed inevitable, it follows from this that, by early 56, the ex-quaestor was supporting the *boni* and their friends against the "tyrants" and theirs.

Another question arises: that of the Antistii and their *cognomina*. The two chief families at the time are the Veteres and the Regini. Since the association of an Antistius Reginus with Caesar can be demonstrated at almost this very time, the tribune supporting the *boni* cannot lightly be identified as a member of that family; indeed, he would have to be the brother of Caesar's officer. I used this as an argument for seeing a Vetus in Caesar's would-be prosecutor. Gruen demurs: the man need not have had a *cognomen* at all. "But why search for a *cognomen*? The sources are full of Republican Antistii without *cognomen*." His note refers to the index of *MRR* for support.[14]

Actual consultation of that source does indeed show many Antistii listed without *cognomen*: in fact, an impressive total of thirteen. But perhaps analysis is needed, rather than arithmetic. All those before 150 B.C. lack a *cognomen* in our record. Two of them belong to the fifth century, two to the fourth; three more appear as envoys in the Hannibalic War, one of them in a fictitious story and another in a corrupt text where the name is uncertain.[15] No Antistii are documented between the Hannibalic War and the middle of the second century, and there is thus no way of connecting those after that gap with those before. Though it is reasonable to suppose that at least those with the *praenomen* Lucius are related to Antistii of the late Republic and early Empire. In any case, the *gens* (like others we know) quite possibly did not use *cognomina* before 200 or so — their complete absence, in seven known (if not always authentic) cases, may not be due to mere accident. These seven must, however, be struck off the list, for our present purpose.

When we pick the *gens* up again about 150, the situation (as in many other cases) has changed and continues to change. Two Antistii (or Antestii)[16] appear on the list of the *consilium* of 129, naturally without *cognomen*: no *cognomina* at all are used on that list or on any official document as early as this.[17] The first of these men is L. Antistius C.f. Men., the second is clearly L. Antistius, but the rest is lost: the end of his tribe appeared on a small fragment (*d*) known to Passerini, but not found by Sherk. Passerini read the last two letters as -NA, and this is generally accepted by scholars. Unfortunately Passerini's readings are shown by Sherk to be unreliable, and we cannot exclude the possibility — though, of course, we should not assert it as a fact — that the tribe was again Menenia.[18] On the other hand, it seems more likely that Passerini made the easy error of reading ΛIA as NA and that this man's tribe should be Aemilia, which is known to have been the tribe of the Antistii Veteres.[19] In that case, we may here have the ancestor of that great family, and be able to distinguish, as early as this, two different families of Antistii of senatorial (or at least potentially senatorial) standing. We should in any case expect the Veteres to be in the Senate by this time — though not necessarily using their *cognomen*.[20]

We can certainly at this time trace two families of Antistii on coins. Two moneyers calling themselves Antestius are known, the first a C. Antestius, put by Crawford in or just before 150, the second a L. Antestius Gragulus, who from Crawford's hoard list seems to be *c*. 140.[21] The second duly features a jackdaw as his emblem; the first shows a dog as his, and it is clear that the dog also will refer to the family *cognomen* (e.g. Caninus, Catulus, or perhaps Lupus), which was not put on the coins. This shows that one of our Antistii without *cognomen* in fact had one, but one that does not appear later, any more than that of Gragulus does.

These two different families ought to correspond to the two families in the SC of 129 — if there are two families there, as there certainly are if Passerini was right, and quite probably if he was wrong. (Of course, we cannot positively identify the second of the moneyers with either of the witnesses.) It would be excessive to posit more than two families of this relatively obscure *gens* in or near the Senate as early as this. In any case, we may now recognise that the Antistii Veteres probably at one stage changed their original *cognomen* to the proud one asserting their antiquity: we might compare the Fulvii Nobiliores, whose *cognomen* appears comparatively late. They will originally have borne the less distinguished one of the dog or the jackdaw. Since the more recent name was already that of Caesar's commander in Spain, who, as praetor c. 70,[22] must have been born c. 110, it was presumably either he or his father who made the change, perhaps at the same time modernising the spelling of the *nomen* to "Antistius."[23]

The next family we must consider are the Regini. A Reginus appears as tribune in 103, helping Q. Servilius Caepio to escape from prison and sharing his exile.[24] He is quite likely to be the L. Antistius who later prosecuted T. Matrinius.[25] The name Reginus is thus attested before 100. The Veteres, as a family, ought to be older. We may now say that of the four Antistii between c. 150 and 100 one is attested with a *cognomen*, but one other certainly and the remaining two quite probably had one.

No *cognomen* is known, or can be suggested, for the P. Antistius who collaborated with the Cinnani, married his daughter to Pompey and was killed for it in 82.[26] It does not follow that he did not use one: P. Sulpicius Rufus certainly did, but though he is constantly mentioned by Cicero in the *de oratore* and the *Brutus*, the *cognomen* never appears in those works. But in the circumstances, and particularly in view of the unique *praenomen*, we cannot know any more about P. Antistius' lineage. There remains only a T. Antistius, whose *praenomen* is once attested by Cicero in a letter[27] referring to the man's activities as quaestor at the outbreak of the Civil War. This man, since he was (we are told) specially devoted to C. Ateius Capito and left him five-sixths of his estate, may not have been closely related to the other senatorial Antistii. His *cognomen* (if any) is unknown, his *praenomen* (if correctly transmitted) unique.

Nothing firm, unfortunately, can be said about the father and family of the jurist M. Antistius Labeo, except that the father was a friend of M. Brutus, took part in the plot against Caesar and killed himself after Philippi.[28] His name is given as "Labeo" in Plutarch and Appian, as "Pacuvius Labeo" in Gellius (5.21.10), and it appears in *Dig.* 1.2.2.44 in a corrupt passage (*Pacuvius Labeo Antistius Labeonis Antistii pater*) — a passage that also contains such names as *Alfenus Varus Gaius* and *Publicius Gellius.* Modern scholars have made up the name "Pacuvius Antistius Labeo" out of these ingredients — an unlikely name for a Roman senator at this time. Kunkel supports this (as "gesichert") by two arguments: (a) that the son has the father's *cognomen*, hence cannot have been adopted out of his *gens*; (b) that Plutarch (*Brut.* 25) calls the father Antistius. Both are patently false. Retention of a *cognomen* after adoption is in fact the rule, not the exception: we need only point to such eminent men as Cn. Aufidius Orestes, *cos.* 71 (an Aurelius Orestes), and M. Pupius Piso, *cos.* 61 (a Calpurnius Piso). Plutarch, again, on two occasions refers to our man as Labeo (*Brut.* 12 and 51), and his reference in *Brut.* 25 is to a different man, an Antistius Vetus whom we know from Cicero's *Letters.*[29] As Mommsen (*ad loc.*) and others have pointed out, the "Antistius" in the *Digest* passage should be deleted as intrusive. The jurist's name was Pacuvius Labeo, and he is beyond our range here. However, it follows that his son must have been adopted by an Antistius, probably a M. Antistius not otherwise known to us. But there is no difficulty in this: whoever he was, he is probably not relevant to the senatorial

Antistii of the late Republic whom we are here considering,[30] and we do not know whether he had a *cognomen*.

The upshot of this long investigation is that, after c. 150, nearly all known senatorial Antistii can be shown to have used *cognomina* (whether known to us or not). The only certain exception is Cicero's T. Antistius, perhaps not related to the principal families; though P. Antistius, prominent in the eighties, is not known to have used one. The other senatorial Antistii, from the moneyers and the men in *RDGE* 12 down to the Antistii of the Civil Wars (too complex to sort out here) appear to belong to two related families,[31] the Veteres and the Regini. And in view of the eminence attained by P. Antistius, it is even in his case quite probably mere scarcity of data that makes it impossible for us to fit him into one of those families. It should no longer be asserted, *tout court*, that there is no need to try to ascertain the *cognomina* of late Republican Antistii, or that the exercise is necessarily fruitless.

This long and circuitous route brings us back to our L. Antistius, would-be prosecutor of Caesar in one of the years 58, 57, or 56 — or, to be more precise, at some time between *late* 58 (in view of the *mox* contrasted with *statim*) and *early* 56 (in view of the reconciliation of the dynasts during the course of that year, which ended all such projects). Is he identical with Antistius Vetus, known tribune of 56 and — at the beginning of his tribunate — known supporter of the *boni*? Even on formal grounds, there is much to be said for it. It eliminates one of two Antistii who (we are told) held the same office within a space of three years and neither of whom appears in any later post that we know of.[32] It amalgamates these two *gentiles* of whom (oddly enough) each is only once mentioned in our sources, one without his *cognomen* and one without his *praenomen* — yet of whom it can be shown (as I tried to show) that *praenomen* and *cognomen* will combine very plausibly. It fits a L. Antistius into one of the two known leading families of the *gens* at the time, to which all but one or possibly two of the other senatorial Antistii of the time belong. Surely sufficient to

justify a proposal to identify, at least as a working hypothesis.

III. P. Vatinius

It is at this point that Gruen's acumen provides the
decisive evidence, hitherto overlooked by me as by others. He
draws attention to the fact that P. Vatinius was in fact
prosecuted, while a legate of Caesar, for illegalities commit-
ted in his tribunate of 59, on Caesar's behalf. He was recalled
by the praetor of 58, C. Memmius, to face the charge,
returned to Rome to do so — and then avoided it. The
question is: how did he avoid it? Cicero's oratorical pyrotech-
nics do not make the answer at all easy, and the passage (*Vat.*
33 f.) will have to be quoted.

> 33. quaero etiam illud ex te, quod priuatus admisisti; in quo
> certe iam tibi dicere non licebit, cum clarissimis uiris causam
> tuam esse coniunctam; postulatusne sis lege Licinia et Iunia?
> edixeritne C. Memmius praetor ex ea lege ut adesses die
> tricesimo? cum is dies uenisset, fecerisne quod in hac re publica
> non modo factum antea numquam est, sed in omni memoria est
> omnino inauditum? appellarisne tribunos plebis, ne causam
> diceres — leuius dixi, quamquam id ipsum esset et nouum et non
> ferendum — sed appellarisne nominatim pestem illius anni, furiam
> patriae, tempestatem rei publicae, Clodium? qui tamen cum iure,
> cum more, cum potestate iudicium impedire non posset, rediit ad
> illam uim et furorem suum ducemque se militibus tuis praebuit.
> in quo, ne quid a me dictum in te potius putes, quam abs te esse
> quaesitum, nullum onus imponam mihi testimoni; quae mihi
> breui tempore ex eodem isto loco uideo esse dicenda, seruabo,
> teque non arguam, sed, ut in ceteris rebus feci, rogabo.
>
> 34. quaero ex te, Vatini, num quis in hac ciuitate post urbem
> conditam tribunos plebis appellarit, ne causam diceret? num quis
> reus in tribunal sui quaesitoris escenderit eumque ui deturbarit?
> subsellia dissiparit? urnas deiecerit? eas denique omnes res in
> iudicio disturbando commiserit, quarum rerum causa iudicia sunt
> constituta? sciasne tum fugisse Memmium? accusatores esse tuos
> de tuis tuorumque manibus ereptos? iudices quaestionum de
> proximis tribunalibus esse depulsos? in foro, luce, inspectante

populo Romano quaestionem, magistratus, morem maiorum, leges, iudices, reum, poenam esse sublatam? haec omnia sciasne diligentia C. Memmi publicis tabulis esse notata atque testata? atque illud etiam quaero, cum posteaquam es postulatus, ex legatione redieris — ne quis te iudicia defugere arbitretur — teque, cum tibi utrum uelles liceret, dictitaris causam dicere maluisse, qui consentaneum fuerit, cum legationis perfugio uti noluisses, appellatione improbissima te ad auxilium nefarium confugisse?

Cicero — to put it mildly — does not go out of his way to make it clear what happened. However, in this case we should not assume that he is seriously trying to mislead (as he often does): these events had taken place two years before, and they were not of the kind that could be kept secret or forgotten. Cicero's upper-class audience, which heard his speech, will inevitably have included men who had, in 58, taken a prominent part in the events he describes, almost certainly even some who had served on the disrupted jury, or were closely related to men who had. Of course, the advocate makes the most of his material. But for once we can be reasonably sure that the outline of the facts, at least, is accurate.[33]

Vatinius waived the immunity he could have claimed as *absens rei p. causa* and returned to Rome. However, as Gruen shows, he had no intention of standing trial. It is commonly believed that he appealed to the board of tribunes. This has raised a dilemma: how did the tribunes respond? Gruen rightly notes that they cannot have dismissed the appeal: it would be unthinkable for Cicero not to mention this shattering argument. Hence it must be concluded that the board as a whole accepted the appeal and halted proceedings. Yet proceedings in fact continued and were disrupted by Clodius, acting on his own. There is no way of escape between the horns of this dilemma. It can merely be concealed by imprecise formulation.[34]

In a case like this, it is an obvious suggestion that our interpretation of the source may be at fault. As we have seen, Cicero is not fully clear in his statement of the facts, both for rhetorical reasons and because everyone knew them. What

Cicero does is to build up his picture of abominable violation of *mos maiorum* and law in the form of a climax. The first enormity he alleges is that Vatinius appealed to the tribunes against having to stand trial. But then he *corrects* himself: "leuius dixi, quamquam id ipsum esset et nouum et non ferendum."[35] In fact, Cicero had understated the enormity: what Vatinius did was to appeal to one tribune – P. Clodius – by name! Hence there is, after all, no dilemma. The board of tribunes never considered the case. Vatinius exercised what some (though obviously not all) might regard as one of the basic rights of a citizen – the right of appeal for protection to the *auxilium* of one individual tribune. Though perhaps never practised on a similar occasion, it was in itself far from unheard of in Roman history.

We cannot be sure what happened next. Did Clodius try to veto the trial and was the veto ignored as allegedly unconstitutional? Or did he not even make the gesture, but at once resort to the use of force, which would ensure that there was no failure? It could even be represented as within the tribune's legal exercise of his powers – and might find popular support in this form. But Cicero (*cum . . . non posset*) does not permit us to decide.[36]

Although the praetor duly recorded his protest, as a basis for possible later action, Clodius' tactics were, as usual in 58, successful. Vatinius did not stand trial. But what had been the purpose of the whole exercise? Historians, as so often, spin complex webs of conjecture, preferring "conspiratorial" schemes to the simple and obvious. Pocock, to whom belongs the credit for rescuing this speech (for the first time in generations, if not the first time ever) from undeserved neglect and revealing it as a historical source of outstanding importance, got many points right in his discussion of this prosecution;[37] but he was a little too ingenious on this point and thought that it was all planned "in order to uphold a cardinal principle of the Popular Party." Gruen rightly rejects this, but is again content with mere vagueness: "It was a game of propaganda and counter-propaganda." That both parties would exploit every situation, as it arose, for intensive propaganda cannot be denied. But it should not be over-stressed. Caesar and Vatinius, like their enemies, had their concrete and immediate objectives, even though either success or failure in attaining those objectives could then be interpreted to best effect.

Vatinius' reason for giving up his immunity and coming to Rome, and then (as Gruen shows) taking all possible steps to escape having to stand trial, was evidently too simple to occur to the modern student. Vatinius wanted the aedileship for 57. In fact, he stood for that office and failed, as Cicero reminded him in 56.[38] Now, in order to stand for office, he had to come to Rome for his *professio* (as Caesar had found out in 60). While engaged on this, he would not be regarded as *absens* and would be liable to prosecution — as Caesar later would have been, had he agreed to return for a *professio* in 49. Hence he had nothing to gain by pleading his immunity. We are nowhere explicitly told precisely when, in the course of 58, the trial took place, but obviously before the elections. In fact, in view of what we know of Cicero's habits of *suppressio ueri* and *suggestio falsi*, it could be thought that the prosecution was launched just when it was known that Vatinius was about to return for his *professio*: his candidacy would be actively advertised by his friends in his absence. A prosecution could be used to prevent a man from standing for office, even if he was later acquitted. The stratagem, as it happened, was familiar to Vatinius' protector P. Clodius: he had been on the other side, when it was used against L. Sergius Catilina.[39] This time he perhaps supplied the answer. But the intention might well have been to force Vatinius, technically, to choose between prosecution (if he returned) and giving up his hope of office (if he claimed his immunity as *absens rei p. causa*) — and in fact to try to force him into abandoning his candidacy, whichever course he chose, and threaten him with conviction as well if he came to Rome to profess. The cases of Caesar (both in 60 and in 49) and of Catiline show that such manoeuvring cannot be thought alien to the spirit of politics in the late Republic.

However, though this is a *possible* reconstruction, it is

probably not the correct one. It seems more likely that the prosecution was launched well before the elections, even as early as February or March,[40] when Vatinius was presumably still *ad urbem* with his commander. Yet it was something that had to be faced and got out of the way immediately, if Vatinius wanted his aedileship. Nothing would be gained by waiting. In any case, therefore, it is this simple and obvious motive – his hope for an aedileship, which he no doubt expected his powerful friends to be able to secure for him – that made Vatinius come to Rome when the prosecution was launched. It was this, too, that forced him to find a way of speedily and safely repelling the threat: had he allowed the case to go forward, he not only risked conviction, but even at the best, like Catiline some years earlier, would almost certainly have lost his chance of *professio*. The course that his interrogator depicts as monstrous, inconsistent, irrational (see s. 34, *fin.*) was in fact the only reasonable course for him to take – and fortunately we have the evidence to see it.

IV. C. Iulius Caesar

In due course (*mox*), as we saw, Caesar himself was accused. He appealed to the tribunes, and they ruled – correctly – that he could not be attacked while *absens rei p. causa*. It was an important victory for him: as is known, that declaration became the basis for his position in the negotiations over the termination of his proconsulate and election to a consulate. Gruen pointed out that Caesar and Vatinius adopted similar ways of escaping prosecution, except that Vatinius appealed after giving up his immunity, Caesar before he could be forced to. But for reasons he does not give, Gruen places the prosecution of Caesar before that of Vatinius. This is purely an *a priori* assumption, often repeated (pp. 65f.) but never argued. Indeed, he is so convinced of this order of events that he regards it as the key to the understanding of the whole situation: "Scholarly bafflement is traceable to the failure to make that obvious link" (l.c.).

We have already seen that it is in fact traceable to failure to think in terms of obvious motives. Nevertheless, the link discovered by Gruen is a vital one, and indeed furthers understanding. However, it needs to be scrutinised: did Caesar's indictment really precede that of Vatinius?

It should certainly never have been simply assumed that it did — especially if that assumption was to become a basis for historical explanation. Our reports come from two different sources, one in each source: Cicero does not mention the attempted prosecution of Caesar, nor Suetonius that of Vatinius. We have now already gone as far as independent chronology can take us: Caesar's prosecution (we saw) may come in 58, 57 or early 56, with *early* 58 highly unlikely; Vatinius' prosecution most probably came early in 58. If these independent conclusions are correct, it follows that Vatinius' prosecution preceded Caesar's. We must test this preliminary conclusion against the detailed evidence we can garner from the *In Vatinium*; for Suetonius, unfortunately, gives only a bare reference.

Our first piece of evidence is at the beginning of s. 33. Cicero is going to interrogate Vatinius on what he did as a private person, and (he adds) here Vatinius can no longer claim that his case is bound up with "very eminent men" (i.e. Caesar). Of course, this may be a technical trick: one could argue that the *causa* was not the prosecution, nor the appeal to Clodius, but the violence used at the trial. Caesar was certainly not directly linked with that.

Next, however, a decisive statement. Vatinius has done what has never been done before, never even been heard of: "*appellarisne tribunos plebis, ne causam diceres?*" He has (we are soon to hear) done worse than that; but for a first charge that suffices. Let us compare Gruen's statement (p. 65): "It is noteworthy that Vatinius, like Caesar, summoned the tribunician college to intercede on his behalf. This anomalous course of events can only be understood in light of the preceding indictment of Caesar."

Cicero, evidently, did not thus understand it. Nor can one plausibly claim that he is merely trying to mislead. If, within the preceding few months (on Gruen's reckoning), Caesar had conspicuously appealed to the tribunes (and successfully so), thus inspiring Vatinius to imitate him, how could an orator say to an audience that had witnessed all this that such a thing had never been done, never even been heard of, within anyone's memory? Memories are short and orators do tell convenient lies, for their own purposes.[41] But this would be outrageous, and surely self-defeating. And he will not leave ill alone — he emphatically repeats it at the beginning of s. 34: *quaero ex te, Vatini, num quis in hac ciuitate post urbem conditam tribunos plebis appellarit, ne causam diceret*? Is it credible that Vatinius could have answered: "Yes, Caesar did it a few months before me"?

It will have to be accepted that Vatinius' trial preceded the attack on Caesar. We may therefore safely put it no later than early March, as other considerations suggest. Of course, this still leaves the date of the Caesar incident open: although it can no longer be encapsulated in 58, between the attack on the quaestor and that on Vatinius, we cannot yet exclude the last nine months or more of 58. Perhaps closer inspection of Cicero's words will yield an answer.

We have already noted Cicero's strong characterization of Vatinius' *appellatio*: he did (33) what was never done before in Rome, what is quite unheard of (*est omnino inauditum*) in all men's memory; and Cicero asks him whether anyone since the foundation of Rome has ever done this (34, *init.*) and continues with a whole succession of perfect subjunctives. In other words, it was not only by 58 that no one had used this wicked *appellatio*, but by the time of Cicero's speech (before March 11th, 56) it could be asserted that the action was as unheard of as it had been two years earlier.[42] It follows that by the date of the speech Caesar's *appellatio* had not yet taken place.

This ultimate result of Gruen's contribution therefore makes certain what I could only hesitantly suggest before. We have seen that the attempted prosecution of Caesar must come before the new agreements of the dynasts at Ravenna and Luca first became known in Rome, putting an end to the hopes of Cicero and other *boni*. That was not before late April or early May 56.[43] It therefore came between about mid-February and the end of April. This confirms that it was indeed a tribune of 56 who tried to launch the prosecution — and identification of this L. Antistius with Antistius Vetus, the supporter of the *boni* interested in *iudicia*, becomes inescapable. The suggestion that the prosecution fits into the context of attacks on the dynasts (and especially on Caesar), which preceded their understanding of early 56 and necessitated it, has also turned out to be reasonable. It merely remains to hazard the conjecture that, when Cicero delivered (or perhaps only when he published) his attack on Vatinius, he placed such extraordinary emphasis on the point we have been investigating because he already had an inkling of what was in the wind. He was not one to take the initiative of April 9th, after the trauma of his exile, unless he could count on widespread support in the Senate, in a climate of intensifying attacks *in arcem illius causae*. It is to be expected that the attack on Caesar had by then already been made. Since he would probably be well informed of moves against the dynasts, he may well have known by February or early March what his supporter L. Antistius Vetus was planning. But this must be left as a mere suggestion, impossible to test.[44]

Harvard University   *E. Badian*

NOTES

1. See *CQ* 1969, p. 201[1] (confined to *DJ*).
2. Ibid. pp. 201-2. *Early* 58 is excluded by the contrast between the prosecution of Caesar's quaestor (*statim*) and the attempt (*mox*) by Antistius to impeach Caesar himself (*ibid.*) — not noticed by Gruen.
3. *Athenaeum* 1971, p. 63. He does indeed continue: "And there are other difficulties." But these turn out to be entirely concerned with the proposed identification of Antistius (on which, see below), not with

the interval that may be covered by *mox*.

4. Cic. *Att.* 1.13.3, 14.2 and 5, 16.1-5; Asc. 53C, Schol. Bob. 89 St.

5. See Livy 38. 39.14 and 39.27.5. This, of course, is intended to illustrate only how the word was understood in Livy's day. There is no reason to assume there had been a radical change in Roman thinking by the time of Suetonius.

6. Cic. *Fam.* 1.9.8. For scepticism, see Balsdon, *JRS* 47, 1957, pp. 18 f. Against this (rightly) Stockton, *TAPA* 93, 1962, pp. 471 ff.

7. Plut. *Caes.* 5.

8. *CQ* 1969, pp. 202f., with notes — no reference to this in Gruen. For the later career of C. Antistius, see *MRR* II, pp. 407, 411 and Index.

9. See Cic. *ad Brut.* 1.11.2. Cf. *MRR Suppl.* 6 (not noted by Gruen), where T. J. Cadoux is quoted as suggesting that this man may be a quaestor of 45. That would perhaps make him excessively ambitious. More probably a *legatus* (*pro quaestore*, possibly) who had been quaestor some years before. I suggested — in view of his eagerness to join Brutus — that he may have been an old Pompeian. There is, of course, no proof.

10. For a full account of what Cicero tells us, see *CQ* 1969, p. 203. Gruen's version (p. 64[37]) is incomplete in one important respect: it omits Antistius' enthusiastic and eloquent ("non mehercule indiserte") support for Cicero.

11. *Phoenix* 20, 1966, pp. 120f.

12. See, conveniently, *MRR* II, p. 207.

13. Cf. Cic. *Q.fr.* 2.4.5.

14. Gruen, p. 64, citing *MRR* II, p. 530 (Also *Historia* 15, 1966, p. 49 n. 100).

15. *MRR*, I, p. 239 (I see no reason to believe the names authentic, as neither man ever again appears in the accounts of the war); p. 256 and p. 258 n. 6. There are no positive grounds for suspecting the third (Sex. Antistius (*ibid.* p. 293) — a unique *praenomen*), though he too is otherwise unknown.

16. Ἀνθέστιος is the spelling in the correct copy of the SC, as also in Diod. 15.51.1 (corresponding to "Antistius" in Livy 6.30.2). The earlier Latin form was "Antestius" (thus the two moneyers: see below), and this must have been transmitted as the name of Diodorus' military tribune. The later "Antistius" is duly rendered Ἀντίστιος in the Greek sources (Josephus, Plutarch, Dio).

17. *RDGE* 12, nos. 22 and 53. These known facts of epigraphic

usage are ignored by Gruen, *Historia*, 1.c. (n. 14).

18. Thus in l.40 Sherk found MAI]KIA, reporting (p. 67) that "Passerini failed to notice the *iota* between the *kappa* and the *alpha*."

19. At least under the Julio-Claudians, hence probably from the start. See Taylor, *VDRR*, p. 192. That Passerini was right is also possible; but we do not in fact know of any eminent Antistii in a tribe ending in -na; and the presence of Veteres will in any case have to be assumed by now (see next note).

20. The *cognomen* of the Veteres makes it likely that they had been in the Senate longer than any other family of Antistii (or at least claimed to have been): they presumably adopted it to distinguish themselves from more recent families, such as the Regini. They were the "old Antistii." They must in any case, therefore, go back to the second century at least.

21. Crawford, *RRCH*, tables III (near end) and X; for the coins, see Sydenham, *CRR*, nos. 406, 407, 411; 451, 452.

22. *MRR* II, pp. 133, 137[9].

23. If the conjecture advanced on Passerini's reading is right. this younger Antistius in the SC (followed by only two more men) can clearly be the father of Caesar's commander: he will only have been 20 or even less in 129. (Cf. the youngest members of Cn. Pompeius Strabo's *consilium*, *ILLRP* 515: I must here reassert my view that it seems impossible for all the 55 men on the consilium of *RDGE* 12 to have been actual members of the Senate, as is often claimed.)

24. Val. Max. 4.7.3.

25. See my *Studies in Greek and Roman History*, pp. 48f., accepting a suggestion by Niccolini. It is rather captious to deny the attested tribune L. Reginus his *nomen* Antistius. (Thus Gruen, *Roman Politics and the Criminal Courts, 149-78 B.C.*, Index, after accepting it as "plausible" in *Historia*, l.c. (n. 14 above).) No other Republican senatorial family bears that *cognomen*. I should now be less positive about his identity with L. Antistius, the prosecutor of Matrinius, than I was fifteen years ago, but must still draw attention to the fact that "Lucius" is remarkably rare among the *praenomina* of prominent late Republican Antistii: the presumed tribune of 58 is the only instance after 100, apart from Matrinius' prosecutor.

26. *RE*, s.v. "Antistius," no. 19. See especially Plut. *Pomp.* 9, *ad fin.*

27. Cic. *fam.* 13. 29.3.

28. *RE*, s.v. "Antistius," no. 35; *MRR* II, p. 364; Kunkel, *Herkunft u. soz. Stellung d. röm. Juristen*, pp. 32f.

29. *MRR* II, p. 327, and cf. n. 9 above.

30. Kunkel's arguments for placing the home of the family in southern Samnium, at or near Ligures Baebiani, are plausible; but they do not necessarily show the *origo* of either Pacuvius or Antistius (whom Kunkel amalgamates). None of the evidence takes us beyond M. Antistius Labeo, who married a Neratia from that area and may have acquired property there in this way.

31. The relationship between them was strongly stressed by two early Imperial moneyers, a Vetus and a Reginus, both of whom featured the same scene of the *foedus Gabinum* (Mattingly-Sydenham, *RIC* I, pp. 74, 78).

32. On the attempt to identify the tribune of 56 with the officer of 45-44, see n. 9 above and text. That officer, whatever his rank, is probably (as is generally held) the later *cos*. 30: see p. 148 above.

33. See n. 42 below. Schol. Bob. (p. 140 St.), as often, merely rehashes Cicero's words and adds fanciful embroidery: the scholiast clearly had no additional information of any use. Cf. n. 37.

34. Thus Gruen (p. 66): "But the tribunician college as a whole does not seem to have bought that argument [the argument that Vatinius had forfeited his immunity]. One of them, at least, P. Clodius, interceded for Vatinius and attempted to block proceedings." But that will not do. If the board supported Clodius, he would not have acted on his own. The procedure is well attested: the tribunes jointly considered and issued a joint decree, presumably arrived at by consensus after discussion. Had this been done and had Vatinius been supported, the continuation of the trial would be inconceivable. On the other hand, in the case of a negative decision, an individual tribune could (though he normally would not) use his own veto, as the elder Tiberius Gracchus is said to have done in the case of the trials of the Scipios. If this is what Clodius was doing, the majority decision would be on record — and, as Gruen notes elsewhere, inevitably stressed by Cicero. (On the constitutional background, see Mommsen, *Röm. Staatsr.* I^3, pp. 279f.)

35. Note the *esset*, showing (after *quamquam*) that the statement is presented as contrary to fact, and the following *sed*, with repeated *appellarisne*, marking the correction of the "understatement" (*leuius*). As so often in Cicero's best oratory, every word and form counts. *Tribunos plebis appellare* (which he uses initially) was in fact obviously the general form of words for such an action. After the correction, Cicero repeats it in s. 34.

36. The phrase does suggest the second course (*cum ... non potuisset* would be more precise for the first). But it was very much in

Cicero's interest to obscure this distinction and imply that Clodius was conscious of having no legal case. Note that, just as Vatinius' *appellatio* is *improbissima*, Clodius' response, the *auxilium* granted, is *nefarium*.

37. L. G. Pocock, *A Commentary on Cicero in Vatinium*, pp. 186-90. He noted, i.a., the fanciful and worthless nature of Schol. Bob. — too often ignored, both here and in other cases. Gruen (pp. 66f.) selectively accepts the scholiast's information and bases part of his case on the selected items, while recognising that the account is "hopelessly confused" and "contains several errors."

38. Cic. *Vat.* 16; perhaps 36, *fin.*

39. Sources and discussion Drumann-Groebe V, p. 419. See now Gruen, pp. 59-62.

40. Pocock (p. 122) thinks it was early in the year, "not long after Clodius had taken over executive control of the 'popular party,'" but adduces no strong argument. One would expect Cicero to make it clear whether or not he himself was in Rome when these events were taking place; and it seems reasonable to take his phrase "nullum onus imponam mihi testimoni," followed by his promise that he would soon be speaking against Vatinius as a witness ("ex eodem isto loco" — Pocock has no comment on all this), as meaning precisely that he could speak on the whole affair as an eyewitness. If this interpretation is correct — it cannot be claimed to be absolutely certain — then the trial did indeed take place not later than March, when Cicero left Rome (Gelzer, *Cicero*, p. 139). Perhaps the statement that Clodius *ducem se militibus tuis praebuit* may point in the same direction: if part of Caesar's army was still *ad urbem*, the *milites* may well have been real soldiers sent in to protect their *legatus*.

41. Cicero must have known that his consular colleague C. Antonius had done something very like what he called quite unheard of and unimaginable — *tribunos appellare* to avoid standing trial — in the seventies (Asc. 84 C). Of course, he had received a *nota* for it from the next censors, so that the practice was by no means approved, and in any case the legal situation had been different (and hard for us to disentangle). But since Cicero had become officially reconciled to him, had defended him, and in this very speech deplored his fate (*Vat.* 27f.), that old story was best forgotten.

42. For the date of Sestius' acquittal, see Cic. *Q. fr.* 2.4.1. The trial began on February 10th: Cic. *Q. fr.* 2.3.5. We do not know precisely when the *In Vatinium* was delivered, nor whether in anything like the published form. (See Pocock, pp. 4f.) But it hardly matters for our purpose whether the statements we are analysing were actually

made in court or published as having been thus made, for the benefit of a larger audience of the same type.

43. Cic. *fam.* 1.9. 8-10. On April 5th Cicero announced his intention to bring up the question of the *ager Campanus* on May 15th. It was after that announcement that Pompey left Rome and met Caesar at Luca, and some time after that again that Cicero heard from his brother and from Pompey himself that his intention would have to be given up.

44. I should like to thank Professor M. G. Morgan (University of Texas) for commenting on a draft of this paper; also to express my pleasure at being asked to join in showing my admiration for a distinguished colleague, from whom I have learnt a great deal. I hope he will find the gift acceptable as shedding a little light on a corner of a period that has been one of his main interests.

[Added in Proof]

H. B. Mattingly, *AJP* 93, 1972 (published 1973), pp. 412 ff., proposes the date of 101 instead of the traditional 129 B.C. for the *SC de Agro Pergameno*. If his argument is accepted, prosopographical conjectures based on the traditional date (including the comments made on the Antistii in this paper) will have to be modified. Mattingly shows that about eight of the men named on the list can be identified with known characters about as plausibly as several could on the earlier date. As for the composition, he comments (p. 419) that "many of the later names look equestrian" — he does not explain the meaning of this or illustrate it, and in fact, in the light of his own suggestion on no. 33 (ibid.), the remaining men ought to be quaestorians. Until the date of the decree (and, if possible, its composition) can be settled on other grounds, it should not be used as a basis for prosopographical conjecture. As regards the two Antistii, on the new date neither of them can be identified with, or readily related to, either of the moneyers or the tribune of 103.

The Roman Inns and the Law
The Inns of Ostia

Two puzzling phenomena face an observer of Roman city life of the first century of the Christian era: a) the seemingly erratic Roman legislation about restaurants and inns, and b) the fundamental difference in appearance between an inn in Herculaneum-Pompeii and one in Ostia. Although the time-gap between the latest taverns of Herculaneum-Pompeii and the earliest in Ostia may be less than fifty years, they seem to serve different purposes: while the counters of the inns of Herculaneum-Pompeii all have big, built-in storage jars, the counters of Ostian inns have bare tops but built-in basins on the floor level (Figs. 1 and 2).

That there is a close relationship between Roman legislation and the change in appearance of the taverns seems quite likely.

I. Imperial Legislation

The official Roman attitude towards the inns was anything but friendly. What is most conspicuous is the severe limitations which were put on the kind of food which could be sold in the taverns. Tiberius (Suet. *Tib.* 34) decreed that the price of foodstuff should be controlled and that restrictions should be placed on *popinae* and *ganeae* to the extent that not even baked goods could be sold there.

Claudius is said (Cassius Dio 60.6.6-7) to have dissolved *collegia* which had been allowed by Gaius, and in order to attack the evil at the root he closed the taverns where college members used to meet and drink; he further promulgated the law that cooked meat and hot water could not be sold. This last provision, outlawing hot water and meat, would presumably refer to the inns and hotels where the colleges did not meet. In this context Tönnes Kleberg[1] quotes the incident told by Suetonius (*Claud.* 38.2) about Claudius' renters who sold cooked wares (*cocta*) and were punished by the aedile. The story, however, does not necessarily refer to an infraction of this particular law.

Regarding Nero, it is said by Suetonius (*Nero* 16) as well as by Cassius Dio (62.14.2) that he would not allow any other cooked food but vegetables and cabbage to be sold in the *popinae* where previously all kinds of meat were available. This indicates that Nero repeated Claudius' prohibition. Under Vespasian (Cass. Dio 65.10.3) the same law was confirmed, and we are informed that specifically only peas and beans could be served.

Our information about these laws is, of course, very limited and lacks detail. Tiberius took action against *popinae* and *ganeae*, both of which were eating places, and decided that not even bread and pastry could be sold. Kleberg points out that *popina* is the word for a place where prepared food, including wine, is sold.[2] *Ganea* has a similar meaning but has lower standards than a *popina*. *Caupona* was at the same time hotel and restaurant, and after the word acquired a bad implication it was replaced by *hospitium* when used in the meaning of hotel, and by *taberna* as a place for wine sales.[3]

Tiberius' provisions can only mean that while the activities of *popinae* and *ganeae* were restricted, the *cauponae* and similar establishments could still cater to the public and that the hotels continued to be unrestricted. Some public services are too vital to be completely shut down. Claudius went one step further, and in a radical move closed down some taverns and outlawed meat and hot water in others. The move may have been temporary since Nero reintroduced or confirmed the law, which now will allow only vegetables and cabbage to be sold; this is also the content of Vespasian's legislation: it is mainly the preparation and sale of meat which is being prohibited. But to what extent this law was enforced, whether it governed all or just some specific type of inns, is unclear.

It is only fair to raise the question whether these laws would be in force in all the Empire, or in all of Italy, or just in Rome. Rome has a special status in many respects. The right of association, for instance, is much more limited than elsewhere, and it might well be that for the sake of peace in Rome only the capital was subjected to these restrictions.

If a conclusion *e silentio* is acceptable, the finds in Herculaneum indicate that the tavern-keepers observed Vespasian's laws. During excavations remains have been found of the merchandise which was sold in the taverns. *Insula* IV.10-11 has produced insect-infested, carbonized grain in a big counter *dolium*.[4] *Insula* V.6: beans and peas in counter *dolia*.[5] *Insula* V.10: grain deposits found in an upstairs store room over the inn.[6] *Insula Orientalis* II.13: grain, chickpeas and beans in counter *dolia*.[7] Grain, peas and beans, but never meat. On the other hand, bones and eggs are found in several places outside the taverns.[8]

Why meat in particular would be prohibited is not too clear, *per se*: ancient medical, agricultural, and culinary literature gives no indication that meat would have a special position. The price is not particularly prohibitive, either. It is true that Diocletian's Price Edict belongs to a much later time, but in the main it gives a reliable picture of the proportionate price levels: while wheat is 100 den. a bushel and beans and peas are 60 den., pork at 12 den. a pound, beef at 8 den., and kid and lamb at 12 den. is no luxury. Vegetables were proportionately cheaper, as today, and it was of course cheaper to make up a meal with cabbage and beets at 5 for 4 den.[9]

II. Political Motives of the Legislation

Erratic as it seems to be, Roman legislation can only be accounted for if one considers the political motives behind it. A key witness for the understanding of the problem is Philo, *legatio* 311-12, where it is said of Augustus that "he ordered the Jews alone be permitted to assemble in synagogues. These gatherings, he said, were not based on drunkenness and disorder, they did not create conspiracy and did not endanger peace but were schools of temperance and righteousness...." This states the philosophy behind the very restrictive policy against the taverns: the taverns were social centres, and when wine had loosened the tongue they became breeding grounds for political conspiracies. There is often talk about the closing of inns. Mention has already been made of the closure ordered by the emperor Claudius (Cass. Dio, 60.6.6-7), and to illustrate the official attitude further it may be enough to refer to the tribune Clodius' earlier activity in Rome. In January of 58 B.C. Clodius introduced a law which legalized all the clubs and associations that had been outlawed five years before by Cicero. From that moment on the *collegia* were used as a front for the organization of armed gangs, a development which led to the state of lawlessness so well illustrated by the tragic fights between Clodius and Milo.[10]

To Kleberg the restrictions that were laid upon the inns are part of a great scheme to introduce social improvements.[11] The deeper motive, however, was very likely political: the restrictions would limit the usefulness of the inns to the public and, consequently, make them less attractive as social centres. The fear of all organizations and assemblies was very great. In a famous correspondence between Trajan and Pliny (*Ep.* 10.33; 34) Pliny asks permission to organize a fire brigade in Nicomedia. Despite the recent sufferings of the inhabitants of that city the emperor refuses. He considers similar organizations potentially very dangerous and tells Pliny so.

When the emperor can deny the citizens of Nicomedia a

fire brigade for political reasons, he can for the same reasons deny Roman citizens the benefit of hot meals or meat in their inns.

After Vespasian there is no mention of Roman legislation about inns until a much later date. The Roman emperors may have attained the goal of their legislation. The fact that we hear about successive confirmations of prohibitions under Tiberius, Claudius, Nero, and Vespasian is not in itself an indication that the law was held in contempt and had to be repeated, as Kleberg is inclined to believe.[12] What we see are several re-writings of the law, each of which modifies its regulations. It would be equally wrong to claim that Vespasian's law did not apply later simply because we do not hear about it.

The prohibitions of Claudius and his successors seem to have taken hold: according to Cassius Dio (60.6.6-7) it was Claudius' idea that it would be unrealistic simply to close some of the taverns unless he at the same time tried to change the habits of his people. In fact, the emperors do seem to have changed the habits of the Roman people.

While in the inns of Herculaneum-Pompeii the characteristic food jars are built into all counters, these same jars are missing altogether in the counters of Ostian inns. One might conceivably infer from this that the sale of food had become less important, and that the legislation had forced the dinner guests out.

III. Where did the Roman Commoner Eat?

Kleberg sees a social scheme behind the restrictions on inns: When the emperors took the food away from the inns, they gave at the same time better houses to the Roman lower classes. Originally, he argues, the miserable living quarters of the humble Roman did not even have a place to cook in, and in the German edition of his book he mentions that in many cases portable braziers may have been used.[13] But this miserable life was improved by the new look of Roman city architecture. New Rome, as it was built by Nero on a well-prepared plan, gave good and adequate housing to the Romans "with a possibility of having fireplaces and of cooking their food." Also, he stresses the importance of the *thermae*, which were hygienic establishments as well as social centres.

Unfortunately there is not much evidence of kitchens or fire-places in Ostia. There are only two kitchens in Ostia, both in the same house (Casa delle volte dipinte). Kleberg's countryman and teacher Axel Boëthius was of the opinion that humble Romans in the cities must have eaten out, – or they could buy hot water in the restaurants for use at home. He referred to Rotterdam, where he had seen hot water being sold from the restaurants in the working class area.[14] The eating place is a problem of concern also to H. T. Rowell: he thinks that the obvious lack of kitchens in Ostia perhaps was offset by the existence of so many guilds (*collegia*), which all had eating facilities in their meeting places. The guilds, however, were under just as heavy restrictions and close supervision as the inns: They were mostly restricted to one or a few meals every month[16] and cannot have offered stable, regular facilities.

The truth is that the common man ate at home, and there are clear indications where the dining area was. The central room in the Roman apartment, as it is known to us from Ostia and Rome, was the *medianum*.[17] The *medianum* was shared by everybody who shared a Roman apartment. From the *Itala* we have two examples of the use of the word *medianum* to designate a dining room. When two disciples are sent into Jerusalem to find a place for the Last Supper, they are told by Jesus that a man with a pitcher on his shoulder will lead them to a *medianum* where they all can have their supper. (Luke 22.12: *ille vobis ostendet maedianum stratum magnum* and Mark 14.15: *ipse vobis ostendet locum medianum stratum in superioribus magnum.*)

The language that we are confronted with in this place is the language of humble Romans of the second century. When the dining place is called *medianum*, it is simply because the *medianum* was the place where the humble apartment dweller ate and prepared his meals. He prepared it, of course, on the portable charcoal brazier that had been with the Romans since prehistoric times.

IV The Inns of Ostia

If the inns of Ostia were not allowed to serve meals to their clients, what could they offer?

A study of the remaining inns in Ostia will partly answer that question. There are not too many places in Ostia which can be identified as inns, with absolute certainty. Many of the certain marks and criteria are vanishing. The cement and rubble counters of the tavern-inns crumble away as they are exposed to the climate, to the rich weed growth, and to the yearly hay-cutting. There are places which have nearly disappeared today. Kleberg, in the French edition of his book, has listed an inn Reg. II.ii.3, because there was a counter with a water basin.[18] Today there is only a low pile of rubble to be seen in a corner. What Kleberg calls a "fourneau" and "tuyauterie" has also disappeared. The counter as shown in the plan of the official publication[19] is no different from the drinking fountains which can be observed in the vestibules of Casa di Bacco e Arianna Reg. I.xvii.5 and of Reg. V.iii.1. The latter two places may have been college seats. In the Pianta delle regioni are indications of counters with water basins in Reg. V.iv.1 on the corner of Via dell'invidioso and Semita dei cippi, in Reg. I.xvii.5, corner of Via della foce and Via del Serapide, and in Reg. IV.v.7 and 10, but very little or nothing at all is left of the construction in those locations, not enough at any rate to tell what there was. Moreover, identifications may be difficult: Kleberg's no. 10 is given as "Reg. III.8 à 50 m. environ de la Porta marina."[20] He is probably referring to one of the taverns in Reg. III.vii.3, but which one? There are six taverns in the neighbourhood of Porta marina. Kleberg's no. 14[21] is in Reg. I.xii.10, not in Reg. IV. A great help in the work in Ostia is the excellent Pianta delle regioni in *Scavi di Ostia* I, but here, too, there are pitfalls. There is no consistency in the

Fig. 1 Pompeian
tavern.

Fig. 2 Ostian tavern.

way in which the counters are indicated. For instance, the counters in Caupona del pavone (Reg. IV.ii.6), in two taverns north of Terme del faro (IV.ii.3), and on the Decumanus (Reg. II.ix.2) represent three different ways of drafting the same type of counter.

The criteria which identify a shop as a tavern are, first, the special counter with the basin at the bottom. The special water basin by itself is not enough for identification, because drinking fountains of similar shape are found in places where many people come and go. Those fountains are mostly built up against a wall. When, however, it is combined with the stepformed shelves for glasses, the identification is more sure. This is particularly true if it is found in one single room with an open front on the street. Moreover, when remnants of foundations of water heaters are found, or where fragments of mortars can be recognized, the identification is quite reliable.

The counter that we now consider so characteristic of Ostian taverns is proved by an ancient grave relief to be an important part of a tavern (see fig. 3). The relief shows to the right two customers at a table, one drinking out of a glass, the other reaching for a glass brought to him by the barmaid. To the left is shown the tavern counter with water basin. Over the counter are three shelves built stepwise against the

Fig. 3 Relief of sarcophagus from Isola Sacra showing Ostian tavern. Counter and shelves for glasses to the left.

wall, glasses on the two upper shelves, glasses and jars on the lower one.

The tavern counters in Ostia are covered with marble slabs on the top and on the sides. The opening at the bottom of the counter is built as a barrel vault, which goes all the way through the counter; the lower part of the vault is closed with marble slabs at both ends to form a basin. Pierre Grimal describes this arrangement as "a counter covered with marble above a charcoal stove on which the food was cooked within sight of the customer."[22] There is, however, no doubt that the basin was meant for water. In the first place, a waterpipe was found in the counter of the inn in Via di Diana.[23] In the second place, basins where people could dip water for drinking and washing were constructed in that manner. They are especially found in busy places: in the entrance to Terme della Trinacria, in Terme della basilica, in the west end of the Portico di Nettuno, in the Tempio collegiale (Reg. V.xi.1), and in the latrine of the domus della Fortuna annonaria. In the third place, the counters in some inns have holes through their sides to accommodate waterpipes. In the inn in Cas. dell'Ercole shop no. 8, Reg. III.ii.3 the floor has been broken up to repair the pipe and the mosaic floor has been relaid in a less careful way. In the inn of Alexander Helix, Reg. IV.vii.4 a similar repair of the floor can be seen, with a piece of lead pipe left in the side of a basin in the middle of the room. In the fourth place, the tavern in shop no. 21 of Cas. dell'Ercole, Reg. III.ii.3, gives additional evidence. In the southeast corner of this tavern is a brick counter, which is built against the wall, with three shelves in a steplike pattern on top (fig. 4). Below is the whole body of a counter, with the difference that the vault and the basin are missing. In this case a solid brick wall goes straight down from the shelves to the floor. There was apparently no basin in the counter because it was not needed in this tavern: Next to the counter on the right is a well out of which water could be drawn.

The basins must have been the main water supply of the inns. From here was taken the water for the *calda* to mix with wine, to make *conditum* or whatever mixture was

Fig. 4 Ostian tavern with shelves, but no water basin. Water was drawn from the vaulted well to the right of the counter.

Fig. 5 Ostian tavern basin with overflow basin in front.

needed. Water, in antiquity as today in modern Roman bars, was the commodity most often sold. I do not think Russell Meiggs' suggestion that the basins were for washing glasses and dishes can be universally applied.[24] Was much dish-washing actually done? Again, an arrangement like the one in the tavern on Via delle corporazioni (Reg. II.vi.5) shows a tendency to keep the two operations apart: from an inner basin the water flows over into an outer one (fig. 5), the inner one being for consumption, while the overflow basin could be used for washing glasses. Glasses were not washed in drinking water. One can see similar divisions in Via tecta degli aurighi, Reg. III.xiv.1, and in domus della nicchia a mosaico, Reg. IV.iv.2.

The next thing of importance is the mortar. This was necessary to mince the pepper which was part of the *conditum*.[25] Pliny gives a short definition (*NH* 14.108) . . . *Aromatiten quoque invenio factitatum . . . nardi etiam et malobathri selibris in musti congios duos additis qualia nunc quoque fiunt et melle addito, quae alii condita, alii pipenta appellant*, and the word is often mentioned and explained in Roman medical literature. Vegetius (*Mulomedicina* 3.8.6) speaks of *conditum bene piperatum*. This mixture of wine, honey and pepper was a standard drink in Ostian taverns and in other taverns of the Empire, and, consequently, mortars must have been standard equipment. Mortars, or fragments of them, are found in several taverns in Ostia and help to identify places where identification otherwise is unsure.

V. List of Ostian Inns

On the basis of the criteria mentioned above, the following list of inns can be made:

1. I.xvi.1, room 18, (first door N. of stairs in Via delle terme del Mitra). Rubble pile where counter was. Marble slabs which formed the water basin. Fragments of mortar.
2. I.xvi.1, room 15, (fourth door N. of stairs). Basin w. shelves against the wall.

3. I.ii.5, room 18-19, (Termopolio in V. di Diana) Kleberg no. 1.[26]

4. I.x.2 corner of Decumanus and V. del pomerio. Counter w. basin; an extra well.

5. I.iii.1, room 16, Western taberna in C. dei molini. Counter w. basin.

6. I.iii.1, room 17, Eastern taberna in C. dei molini. Counter w. basin; heater foundation.

7. I.xii.10, room 12, (corner of Cardo maximus and Terme del foro). Kleberg no. 14.

8. II.ix.2, room 21, (second door from W. on Decumanus). Counter w. basin.

9. II.vi.1 Caupona di Fortunatus. Kleberg no. 7.

10. II.vi.5 V. delle Corporazioni. Kleberg no. 8. See fig. 5.

11. II.v.1 tavern at entrance to Caserma dei vigili. Kleberg no. 5.

12. II.v.1, second tavern at Caserma dei vigili. Kleberg no. 6.

13. II.ii.6, room 4. (in Portico del tetto spiovente, fourth shop W. of Mithraeum.) Kleberg no. 4.

14. II.ii.3. Kleberg no. 3.

15. III.xvii.5, room 9, corner shop N. of C. di Bacco e Arianna. A counter is clearly indicated on the Pianta generale, but little is left in situ.

16. III.xiv.4, room 10. (Annio's corner.) Counter w. basin looks likely, from Pianta generale. Counter top missing as in Alexander Helix' tavern.

17. III.xiv.1, room 18. (Corner across from Casette tipo.) Counter-shelves w. basin.

18. III.v.1, room 3. (N.W. corner of C. delle volte dipinte.) Kleberg no. 9.

19. III.vii.3, room 2. (Two doors N. of entrance to domus fulminata.) Counter-shelves w. basin.

20. III.vii.3, room 6. (one door S. of entrance to domus fulminata.) Counter-shelves w. basin.

21. III.x.2 decorated room in Terme dei sette sapienti (see G. Calza in Die Antike 15, 1940, pp. 99-115).

22. III.i.10, room 1. Counter w. basin standing out from

wall in traditional pattern; lead pipes leading up to it; drain
under wall into next room; 4 rooms, w. mosaic floors, seem
to have belonged together. A second counter w. basin outside
north wall may have been part of same plant; fragment of
lead pipe in wall of second basin. Not in Pianta delle regioni,
Scavi di Ostia, I, Rome 1933.

23. IV.vii.4, room 1. Caupona di Alexander Helix.
Kleberg no. 13.

24. IV.vii.3, room 2, (the middle shop). Remains of
counter, marble slabs forming water basin.

25. IV.vii.2, room 20. (8th door from S.) Counter w.
vault w. marks of basin.

26. IV.vii.2, room 9, (15th door from S.) Rubble
remains of counter, half a mortar.

27. 27. IV.vii.2, room 5, (17th door from S.) Marble
slabs forming a water basin.

28. IV.ii.6, room 10, Caupona del pavone. Kleberg no.
11.

29. IV.ii.2, room 3, (1st door N. of entrance to Terme
del faro). Kleberg no. 12.

30. IV.ii.2, room 8 (5th door N. of entrance to Terme
del faro). Counter w. basin.

31. IV.ii.2, room 21, (13th door N. of entrance to Terme
del faro). See fig. 4.

32. V.iv.1, room 1. Pianta generale shows usual counter
and bench. Nothing left *in situ*.

There is evidence of about thirty-two taverns in Ostia.
The original number must have been considerably higher.
Many taverns have had counters and other equipment in
wood, which now has disappeared. The densest concentration
of inns is around the Porta marina, outside which Aurelian's
forum may have been located.[27] Elsewhere they are found in
the busy sections of the city. The pattern which is known
from Pompeii is repeated in Ostia.

The University of Alberta
Edmonton and Rome   G. Hermansen

NOTES

1. Tönnes Kleberg, *Hôtels, restaurants et cabarets dans l'antiquité romaine*, Uppsala, 1957, pp. 101-2.
2. Kleberg, *Hôtels*, p. 17.
3. Kleberg, *Hôtels*, p. 27.
4. Amadeo Maiuri, *Ercolano. I nuovi scavi*, 1927-58, 2 vols., Rome, 1958, I, p. 432.
5. Amadeo Maiuri, *Ercolano*, I, p. 402.
6. Amadeo Maiuri, *Ercolano*, I, p. 251.
7. Amadeo Maiuri, *Ercolano*, I, p. 465.
8. In the Museo Nazionale, Naples. Cf. J. J. Deiss, *Herculaneum*, New York, 1966, 3.18.156.
9. E. R. Grocer's edition of The Edict in Tenney Frank, *An Economic Survey of Ancient Rome* V, pp. 318-37.
10. About Clodius and the *collegia*, see e.g. David Stockton, *Cicero*, Oxford, 1971, p. 187. Kleberg, *Hôtels*, p. 103.
11. Tönnes Kleberg, *In den Wirtshäusern und Weinstuben des antiken Rom*, Darmstadt, 1966, p. 46.
12. Kleberg, *Wirtshäuser*, p. 40.
13. Kleberg, *Wirtshäuser*, p. 44.
14. Kleberg, *Hôtels*, pp. 10, 53, 55-56: A. Boëthius, *De nya utgrävningarne i Rom*, Stockholm, 1931, p. 52; T. Kleberg, *Värdshus och värdshushiv*, pp. 67, 70-71, 129 and n. 1.
15. *AJA* 62, 1958, p. 124.
16. J. P. Waltzing, *Étude historique sur les corporations professionnelles*, Louvain 1895, I, p. 325.
17. *Phoenix* 24, 1971, p. 342.
18. Kleberg, *Hôtels*, p. 43, no. 3.
19. *Scavi di Ostia* I, Rome, 1953, Pianta delle regioni, section 5.
20. Kleberg, *Hôtels*, p. 46.
21. Kleberg, *Hôtels*, p. 47.
22. Pierre Grimal, *Civilization of Rome*, 1963, p. 226.
23. NSc 1915. 29.
24. Russell Meiggs, *Roman Ostia*, Oxford, 1960, p. 428.
25. Joachim Marquardt, *Das Privatleben der Römer* II Darmstadt, 1964, p. 461.
26. In this list are given the numbers in Kleberg, *Hôtels*, pp. 46-47. Kleberg knows 14 taverns in all. His no. 2 is no. 5 or no. 6 of the present list; his no. 10 is most likely no. 19 or no. 20 of this list.
27. Russell Meiggs, *Roman Ostia*, p. 186.

Autour de la Date
du "Foedus" Rome – Callatis

Depuis une quarantaine d'années les fouilleurs de la ville pontique de Callatis s'enorgueillissent d'avoir mis au jour et fait connaître l'unique traité conclu par Rome avec une ville de l'Orient grec qui nous soit jusqu'ici parvenu dans sa version latine. Outre sa rareté, qui l'impose à l'attention des épigraphistes de partout, le document présente pour l'histoire de la Péninsule Balkanique dans l'antiquité un intérêt que les plus récents travaux dans ce domaine n'ont fait que souligner.[1] Il s'agit, en effet, d'un témoignage de tout premier ordre sur l'expansion romaine au nord des frontières de la Macédoine, en même temps que d'un exemple significatif des méthodes employées par la diplomatie du Sénat afin d'attacher à la République une cité traditionnellement indépendante, sise dans une région du monde ancien où les intérêts de la première puissance militaire de l'époque commençaient à peine à poindre.[2]

On comprend, dans ces conditions, que le problème de la date du *foedus* ait dès le début retenu l'attention de ceux qui s'en sont occupés. Ce n'est pas que le premier éditeur du texte, Théophile Sauciuc-Săveanu, soit arrivé sur ce point à des conclusions dont il convient de tenir compte. N'ayant pas saisi dès l'abord la nature et l'importance du fragment dont il était en train d'assurer la publication, il ne s'est même pas posé la question, se réservant de revenir sur l'interprétation de l'inscription dans un mémoire qu'il n'a jamais publié.[3] Par contre, le second savant qui ait repris l'étude du fragment, Scarlat Lambrino, dans une communication présentée à l'Académie des Inscriptions peu de temps après l'édition de Săveanu,[4] n'a pas manqué d'évoquer, en même temps que le contenu et la portée du traité, les circonstances historiques dans lesquelles il a été signé. Pour arriver sur ce point à des conclusions valables, Lambrino a passé en revue les faits et gestes des proconsuls de la Macédoine dans la première moitié du Ier siècle av. notre ère, s'arrêtant tout particulièrement sur l'activitê de M. Terentius Varro Lucullus au cours de la IIIe guerre mithridatique, quand le frère du grand L. Licinius Lucullus, chargé d'annéantir les postes avancés du souverain asiatique sur la côte ouest de la mer Noire, a réussi, au cours de deux campagnes successives, à s'emparer de toutes les villes pontiques alliées au grand roi, depuis Apollonie, au sud, jusqu'à Istros, au nord, à proximité des bouches du Danube. Après ces brillants faits d'armes, pouvait conclure le regretté savant, le proconsul s'est empressé d'offrir aux Grecs l'amitié de Rome, en transformant en alliées les cités qu'il avait l'une après l'autre soumises et, dans un cas tout au moins, cruellement punies.[5]

Ce qui semble avoir conduit Lambrino à cette conclusion, — dès le premier moment acceptée et défendue par Jérôme Carcopino dans la même séance de l'Académie où la communication venait d'être lue,[6] — c'est, d'une part, la considération qu'à aucun autre moment du IIe siècle ou de la première moitié du Ier la situation politique ou les intérêts de Rome dans la mer Noire n'exigeaient ni n'auraient permis une telle alliance; ensuite, le fait qu'à moins de dix ans après le proconsulat de Varron, en 61 précisément, Dion Cassius, parlant des exactions dont un autre gouverneur de Macédoine, M. Antonius Hybrida, s'était rendu coupable envers plusieurs tribus thraces voisines de la province, cite, parmi les victimes de l'abusif personnage, en même temps que ces peuplades barbares, certains σύμμαχοι ἐν τῇ Μυσίᾳ.[7] Dans ces "alliés de Mésie" qu'aucune autre source ne mentionne, déjà Mommsen avait reconnu les villes grecques du Pont

Gauche.[8] Et Lambrino ne faisait que reprendre l'interprétation du grand historien allemand lorsqu'il proposait de voir dans Varro Lucullus l'homme qui aurait obligé celles-ci à accepter le vasselage de Rome.

La date et la portée du *foedus* callatien, telles que les avait établies l'épigraphiste roumain dans le mémoire à peine cité, ont depuis reçu une confirmation inattendue de la part de Gaetano De Sanctis, qui, dans une note du dernier volume de sa *Storia dei Romani*,[9] s'attardant à relever l'intérêt de notre document pour la connaissance de la politique orientale de la République à la fin de la IIIe guerre avec Mithridate, faisait observer que si, dans la version latine du traité, destinée à être exposée à Rome, on lit l'indication qu'un exemplaire de cet accord devait être placé [. . loc]*o optumo in faano Concor[d(iae). .]*, c'est parce que le temple de Jupiter Capitolin – où le texte aurait normalement dû trouver sa place – avait été incendié en 83 et rendu inutilisable jusqu'en 69, au plus tôt. Dans ces conditions, concluait-il avec raison, non seulement cette clause – insolite, au premier abord – peut s'expliquer de la manière la plus simple, mais elle constitue en même temps un argument décisif en faveur de l'hypothèse selon laquelle l'alliance romaine aurait été imposée à Callatis et aux autres cités grecques de la côte thrace aussitôt après leur foudroyante défaite par M. Terentius Varro.

Cette interprétation du *foedus* callatien qu'avait d'emblée acceptée le regretté Passerini, dans une ingénieuse tentative de restituer le texte mutilé à l'aide des versions grecques de plusieurs traités conclus par Rome au cours des derniers deux siècles av. notre ère avec des cités de la Grèce propre ou de la Grèce asiatique,[10] et qu'un savant aussi averti qu'Attilio Degrassi n'hésitait pas à faire sienne,[11] a été remise en cause à différentes reprises au cours des derniers trente ans, tout particulièrement en ce qui concerne la date à attribuer à l'insigne document. Le premier qui, à ma connaissance, ait avancé à ce sujet une hypothèse nouvelle, semble avoir été Ernst Lommatzsch, lequel, s'en tenant aux caractères paléographiques du document et sans trop se soucier des circonstances historiques qui ont pu l'occasionner, a proposé de l'attribuer à la première décennie du Ier siècle.[12] Quelques années plus tard, revenant à son tour sur cet épineux problème, dans un mémoire publié par les *Epigraphica* de Milan, Demetrio Marin n'hésitait pas à s'attaquer à la fois à la restitution de Passerini et aux conclusions historiques de Lambrino.[13] Il ne saurait naturellement pas être question de discuter à cette place, dans le détail, l'exactitude des conjectures de Passerini (sur la littéralité desquelles, au demeurant, ce savant n'avait pas manqué de faire lui-même les réserves qui s'imposaient),[14] ni de celles de Marin, dont le bien fondé est loin de s'imposer et qui, dans l'ensemble, s'éloignent du schéma soigneusement étudié par le prédecesseur, sans compenser cet écart par la clarté du contenu ou par la rigueur de l'expression. Sur ce point je préfère m'en remettre à l'autorité de Gaetano De Sanctis, qui jugeait les restitutions de Passerini "assai felici . . . sobrie e originali,"[15] me contentant de faire remarquer que, vu le caractère du document, on ne saurait s'attendre à trouver dans le *foedus* callatien des clauses qui ne figurent pas dans les textes rapprochés par Passerini, ce qui nous fait un devoir de nous en tenir, quant à l'économie du traité, au modèle esquissé une fois pour toutes par Täubler.[16]

Ceci dit, arrêtons-nous un instant sur les arguments qui, dans l'étude de Marin, sont tour à tour invoqués en faveur de l'hypothèse selon laquelle le *foedus* aurait été conclu non pas à la fin des campagnes de M. Terentius Varro Lucullus, mais bien au IIe siècle, et plus précisément, aux environs de 140 av. notre ère.[17] Ces arguments — paléographiques, linguistiques, historiques — sont, il faut bien le dire, de valeur inégale et, dans l'ensemble, assez peu convaincants. Ainsi, pour ce qui est de l'écriture, il me paraît que prétendre distinguer à vue d'oeil entre une inscription de la deuxième moitié du IIe siècle et une autre de la première moitié du Ier, c'est faire preuve de plus de présomption que de familiarité avec la paléographie latine. D'aussi bons connaisseurs en la matière que les Gordon ou Degrassi ne se flattent pas d'arriver, eux, à une telle précision, même quand il s'agit d'intervalles plus

longs que quelques dizaines d'années.[18] Aussi ne m'attar-
derai-je pas à réfuter ce qui, après tout, n'exige pas une
discussion approfondie, et passe à l'examen des considérations linguistiques à l'aide desquelles on voudrait nous
persuader que notre traité n'a pu être rédigé sinon au IIe
siècle.

Sur ce point, il faut dire que Marin est plus à son aise et
que les faits qu'il cite sont incontestables. On ne saurait nier,
en effet, que la langue du document présente plus d'un aspect
archaïque et que des graphies comme *poplus, adiouanto,*
pequnia, utei, faano trouvent des parallèles dans nombre de
textes de la première moitié du IIe siècle, à commencer par le
fameux *s.c. de Bacchanalibus*.[19] Lambrino lui-même s'en était
aperçu et, s'il n'a pas cédé à la tentation d'attribuer au *foedus*
une date aussi ancienne, c'est que, d'une part, il s'est bien
rendu compte qu'on est là en présence d'une convention qui
voulait que des actes intéressant la vie publique, comme les
lois, les *senatus consulta* et les traités, fussent rédigés dans
une langue tant soit peu archaïsante, d'autre part parce que
l'examen de la situation dans les Balkans depuis la constitution de la province de Macédoine jusqu'à la IIIe guerre
mithridatique exclut la possibilité que le *foedus* callatien ait
été conclu à un quelconque moment du IIe siècle.

Pour ce qui est de la langue du document, tout d'abord,
l'erreur méthodologique de Marin est d'avoir cherché des
exemples à rapprocher uniquement dans des textes antérieurs
ou contemporains de la conquête de la Macédoine,[20] tandis
qu'il lui aurait suffi de descendre au Ier siècle pour en trouver
d'autres, tout aussi clairs et probants. Que n'a-t-il pas jeté un
coup d'oeil sur la *lex municipii Tarentini*,[21] de 89, sur la *lex*
Cornelia de XX quaestoribus,[22] de 81, ou encore sur la *lex*
Antonia de Termessibus,[23] qui est de 71 av. notre ère, date
présumée du *foedus* callatien? Il y eût trouvé à foison non
seulement des exemples de *aei* pour *ai* ou *ae*, de *ei* pour *ai* ou
ae, de *ei* pour *i* et de *ou* pour *u*, mais aussi des graphies
comme *pequnia, quoia, queicomque*, des vocales géminées
comme *iuus* (et aussi *ious, iouris*), en un mot la plupart des
particularités phonétiques et morphologiques relevées dans le

fragment qui retient notre attention, ce qui prouve, s'il en
était encore besoin, qu'il serait pour le moins imprudent de
fixer la date d'un texte de cette sorte en se fondant
uniquement sur des faits de langue.[24]

Nous arrivons ainsi à la dernière catégorie d'arguments
invoqués par Marin en faveur d'une datation haute du traité,
je veux dire aux circonstances historiques qui, à l'en croire,
auraient poussé les deux parties à conclure une alliance. Pour
arriver sur ce point à la solution qu'il voudrait nous voir
adopter, il commence par écarter l'interprétation donnée par
Mommsen au passage de Dion Cassius mentionné plus haut,[25]
selon laquelle, en 62-61, les σύμμαχοι ἐν τῇ Μυσίᾳ aux prises
avec le gouverneur de Macédoine M. Antonius Hybrida
auraient été les cités grecques de la rive occidentale de
l'Euxin. En supposant qu'en réalité il s'agirait d'une ou de
plusieurs peuplades barbares vivant à l'écart de la Scythie
Mineure — "può darsi proprio tribù di Mesi —,"[26] alliées aux
Romains à un moment qu'il n'essaye même pas de préciser,
mais qui de toute façon se situerait *avant* l'expédition de M.
Terentius Varro Lucullus, Marin se flatte d'avoir brisé le lien
qui, selon Lambrino, aurait rattaché les deux événements. En
réalité, cette manière d'envisager le problème ne fait que le
compliquer inutilement, puisque — au lieu de nous aider à
fixer un seule date, elle nous fait un devoir d'en établir deux,
sans qu'aucun nouvel indice dégagé de l'analyse des faits
vienne faciliter notre tâche. De plus, à moins que je ne me
trompe, et fortement, je ne sâche pas que les Romains aient
jamais conclu une alliance formelle avec une peuplade
barbare vivant loin des frontières de la République et séparée
de celles-ci par d'autres peuplades indépendantes et, de plus,
hostiles. Le seul exemple de cette sorte que Marin se plait à
nous citer ne prouve en réalité rien, pour la bonne
raison que la prétendue alliance entre Romains et Dardaniens,
qui aurait poussé ces derniers à attaquer Philippe V à un
moment où le roi s'apprêtait à pénetrer en Elide, n'a jamais
existé, le tout se réduisant à la tactique habituelle de ces
tribus guerrières, toujours prêtes à envahir la Macédoine alors
que les troupes du royaume se trouvaient engagées sur
d'autres fronts.[27]

Reste dès lors à se demander si l'alliance entre Rome et Callatis (ou entre Rome et les autres cités grecques du Pont Gauche) a pu vraisemblablement être conclue vers 140 av. notre ère, comme voudrait nous le faire croire Marin, qui invoque à ce propos la nécessité "absolue" où se seraient trouvées ces cités d'arriver avec la République à un accord leur permettant de continuer avec le Sud Egéen les échanges commerciaux qui pendant des siècles avaient constitué la base la plus sûre de leur prospérité.[28] Cette fois encore l'argument est spécieux, vu qu'après la conquête de la Macédoine – et même plus tard, après la création de la province d'Asie – on ne voit pas que les Romains aient en quoi que ce soit contrôlé les relations économiques entre les cités de la Grèce, ou entre celles-ci et les anciennes colonies de la mer Noire, et cela indépendamment de la question de savoir si, dans la seconde moitié du IIe siècle, ces dernières activités pouvaient encore avoir l'ampleur et l'intensité qu'elles avaient eues pendant longtemps. Depuis quinze ans au moins, il m'est arrivé de signaler à plusieurs reprises le fait qu'à l'époque hellénistique les cités du Pont ont traversé une crise qui est allée s'aggravant jusqu'à la conquête romaine et qui, en même temps que leurs activités productives, mettait en cause leur liberté et leur indépendance.[29] Des documents épigraphiques on ne peut plus explicites nous apprennent que pour cultiver leurs χῶραι, pour circuler dans l'arrière-pays ou même pour pêcher dans le delta du Danube, les cités de la côte étaient à la merci des "barbares" de l'intérieur – tantôt venus de loin, tantôt autochones – qui, afin d'en tirer des φόροι et des δῶρα ne se gênaient pas pour piller et ravager leurs territoires. Dans ces conditions, peut-on encore parler d'une exportation régulière de grains et d'autres denrées vers le Sud, comme cela c'était fait des siècles durant et en vue de laquelle ces Grecs périphériques auraient éprouvé le besoin de s'assurer l'amitié des Romains? Ce qu'on voit surtout, ce sont leurs propres difficultés à se procurer le nécessaire, les ἀφορίαι et les σιτοδεῖαι dont parlent les inscriptions, l'intervention providentielle des évergètes qui s'ingénient à nourrir leurs concitoyens et même l'obligation des autorités de faire venir le blé de l'extérieur, parfois de très loin.[30]

Il n'a donc pu y avoir dans la seconde moitié du IIe siècle, chez les Grecs de la Dobroudja, le désir de s'assurer des débouchés commerciaux en Grèce métropolitaine, puisque leur propre existence dépendait à cette date des Scythes, des Bastarnes et des Gètes dont la mention revient dans les textes avec une inquiétante fréquence. On ne voit non plus à quoi aurait servi à la République l'alliance des Callatiens (pas plus que celle des autres villes du littoral roumain, puisqu'on peut considérer comme sûr que jusqu'à leur conflit avec le roi de Pont — et plus précisément jusqu'à la troisième guerre mithridatique —, les Romains ne semblent guère avoir conçu l'idée d'une alliance ou le projet d'une annexion territoriale du côté des bouches du Danube. Pour y arriver, pour qu'ils en viennent à comprendre l'utilité de certains postes avancés à proximité d'une frontière naturelle qui par la suite était destinée à jouer un rôle des plus importants dans leur système défensif, il a fallu Mithridate et la mer Noire transformée en lac "pontique," et des garnisons royales dans chacune des colonies naguère indépendantes, d'Olbia à Apollonie de Pont. Des lors, et en attendant l'établissement d'un *limes* danubien des Alpes à la mer Noire, et la création d'une province impériale de Mésie suivie à brève échéance par l'annexion du royaume clientelaire de Thrace, le Sénat pouvait trouver intéressant de s'assurer, sur ces rives lointaines et à proximité des indomptables tribus de l'arrière-pays thrace, des points d'appui pour des entreprises futures, diplomatiques et militaires. D'autre part, il fallait la disparition de Mithridate — retiré pour mourir dans ce Royaume du Bosphore dont la conquête, aux dernières années du IIe siècle, avait marqué l'essor de sa gloire de jeune conquérant[31] — pour que les Grecs éprouvassent le besoin d'un autre protecteur, capable de les défendre contre la vague montante des peuples de l'intérieur. Ces deux conditions étant remplies à la fin des campagnes de M. Terentius Varro Lucullus, il n'est pas étonnant que l'alliance qui retient notre attention ait été conclue dès la fin des hostilités. Et l'on ne peut considérer que comme un argument de circonstance l'objection selon laquelle un *foedus aequum* comme le nôtre n'eût pu être signé le lendemain d'une guerre qui avait vu s'affronter les armes de Rome et celles de ses chétifs adversaires. Précisément à ce sujet, je dois rappeler qu'ayant eu à m'occuper récemment des premiers rapports de Rome avec les villes de l'Euxin, j'ai fait observer que les termes dans lesquels sont racontés les exploits de M. Terentius Varro Lucullus dans le *Bréviaire* d'Eutrope, entre autres (... *Apolloniam euertit, Callatim, Parthenopolim, Tomos, Histrum, Burziaonem cepit*),[32] permettent de supposer qu'Apollonie ayant opposé au proconsul une résistance acharnée (grâce, sans doute, à la garnison royale dont la présence dans cette ville nous a été révélée par un décret fragmentaire publié en 1937 par Danov),[33] elle en a subi les conséquences,[34] tandis que les autres villes situées plus au nord, jusqu'à la lointaine Istros, ont pu, instruites par l'événement, rénoncer à se défendre, ouvrant leurs portes au vainqueur et s'assurant ainsi sa bienveillance.[35] Callatis étant du nombre et – tout au moins à cette date – la cité du Pont gauche la plus puissante,[36] on comprend très bien qu'elle ait été sinon la seule, au moins l'une des premières à saisir la main que Rome lui tendait en devenant presque sans délai son alliée.

A ce point de mon exposé, il ne sera pas inutile de m'attarder un instant sur une clause du *foedus* restituée et interprétée différemment par Lambrino (suivi par Marin) et par Passerini. Dans sa communication à l'Académie des Inscriptions, le premier avait cru reconnaître dans certaines lettres conservées à la ligne 4 et qu'il lisait [*p*]*equ*[*n*]*ia adiouua*[*n*]*to*, l'allusion à une stipulation aux termes de laquelle les Callatiens auraient été tenus d'aider Rome financièrement, ou tout au moins de lui verser certains subsides, peut-être à titre de réparations. C'était, évidemment, aller vite en besogne et, encore que les approbations sur ce point ne lui aient guère manquées,[37] faire fi de la règle méthodologique qui veut que dans l'interprétation d'un texte fragmentaire il convient d'expliquer le particulier par le général et, en l'occurrence, le sens d'une clause isolée par le caractère d'ensemble du traité étudié. C'est ce qu'a fait pour la première fois Passerini, dans le mémoire déjà cité, et c'est ce qui confère à son travail une valeur exemplaire, quelles que soient par ailleurs les réserves qu'appelle sa tentative de restitution.

Or, en retraçant, après Täubler, le schéma des traités conclus par Rome aux IIe et Ier siècles avec des villes de l'Orient grec, Passerini a bien fait resortir le fait qu'à cet endroit du texte on s'attend à lire ce qu'il appelle "la clause de neutralité," qui prescrivait aux parties contractantes de s'abstenir, en cas de guerre, d'aider l'une les ennemis de l'autre de quelque manière que ce soit, et plus particulièrement en leur fournissant des armes et des subsides en argent. Dans le texte passablement bien conservé du *foedus* avec Astypalée, cette clause a la teneur suivante: ὁ δῆμος ὁ Ῥωμαίων τοὺς πολεμίους καὶ ὑπεναντίους . . . τοῦ δήμου τῶν Ἀστυπαλαιέων διὰ τῆς ἰδίας χώρας καὶ ἧς ἂν [κρατῇ ὁ δῆμος ὁ Ῥωμαίων μὴ διέτω] δημοσ⟨ίᾳαι βουλῇ δόλῳ [πονηρῷ, ὥστε τῷ δήμῳ τῷ] Ἀστυπαλαιέων καὶ τοῖς ὑπ' αὐτοὺς τασσομένοις πόλεμον ἐπιφέρωσιν· μήτε [τοῖς πολεμίοις μήτε] ὅπλ⟨οις⟩ μήτε χρήμασι μήτε ναυσὶ βοηθεί⟨τω⟩ δόλῳ πονηρῷ³⁸ ce qui devient, dans le fragment restitué par Passerini: [*Poplus Romanus hostes et inimicos popli Callatini per suos agros et quibus imperat poplus Romanus ne sinere transire debeto dolo m]alo quo po[plo Callatino queiue sub imperio eorum erun]t bellum face[re possint neue hostes neue armis neque p]equnia adioua[n]to publica uoluntate dolo malo.*³⁹

Dans cette version, il est clair que les mots *pequnia adiouanto* prennent une toute autre signification que dans l'interprétation Lambrino-Marin-Carcopino et que, pour ce qui est du caractère du traité plus particulièrement, on ne saurait en aucun cas y voir un *foedus iniquum*, mais bien un *foedus aequum*, garantissant aux deux signataires les mêmes droits théoriques. S'il en était encore besoin, ce comportement à l'égard des ennemis de la veille, en qui il leur était permis de reconnaître des victimes aussi bien que des alliés de Mithridate, témoigne de la part des Romains d'un fin sens politique, grâce auquel à un moment où les opérations militaires se poursuivaient sur le front asiatique et après avoir démantelé à peu de frais les bases européennes de Mithridate —, ils réussissaient à se ménager pour l'avenir les points d'appui d'une politique balkanique qui, aux yeux du Sénat, n'était qu'à ses débuts.

J'en viens maintenant à la dernière tentative d'attribuer au *foedus* callatien une date différente de celle proposée par Lambrino, j'entends celle d'Alexandre Suceveanu, qui, dans une note publiée par la revue *Pontice*, organe du Musée archéologique de Constantza,[40] se flatte d'avoir supprimé ce qu'il appelle "une fausse certitude," en repoussant l'explication fournie par Gaetano De Sanctis de la clause qui, aux lignes 14-15 du texte conservé, prescrit l'exposition du traité *loc*[*o*] *optumo in faano Concor*[*diae*]. A ce propos, j'ai déjà eu l'occasion de rappeler que pour l'auteur de la *Storia dei Romani* le choix à première vue insolite du temple de la Concorde pour y placer un exemplaire de notre *foedus* serait dû à la circonstance qu'à partir de l'an 83 (date de l'incendie du temple de Jupiter Capitolin) et jusqu'en 69, au plus tôt, les documents ordinairement exposés dans ce sanctuaire l'auraient été dans celui de la Concorde,[41] bien connu par de nombreux témoignages littéraires et épigraphiques. Cette explication, qui présente l'intérêt de permettre une datation assez précise du *foedus* et qui, de ce fait, constitue une forte présomption en faveur de l'hypothèse Lambrino, est rejetée catégoriquement par Suceveanu pour des raisons dont il ne sera pas inutile d'examiner la validité.

Il s'agit d'abord de ce qu'à en croire notre auteur, en parlant d'un sanctuaire aussi connu que celui de la Concorde, les rédacteurs du traité n'auraient pu user le terme *fanum*, exclusivement employé pour désigner des édifices religieux d'une moindre importance, sis en général en dehors de l'Urbs.[42] Il s'agit, en outre, du fait qu'un ἱερὸν τῆς Ὁμόνοιας étant attesté a Callatis dès le IIᵉ siècle av.notre ère,[43] la tentation est forte de penser que c'est de ce *fanum* local qu'il est question dans notre fragment, ce qui, bien entendu, écarterait le repère chronologique invoqué par De Sanctis, permettant d'attribuer au *foedus* callatien soit la date défendue par Marin, soit une date plus récente, au Iᵉʳ siècle, mais qui ne serait pas la date proposée par Lambrino.[44]

Maintenant, pour ce qui est de l'emploi de *fanum*, il me paraît excessif de prétendre que le terme n'a jamais été employé qu'en dehors de Rome et uniquement pour indiquer des édifices religieux voués à des divinités étrangères. La différence — si différence il y a — entre *fanum* et *templum* me paraît résider ailleurs, à savoir dans le fait qu'au début *fanum* désignait un *lieu consacré* et que ce n'est que plus tard qu'il acquiert l'acception de *templum, delubrum, aedes*, au point que dans l'usage courant il est difficile de les distinguer. Tout au plus pourrait-on observer qu'en bon latin l'usage se crée d'employer *fanum* pour parler d'un sanctuaire (en entendant par ce terme l'édifice sacré et l'enclos où il est errigé), tandis que *templum* désigne plus spécialement la bâtisse destinée à la divinité, sa maison.[45] Encore faut-il ajouter que même cette nuance n'est pas toujours facile à saisir, comme on peut s'en rendre compte par ce texte de Tacite où, parlant des dommages causés à l'Urbs par l'incendie néronien, l'historien commence par déclarer:

'Domuum et insularum et templorum, quae amissa sunt, numerum inire haud promptum fuerit,' après quoi il passe à des indications plus précises, en s'ingéniant à varier autant que possible ses expressions: '... magna ara *fanumque*, quae praesenti Herculi Arcas Euander sacrauerat, *aedesque* Statoris Iouis ... et *delubrum* Vestae ... exusta.'[46]

Soit dit en passant, il est ici question de Rome et d'un sanctuaire aussi fameux que celui d'Hercule au *forum boarium*, ce qui n'empêche nullement notre auteur de l'appeler *fanum*, tout comme, dans un autre contexte, il l'aurait sans doute appelé *templum*. Il ne manque d'ailleurs pas d'exemples où — dans la même phrase et en parlant du même édifice sacré — *fanum* apparaît comme synonyme de *templum* et d'*aedes*, telle la *lex uicana Furfensis*,[47] où, après avoir été question d'abord de l'*aedes Iouis Liberi*, ce même sanctuaire est à plusieurs reprises appelé *templum* et, dans les tout dernières lignes du texte, alternativement *fanum* et *templum*: "*Sei quei ad huc templum rem deiuinam fecerit Ioui Libero aut Iouis Genio, pelleis, coria fanei sunto.*"

Reste la difficulté de savoir si, dans le texte qui retient notre attention, il est fait allusion au temple de Rome ou à celui de Callatis. A mon avis cette question n'aurait même pas dû se poser, vu que, suivant une règle qui ne connaît point d'exception un *foedus* était gravé au moins en deux exemplaires, dont l'un en latin, fait pour être exposé à Rome (le plus souvent sur le Capitole), l'autre en grec, destiné à trouver sa place dans un endroit quelconque de la ville avec laquelle l'accord était conclu. Ainsi, dans le *foedus* avec Astypalée, datant de 105 av. notre ère, on lit aux lignes 48-50: [ἀναθέντων δὲ] ἀνάθημα ἔμ μὲν Ῥωμαίων ἐν τῷ καπετολίῳ ναῷ τῶ Διὸς, ἐν δὲ Ἀστυπαλαιέων ἐν τῷ ἱερῷ τῆς Ἀθηνᾶς καὶ τοῦ Ἀσκλυπίου καὶ πρὸς τῷ βωμῷ[48]

Telle étant la règle, il est, je pense, permis d'inférer que dans le cas du *foedus* avec Callatis également l'exemplaire latin du document était destiné à être exposé à Rome — que ce soit dans le temple de Jupiter Capitolin ou dans celui de la Concorde — et que ce n'est qu'accessoirement qu'un second exemplaire de la même version a dû être envoyé à Callatis — on ne sait si pour y être exposé conjointement avec le texte grec ou pour toute autre raison.[49] Ajoutons que, dans le fragment qui retient notre attention, la clause concernant la transcription et le placement d'un exemplaire du traité dans le temple de la Concorde suit de près la clause qui accordait aux deux parties la latitude d'ajouter ou de supprimer, de commun accord, une stipulation quelconque du texte initial. Cette disposition, qu'on lit clairement dans le *foedus* Rome-Astypalée (ἐαν δέ τι[ς] πρὸς ταύτας τὰς συνθήκας κοινῇ βουλῇ προσθεῖναι ἢ ἀφελεῖν βούλ⟨ω⟩νται δημοσί⟨ί⟩ᾳ βουλῇ [ὃς?] ἂν θελήσῃ ἐξέστω ...) et qui se retrouve à peu de différences près dans les traités avec Cybira[50] et Methymna,[51] a été restituée de la manière la plus vraisemblable par Passerini à partir des quelques lettres conservées sur la pierre d'où il ressort que la clause immédiatement suivante indiquait l'endroit de Rome où une copie de l'accord devait être placée, ce qui exclut la possibilité qu'aux lignes 14-15 il ait pu être question de l'"affichage" du document à Callatis. Marin s'en est bien aperçu, qui proposait de lire à cet endroit: [*in tabola*]*m aenam utei scriberetur hoc* [*Romae in*] *loco optumo in faano Concord*[*iae*], mais pas Suceveanu, qui n'hésite nullement à restituer . . . *scriberetur ho*[*c Callati loc*]*o optumo in faano Concor*[*diae.* .]. Soit dit en passant, cette phrase n'est même pas correcte au point de vue de la langue, puisqu'on ne saurait dire en latin: . . . *scriberetur loco optumo* (ce qui n'a guère de sens), mais, comme l'a parfaitement vu Passerini: . . . *scriberetur ac* [*figeretur* . . . *loc*]*o optumo in faano Concor*[*diae*][52] (de même qu'en grec, dans les mêmes circonstances, on ne manque jamais de prescrire: ἀναγράψαι καὶ στῆσαι, ou: ἀναγράψαι καὶ ἀναθεῖναι, ou encore: τὰ ἀντίγραφα . . . ἀναγραφέν[τα] . . . ἀνατεθήτῳ ἐν τοῖς ἐπιφανεστάτοις Τό[ποις].

Ces quelques considérations en marge des discussions suscitées par l'interprétation du *foedus* Rome-Callatis, et plus particulièrement par la chronologie de cet important document, peuvent s'arrêter ici. Il en est résulté, si je ne m'abuse, au moins une raison supplémentaire d'accorder foi à ses premiers exégètes, Lambrino et Passerini, en dépit des tentatives récentes de mettre en doute leurs conclusions. Car, en histoire, autant et plus qu'en d'autres domaines du savoir, il convient, je crois, de ne pas oublier l'avertissement qu'un des fondateurs de l'épigraphie grecque s'est plu à formuler, il y a plus d'un siècle, et que d'autres après lui ont jugé opportun de nous rappeler à l'occasion: "il ne s'agit pas de remuer la science, il faut la faire avancer."[53]

Université de Bucarest   *D. M. Pippidi*

NOTES

1. Cf. en dernier lieu mon livre *I Greci nel Basso Danubio*, Milano, 1971, pp. 143-44, et pp. 275-76 (avec toute la bibliographie plus ancienne du sujet).

2. Sur ce problème, outre l'ouvrage cité à la note 1, voir aussi D. M. Pippidi, "Les premiers rapports de Rome avec les villes de l'Euxin," *Riv. storica dell'antichità* 2, 1972, pp. 17-37.

3. *Dacia* 3/4, 1927-32, p. 458.

4. *CRAI*, 1933, pp. 278-88.

5. *Infra*.

6. Cf. *La République romaine de 133 à 44 av. J. C.* ("Histoire Générale dirigée par Gustave Glotz"), Paris, 1935, p. 542 et n. 1.

7. Dion. Cass. 38.10.

8. Röm. Geschichte V, 11 n. 1.

9. IV 2,1, 1953, p. 299, n. 785.

10. "Il testo del 'foedus' di Roma con Callatis," *Athenaeum* n.s.13, 1935, pp. 57-72.

11. *Inscr. Lat. lib. Rei publicae*, II, 1963, p. 37, commentaire au no. 516; id., *Scritti vari di antichità*, Roma, 1962, I, p. 442 et n. 115.

12. *CIL* I^2 2676. Je ne cite que pour la mémoire l'opinion des auteurs du recueil *Ancient Roman Statutes*, Austin, Tex., 1961, p. 58, qui, eux-aussi, assignent comme date à notre document les dernières années du IIe siècle.

13. D. Marin, "Il foedus romano con Callatis," *Epigraphica* 10, 1948, pp. 103-30.

14. Passerini, (N.10): "Con tale ampiezza di lacune naturalmente non si può pensare a una ricostruzione della lettera, ma solo a una del senso e pur così molto rimarrà ipotetico."

15. *RivFC* 63, 1935, p. 424.

16. Eug. Täubler, *Imperium Romanum*, 1913, I, pp. 44 sqq: avant lui, déjà P. Viereck, *Sermo Graecus quo Senatus Populusque Romanus magistratusque usque ad aetatem Ti. Caesaris in scriptis publicis usi sunt examinatur*, Göttingen, 1888, p. 84.

17. Marin (n. 13), p. 127.

18. Joyce S. and Arthur E. Gordon, *Contributions to the Palaeography of Latin Inscriptions* (Berkeley-Los Angeles, 1957), pp. 208 suiv. et plus particulièrement p. 217; encore plus énergiquement, Degrassi, *Scritti vari di antichità*, I, 657: "Conviene reagire contro la presunzione di datare con sicurezza epigrafi dalla forma delle lettere al decennio o anche al cinquantennio ... Ben di rado il Mommsen nei volumi del *Corpus* da lui pubblicati si arrischia a proporre datazioni sia pure molto larghe. Troppi sono gli elementi di incertezza che possono fuorviare il giudizio. . ." C'est toujours Degrassi qui, dans la même leçon inaugurale d'ou je viens de reproduire les lignes qui précèdent, cite ce jugement de Lothar Wickert selon lequel ... "l'incompetenza

dell'editore di un'epigrafe si palesa meglio di tutto dalla sicurezza con la quale sa datarla dai caratteri paleografici."

19. *CIL* I^2 581 = *Inscr. Lat. lib. Rei publicae*, 511.

20. Marin (n. 13), pp. 116-18.

21. *CIL* I^2 590 = *ILS* 6086.

22. *CIL* I^2 587.

23. *CIL* I^2 589.

24. Cela est si vrai, qu'on peut relever quelques-unes des particularités dont il vient d'être question jusque dans la *lex Iulia municipalis* (*CIL* I^2 593 = *ILS* 6085), qui est de 45 av. notre ère.

25. *Supra*.

26. Marin (n. 13). p. 121.

27. Tite Live 27.32.10 − 33.1 et, en outre, 28.8.14; 31.28.1-3; 31.38.7-8; 31.40.7-8. Cf. M. Holleaux, *Rome, la Grèce et les monarchies hellénistiques au IIIe siècle av. J.-C.*, Paris, 1921, pp. 299-300 et, en général, Fanula Papazoglu, *Srednjobalkanska plemena u predrimsko doba*, Sarajevo, 1969, pp. 111 et suiv.

28. Sur ces échanges et, en général, sur le développement économique des colonies grecques du littoral roumain de la mer Noire, depuis l'époque archaïque jusqu'à la conquête romaine, voir mon livre déjà cité, *I Greci nel Basso Danubio*, châpitres II-IV.

29. Outre l'ouvrage cité dans la note précédente, pp. 114-16 et pp. 263-64, voir mes *Epigraphische Beiträge zur Geschichte Histrias in hellenistischer u. römischer Zeit*, Berlin, 1962, pp. 11-34, pp. 75-89, et aussi *Contributii la istoria veche a României*^{2}, 1967, pp. 186-221.

30. Cf., à ce sujet, le décret histrien en l'honneur d'un marchand carthaginois récompensé pour avoir livré à la ville un chargement de blé dans des conditions avantageuses (Lambrino, *Dacia* 3/4, 1927-32, pp. 400 suiv.). Ce texte, qui est de la première moitié du IIe siècle, ne fait d'ailleurs que confirmer sur un point précis les informations plus générales de Polybe 4.38.5: σίτῳ δ' ἀμείβονται (scil. οἱ κατὰ τὸν Ἴστρον τόποι), ποτὲ μὲν εὐκαίρως διδόντες, ποτὲ δὲ λαμβάνοντες ... Voir également *Contributii la istoria veche a României*^{2}, 49 et suiv.

31. Sur les premières années de règne de Mithridate, ainsi que sur les campagnes de Diophante dans la Péninsule Taurique, on consultera toujours la monographie de Théodore Reinach, *Mithridate Eupator, roi de Pont*, Paris, 1890, pp. 66 et suiv. (à compléter par l'étude pénétrante de S. A. Žebelev, *REG* 49, 1936, pp. 17-37.

32. Eutr. 6.10; cf. Ruf. Festus 9; Amm. Marcell. 27.4.11; Oros. 6.3-4; Eusèbe-Jérôme, *Chron.* 152 Helm.

33. *JOAI Beibl.* 30, 1937, pp. 87-94.

34. L'hypothèse avancée dans le texte, selon laquelle Apollonie aurait été en cette occasion plus sévèrement traitée que les autres cités grecques du Pont Gauche est confirmée par Strabon 7.6.1 qui nous informe que Varro Lucullus a enlevé du principal sanctuaire de la ville une statue colossale d'Apollon sculptée par Calamis, que Pline l'Ancien pouvait encore admirer sur le Capitole, où l'avait fait transporter le vainqueur (34.39).

35. J'ai développé ce point de vue dans une étude citée *supra*, n. 2, parue dans la *Riv. storica dell'Antichità* 2, 1972, pp. 17-37.

36. Pour la situation de Callatis à l'époque hellénistique on consultera mes *Epigraphische Beiträge zur Geschichte Histrias* ..., 11-34; sur les relations entretenues par cette ville avec d'autres cités grecques du Pont et de l'Egée pendant la même période, *Dacia* n.s. 6, 1962, pp. 469-74.

37. Carcopino, *La République romaine* ..., p. 542 et n. 9. Sur ce point l'interprétation de Marin diffère à la fois de celle de Passerini et de celle de Carcopino-Lambrino; à l'en croire, le *foedus* aurait prescrit aux Romains aussi bien qu'aux Callatiens l'obligation de s'entraider financièrement en cas de guerre avec une tièrce puissance (*art. cit.*, pp. 110-12).

38. *IG* XII 3,173 = R. K. Sherk, *Roman Documents from the Greek East. Senatus Consulta and Epistulae to the Age of Augustus*, Baltimore, 1969, no. 16, lignes 35-40.

39. Marin (n. 13), pp. 61-62.

40. II, 1969, pp. 269-74.

41. Toujours dans cet ordre d'idées, il ne sera pas sans intérêt d'ajouter que, selon Degrassi, dans une étude déjà citée, l'érection sur le Capitole d'un monument spécial destiné à recevoir les dédicaces de plusieurs peuples et rois asiatiques au peuple romain et à Jupiter Optimus Maximus, au cours des années ayant suivi la paix de Dardanus, s'expliquerait également par l'impossibilité d'utiliser à cette fin le temple incendié en 83 ("Le dediche di popoli e re asiatici al popolo romano e a Giove Capitolino," *Scritti vari di antichità*, I, pp. 415-44, et plus spécialement pp. 438-42).

42. Suceveanu reprend ici, en l'exagérant, une affirmation de Samter (*RE* 6, 1996), qui en réalité n'en a jamais dit autant: "*Vorwiegend* werden aber *aedes* ausserrömischer Gottheiten als *fana* bezeichnet" (se contente-t-il d'écrire, en citant plusieurs textes littéraires ou des temples de Rome sont dits sans distinction *fana*).

43. Th. Sauciuc-Săveanu, *Dacia* n.s. 2, 1958, pp. 207 et suiv.

44. Marin (n. 13), p. 273. Notons qu'avant Suceveanu

Sauciuc-Săveanuu avait déjà envisagé la possibilité que dans le texte qui retient notre attention le *fanum Concordiae* soit précisément le ἱερὸν τῆς Ὁμόνοιας (*Dacia* n.s. 2, 1958, p. 220).

45. J'y verrais volontiers la différence qu'il y a en grec entre ἱερόν – ναός et, précisément, dans un document bilingue de Kyme, lettre du proconsul Vinicius aux habitants de cette ville (H. W. Pleket, *The Greek Inscriptions in the Rijksmuseum van Oudheden at Leyden*, 1958, no. 57 = Sherk, *Roman Documents from he Greek East*, no. 61), le même sanctuaire est désigné dans le texte latin par *fanum* et dans la traduction grecque par ἱερόν.

46. *Ann.* 15.41.

47. *CIL* I² 756 = *Inscr. Lat. lib. Rei publicae* 508.

48. Lignes 16-19.

49. Dois-je faire observer que Suceveanu se trompe, à n'en pas douter, lorsqu'il suppose sans raison apparente que, tout au moins au début, il aurait été de règle à Rome de rédiger *en grec seulement* les traités conclus avec des cités de l'Orient?

50. *OGIS* 762.

51. *IG* XII 2, 510 = *SIG*³ 693.

52. Marin, n. 13, p. 70.

53. L. Robert, *Opera minora selecta*, I (Amsterdam, 1969), p. 600.

Who Designed the Anglican Church of St. Paul in Athens?[1]

The whole subject of English places of worship abroad is one that it is to be hoped ... will at long last find its qualified historian. No more striking testimony to the self-confidence and unshakable convictions of the Victorian Age exists than that provided throughout the Continent of Europe by these innumerable examples of Anglo-Saxon mediaevalism standing where they ought not: nothing demonstrates more forcibly the woolliness and love of compromise of a later generation than those pathetic monuments of nervous instability which, in a desperate effort to achieve "good taste," vainly seek to establish an unworthy and unattainable harmony with their exotic surroundings. . . .

St. Andrew's in Athens makes no greater concession to local taste than that provided by a cruciform plan, a pleasing gesture acknowledging the mutual recognition of each other's orders existing between the Anglican and Orthodox churches; in all other respects it is demonstratively British. It is no fault of the designer that the Aberdeen granite of which it is built, imported from Scotland at immense expense, should have weathered to a texture to-day almost indistinguishable from the local limestone. Built from funds collected by C. H. Bracebridge, Esq., of Atherstone, Warwickshire, it was consecrated by the Bishop of Gibraltar in 1843. If Murray's Handbook of 1897 . . . is correct and the building has undergone no radical restoration since, it is a very remarkable achievement of that date. The interior, in an austere version of Trans with plain continuous mouldings around the Chancel Arch, is entirely devoid of frills and seems to foreshadow with its marked emphasis on height the work of Comper. The name of the architect I have, unfortunately, been unable to discover.

Osbert Lancaster[2]

*   *   *

The story of the "English Church at Athens" began with the British residents in 1836.[3]

At a time when the duty of providing suitable Edifices for the Public Worship of Almighty God is so deeply felt, and so honourably fulfilled, by the Inhabitants of Great Britain in their Native Land, it will not appear surprising, that their Fellow-citizens, living either permanently or temporarily in Foreign Countries, should desire to have this important want supplied in their respective residences; in order that they may not only enjoy, as individuals, the advantages derived from Divine Worship, but also escape the danger of becoming indifferent to it: while, at the same time, many prejudices entertained in Foreign Countries respecting our Religion might by this means be effectually removed, and the Doctrines and Rites of the Church of England be presented to public view, in their true character.

Among others, the British Residents at Athens here, for sometime past, felt, that, both for themselves and the numerous Travellers visiting that celebrated spot, once hallowed by the footsteps of an Apostle, it is very desirable that a Church should be erected in the rising Capital of the Greek Kingdom.

Subscriptions were solicited both at Athens and in England. Among the first to contribute were Colonel W. M. Leake, £5 on Feb. 3, 1836, the Marquess of Bristol, £50 on March 28, and the Society for Promoting Christian Knowledge, £100 on April 18. The Society for Propagating the Gospel matched this last sum a year later on May 24, 1837, Victoria's last birthday as Princess. So immediate and generous was the response that on Tuesday, April 6, 1837, Henry Daniel Leeves, priest, bought from

Chrestos Joannousis by deed No. 793 a plot of land consisting of 3551.07 pikes, situated at the place in this town called Nicodemos and bounded on the west by the property of

Spyridon Mouritzis, on the north by property of Mr. John Papparigopoulos, on the east by the old wall of the town, on the south by the street and also on the west by (property of) Anastasios Roumbesis.

For this site Leeves paid 9942 drachmas, a little over £350.

Events continued to move rapidly, and on August 29, to a meeting of twelve subscribers assembled at the residence of the British Minister, Sir Edmund Lyons, and chaired by him, Leeves was able to announce not only the purchase of the ground with part of the subscriptions, which at the time of the meeting totalled £912=11=6, but also the permission of the Greek Government for the erection of a church "for the administration of Divine Service according to the rites of the United Church of Great Britain and Ireland," and the inclusion of the English Church in the official "Plan for the Quarter of the City adjoining the New Palace" approved by H.M. The King of Greece. The subscribers found these developments entirely satisfactory, and, so that their wishes might be carried out "in a manner honourable to the character of the British Nation" and "within the shortest period possible," they both requested the British Minister to petition Her Majesty's Government for "benevolent aid," and established a Commission of Management, the members being Lyons, Leeves, and George Finlay, the noted Philhellene and historian.

A month after the meeting of the subscribers Lyons wrote to Her Majesty's Foreign Secretary, Lord Palmerston, concerning the matter of government support for the proposed church and its chaplain.

> I have the honour to inclose to your Lordship a Petition from the British Residents in Greece and Athens, praying Her Majs. Govt to aid us in our undertaking of building a Protestant Church at Athens.
>
> In addition to the subscriptions set forth in the Petition and in the accompanying printed list we have information of further sums having been submitted in London which raises the amount to rather more than £1000, and if Her Majs. Govt should be pleased to extend to us the benefit of the Act of the 6th of

George the 4th we should be enabled to complete our undertaking in a proper manner.

The subscribers will cheerfully acquiesce in any arrangements Her Majs. Govt may adopt respecting the appt. of a Chaplain but their own choice would I believe fall upon the Revd. H. D. Leeves who resides in this Capital and who has been for many years honourably occupied in the Levant as a pious, benevolent, zealous and orthodox Clergyman of the Church of England.

The Act referred to by Lyons allowed Consuls or Consuls-General to make payments to chaplains and "for the building of churches under certain circumstances."

Be it therefore enacted, That at any Foreign Port or Place in which a Chaplain is now or shall at any future Time be resident and regularly employed in the Celebration of Divine Service according to the Rites and Ceremonies of the United Church of *England* and *Ireland*, or of the Church of *Scotland*, and maintained by any voluntary Subscription or Rates levied among or upon His Majesty's Subjects resorting to or residing at such Foreign Port or Place, or by any Rate or Duty levied under the Authority of the Acts herein after repealed, it shall and may be lawful for any Consul General, or Consul, in obedience to any Order for that Purpose issued by His Majesty through One of His Principal Secretaries of State, to advance and pay from Time to Time, for and towards the Maintenance and Support of any such Chaplain . . . any Sum or Sums of Money not exceeding in any One Year the Amount of the Sum or Sums of Money which during that Year may have been raised at such Port or Place . . .

Section XI of the same act provided for the payment of "One Half Part of the Expenses of Erecting" a church "at any Foreign Port or Place wherein any Consul-General or Consul appointed by His Majesty shall be resident."

On December 8, 1837, Palmerston gave his reply to the petition addressed to him by Lyons on behalf of the subscribers to the English Church at Athens.

I have had under my consideration your despatch No. 104 of the 27th Septr. last, enclosing a petition from the British Residents in Athens, soliciting the assistance of Her Majesty's Government towards building a British Protestant Church in that

City; and I regret to acquaint you that as there is no British Consul stationed at Athens, Her Majesty's Government are not empowered to afford the assistance required consistently with the Provisions of the Act 6 Geo: IV.cap. 87.

Highly approving however of the exertions which have been made by the British Residents to raise funds for this laudable purpose, I shall have great satisfaction, upon receiving from you the further necessary explanations, in referring the matter to the consideration of the Lords Commissioners of Her Majesty's Treasury, and in recommending that some allowance may be granted by Her Majesty's Government towards the Building of a Chapel.

You will therefore transmit to me, to be laid before their Lordships, Plans and Estimates for the proposed Building, together with a statement of the measures proposed by the Residents for providing funds for the future maintenance of the church establishment.

It is indispensable that the Estimates be framed in the most economical scale, and that they be accompanied by a guarantee from Two or more Residents that any expenditure beyond the sum which may be deemed by Her Majesty's Government to be adequate for this purpose, shall be paid by the Residents without any further call upon the Treasury.

This reply arrived in Athens on January 6, 1838, and two days later the Committee of Management was convened. After they had considered the Foreign Secretary's despatch — not the clear subsidy asked for, but on the other hand the letter did stress the willingness of Her Majesty's Government to cooperate — Leeves informed his colleagues that he had received "several plans" for the church. Although there are no records to prove it, it is obvious that in the autumn of 1837 Leeves must have advised the local architects that an Anglican church would soon be erected and that he and the Committee would welcome their submissions. By the beginning of 1838 the number of such proposals was four, two of which Leeves thought of sufficient interest to be considered by the Committee. Ludwig Lange, Professor of Drawing in the Academy of Athens, was the author of one of these plans, Christian Hansen, one of the foreign artists in the service of the Greek Government, of the other. The name of those architects whose plans the Committee did not pursue in any way are unknown, although a strong tradition maintains that Stamatios Kleanthes entered the "competition" for the design of the Anglican church.[4] If Kleanthes did, his entry was unsuccessful, for the Committee ended their meeting of January 8 by deciding to "ascertain the sum necessary to carry" the plans of Lange and Hansen "into execution."

On February 16, the Committee of Management met at the British Residency to consider in detail the designs prepared by Lange and Hansen. On this occasion the three members invited Henry Wentworth Acland to join them. Acland, twenty-seven years old, and John Ruskin's closest friend, was travelling in the Middle East for his health. He later returned to England, studied medicine, and became Regius Professor of Medicine at Oxford. But in 1838 it was his artistic talents that appealed to the Committee. Together, the Committee and Acland rejected the two schemes before them as "too expensive and too large for the Circumstances of the British Church at Athens." Yet Lange's ideas must have seemed attractive to the Committee, for, instead of immediately seeking new plans, it asked Leeves, Finlay, and Acland "to speak personally with Mr. Lange and explain to him the size, nature and expense of the church for which a plan was required and request him to make new plans on this reduced scale of size and expense."

Four days later, the Committee, still augmented by Acland, met again. Lange had apparently in the meantime prepared a new plan with a schedule of costs. However, it fared no better than his original proposal, and was rejected. Indeed, the members were of the opinion that to build Lange's church would take four times the funds already subscribed. Although the Committee may have thought that this second rejection ended its association with Lange, the Professor of Drawing felt differently, and in April submitted a bill for the time he had spent working on the plan and costs at the Committee's request. The amount claimed was twenty louis d'or, equivalent to about 450 drachmas. The Committee responded late in May with 250 drachmas, somewhat reluctantly, for Leeves in a letter to Lange pointed out that the latter's design was impracticable insofar as it called for monies greatly in excess of the sum "qu'on vous avoit marqué pour vôtre règle."

The rejection of Lange's modified proposals was only the first item decided by the Committee of Management at its meeting of February 20, 1838. Acland now presented a sketch and ground plan of an "English Chapel on the plan of the plainest cottage gothic," large enough to contain one hundred persons.[5] Although the Committee was at once in general favour of Acland's idea, at the suggestion of Lyons it was decided to put off a final decision until Leeves and Finlay "should inform themselves accurately on the subject of the expense of carrying out the plans presented to the Committee into execution rejecting all superfluous ornament."

Five weeks later, on March 29, the Committee of Management considered the estimates secured by Leeves and Finlay. Acland's chapel was declared clearly the most economical to build, and, because it was "appropriate for the circumstances and funds of the future congregation," the Committee

> resolved to lay the foundations of the English Church on Easter Monday according to the plan of Mr Ackland . . . . reserving the power of completing the building in such a style with regard to the furnishing as the grant from Her Majesty's Government may authorize.

Acland's ground plan exists in a copy made by Finlay (Pl. 1, p. 208, redrawn from the original). We can therefore gain some idea of the structure that the Committee of Management had resolved to build. The main element was a single nave, 21 ft. 6 in. by 44 ft. 3 in., with added chancel, 16 ft. by 8 ft. 6 in., the two separated by steps. On either side of the nave were two symmetrically placed projections, both 9 ft. 2 in. by 8 ft., the one to the north a baptistry, the one to the south a porch with four steps between buttresses. All corners,

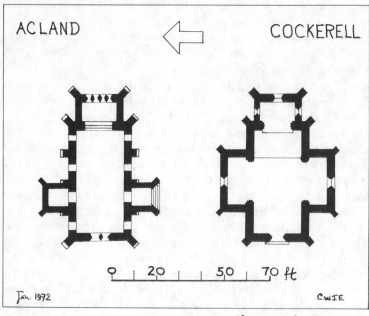

ACLAND   COCKERELL

0   20   50   70 ft

Jan. 1972   C.W.J.E.

Plate 1. Acland's ground plan, redrawn from the original.

Plate 2. The Anglican Church of St. Paul in Athens.

except those where the baptistry and porch joined the nave, had angled buttresses. In addition to these, two other buttresses were set against the nave between the projections and the eastern end of the nave. Most of the walls were 3 ft. 6 in. wide, but the lateral walls of the chancel were a few inches wider, while those of the porch and baptistry were appreciably thinner, 2 ft. 4 in. Lighting was provided by a 4-light window at the chancel end, a 2-light window at the back of the nave, and three single light windows on either side of the nave. Such was the plan of the church designed by Henry Acland.

On Easter Monday, April 16, the foundation stone of the English Church was laid "with the due solemnities, in the presence of all the subjects of Her Britannic Majesty residing in that city, of many other individuals of different nations, and of a considerable number of the Greek inhabitants." Leeves' description of the happy event continues.

> The Ceremony was performed by Her Britannic Majesty's Minister Plenipotentiary at the Court of Greece Sir Edmund Lyons assisted by John Green Esq British Consul at the Piraeus and George Finlay Esq one of the committee for the execution of the building; coins of the Kingdom of Great Britain and of Greece and an appropriate medal having on the one side the head of Our Blessed Saviour and on the reverse his distinctive injunctive to his disciples "love one another" being deposited under the stone. The religious services were conducted by the Revd H. D. Leeves Minister of the Church of England, and one of the members of the Building Committee assisted by the Revd J. H. Hill minister of the Episcopal Church of the United States of America.
>
> It was gratifying to observe the impression made by this interesting and solemn ceremony upon all present and especially upon the Greek portion of the Assembly, who, on this occasion, the first of the kind which has occurred in this country, shewed not only the most tolerant but the most kind and friendly feelings towards the British Nation: and as the weather was beautiful, and the site selected for the edifice is eminently striking being within view of many of the celebrated monuments of Ancient Athens, the whole scene was one, which will long be remembered with pleasure by those who took part in it.

The building of a church from plans prepared by Acland in the "Most Ancient and Simple English Gothic" had begun, properly blessed. The following Monday, Leeves authorized Finlay to proceed with the foundation: "as we have no architect, we must depend on you for the accurate laying out of the foundation with its buttresses etc." It was for this that Finlay needed a copy of Acland's plan.

*   *   *

However auspicious the proceedings that initiated the English Church, the matter of funds was far from solved. To this end Leeves returned to England in the summer of 1838, and in the name of the Committee appealed "to the liberality of the British Public." A flyer was published, dated July, sketching the aims and activities of the Committee and listing the subscribers and the amounts each had donated. The Committee's closing plea is worth recalling.

> They hope, that among their Countrymen many will be found — and particularly among those connected with the Universities of our Land — not unwilling to make some return for the inestimable benefits which Great Britain, in common with the whole civilized world, owes to Athens, as the cradle of all that is elegant and intellectual, by contributing towards the erection of the first Protestant Church in that remarkable city, now emerging from its ruins, and recovering from the wounds inflicted upon it by Mussulman Barbarism.

The response to this approach and to Leeves' preaching was such that on his return to Athens in late autumn he was able to announce additional subscriptions amounting to above £400.

Leeves did not go to England empty handed: he took with him Acland's plan. This he showed early in the summer to the famous architect and archaeologist Charles Robert Cockerell, who immediately consented to have his name publicly linked with the subscribers' project. But the association of Cockerell with the building of the English Church did not stop there. Leeves clearly invited the Architect to the

Bank of England and Surveyor and Curator of St. Paul's Cathedral to look critically at the plans of the building for which the foundation had already been laid. And on August 25 Cockerell offered his suggestions to Leeves.

I have carefully considered the designs for the English chapel at Athens, offered by the ingenious Mr. Acland; and which I understand to have been approved and in part proceeded upon, by the local committee.

I beg leave to offer my entire concurrence in the selection of the *style*, as that which is most truly consonant with English feelings, especially in a foreign land; and as best contrasting with the inimitable style of the inimitable Athens; and as best evading the fruitless attempts at a copy of any description, in the neighbourhood of those splendid originals.

As respects the details of those designs I gladly avail myself of your permission to offer some remarks, (in my professional capacity), and to present to you a modification of those designs in three sheets; which I believe to be worthy of your attention. Also to offer some suggestions with regard to the execution of the work. My long acquaintance with the happy site of this chapel enables me to do so with the more confidence.

First, I consider (under correction and better advice) 60 sittings as hardly adequate to the probability of residents and commercial and naval visitors; and that there should be *provided* in the building the means of future increase of accommodation by galleries. The extension of the transept by removing eastward the east sides (see drawing: No. 1) and the increased elevation of the building would enable it to contain nearly 300 persons, should so large a congregation ever be assembled. Without the galleries 180 persons would be easily accommodated.

Secondly I consider the height insufficient, both for due ventilation in that hot climate, and for that effect externally, which the *English chapel* would be expected to produce in such a town or city. The number and size of the windows, so desirable in our cold climate, do not suit that in which the sun's rays should rather be excluded; I propose therefore six only. 3 large and 3 small. The lower part of those windows, as well as smaller windows below, should be made to open readily with small wooden shutters, to give a speedy and complete ventilation. The roof should have ventilation with open cinq foils (see elevations) and an intermediate surface or ceiling of wood planking laid on the beams and binders in the fashion of the East, – protecting the chapel from heat thro' the external roof. I think that the simple ceiling and roof of my design will be found much less expensive, and sufficient (the greater internal height considered) for all purposes. For however picturesque and characteristic the ceiling and roof of Mr. Acland's design, the objections are varied and great. The expense – its inapplicability in so small a space, this scheme being suited to the widest bearing attempted by our ancestors, as in Westminster and other Halls, and its acute angle externally – so well suited to a wet and snowy climate, but ill adapted to one in which those inconveniences are seldom or never felt, and in which a flat or obtuse angle of roof is ideal. And in this case where (as I trust) English slate will be used, which is laid at this angle, and requires no higher pitch. I suppose the vestry to be placed under the chancel so as to give all the internal space to the congregation, baptismal Font etc. The pulpit and reading desk and the communion rail to be elevated and arranged as in this plan, and as approved by the venerable Bishop Heber. The Porch an essential feature in this hot climate should be capacious, and so contrived as by the door and a window, to permit the late comers to participate in the ceremonies without disturbing the congregation, if the chapel be full. It may also contain the stairs to the whole of the galleries and to the future organ.

With respect to the materials and workmanship I presume that the buttresses, quoins, copings, jambs of windows and doors and label over them and the whole of the lower part of the porch, to be of Egina stone, ashlar. The rest of the building to be in Lycabettus limestone in irregular courses, – with respect to the window frames, it is obvious that it may be impossible to have them executed with the character and nicety suited to the English Eye, by foreign hands, therefore I have strongly to recommend that they be sent from this country in artificial stone ready to fix, from Mess. Greenwoods, who have the patterns and have offered me the subjoined estimate or tender.

I feel also persuaded that the paving would be sent more cheaply and much more advantageously from this country according to the subjoined tender.

The slating in Welsh rag could also be sent according the price I have inserted. The iron gates and glazings (which ought if possible to have some coloured glass) might also be sent from thence, and I feel confident that the committee would be better and more cheaply served especially if Government would afford the freight, than by your local markets or artificers. I can only say that I shall gladly offer my services if the committee should desire to employ them. And you will please to remember that I have tendered you the cross should its style and character be approved. As Surveyor and Curator of St. Paul's Cathedral, it has been my proud lot to reerect the Ball and Cross of that Metropolitan Fabrick — and I should for many reasons be happy [to] offer this humble symbol for the Athenian Chapel, if your committee will permit me.

I beg you will at the same time assure them of the pleasure this occupation has given me, in company with yourself — that I shall always be an affectionate Athenian. . . .

*　　*　　*

Armed with additional subscriptions and a new plan, Leeves arrived back in Athens in November. A meeting of the Committee of Management was held at once. Cockerell's designs — only Cockerell, with tact and modesty, referred to them as modifications — were enthusiastically received, and it was decided to proceed with their execution. To that end Christian Hansen, whose own plan for the church the Committee had rejected six months before, was appointed architect to superintend the project. His first task was to prepare an estimate of the cost of building Cockerell's church. Acland's "plainest Cottage Gothic" was never to rise above the foundation.

Hansen's first reaction to Cockerell's plans was very reminiscent of Cockerell's to Acland's. Far from preparing an estimate of costs, he sent the Committee a revised set of plans and a letter in which he set forth his modifications. On Boxing Day the Committee framed its reply, a restrained one seeing that Hansen had deliberately ignored his charge and thus delayed the submission to the Foreign Office for financial aid. Leeves acted as spokesman.

I have shewn the plans you had the goodness to send Sir

Edmund Lyons and Mr Finlay who feel much obliged by the trouble you have given yourself and admire the ingenuity you shew in many of the suggestions, but we agree in opinion that we are not justified in departing from the plan we have obtained from Mr Cockerell and that our object must be as we explained to you at first in my interview with you in company with Mr Finlay to obtain an estimate of what the expenses of the building would amount to on this plan.

We are anxious that you should understand that we are far from undervaluing the suggestions you have made or from supposing that in the course of execution local circumstances may not require some modifications in the plan sent us by Mr Cockerell but we feel that our object must now be to obtain an estimate which we may send to England and which will be entirely in conformity with the plan before us; and we should be much obliged to you if you would as early as possible execute the commission for us, for which purpose I send you the papers.

Early in 1839 Hansen presented his estimates. When these were added to the costs of land, the total sum required to build the church in accordance with Cockerell's plans reached £3013=10=0. On March 9, Finlay and Dennison G. Dixon, who was later to become Treasurer of the Church Building Fund, declared that any expenses beyond this amount would be the responsibility of the residents. John Green, Her Majesty's Consul at the Piraeus, was now in a position to act. And so, on March 13, in a despatch to Palmerston that included plans, estimates, amount of subscriptions, and the required guarantee, he renewed the petition for assistance in the building of a Protestant Church at Athens. Since subscriptions at this time totalled little more than £1600, clearly the Committee hoped to secure an allowance from the Government of very close to "One Half Part of the Expenses."

*   *   *

13 months later, April 13, 1840, the Committee gathered at the British Residency to hear the Consul read the reply that he had received from the Foreign Office, dated March 12.

Viscount Palmerston having referred to the consideration of the Lords Commissioners of Her Majesty's Treasury your Despatch No 6 of the 13th. of March 1839, in which you request pecuniary assistance from Her Majesty's Government, under the Act 6 Geo IV. c 87 towards building a British Protestant Chapel at Athens, I am directed by His Lordship to transmit to you the copy of a letter from the Treasury, stating that while their Lordships readily admit the expedience, of constructing a Church of dimensions suitable to a probably increasing congregation, they cannot authorize a larger grant than the sum of £800 towards that object; and as their Lordships have suggested that the British residents at Athens should either engage to complete the present proposed building by making up the deficiency themselves, or that they should send for approval, a Plan and Estimate on a reduced scale, I am to desire that you will ascertain what course the Residents propose to pursue, and that you will report thereupon to Lord Palmerston.

The enclosed letter of Mr C. E. Trevelyan, dated "Treasury Chambers, 22 Feb 1840," to The Hon. W. Fox Strangeways of the Foreign Office, made clear the principles by which the Lords Commissioners had come to their decision.

. . . it appears to My Lords that they should be governed less by the actual estimates and plans submitted to them, than by the expense which would be required for building a place of worship of Sufficient Capacity of the simplest materials and of the simplest form consistent with the variations of structure which the peculiarities of climate may render necessary.

Since Cockerell's plans were not of this austere nature,

they are of the opinion that Government cannot be expected to contribute the whole sum required beyond the subscriptions to complete a church, which is designed for a congregation so much larger than the British inhabitants of Athens will probably afford for many years to come, and which it is prepared to construct in an expensive form even supposing it to be desirable to erect a church capable of accommodating 300 persons.

Thus they justified the grant of £800, which in their view was "a fair contribution on the part of the Crown." They were probably right.

Fair or not, there was no disputing the decision of the Lords Commissioners, and the Committee had to choose between raising more money or reducing the estimates. It lost no time in adopting the latter, and before the meeting ended Leeves and Finlay had been authorized to consult with Hansen

> as to the necessary alterations to be made in the plan and estimate, it being decided by the Committee . . . to endeavour to carry out as expeditiously as possible Mr. Cockerell's plan, subject only to such alterations as are necessary to bring the estimate within the amount at its disposal.

A few days later Finlay was able to report to Green.

> Mr Leeves and Mr Hansen have just been with me. Mr Hansen gave us his reduced estimate which amounted to 46,821 drachmas. Our funds are £2100 of which I understood the Committee to decide that the estimate should only appropriate 2/3rd or 39,200 — Now if Mr Hansen leaves out the galleries I think the church might be executed for the sum in our hands.

That same day Leeves informed the British Minister that the "diminished estimate" would be "ready by to-morrow morning," and asked him to "have the kindness to call a meeting."

The next day, April 22, Tuesday in Easter Week, with the laying of the foundation stone now two years in the past, the Committee, in addition to some other subscribers, met to consider Hansen's proposed alterations in the estimate. There was much discussion, particularly between Finlay and Hansen, the latter present at the request of the Committee. Finlay was not prepared to accept Hansen's list of reductions. More savings had to be made, especially since he was quite certain that some items had risen in price since the time of the original calculation. On at least one issue Hansen stood firm: the estimate for walls could not be further reduced without imperilling the solidity of the building. Finally, the meeting agreed that the only way it could proceed with Cockerell's plan "would be by making the following deduc-

tions and alterations:" walls of rough instead of cut stone; no
vestry; tiles instead of slate on a lighter roof; no furnace; no
pews; no galleries: a wooden, rather than a marble, floor; two
bells omitted; walls unplastered. These items represented an
estimated saving of slightly more than £800, a larger
reduction than Hansen had originally proposed, but then
Finlay had had his way over the galleries. The Committee had
done its best to meet the demands put upon it by the Lords
Commissioners of Her Majesty's Treasury and its own
financial resources. It had sacrificed comfort, convenience,
refinement. It refused to sacrifice Cockerell's plan. There is
no doubt that the Committee was right on April 22, 1840.

Three weeks later Finlay and Dixon once again furnished
the guarantee required by the Foreign Office. Their bond
fully attests the decisions reached by the Committee.

> We the undersigned British Residents at Athens and at the Piraeus
> do hereby engage and hold ourselves responsible that the
> Protestant Chapel at Athens shall be built according to the plan
> proposed by Mr. Cockerell and according to Mr. Hansen's detailed
> Estimate (subject to the modifications and alterations agreed
> upon by the meeting of Subscribers on the 22nd April last) with
> the funds at the disposal of the Committee including the £800 to
> be granted by Her Majesty's Government; and that Her Majesty's
> Treasury shall not be called upon for any further grant of funds
> for this purpose.

Once again the Consul wrote to the Foreign Secretary,
but this time there was no delay in receiving his answer,
dated June 19. Acting on this letter Green was able to
address the Committee of Subscribers on July 31.

> I have the honor to inform you that I am authorized by Her
> Majesty's Government to draw a bill at thirty days sight on the
> Lords Commissioners of Her Majesty's Treasury for the sum of
> £800, *in favour of the Treasurer and Trustees of the Church
> Building Fund*, and that I am ready to hand you this bill, on the
> understanding that the written engagement signed before me on
> the 4th day of May last by Mr Finlay and Mr Dixon, and of which
> I forwarded a copy to Her Majesty's Government, will be strictly
> attended to in every respect.

The Committee of Subscribers received this gratifying intelligence at its meeting of August 10. It now had £1835=16=5, or 51,403 drachmas, enough to cover Hansen's revised estimate with a slender margin. To manage these monies a Treasurer and Trustees were appointed. As for the purpose of the fund, Finlay agreed "to become the immediate means of communication with Mr Hansen the architect," and to advertise "for contracts for the supply of the requisite materials for enclosing the ground and building the church." The construction of the first Protestant Church in Athens had begun in earnest a second time, with every hope that with a practical concern for thrift the plan prepared by Cockerell and modified by Hansen would be executed.

*   *   *

The Church that was consecrated on Palm Sunday, April 9, 1843, and dedicated to St. Paul,[5] was in most respects the structure agreed upon by the Committee of Management three years before. The credit for this achievement must largely go to Finlay, who for two years was tireless in his efforts to keep the cost of the building within the estimate. To do this, he often had to struggle with Hansen, who, quite naturally, did not appreciate stone lacking mouldings or ornament. There was something of a crisis early in 1841 when Hansen made "a plan of the mouldings prepared for the door and windows," and "spoke very strongly of the great advantage which would arise to the building if the cut stone . . . could be executed and put up at the same time with the walls themselves." Finlay was not swayed.

> . . . we must abide by the decision of the Committee to complete the walls before engaging in any ornamental work. . . . The doorways and windows will therefore be plain hewn stone like the rest of the building without mouldings.

Hansen profitted from this encounter. Two months later, April 1841, Finlay realized, not from a plan, but from the first of the blocks set in place, that Hansen had designed moulded cornices for the buttresses. He was understandably annoyed, and conveyed his views in a very direct fashion to Green.

> As I cannot render myself responsible for the marble[6] cornices against which I protest I must beg you to call a meeting of the Committee in order to put a stop to the possibility of any future attempt to incur expenses in an unauthorized manner.
>
> I shall stop the progress of the remaining cornices even though they be made now as understood they were to be cut of a plain profile. I have told Mr. Hansen that he should have my final answer tomorrow morning and I shall tell him to make the remaining ones plain and that I consider the ornamental work of the others done at his expense until the decision of the committee be known.
>
> My only object is to finish the church for the money in hand and I should not mind to see it of polished porphyry, but I must now guard against being called upon to pay for the deeds of others and on these marble cornices I make my stand, preparatory to the grand operation concerning the roof where I foresee I shall have a hard struggle.

The Committee met three days later, April 7. As it had a year before, the Committee found a way to preserve the dignity of both contestants. It resolved

> that Mr Finlay be authorized to pay for those [cornices] now in progress and which may be necessary to complete the buttresses but that Mr Hansen be informed that in future no expense for ornamental work must on any account be incurred. . . ."

Although Finlay lost this round, he had in fact won the battle, and when, on the point of leaving Greece a year later, he presented his accounts to the Committee at a meeting held on April 2, 1842, it was clear that the church would be built for the money in hand. Moreover, the building was no longer as austere as once planned, for strict economy and additional subscriptions had restored Cockerell's slate roof and made possible a surrounding wall with iron railings. And there was still uncommitted a margin of over £250. Finlay fully deserved the Committee's unanimous vote of thanks for "his attention to this duty."

With Finlay's departure the Committee requested Leeves "to take charge of the business relating to the work necessary for the completion of the church." The margin allowed certain items once viewed as expendable, and on July 13 the Chaplain wrote to the Consul that he had

> given Mr Hansen instructions for proceeding with the objects we talked over the other night, namely ... making ten benches, painting and covering them with leather, and for making the vestry.

That same day he asked the Treasurer to make payments for the font "and the stone cutter's work in the front of the Church," two projects that a Mr. Blayd of Leeds had unexpectedly agreed to pay for.

The church consecrated by Bishop Tomlinson could no longer be described as all finished "in a plain and becoming style." At least one part had the true character of "a particularly neat and ornamental Gothic edifice."

*   *   *

This account of the planning and building of the English Church of St. Paul leaves no doubt concerning the identity of its architect. He was C. R. Cockerell, and the Committee, insofar as it had the means, followed the designs that he had offered Leeves in August, 1838. Where modifications had to be made or a detail improvised, these were done by the supervising architect Christian Hansen. But these departures from the original intentions were neither so many nor so radical as to change the basic elements, disposition, and style – in a word, the personality – of Cockerell's plan. Nor have subsequent alterations significantly affected that personality (Pl. 2, p. 208).

But in giving Cockerell his proper recognition, we must not forget Henry Acland, the convalescent whose design the Committee had first accepted. A comparison of the ground-plan of his proposed church, for which the foundation was laid, with that of the church as erected – later structural additions have been omitted – makes obvious that Cockerell quite literally built upon Acland's foundations (Pl. 1). Presumably he recognized that in trying to help the Committee he could not ask that the foundation be ignored. Thus both plans have much in common: length; floor-plan of chancel; width of nave; maximum width. Even the dimensions of the two arms of the transept — the feature that most distinguishes Cockerell's plan from that of Acland — were determined by the size and location of the porch and baptistry and by the position of the buttress to the east of both. Cockerell's design thus incorporated the beginnings made by Acland.

*　　*　　*

As one enters the church, there is set on the wall immediately to the left a plaque in memory of Henry Wentworth Acland, the dedication of his children. The beginning of the last sentence reads: "From his designs made in 1837 this church was built . . ." There is a truth contained in these words, but it would be more easily apprehended (and less often misunderstood) if there were a corresponding plaque for Charles Robert Cockerell.

American School of Classical Studies
at Athens   *C. W. J. Eliot*

NOTES

1. Were it not for E. Togo Salmon's magnanimity, his breadth of mind and interest, it might appear that the subject of this essay is ill-chosen to honour a Roman historian. I can only claim as an apology that, when I returned to Greece in 1971, everyone was celebrating the hundred and fiftieth anniversary of the beginning of the Greek War of Independence. Thus my thoughts and readings were directed to the Acts of the early travelers and Philhellenes. The building of St. Paul's Church is part of their story, a symbolic epilogue.

2. *Classical Landscape with Figures*, London, 1947, pp. 59-60. The same material is printed in the second edition, London, 1963. (Quoted

by kind permission of the publisher, John Murray.) The reference to St. Andrew is easily explained in one of two ways: there is a second Protestant church in Athens dedicated to that apostle, and a third in Patras. The author has presumably confused St. Paul's Church with one or other of them. The description of Bracebridge as fund-raiser derives from Murray's *Handbook* of 1854, and is incorrect. Mr. and Mrs. Bracebridge were indeed generous subscribers, and the latter allowed one of her views of Athens to be published and "sold for the benefit of the fund for building a Protestant chapel at Athens" (*Notes Descriptive of a Panoramic Sketch of Athens, May, 1836*, Coventry, n.d., repr. 1972 and sold in aid of St. Catherine's British Embassy School, Athens) a privilege that she also gave to the London Benevolent Repository (*Notes Descriptive of a Panoramic Sketch of Athens, Taken May, 1839*, London, 1839), but the records do not show either of them as prominent canvassers. The myth about Aberdeen granite — sometimes it is said to have been brought to the Piraeus in the bottoms of English ships as ballast — is well established, but I have not been able to trace its history.

3. All the quotations come from the records and papers of the Anglican Church of St. Paul. I am very grateful to the Church Council for allowing me to study and publish these documents. I have not in all cases been able to check quotations against the originals. Nor have I thought it necessary to footnote the source of individual citations. I am also in debt to Eberhart Slenska, who made it possible for me to understand L. Lange's letters. William Miller used the same material for the "Centenary Souvenir" that he wrote in 1938 titled *English Church of St. Paul, Athens*, a work freely used by W. G. Angus in the most recent edition of *The Anglican Church of St. Paul Athens. A Short History*, dated February, 1968. Both contain a brief account of the period covered in this essay. Neither is entirely right on the question of the church's architect. Miller's claim that "ultimately the famous Kleanthes ... was the architect," even though he (Miller) knew about the plan "submitted by Cockerell and approved," is demonstrably untrue, while Angus' statement that Acland's plans were "amended by Cockerell ... and Hansen" does not do justice to Cockerell.

4. E. Bires, Σταμάτιος Κλεάνθης, Athens, 1959, p. 6, where a Bavarian, an Englishman, and a Dane are also mentioned as competitors. In a later work Bires identifies these people as Lange, Acland, and Hansen (Αἱ Ἀθῆναι ἀπὸ τοῦ 19ου εἰς τὸν 20ον αἰώνα, Athens, 1966, p. 115), and says that although Acland's design was at first judged successful this decision was later reversed and Kleanthes' plan accepted

in its place. A footnote (*op. cit.*, p. 426) gives Miller and his "Centennial Souvenir" as the source. Where Miller got the notion that Kleanthes was the architect, which he expressed publicly at least as early as 1925 (*The Early Years of Modern Athens*, London, 1926, p. 19), I do not know. Bires' identification has been followed (among others) by J. N. Travlos, Πολεοδομικὴ Εξέλεξις τῶν Ἀθηνῶν, Athens, 1960, p. 247. V. Scully ("Kleanthes and the Duchess of Piacenza," *Journal of the Society of Architectural Historians*, 22, 1963, pp. 144-45), aware of the differing accounts of Miller and Angus (see above, n. 3), and unhappy about the attribution to Kleanthes for artistic reasons, proposed a compromise solution: "He probably collaborated, since his touch on his own, even in Gothic Revival design, tends to be somewhat more taut."

5. This figure is taken from the minutes of the meeting. It is in conflict with Cockerell's estimate of sixty persons. Such a difference is probably not significant. Probably Acland and Cockerell each had his own method for establishing the church's capacity.

6. To a Protestant in Athens, the dedication of the church to St. Paul would be so obvious as to require no argument. And indeed nowhere is there recorded any debate by the subscribers on the subject of the name of the church. To an Orthodox Greek, on the other hand, such a dedication would have been most unusual, St. Paul being held in little favour. Even today there is in Athens only one Orthodox church dedicated to him (O.F.A. Meinardus, *St Paul in Greece*, Athens, 1972, p. 52). It dates from 1910, and the choice of saint may represent a western influence, particularly since by this time Crown Prince Constantine had named one of his sons Paul.

7. The cornices now in place are of the same limestone as the walls. It is hard to see them as anything but the original ones. The mistake is probably Finlay's, who, in the heat of the moment, thus made Hansen's action seem all the more extravagant than it really was.

8. There is no mention of restoring the furnace. Perhaps this decision had been taken earlier, for in Finlay's opinion at least the provision of heat was more important than that of pews: "It seems to me that the Trustees *must warm* the church but the sitters may send their own chairs though they cannot bring their own fires." As for the vestry, the one planned by Cockerell beneath the chancel was not carried out, nor was a suitable alternative provided until 1891 when the two rooms were added, one to the east of the east wall of each arm of the transept, that to the north for the organ, the other for the vestry. Assuming that Hansen executed his instructions, I think that he may

have hollowed out the space beneath the southern arm of the transept, where today there is an austere room accessible from the outside only. One can well appreciate the prolonged cry for a vestry if this subterranean chamber was originally all that was available.

The Site of the Battle of Zama

It is a notorious fact that we do not know the precise site of one of the greatest battles of antiquity in which Scipio defeated Hannibal in 202 B.C., although on the authority of Nepos who wrote a century and a half after the engagement we generally follow his lead and call it the Battle of Zama. Numerous attempts have been made to fix the site but none is conclusive. Indeed anything like certainty is impossible and could be claimed only if new archaeological evidence turned up, such as an inscription naming the unknown Margaron (which Polybius, or his MSS, give as the site) or traces of camps with closely dateable material. A new attempt to determine the site has been made by Mr. F. H. Russell, until recently American Ambassador to Tunisia (see *Archaeology* 1970, pp. 122 ff.). The purpose of this present note is not to try to show that his view is wrong (it is in fact quite attractive), but to suggest that he has rejected in too cavalier a fashion the possibility of other sites which may have equal claims to consideration.

The topic bristles with well-known difficulties: here brevity demands focussing attention on a few crucial points. First, Mr. Russell (surely rightly) rejects the Siliana Valley as a possible site and then argues for one in the valley of Le Sers, just east of Ou. Tessa, west of the slopes of Les Massouges, and thus a little west of Jama and Seba Biar (in

general terms west of Zama). Unfortunately he gives no plan
of the plain (and thus no indication of the precise battle
positions), nor do his air-photographs include this critical
area; thus there is no chance of seeing whether any traces of
camps could be discerned. However his ground photographs
of the plain and the hill on which he places Hannibal's camp
look attractive.

But what of possible sites further west? These he
dismisses in rather general terms as the area of Sakiet Sidi
Youssef (Naraggara), west of El Kef. Now a site in the
immediate neighbourhood of Sidi Youssef would be eliminated by most scholars (including G. Veith, who once
suggested two possible sites in the area, only later to reject
them), but Mr. Russell does not specifically refer to the site
of Draa el Metnan, 27 km. east of Sidi Youssef which Veith
finally accepted as the most probable battle-ground.

Why does Mr. Russell reject this area? I must quote him
in full (p. 123):

> We can be sure that the battle was not fought there. Sakiet
> (Naraggara) is fifty miles, a three days' march from Zama which
> would hardly be the mere tactical "move to advantageous
> position" that took place during the brief time between Hanni-
> bal's request for a meeting and Scipio's agreement to hold the
> historic conversation. One reason writers have given for regarding
> Sakiet as the location is that Scipio may have wished to move
> that far toward Numidia in order to assure that his ally,
> Massinissa, would join him in time to take part in the battle.
> Polybius says, however, that Massinissa joined Scipio the day
> after Hannibal asked for a meeting and *before* Scipio moved his
> camp. So the move was not motivated by Scipio's desire to
> establish contact with his Numidian ally. We can eliminate Sakiet
> and other suggested spots in the area around it.

The argument appears to be that Scipio made a short
tactical advance from his camp where Massinissa had joined
him and then met Hannibal near Zama; since Naraggara is
fifty miles from Zama the battlefield cannot have been near
Naraggara. But there appears to be some misunderstanding
here in referring to a "mere tactical 'move to advantageous

position.'" This is based on Mr. Russell's translation of Polybius which is given as follows (p. 122): "Scipio broke camp and moved *to* (my italics) establish himself at Margaron in an advantageous position." This translation seems to suggest that Scipio moved in order to obtain a stronger position, but what Polybius says is (and I quote W. R. Paton's translation) that Scipio "then (i.e. after being joined by Massinissa) broke up his camp and on reaching a town called Margaron (I retain the MSS reading) encamped there, selecting a spot which was favourably situated in other respects and had water within the throw of a javelin." Thus Polybius in no way suggests that Scipio moved east (i.e. against Hannibal) because he needed a stronger position, but merely states that he advanced and then chose a good position. Thus while Mr. Russell says that the "battle was not fought there. Sakiet (Naraggara) is fifty miles, a three days' march from Zama which would hardly be a mere tactical move to more advantageous position," Scipio will in fact have moved for other reasons than that of obtaining a more advantageous position, namely that after waiting for the arrival of Massinissa and his invaluable cavalry and having received this aid he was then ready to face Hannibal.

There is of course no doubt (as Mr. Russell stresses) that Scipio was joined by Massinissa before he made the final advance, i.e. to the battlefield, but it is well to distinguish two movements, (a) Scipio advanced south-west in order to meet Massinissa (which may well have occurred at Naraggara: this would help to explain the linking of this name with the campaign) and (b) his subsequent advance east with Massinissa to meet Hannibal. Mr. Russel insists (p. 125) that Scipio must have been coming from the north. This is true of (a) but not necessarily of (b) which was the move that led to the battle itself.

We may now look at the position from Hannibal's point of view. He advanced westwards, seeking Scipio, but did not know where he was. When at Zama he sent scouts to find out (the scouts were caught, treated well and sent back by Scipio). Scipio may well have been at Narraggara; the fifty miles is surely no objection, and in fact, as pointed out by F. W. Walbank, Polybius implies that the distance was considerable when he records that Scipio provided the scouts with provision for the return journey (ἐφόδια). Having thus located Scipio and believing that he had not yet been joined by Massinissa (not only the scouts but also Hannibal's subsequent herald had left Scipio's camp before Massinissa's arrival), Hannibal would wish to meet him either to negotiate or failing that, to fight it out before Scipio was joined by Massinissa and could negotiate from greater strength. Scipio in reply to Hannibal's suggestion for a meeting said that he would let him know the time and place. The next day Massinissa arrived; Scipio was strengthened and then advanced to meet Hannibal.

How soon news of Massinissa's arrival reached Hannibal at Zama we do not know, but presumably he will have heard before he actually met Scipio and will thus have realised that the tables had been turned on him. He had hoped to negotiate before Scipio was strengthened in his cavalry, and had failed.

There is no good reason to think that the battle was fought in the immediate neighbourhood of Zama. Polybius does not say this, and to assume it is to fall into the same mistake that Livy made when he implied that the battle of Ilipa was fought near Baecula (whereas in fact Scipio joined up with other troops at Baecula and then marched south to Ilipa). In neither case is the actual distance of the advance from the last named base given. It may have been short or long; before the battle of Ilipa it was some 150 miles, while from Zama to Veith's site is only 30 miles. All that Polybius says is that "Hannibal broke up his camp and on getting to within a distance of not more than thirty stades of Scipio he camped on a hill"; no hint of the length of his march is given.

Thus a position at any point between Naraggara and Zama is indicated and Veith has found a suitable site at Draa el Metnan. Although this reconstruction cannot claim anything like certainty, it does supply a reasonable account of events and provides a battlefield which suits the physical

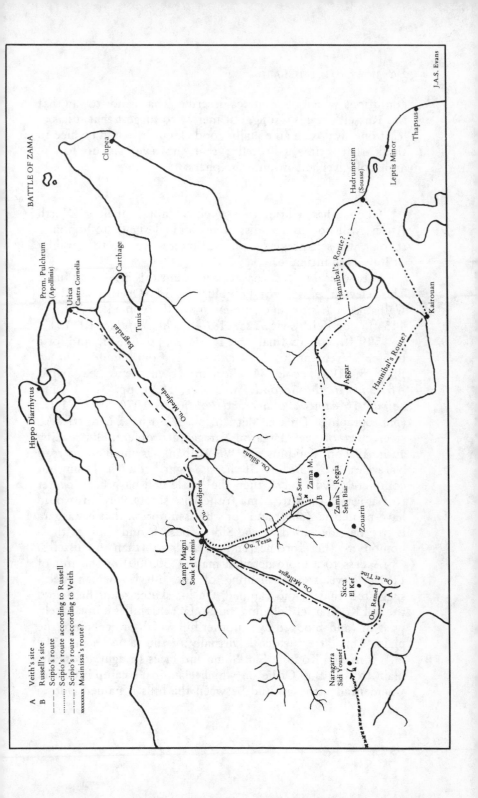

BATTLE OF ZAMA

A   Veith's site
B   Russell's site

——— Scipio's route
— — — Scipio's route according to Russell
·········· Scipio's route according to Veith
xxxxxxxx Masinissa's route?

J.A.S. Evans

conditions which our sources describe. That is not to say that Mr. Russell's site is wrong, but merely to suggest that it has at least one rival with an equally good claim. It would be nice to think that "time will tell"; that, however, is up to the archaeologists and air-photographers.

*   *   *

I hope that a brief topographical note, albeit of North Africa, will not come amiss in a volume designed to honour a scholar whose knowledge of and interest in the topography of Italy is so intimate.

It is scarcely necessary to document this brief note fully. The relevant passage of Polybius is 15.5. On this see F. W. Walbank, *A Historical Commentary on Polybius* II, 1967, pp. 445 ff. For Veith's views see *Antike Schlachtfelder* III, 1912, pp. 599 ff., for his final site, IV, 1931, pp. 628 ff., and for a briefer statement his *Schlachtenatlas, Römische Abteilung*, Blatt 8, 1922, col. 34. For my own views see *Scipio Africanus in the Second Punic War*, 1930, pp. 310 ff. and *Scipio Africanus: Soldier and Politician*, 1970, pp. 271 ff., (photograph of Draa el Metnan, pl. 33). I have here tried to steer clear of the Margaron-Naraggara problem. Our leading authority on Polybius, F. W. Walbank, is inclined to read Naraggara at 15.5.14. If he is right (though I am not completely won over), then the battle will have been nearer to Naraggara than to Zama (otherwise surely Polybius would have named it Zama) and (on the assumption that Naraggara is to be identified with Sidi Youssef and not with a homonym) therefore nearer to Veith's site than to Russell's.

Access to a more detailed map (1:50,000) of the area of El Kef reveals a misnaming of the hill on which Veith suggested that Scipio camped. On his sketch-maps he names the hill Koudiat el Behaima, but in fact this hill is immediately west of (and blocked by) another hill which projects into the plain. This latter, which is virtually of the same height (518 m.), is named Koudiat Sidi Slima and faces straight across the plain to K^{dt} Bou Grine on which Hannibal's camp is placed. (Incidentally, the ground between the hills is named Outate

Zemmal and not Draa el Metnan, as on Veith's map, a name which no longer appears on the 1:50,000). Thus if the whole site is accepted, Scipio will have camped on K^{dt} Sidi Slima.

University of London,   *Howard H. Scullard*
King's College

Trajan's Character in the Literary Tradition

By common consent the most admirable and pleasing character amongst the Roman Emperors was Trajan. Occasionally, it is true, there has been a slight suspicion that all was not well with the powerful and prevailing literary tradition; that just as the falsity of the slanderous accusations against Tiberius and Domitian could be proved, it was likely that there were chinks in the armour of righteousness in which Trajan paraded on the stage of history; and indeed even in antiquity the malicious pen of Julian was only following an existing hostile tradition in attributing certain faults to the exemplar of imperial virtue. In his judicious summing-up of the character and achievements of Trajan, Professor E. T. Salmon said, "The ancient picture of Trajan as an emperor of almost superhuman excellence cannot be fully endorsed,"[1] but in general he accepts the main tradition, giving some sound reasons both for a high estimate of Trajan's achievements and the attitudes of Senate and people towards him. It is my purpose in this paper to examine the tradition itself, rather than the character and achievement of the Princeps, and to suggest reasons other than his own excellence for the unique place Trajan held (and to some extent still holds) in the received version of Roman Imperial history.

In the case of Trajan, just as in the converse case of

Domitian,[2] the literary tradition has played the dominant part; it is true that we may attempt to evaluate a man's character from his recorded acts, but the public acts of an Emperor are matters of policy, decisions of the Consilium, the outcome of strategic considerations or economic circumstances, no less than of his individual character; and of Trajan's private life we know practically nothing. Again, even the most weighty decisions of the emperor's reign may meet with differing interpretations as to motive; for example it is still very much an open question whether vaingloriousness or sound "defence" policy motivated both the original invasion of Parthia and its southern extension.[3] I do not intend to repeat the arguments put forward or rejected by Lepper, nor to examine in detail other important actions or policies;[4] my method will be to consider the traditional literary portrait, with a brief examination of the sources and of parallels, with a view to determining how far the qualities and attributes they describe are derived from the individual himself, and how far they are merely the stock-in-trade of flattery and official propaganda, which could be, and frequently was, applied to any emperor of whatever calibre.

Our "knowledge" of Trajan's character is distinguished from our information about most other emperors by the peculiar nature of its sources. Pliny's Panegyric, ostensibly composed and delivered early in the reign, is of course largely discounted as historical evidence today by the recognition of its programmatic nature,[5] as well as for its glaringly hyperbolical flattery. None the less it continues to produce some impression, since its view of the Optimus Princeps may be thought to gain some support from the contemporary utterances of Tacitus in the prologues of the Agricola and the Histories, and the high-flown rhetoric of Dio of Prusa in the Orations "On Kingship" and elsewhere. Later sources, such as they are, not unexpectedly echo the canonical view; naturally we need not pay much attention to these, though interesting parallels regarding other individuals may be found therein. As for Tacitus, it is now generally recognised that his statements on freedom of speech and thought reflect the official propaganda of the new dynasty equally with the effusions of Pliny; the flush of enthusiasm, real or simulated, for the new regime appears to have evaporated before long, since Tacitus forebore to comment explicitly at all on the events or policies of the reign, and disillusion has been suspected.[6]

The orations of Dio should be totally disregarded, as I shall attempt to show, since on the one hand they merely reflect the traditional quasi-philosophical view of the ideal monarch[7] and on the other cannot be proved to have any direct connection with Trajan at all (v. infra).

Trajan's "own" letters to Pliny have been laid under contribution for evidence as to his character. The dangers of circularity of argument are obvious; only from what we know of Trajan can we point to anything in these documents as likely to have been his personal contribution. If we had the slightest external evidence to prove that he had anything to do with their style and wording, or even indeed their content other than the giving of approval to the drafts laid on his desk by officials, some progress might perhaps be made; as it is, large assumptions are unavoidable, in general necessitating acceptance of the official line as representing the inner nature of the Princeps; and this I find myself unable to concede. Although the imperial bureaucracy had not reached its height, with Hadrian and Severus still to come, this machinery was working well enough and there had been time since Augustus or Claudius for bureaucratic conventions for correspondence to develop.[8]

A complicating factor in the situation is the absence of literary accounts of the reign; even a "Life" from the forger of the *SHA* might have been better than nothing as assistance in restoring a due perspective. Other emperors were unfortunate enough to have their biographies composed under a new and often hostile dynasty, or by a man with scant regard for historical truth. Trajan has gone down in history almost unscarred by hostile witnesses, though there are traces of a different tradition in Fronto, the Xiphilinus excerpts from Cassius Dio, and Aurelius Victor, which will be examined a little later.

The qualities for which Trajan is commended by Pliny are almost innumerable; he uses at least forty complimentary abstract nouns, supported by their cognate adjectives, often in the superlative degree. Though many of these are virtually synonyms, the qualities denoted are further reinforced by phrases expressing the absence of bad qualities. The first two orations of Dio of Prusa contain exact verbal equivalents or close periphrases for about half of them — and it is easy to see why, if any credence is placed in Pliny's "portrait," Dio might be thought to corroborate it.[9] But two considerations tell heavily against such an inference; first, the appearance of identical or similar terminology both in the earlier literature on kingship, which can be shown to be the source of the general ideas and even the specific images and expressions[10] used, and also in the official language of inscriptions and the like; second, the prescriptions for kingship are not altogether appropriate for the Roman institutions and ideas of the early second century, and indeed there is, in some of the other orations, implicit criticism of the whole institution of rule by an individual, for instance in the unfavourable presentation of Alexander's φιλοτιμία, in the Fourth oration.[11] Against this, admittedly, may be set such passages as 2.65, a justification of the "election" of a king — if a man is chosen by all he must be "the best" — but this tells us nothing about Trajan except perhaps that, as Pliny shows, he felt it advisable to emphasize both the legitimacy of Nerva's accession and the propriety of his own adoption. (The similarity of Galba's justification of the adoption of Piso, as reported by Tacitus, with the propaganda surrounding Nerva's action has often excited remark.) However, in general, as in the converse case of the attacks on tyranny made by Epictetus, the monarch is a composite figure, drawing one traditional trait from Xerxes, another from Sardanapalus, or their more admirable counterparts. A good example is 2.77, where the king who is both valiant and humane, the suppressor of evil and encourager of virtue, is compared to Cyrus and Deioces, Idanthyrsus the Scythian, Leucon, many (!) of the Spartan kings, and some of the early

Pharaohs. The basis of the specification for kingship goes back certainly to Aristotle, and no doubt beyond, maybe to Pythagoras;[12] the point here is that it is the merest hypothesis to imagine any of the characteristics listed here or in other passages of Dio as having any direct relevance to Trajan. The only exception would be if we were to regard the compositions as sermons, or moral tracts intended to encourage the monarch in virtuous attitudes and actions.

Were the speeches actually delivered before Trajan, and was Dio in any way intimate with the Princeps, as he himself suggests ? The "dramatic framework" of the orations is in my view, totally fictitious; they may, in substance, have been orally delivered, but the presence of the Emperor need not be anything but a convenient device, no more meaningful than the "Prisce, iubes - -" of the unfortunate Passennus Paulus.[13] But this does not answer the second part of the question. Now while there is no reason totally to reject Dio's own claim (45.2) that he was acquainted with Nerva, it is not necessary to suppose that $\phi\iota\lambda o\varsigma$ means much more than some degree of official communication. The cognomen Cocceianus, too, may indicate a connection, but no precision is possible. However it is extremely unlikely that this relationship, whatever it was, was inherited by Trajan; Trajan it is true inherited *amici* from Nerva and also from Domitian, but a mere provincial rhetor is not to be counted among these, nor in the social circle of a *vir militaris*. The references to Dio in the Pliny-Trajan correspondence do not provide even the faintest hint of any acquaintance, let alone *amicitia*. An extraordinary anecdote in Philostratus (*V. S.* 1,7), asserts that Trajan invited Dio to ride with him in his triumphal chariot, a clear impossibility, and that he continually turned towards Dio repeating "I don't understand what you are saying, but you are as dear to me as I am myself." Was it Greek that Trajan did not understand, or the sophist's rhetoric? In either case, rather chilling for the reception of the orations on Kingship! And the dramatic device of the Imperial addressee is revealed as fraudulent. But one may suppose Trajan to have had some Greek, and in fact the whole fictitious episode is part of the sophistic hagiography to which Philostratos was addicted and which became quite fashionable in the second century.[14]

The orations of Dio, accordingly, may be neglected as evidence for the real character of Trajan; but if they had any vogue in later years, they may very well have been taken as confirming the conventional view of his ideal character as monarch. There is no doubt that Pliny's Panegyric did remain current, and was probably used as a model for the innumerable *gratiarum actiones* and other laudatory speeches demanded by the Imperial calendar, and its influence may be detected in some of the other Panegyrics that have survived from the Fourth century. That in honour of Theodosius ascribed to Pacatus, for example, beginning with the time-worn claim "cum te semper ultra omnes retro principes laudari oporteret"[15] goes on to claim that now at last there is freedom to speak — or to refrain from speaking! A most Plinian conceit. If there had been an election everyone would have voted for Theodosius, says Pacatus; Spain has given the Empire a very god on earth (thus outdoing the "dis simillimus princeps" of his model).[16]

Theodosius, like Trajan, unites in himself all the virtues which others may claim singly; specifically, his *frugalitas benignitas* and *amicitia* are emphasised, and stress is laid on three aspects showing a remarkable coincidence with the career and situation of Trajan; lengthy military experience in youth[17] (so that he is to be compared favourably with Africanus Minor, Hannibal, and Alexander!), that his father ought to have been Emperor and this is a guarantee of the son's fitness, and that he habitually appears in public freely and unguarded.

It may be objected that Theodosius deserved some of these praises, and indeed they are echoed by the Epitomator *de Caesaribus* in a passage to be discussed later. But in reality these phrases and ideas are the stock-in-trade of panegyrists; we find in the case of Maximian, who does not elsewhere rejoice in a good press, that he too held a strenuous military career — indeed too long for the orator to relate, and that he was distinguished for fortitude, clemency, forethought or wisdom, generosity, justice, and harmony with his co-Augustus. Thus it becomes clear that if only the right sources were extant, every emperor would possess all the admirable qualities.

Confirmation comes from the inscriptions. No single princeps receives epigraphically the lavish complement of praise that can be set forth in a three-hour oration — for the stone-cutters were only human; but single virtues or whole groups of them are omnipresent. We recall that *virtus clementia iustitia* and *pietas* were first publicly proclaimed on the golden shield that honoured Augustus, and it will hardly astonish us to find most of the admirable qualities that made a Trajan or a Theodosius attributed to emperors of a different stamp. The following brief list is taken merely from Dessau's selection; even before flattery came into its own (as is thought), Tiberius is "princeps optimus ac iustissimus conservator patriae" (*ILS* 159); Claudius is "vindex libertatis" (217); Antoninus Pius is "optimus maximusque princeps et cum summa benignitate iustissimus" (341, cf. 345); Septimius, "vindex et conditor Romanae disciplinae" (446) displays "indulgentia caelestis" (432); Mactinus is "providentissimus et sanctissimus" (463); Gallienus (in an official statement) is "clementissimus" and his "invicta virtus" is only surpassed by his "pietas" (548). In later years of course the laudation of emperors continues unchecked, with variations on the well-established themes; it is fascinating to find Constantine described as "clementissimus" (709) and his son Constantius II as having surpassed all previous princes in *virtus, gloria, pietas* and *iustitia* (733), terms which practically take us back to the Shield of Augustus.

The official claims of emperors to all manner of virtues would of course be amply illustrated by the coinage; but I do not intend to discuss it here, since my topic is not directly concerned with what Emperors thought or wished to be thought of themselves.[18]

The poets are also ignored here, but for different reasons; the grossness of their flattery takes advantage of the

conventions of poetic language to indulge in all kinds of
hyperbole. It is however not irrelevant to my general thesis to
observe that a man like Martial can change the recipient of
his adulations as readily as his clothes; this tends to confirm
the existence of a norm for the virtues of princes.

It may seem inconsistent that after rejecting the poets I
should turn to the *Historia Augusta*. Despite the total
dishonesty of its author which renders it almost valueless for
evidence of historical fact, it provides in the Life of Hadrian
yet another piece of confirmatory evidence. The writer was
obviously under no particular obligation to flatter Hadrian; it
is however Hadrian, not his predecessor, who is depicted as
the ideal "commilito," (*SHA Hadr.* 10), eating the same
rations as his troops, engaging in the same training exercises,
with all the other legendary trappings; at the same time he is
the restorer of discipline, which had become lax under the
previous Emperors since Octavian![19] Of Trajan and his
campaigns, no hint. This piece of fiction then is but one more
of the commonplaces attaching to the momentary object of
laudation; the objection that the *SHA* fails to give consistent
portraits of its subjects is immaterial, as this is merely part of
the accepted pattern of description of the good emperor.

Another fourth century author, the writer of the *Epitome de Caesaribus*, makes Trajan an ancestor of Theodosius.
To improve even upon that fanciful warrant of nobility, they
resembled each other in both physique and character; as to
the former, pictorial evidence is alleged. Theodosius was
noted for his clemency, affability, generosity and love of his
subjects; he liked simple souls, but admired the intellectuals
provided they were harmless.[20] Rather naive is the praise of
Theodosius for bestowing offices, money and other benefits
on his personal friends, especially as rewards for service to
himself or his father. However, unlike Trajan, Theodosius was
distinguished for his strong objection to wine-bibbing and to
love of triumphs; less aggressive than Trajan, he did not start
wars, and more moral, he passed sumptuary legislation
against female guitar-players at dinner parties (o si sic
omnes!) and even forbade marriage between cousins. (*Ep. de*

Caes. 48). One would expect that this paragon (for I have by no means exhausted the catalogue) would have been living and reigning at the time of composition, and it is perhaps a little unfortunate for my theory that he was deceased, though his sons were reigning and flattery of their father was obviously in order. This and other versions of Theodosius' reputation make it clear that Trajan was, in the tradition, still the ideal emperor, only surpassed by the actual incumbent. Optimus Princeps had been accepted as denoting a fact, and it was the sheerest wishful-thinking to cry "Felicior Augusto, melior Traiano" at the accession of new emperors.[21]

But the fulsome author of this epitome may admit rivals for the preeminence of Trajan. The "foreign" emperors raised Rome to new heights — Nerva by his prudence and moderation, Trajan by his godlike quality (Quid Traiano divinius?) and Hadrian by his excellence (*praestantia*) (*Ep. de Caes.* 13)[22] The account which follows, while generally laudatory in the extreme, allows the accusation of intemperance with food and wine; the shortcomings of Trajan's literary education are excused; and it is admitted that Trajan's good qualities were magnified by contrast with the faults and vices of several appalling tyrants who preceded him! The divine providence which proclaimed his appointment, e.g. per a Greek-speaking raven, enabled him to cope like a veritable Superman, with floods in the Tiber, earthquakes in the provinces, a terrible plague, famines and fires — all of which, it seems to be implied, were dealt with by such resolute measures as limiting the height of buildings to sixty feet. However despite the foolishness, inaccuracy and inconsistency of which the Epitomator is capable, he provides good evidence for the traditional equation, Trajan = ideal prince = Theodosius.

Some other historical accounts of Trajan are perhaps less flattering. The serious and weighty historian Cassius Dio, unfortunately represented in the main only by the Xiphilinus excerpts, with their disproportionate interest in such matters as the Antioch earthquake, begins with the conventional eulogy (68.6-7) but appends the principal reproaches known to have been directed against Trajan — and accepted as factual by the historian. Intemperance and homosexuality are however comparatively minor defects; more serious is δόξης ἐπιθυμία, stated at 68.17 as the real reason for the invasion of Parthia. This last tends to be confirmed by the recorded emulation of Alexander (29.30). If little corroboration for the charge can now be found in Dio's Fourth Oration (above), it may on the other hand be explained away as the alleged justification for Hadrian's reversal of strategic policy. The accusation of pedication is of course a normal feature of Roman political denigration; considering the general chorus of praise, one suspects it of some basis of truth. There would have been little point in inventing it long afterwards. Trajan was not the last of a dynasty,[23] and in any case the dynasty never underwent the vilification suffered by its predecessors. On the contrary, the name of M. Aurelius Antoninus was adopted by the Severans, and even the last of the Antonine line, Commodus, though liable to be labelled with the same tags as Nero and Domitian,[24] was partially rescued by the emphasis which Septimius placed on him as legitimate predecessor and fictive kin. Possibly the story of Pylades is evidence of homosexuality in Trajan; the restoration of pantomime to legitimacy and to imperial favour is indubitable, since Pliny has to try to justify it. (*Pan.* 46), though he cannot condemn Nerva's contrary action. The charge of drunkenness is repeated by both Aurelius Victor, who explains that it was no serious problem, in an emperor who made it a rule not to conduct official business after lengthy dinners (13.9) and, as we saw above, the Epitomator who claims superiority for Theodosius on this account.

Fronto, much closer in date to Trajan, does not, of course, give a direct account but a number of observations on the Optimus Princeps are included in his address to Lucius Verus. As the *Historia Augusta* was to transfer Trajan's merit as "commilito" to Hadrian, Fronto attributes to Verus most of those virtues which in the *Panegyric* and elsewhere are normally ascribed to Trajan; while Antoninus, his own imperial patron, is "divinus ille vir, providentia pudicitia frugalitate innocentia pietate sanctimonia omnes omnium virtutes supergressus" (Haines II 8); the nearer we get to the reigning monarch, the more numerous the virtues.[25] On the other hand the first great figure of the dynasty is no longer totally free from vices; the drinking and the *histriones* are noticed (while Hadrian also was not completely *severus*, being fond of music and good food); again, while Trajan was popular with his troops, he was jealous of his generals' prowess and renown; his own glory was of more concern to him than the blood of his own men, and neither his justice nor his clemency were as unquestionable as those of Lucius.[26]

These, as we have seen, are on the whole the standard accusations, though more precise; but however injudicious in flattery, Fronto was perspicacious enough to observe that there may have been reasons for some malicious attacks on Trajan's memory, whether inspired by Hadrian or not; and also that there were reasons other than philosophic, moral and manly virtues for his reputation. His summing-up provides a starting-point for the next section of this paper: "Whether Trajan is to be accounted more illustrious in war or in peace for my part I leave undecided – in the arts of peace scarcely anyone has equalled Trajan in popularity with the people."[27] The reason, says Fronto, was that he understood the "dual principles of governing the Roman people – *annona* and *spectacula.*"[28] For neglect of serious matters may bring greater harm to the state, but neglect of the amusements of the populace brings greater unpopularity.

Much of the foregoing has tended to ignore the possibility that Trajan in fact did possess at least some of the almost incredibly lengthy catalogue of merits attributed to him, in the attempt to show that other princes, perhaps less worthy, gained in their own time an apparently equal celebrity for virtue. Whether or not he did possess these qualities, we can identify factors in the situation which encouraged the acceptance of the official view, not only at the time, but subsequently, so that Trajan became the paradigm of the good emperor – Τραιανὸς ὁ χρηστός, as Arrian summarily put it.[29] Popularity, as Fronto suggested, is indeed the key, or one of the keys — for favour only from the lower orders could not have influenced the literary accounts so powerfully. The city populace were, naturally, not unimportant to the general aspect of a reign; for prestige reasons, as well as for comfort, it was desirable to keep them in a friendly frame of mind. Yet one tends to suppose that the *turba Remi* was as fickle as Juvenal maintains, and had a short memory both for alimentary and spectacular offerings. Trajan took no chances.

The *liberalitas* and *munificentia* emphasised by Pliny were genuine enough, almost embarrassingly so when one considers the amount of *congiaria* recorded by the Chronographer of 354, the 10,000 pairs of gladiators mentioned by Dio; but whether it was so virtuous might well be questioned. However the panegyrist at least is bold enough to assert that Trajan was careful with his money (having it both ways as usual; in Domitian parsimony was a crime!) and even "parcus in aedificando" — a claim so absurd as to need no refutation. One of the major policies of Trajan seems to have been to impress the urban (and to a lesser extent the municipal and provincial) populace with fora, baths, harbours, aqueducts, roads, bridges, arches and columns. Some of these, undoubtedly, were extremely useful, if not utilitarian; our present concern is with their value in gaining popularity. A measure which seems to be more philanthropic was the extension of the *alimenta*, not a great vote-winning project, but indicative of a buoyant state of the Treasury. Whether it was in reality "L'Or des Daces" which enabled him to adopt this free-spending policy lies outside the scope of this paper; the acquisitions of fresh capital from barbarian lands would undoubtedly be conducive to general approval of the ruler, since the public would suppose that it was not their money, contributed in taxation, which was being expended.

But conquest itself, rather than financial profit resulting from it, was a greater means of winning general approval, and not only at the lower levels of society. I forbear to cite the poets from the Augustans on who celebrated conquests, whether achieved or foreshadowed, and turn instead to the sober testimony of Tacitus. "In those days, the historians were dealing with great wars, the capture of cities, the routing or taking prisoners of kings — I labour in a narrow field and shall reap no glory. Mine is the theme of a peace unbroken. . . ."[30] Clearly military conquest and glory are the most praiseworthy preoccupations of an emperor; even the ideal king of the pseudo-philosophic Dio will be "terrible to his country's enemies." In this way he becomes the "saviour and guardian of all mankind" — the lesser breeds without the law apparently excluded from consideration. Trajan obliged. The Dacian Wars (which Decebalus may have precipitated, thus justifying in this case at least the claim that Trajan did not initiate wars unless provoked) saw a vast assemblage of troops, an unexampled logistic train — and the loot that justified the whole operation only less than the glory of advancing the Empire's boundaries. Had Trajan done no more, he might well have escaped the imputation of $\phi\iota\lambda o\tau\iota\mu\acute{\iota}a$, even despite the ostentatious memorial he erected and the lavishness of the triumphal celebrations. It was of course the Eastern campaigns that gave the opportunity for this accusation, whether sincerely made because others agreed with Hadrian that the operations were too costly, the new frontiers untenable; or as propaganda to justify the obviously unpopular surrender of Trajan's territorial acquisitions. Dacia had been left over, as it were, from the Flavian period; Trajan's campaigns here were a logical continuation of those of Domitian. But the Eastern venture too, whatever the strategic or other motives which actually set it in motion,[31] had long been on the ostensible or propagandist agenda; furthermore Parthia was the one external power whose strength could be even remotely compared with that of Rome; her "king of kings" was the next most powerful individual in the known world after the Princeps; any success against Parthia (non-military examples included) was a guarantee of popularity in all circles, from the senators whose high commands were richly rewarding, to the plebs Romana who benefitted from the triumphal shows and largesses. The moral effect of Trajan's operations, even though apparently not a lasting success, should not be underestimated in its impact on the Roman world, whether or no there was any substantial change in the power-balance in the East.

Trajan had devoted a larger part of his energies (not to mention the imperial resources) over a longer time to aggressive or expansionist warfare than any of his predecessors since Augustus. In addition to this leading qualification for popularity, and the generosity already discussed, we must consider a factor for which Trajan himself was not directly responsible; namely, the length of time during which the dynasty of which he was the virtual founder remained in control — that is, almost a century, and comparable with the duration of the First dynasty established by Augustus. This lengthy period facilitated the consolidation of the Trajanic legend, in much the same way as Augustus' reputation survived — in his case despite the vagaries of certain of the Julio-Claudians, and the abandonment of the "republican façade" which was the key to his initial acceptance by the Senate, if not the people. Not only the passage of time without a change in the dynasty, but the calibre and success of most of its later representatives, assisted to propagate the belief that its founder must have been a great man. Visual reminders of his fame, mentioned earlier as winning renown in his own day, could still be seen under his successors; his names and honours were not erased, nor his buildings usurped as later the basilica of Maxentius was usurped by Constantine.

Despite some differences in policy between Hadrian and his predecessor it was generally in Hadrian's interest to conserve, indeed to promote, the reputation of his adoptive father. The first coinage issues of the reign[32] heavily emphasise the adoption by Trajan; then duly comes the consecration of the deceased emperor, and *Divus Traianus* is amply displayed for some time, even the legend *TRI-UMPHVS PARTHICVS* appearing in this connection,[33] somewhat unexpectedly in view of Hadrian's change of policy in the East (but confirming my observation on Trajan's glory above). Throughout the first seven years of his reign Hadrian continues to be entitled *Traianus*; by 125 begins the

HADRIANUS AUG COS III series and Trajan is no more in evidence; but by that time the regime is solidly established and the motive of asserting the respectability of Hadrian's claim to the throne no longer operated. (One is reminded of Augustus' early emphasis on *Divus Julius*; in that case however a more positive motive for dropping the theme can be shown to have existed).

But possibly an even more important factor was the Senate, which amidst increasing autocracy was still honoured in appearances and continued to maintain a certain influence over climates of opinion and a considerable influence on literature.[34] The detailed examination of the reasons for the acceptance by the Senate would take long, and many of its aspects have been much discussed; the general conclusion is that (if we have not been deceived by Trajan's propaganda!) the Senate and the Emperor do appear to have arrived at a *modus vivendi* more satisfactory and more equable than previously. Caution is necessary however, for this view partly rests on a negative, the absence of contemporary or near-contemporary evidence to the contrary, while by contrast there seems to be convincing evidence for the bad relations which had prevailed between the Senate and Tiberius, Nero, and Domitian. Again in the period immediately following the death of Trajan, two alleged conspiracies and the liquidation of the Four Consulars undoubtedly produced an atmosphere in sections of the Senate of hostility to Hadrian or at least distrust of a potential "tyrant"; no such untoward events marred the internal tranquility of Trajan's rule.[35] It is vain to place much reliance on the Senate's offers of titles, which indeed might be interpreted not as goodwill but as the reverse — they flattered because they feared. Yet there were reasons why the senators should be reasonably content, or appear to be so; in the first place, it was they who had engineered the assassination of Domitian, with a candidate of their own ready to replace him. Within a short time however it became clear that an Emperor's reliance on the support of the Senate was nothing but a bad joke, unless the favour of the army could be won as well. Hence the Senate had no alternative but to welcome the adoption of Trajan, with its "constitutional" form and its dynamic reality; if any of the august body were indeed apprehensive about the possibility of a more openly military government, they were not in a position to protest; instead they joined in the chorus of praise led (for us) by Pliny. Secondly, there was no deterioration in their actual position, as an institution; no deliberate snubs, rather some attempt to disguise the hard facts of autocracy instead of advertising them.[36] The campaigns of Trajan may have brought distinction and financial profit to some senatorial individuals who would not have obtained them under a more pacific emperor; military glory had as much appeal for them as for other sections of the community. The general attitude of senators to the service of the emperor was particularly cooperative at most times, and more so at this juncture since the slogans of the "Stoic opposition" had been largely silenced by the change of dynasty. Nerva and Trajan went out of their way to emphasis "libertas" for the Senate.[37] In so far as his orations are relevant to the situation at all, Dio of Prusa seems to represent the senatorial "programme" rather than that of the Emperor; however little congruence with the actual policies and administration of Trajan's government eventuated, it would be difficult – and unwise – to start complaining again so soon. Lastly, the Senate consisted almost entirely of individuals who held or had held, or more importantly were looking forward to holding, offices of profit under the Princeps; they seem to have realised which side their bread was buttered on, and abandoned the endeavour to put the political clock back in conformity with an obsolete ideology – a change which offended neither expediency nor honour.

For these reasons, and possibly also because of a genuine admiration for Trajan – there is certainly no evidence of unprepossessing traits – the Trajanic Senate adopted an attitude of enthusiastic support for the Princeps. My insistence, above, on the universality of laudable imperial qualities in favourable sources, is not meant to deny that Trajan possessed some, or even many, of these virtues. But it is clear that both his immediate reputation was advantaged by the contrast with his predecessor Domitian, who was unable to suffer gladly fools, knaves and flatterers, and his subsequent renown by comparison with his successor Hadrian, who like Domitian was a mite too intellectual — always a cause for resentment in political circles — and became through ill-health very difficult in personal dealings towards the end of his reign, even if we discount the irresponsible cruelty depicted by the Historia Augusta. Thus the memory of Trajan was regarded as light between two pools of darkness, and this is at least in part the explanation of the perpetuation of his fame as the ideal Emperor.

The first part of this paper was devoted to showing that to their supporters or flatterers, all emperors are alike; the survival of almost none but wholly favourable sources[38] was exceptional in the case of Trajan, and this together with the particular external reasons shown to operate in the last section, accounts for the somewhat exaggerated notion of Trajan as uniquely virtuous.

The University of Tasmania   *K. H. Waters*

NOTES

1. E. T. Salmon, *A History of the Roman World 30 BC to AD 138*, 6, London, 1968, p. 294. I owe a great deal to Professor Salmon for his encouragement and criticism of my early studies in the history of this period.

2. K. H. Waters, "The Character of Domitian," *Phoenix* 18, 1964, pp. 49 ff. and other discussions there referred to.

3. F. A. Lepper, *Trajan's Parthian War*, Oxford, 1948, pt. III.

4. Some, e.g. Dacian wars, dictated by the situation, others, e.g. the alimenta, a legacy from a predecessor.

5. M. Durry, *Pline le Jeune: Panegyrique de Trajan*, 1938. R. Syme, *JRS* 28, 1938, p. 223; id. *Tacitus* 1958, pp. 94 ff.; D. Kienast, Nerva und das Kaisertums Trajans. *Historia* 17, 1968, pp. 54 ff.

6. E.g. R. Syme, *Tacitus*, Oxford, 1958, pp. 495 ff. F. Taeger, *Charisma*, II, 1960, p. 370 suggests that the "break" between princeps and historian came about through the increasing emphasis on the divinity of the Emperor.

7. F. Taeger, *Charisma* II, pp. 364-65: he discounts Dio even as evidence for the charismatic aspects of the Imperial institution, as Dio, like his predecessors, is defining a βασιλεύς- and the equation would still have been unacceptable.

8. The question is sensibly discussed by A. N. Sherwin White, *The Letters of Pliny*, Oxford, 1966, pp. 536-46. See also F. Millar, "Emperors at Work," *JRS* 57, 1967, p. 9.

9. Pliny's list includes the following which have obvious equivalents in Dio; abstinentia, benignitas, comitas, clementia, continentia (ἔλαττον βουλόμενος τρυφᾶν) fortitudo frugalitas humanitas (εὔνους τοῖς ὑπηκόοις) iustitia labor moderatio pacificus pietas patientia (πρᾶος) reverentia legum sapientia verecundia; of the score or so of other (or complementary) qualities not a few are implied, without being expressly stated in a single word or phrase. Perhaps it is significant that *no* quality listed by Dio fails to appear in the Panegyric. Cf. the indices in Taeger, *Charisma*, v. 2, 1960, pp. 711-15.

10. von Arnim. *Leben und Werke des Dio von Prusa*, 1898. F. A. Lepper, *Trajan's Parthian War*, pp. 194 ff.

11. Obviously the parallel Alexander/Trajan must suggest itself to Dio's public once the Eastern campaigns were under way; earlier perhaps if Trajan's aspirations (or alleged aspirations!) were suspected.

12. V. Valkenberg, "La theorie monarchique de Dion Chrysostome," *REG* 40, 1927, pp. 142-64; E. R. Goodenough, "The Political Philosophy of Hellenistic Kingship," *YCS* 1, 1928, p. 55. F. A. Lepper, *Trajan's Parthian War*, p. 203, characterises the Dio orations as "an appropriate restatement of the doctrine of the good king." I would hesitate to use the word "appropriate."

13. Plin. *Epp.* 6.15.1.

14. G. Bowersock, *Greek Sophists in the Roman Empire*, 1969.

15. Plin. *Pan.* 88.7 "Omnibus imperatoribus et Caesaribus et Augustus melior" and cf. the epigraphic tag "super omnes retro principes," *vel sim.* and see further below.

16. One must expect such "progress" in these matters, though it seems remarkable that such a phrase is applied to a Christian monarch. However the 4th century Panegyrists, perhaps because writing for state occasions of Roman origin and associated with the traditional gods of the state, studiously avoid all notice of Christianity and the Christian god.

17. One ancient writer alleged that Trajan was "senex" when he came to power! See Syme's comment, *Tacitus*, Oxford, 1958, p. 36, on *SHA Tac*, 5.1.

18. For this see in general Mattingly and Sydenham *RIC*, and for the Trajanic period esp. P. L. Strack, *Untersuchungen zur römischen Reichsprägung des zweiten Jahrhunderts* I, 1931. M. P. Charlesworth, "The Virtues of a Roman Emperor; Propaganda and the Creation of Belief," *Proc. of the Brit. Acad.* 23, 1937, p. 105.

19. It is to be observed that *all* successful commanders in Roman history have to "restore discipline" — so much for the vaunted discipline of the legions! It is even more essential when they take over an army in the East, which (according to another pseudo-philosophic commonplace) must have become demoralised by Oriental luxury. Hannibal's army never recovered from a winter's dissipation at Capua; Sulla's troops were demoralised by the drink, women, statuary and pictures available in the East (Sall. *Cat.* 11.5) Lucius Verus had the same problem at Antioch, Fronto *Princ. Hist.* 19 (Haines II 148). Aurelian was disciplinae militaris corrector, Eutro. 8.14.

20. On Trajan's non-intellectualism see K. H. Waters, "Juvenal and the Reign of Trajan," *Antichthon* 4, 1970, pp. 73 ff.

21. Eutropius 8.5.3. According to R. Syme, a statement rather than a prayer (*Tacitus* 1958, p. 36, n. 5).

22. The *Historia Augusta* has a more elaborate list, at *Trig Tyr* 6.4; Victorino, qui Gallias post Postumum rexit, neminem aestimo praeferendum (sic!), non in virtute Traianum, non Antoninum in clementia, non in gravitate Nervam, non in gubernando aerario Vespasianum, non in censura totius vitae ac severitate militari Pertinacem vel Severum. The effect of this extraordinary hyperbole is immediately destroyed by the following sentence: sed omnia haec libido et cupiditas mulierariae voluptatis sic perdidit. . . .!

23. See on this aspect K. H. Waters, "The Character of Domitian," *Phoenix* 18, 1964, p. 49.

24. Both totally dissimilar to each other and to Commodus — but the very type of a "Bad Emperor"!

25. Pius receives an eulogy from Eutropius also, at 8.8.1. As Trajan to Romulus, so Pius should be compared to Numa; possessing many of the desirable qualities, despite his "moderata gloria" in military matters, he was "terribilis" as well "venerabilis" to client kings; his cognomen was due to his "clementia" and altogether he fits into the Dio of Prusa pattern.

26. He instances the case of Parthamisiris, which Pliny tries to gloss over, *Pan.* 16. Arrian ap. *Suda* s.v. γνῶσις says it was Trajan's own

decision to execute Parthamisiris.

27. *Pr. Hist.* 17. (Haines II 216) "ad populum acceptior."

28. Cf. Juvenal's notorious phrase, *panem et circenses* (10.81), where the community is blamed for confining its interests to these matters.

29. Reported by Lydus *de Mens.* 3.13 (= Parth. 6). Centuries later Malalas referred to him as Θειότατος βασιλεύς.

30. Tac. *Ann.* IV.32. trs. Dudley (in part). Many other passages reveal such a view, for example Tacitus' implication that Agricola ought to have been allowed to complete the conquest of Britain, *Agr.* 39, 40, and many references to *longa pax* as detrimental: cf. Juv. 6.92 "nunc patimur longae pacis mala." Eutropius 8.8.2 bears the same implication: Romani imperii quod post Augustum defensum magis fuerat quam nobiliter ampliatum. . .

31. F. A. Lepper, *Trajan's Parthian War*, 1948, Pt. III. R. Syme, *Tacitus*, 1958, pp. 217 ff., pp. 226 ff.

32. Mattingly and Sydenham, *RIC* II, pp. 341 ff. P. L. Strack, *Untersuchungen*, II, 1937, p. 41.

33. At a somewhat later date appears a reference to DIVI PARENTES, Mattingly and Sydenham, *RIC* II, p. 367, nos. 232 A & B.

34. The senatorial attitude is notoriously strong in Cassius Dio and even in the *Historia Augusta*.

35. The "conspiracies" which occurred in most reigns, even in the brief tenure of the beloved Titus, were not totally lacking under Trajan. One or two banishments are mentioned e.g. Calpurnius Crassus Dio Cass. 78, 3 and 16, and Laberius Maximus *SHA Hadr.* 5.5.

36. I regard this as one of the main differences between the autocracy of Trajan and the autocracy of Domitian; see "Traianus Domitiani Continuator" *AJP* 90, 1969, pp. 385-405.

37. See e.g. Ch. Wirzubski, *Libertas as a Political Idea at Rome*, Cambridge, 1960, pp. 167 ff.

38. Fronto's criticisms, discussed above, are fairly mild; Julian's rather frivolous "Caesares" need hardly be taken into account.

O Patrona Virgo

Do not be fooled, my dear Togo, into believing that what editors serve up as Catullus's first poem accurately reproduces what he wrote or meant. I make no fuss about the first line, though Friedrich was quite right to insist that the spelling *lepidum nou*om *libellum* avoids a dull homoeoptoton, as the poet avoided another at 46.11 *diuersae uarie uiae*; nor shall I quibble about the second line, though the reckless alteration of the manuscript tradition (*arido*), corroborated as it is by several independent witnesses and the testimony of the poet's arch-imitator Martial (8.72.2), and all to suit an unfocused fiat of the wayward Servius, is enough to try any man's patience. What I should like to establish here is the text of the penultimate line: it is, I contend, the key to the whole poem.

As it stands in the manuscripts, it has lost a syllable. Though scholars and editors are almost unanimously agreed about the way to repair the loss. I hold that they are wrong and that, properly restored, Catullus's poem will become invested with an interest and significance which at the moment it lacks. This lack of significance prompted a paper by Frank Copley over twenty years ago, in which he spoke of the poem as pleasant but pointless (*TAPA* 82, 1951, pp. 200-206), though neither his discussion nor subsequent ones by Elder (*HSCP* 71, 1966, pp. 243-49) and Levine (*CSCA* 2,

1969, pp. 209-16) have succeeded in allaying uneasiness; and as a new example of the search for meaning one may cite an article by Francis Cairns (*Mnem.* 22, 1969, pp. 153-58) viewing the *Chronica* of Cornelius Nepos as a manifesto of neoteric Alexandrianism. In the standard editions the poem presents the pretty new book to Cornelius and prays, on woefully inadequate grounds, for immortality. This is exceedingly flat: Catullus so often closes his lyrics with some forceful point that we should have expected, especially in the first one, a smart and elegant conclusion. When the true text is recovered, I think we shall find some wit in his poem, and in this paper I shall tell you what it was. First, however, I must tell you what it was not.

The hendecasyllable line *qualecumque; quod, o patrona uirgo* contains three unparalleled features. The first is the heavy stop after the fourth syllable. This never recurs in Catullus, and is never found in Martial at all. Although we find examples of sense-pauses |after the first, the second, the third, the fifth, and the sixth syllables, the juncture of the two short syllables cannot, it seems, be weakened by a heavy stop: we may have a word-break after the fourth syllable (usually followed by an iambic word), but not the end of a sentence.

Secondly, Catullus does not use the interjection *o* with an adjective and noun combination: he says O *Colonia* but not O *miser Catulle*. I have argued the matter thoroughly in my paper on Catullus 3.16 (*Phoenix* 23, 1969, pp. 186-203) and will not repeat myself here. However, I should like to take this opportunity of correcting what I said there and in my earlier article (*Phoenix* 12, 1958, pp. 93-116) about Catullus 99.8: Mr. A. G. Lee (in Quinn's edition, page 438) now merits our congratulations for his discovery of the true reading *abstersti mollibus articulis* ("wiped with dainty fingers," cf. Quint. 11.1.70 *molli articulo* "with a dainty touch") and I a dunce's cap for my preposterous explanation of the reading of X: rather, the syncopated form *abstersti* in V prompted some annotator to add *si* above the termination, signifying *abster-si-sti*, and the scribe of X, interpreting this as

an amendment, copied out *abstersi*. But a rigorous refutation
of *o* is in any case unnecessary: in Catullus 1.9 the *o* printed
in our editions is not to be found in the manuscripts: it is a
renaissance supplement, and, since unparalleled, it is clearly
wrong. Now there is another renaissance supplement which
seems clearly right, since it removes at a stroke the two
oddities I mentioned earlier, besides reinstating the metre:
instead of *quod* read *quidem*. The alteration is really no
alteration at all, for the letters *qd* written with a suspension
sign over them signified in the middle ages *quidem*, whereas,
if the suspension were misread as applying only to the letter
d, the abbreviation would be misinterpreted as *quod*. This is
precisely what must have happened here, as it happened
elsewhere: as Madvig points out in the preface to his *De
Finibus* (page xxi), the scribe of the Erlangensis repeatedly
had trouble with the abbreviation for *quidem* and (to go no
farther than the first book) erroneously copied it as *quod* at
1.4.16; 1.16.53; 1.17.56; and 1.19.64.

This brings us to the third and crucial matter, the words
patrona uirgo. They can be construed only as a vocative,
which is very strange, because in Catullus – indeed, in most
Latin poets – vocatives normally have some formal connection with the sentence, whether it is a pronoun *tu* or *uos*, a
pronominal adjective *tuus* or *uester*, or a verb in the second
person. It is true that exceptions occur, though none where
the poem has a special addressee (in such poems a second
apostrophe to the addressee often occurs at the end, cf. 6, 8,
13, 23, 31, 36), and very few of these exceptions cannot be
explained: in 50.1 *Hesterno, Licini, die otiosi/ multum
lusimus* the vocative is explained by the implicit subject of
the verb, namely *ego et tu*, just as in 58.1 *Caeli, Lesbia nostra*
the adjective is equivalent to *mea et tua* and so provides the
vocative with a referend.

But in Catullus 1.9 the vocative *patrona uirgo* has no
referend at all, and further consideration will cast the gravest
doubts on the validity of the reading. Only with difficulty
can one find an example of *patronus* or *patrona* used side by
side with another noun. Sooner or later one comes to Martial

7.72.14, where occurs the phrase *uocem patronam*. However, this means "patron's voice," from which it follows that *patrona uirgo* should mean "patron's maiden." Grant for the sake of argument that *patrona uirgo* means "patron maiden": who is she? Surely not, as Scaliger and Baehrens will have it, Minerva, the presiding goddess of libraries: that deity was unknown to Catullus. The annotator of the Oxoniensis, founding the common opinion, identifies the lady as the Muse. But nowhere is the Muse ever referred to as "patron."

In this dilemma we should enquire what is the practice of the poet himself. How does he regard the Muse or Muses? The answer is unambiguous: in his lyrics and epigrams there is no muse at all; here the poet lives in the real, everyday world, and the composition of verses is no priestly craft, but an activity practised *in meis tabellis* and *per iocum atque uinum*, and the beings responsible for poems are not Muses, but men, poets like Cornificius or poetasters like Suffenus. It is only in the elevated style of the long poems that we encounter Catullus's Muses, and there they invariably constitute a plurality.

There is yet another nail to be hammered into the coffin of the *patrona uirgo*: although Catullus uses the word *uirgo* and its adjective *uirgineus* and its derivative *uirginitas* on more than a score of occasions, he does so only in the long poems, numbers 61, 62, 64, 65, 66, 67, and 68. This is not coincidence; it is not by chance that all these occurrences should form such a cluster in these seven poems: it means that the poet deliberately eschewed the word *uirgo* "maiden" in his lyrics, presumably because he wanted to talk about girls, *puellae* (Virgil's usage, we see, is the exact opposite).

Consequently I hold that the words *patrona uirgo* are corrupt, and will merely sketch the further objections that, having thoroughly disparaged his poems, Catullus was hardly likely to beg the Muse to immortalize them, and that we need a conjunction or some other motivation for the stark and isolated subjunctive in the last verse.

In introducing the correct reading in line 9, let me summarize and elucidate the first part of the poem. "To whom do I give my pretty new book? Cornelius, to you, for you thought well of my trifles when you wrote your *Chronica.*" But good heavens, what is this in Quinn's commentary? Cornelius Nepos has *not* completed his work, for *solebas . . . putare* ("you are always saying") is an epistolary imperfect and *iam tum cum ausus es . . . explicare* means that the historian has "only this very moment had the courage to tackle"! Let us not deride, but let us not pass, this painful exegesis. Not only do epistolary imperfects exclude the second person (i.e., actions of the recipient of a letter), not only does *iam tum* mean "already then" and *explicare* "to complete," but it stands to reason that, if Nepos's history consisted of three books, then the history must have been a finished production. Now we know little of the *Chronica* of Nepos beyond what we may infer from this poem, but we know more than the editors of Catullus choose to tell us. This Universal History contained the dates of the Greek poets (Gellius, *Noct. Att.* 17.21, gives references for Homer, Hesiod, and Archilochus), and in view of the biographer's penchant for comparing Romans with Greeks (Momigliano, *Development of Greek Biography* 97f) he must have included Roman poets, too. As Theodor Bergk saw, Catullus must have received an honourable mention in the *Chronica*: in this poem he returns the compliment ("*Nepos hatte in seiner chronik unter den römischen dichtern auch des Catull ehrenvoll gedacht, zum dank dafür stellt Catull seine poesien unter den schutz des Nepos*" *Phil.* 12, 1857, p. 581). "Wherefore," says the poet in line 8, "accept whatever this little book amounts to," – the language here is marked by legal terms – then, as Bergk splendidly conjectured, the poet concluded with a purpose clause (as in poems 5 and 7 and others) "so that, on account of its patron," *patroni ut ergo*, "it may last for centuries."

The palaeographical probability of the emendation is high. Munro (*Criticisms and Elucidations of Catullus*, Cambridge, 1878, pp. 1ff) points out that the genitive singular *patroni* would have been spelled at an early stage of the tradition *patronEI* and that twice elsewhere in Catullus (7.9;

65.14) confusion between final *ei* and *a* has caused corruption in our manuscripts: it is not unfair to say that the conjecture *patroni* for *patrona* is scarcely any change at all. As for *ut ergo* being corrupted to *uirgo* (not a large change), that is likely to have been a deliberate alteration consequent upon the misreading of *patroni* as *patrona*. Eduard Fraenkel (*Gnomon* 34, 1962, p. 259) regarded the conjecture as *abscheulich*, seemingly because of the elision, but this is sufficiently supported by 45.8 *sinistra ut ante* (which also illustrates the postponement of the conjunction). Munro very reasonably sees in certain passages of Martial the influence of the *patroni ut ergo* tradition of Catullus. In 1.113 the survival of Martial's epigrams is at the end of the poem imputed to Valerianus (not the Muse), *per quem perire non licet meis nugis*; in 3.2, transparently modelled on Catullus 1, the *libellus* is told to secure the patronage of Faustinus (not the Muse) — *illo uindice nec Probum timeto*; and finally in the prose dedication of Book 8, Domitian (not the Muse) is credited with giving life to his *libelli*, and *propter hoc legentur* (here *propter* echoes *ergo*). I must not omit to notice that the conjecture or "something like it" is accepted by David Singleton in the most recent expression of opinion (*CP* 67, 1972, pp. 192-96).

Actually, Bergk inserted an *est* after *quidem*. This, as we shall see later, is wrong. For now be it observed that an *est*, whether after *quidquid* or after *qualecumque*, is not obligatory: Virg. *Aen.* 1.78 *quodcumque hoc regni* adequately sanctions the omission of the copula after *quidquid hoc libelli*, as does Prop. 3.21.16 *qualiscumque . . . uale* after *qualecumque*. Thus we have

> *quare habe tibi quidquid hoc libelli*
> *qualecumque quidem . . .*

But here is something amiss. "Accept whatever this little book amounts to, whatever indeed its quality." How clumsy! The addition of "whatever . . . quality" adds little, if anything, to the "whatever . . . amounts to" clause, and *quidem* seems devoid of point. Fordyce tells us that

"*qualecumque* intensifies the disparaging effect of *quidquid*."
It is hard to see how: *quidquid hoc libelli* is absolute. If
quidquid and *qualecumque* are to be taken in conjunction in
Catullus, we must construe them on the pattern of Tac. *Ann.*
14.55 *quidquid illud et qualecumque tribuisset* "his gifts,
whatever their size or kind" and Plin. *Ep.* 8.22.4 *quisquis ille
qualiscumque sileatur* "his name, his character, had better be
suppressed." This will give us for Catullus: "Accept this little
book however small in size, indeed however slight in kind."
This may sound passable in English, but *hoc libelli* "this little
book" (cf. Lucr. 2.16, Virg. *Aen.* 1.78) makes discrimination
of quantity and quality most inelegant here; and whereas the
Plinian passage might seem to excuse the omission of a
conjunction, the presence of *quidem* in the second half
accentuates the difficulty. A correct analysis of the Latin is
specially desirable, and I should like to thank Professor J. B.
Solodow of Columbia University for much help with the
elucidation of *quidem* which follows.

Attached to the second member of a pair, the particle
directs attention to that member, emphasizing it either as an
extension of the first or as a contrast to it. In the former case
quidem is usually, though not always, preceded by a
conjunction and means "what is more," e.g., Cic. *Att.* 2.19.1
doleo ac mirifice quidem "I am hurt and, what is more,
deeply hurt"; Plin. *Ep.* 3.5.17 *commentarios centum sexagin-
ta mihi reliquit, opisthographos quidem et minutissime
scriptos* "he left me 160 notebooks, and, what is more,
written on both sides in a minute hand." In the latter case
quidem means "on the other hand," e.g., Quint. 10.1.93
*elegia quoque Graecos prouocamus ... satira quidem tota
nostra est.* Adversative *quidem* being out of the question, the
Catullus passage will have to be construed "Accept this little
book, of whatever quantity it be, and, what is more, of
whatever quality." Such an unnatural insistence on quality
over quantity leads me to look for a quite different
interpretation of *quidem*, which I find in Munro's proposal to
divorce the words *qualecumque quidem* from the preceding
verse (all we like sheep have been staring at Orion transported

next to Aquarius) and construe them with the *ut*-clause, i.e., *quare habe tibi quidquid hoc libelli, ut, qualecumque quidem, patroni ergo* . . . "Accept this little book, so that, whatever indeed its quality, it may on account of its patron live for centuries." This gives not merely satisfactory, but perfect sense. *Quidem*, now placed with the first of a contrasting pair, acquires its common concessive force, like the Greek μέν, e.g., Cic. *Tusc.Disp.* 3.35 *tarda illa quidem medicina, sed tamen magna* "though slow, yet effective"; Mart. 1.108.2 *pulchra quidem, uerum transtiberina domus* "though fine, yet across the Tiber," and without an answering *sed, uerum, at,* etc., Livy 2.64.4 *consul . . . ipsum quidem agmen adipisci aequis locis non potuit; populationem adeo effuse fecit* "though unable to catch the column, laid waste the country"; *id.* 9.11.9 *ut quidem tu . . . habeas, ego . . . non habeam* "that whilst you should have, but I not." Thus the antithesis of Catullus 1.9 is "so that my book, though slight, yet because of its patron . . ."

The postponement of *ut* occurs some thirty times in Catullus, but in almost every instance the displacement is by a single word, and the exceptions are trifling: 61.149 *tibi domus* ut; 76.23 *contra me* ut; and 78.4 *cum puero* ut. Nevertheless, in old and legal Latin — such as Catullus seems to be affecting here — postponed *ut* is not unusual, e.g., *CIL* I 2.581, 23 (*Remains of Old Latin*, IV, p. 254 Warmington) *senatuosque sententiam* utei *scientes esetis*; *CIL* I 2.587, 77 (*ROL* IV, p. 310 Warm.) *quei, ante hanc legem rogatam* utei *legerentur, instituti sunt*; also, significantly perhaps, in contexts of entreaty, Plaut. *Rud.* 257f *quisquis est deus, ueneror ut . . . eximat,/ miseras inopis aerumnosas* ut *aliquo auxilio adiuuet*; Cic. *Mil.* 2.6 *obsecrabo obtestaborque uos, iudices, si cetera amisimus, hoc saltem nobis* ut *relinquatur, ab inimicorum audacia telisque uitam* ut *impune liceat defendere*; and Livy 30.12.12 (speech of Sophoniba) *omnia quidem* ut *possis in nobis, di dederunt*. Munro does not fail to cite the most striking parallel, one which may very well have been influenced by Catullus, a hendecasyllable in fact containing a postponed *ut* after an indefinite *qualiscumque*,

Mart. 5.60.3 ff:

> certum est hanc tibi pernegare famam,
> olim quam petis, in meis libellis
> *qualiscumque* legaris *ut* per orbem.

We can now translate the poem. We learn that Catullus is dedicating his slight book of verse to Cornelius Nepos so that it may secure as a result of the historian's authority the immortality it would hardly have merited on its own account. This constitutes an elegant and amusing reversal of the normal relationship in which artists undertake to perpetuate the memory of the patrons who support them.

Let us look a little more carefully at *ergo*, mistranslated by Simpson and Fordyce in the notes to their respective editions as "for the sake of" (correctly, however, Singleton, *op.cit.* 194): the word properly means "in consequence of," "as a result of," as we may see from its significance as an adverb "in consequence," "as a result." By classical times adverbial *ergo* had almost entirely extinguished postpositional *ergo*; only a few occurrences are found, of which practically all are remembrances of legal language. Thus we find postpositional *ergo* in Cicero — but in citing law (*Att.* 3.23.2; *Leg.* 2.23; *Opt.Gen.* 7.19), in Nepos — but quoting an inscription (*Paus.* 1.3), and in Livy — but drawing upon public documents (25.7.4; 40.52.6; 41.28.9); and several inscriptions, some bilingual, dating from the late eighties, attest the commonness of *ergo* (ἕνεκεν) in its significance as "in consequence of" (*CIL* I 2.727, 728, 730, 743, cf. *ROL* IV 138-142 Warm.). Once or twice, however, the word occurs in classical poetry (usually at the end of a verse), e.g., Virg. *Aen.* 6.670f *illius ergo uenimus* "because of him have we come."

But does Catullus really mean what he says? That Nepos will bring Catullus the lasting fame he could not win for himself? Oh, no! The poem is ironical. This we know — as indeed Nepos knew, *et quantum est hominum uenustiorum* — because of Catullus's patently feigned awe at the historian's *tribus . . . chartis, doctis, Iuppiter, et laboriosis* and because of the no less obviously simulated self-depreciation of *quidquid hoc libelli* and *qualecumque quidem*. And the unnaturally solemn language of the conclusion instructs us that we are not to take the poet seriously. Indeed, since the word *ergo* "in consequence of" *is* sometimes used in contexts where its meaning approximates to "for the sake of" looking forward to the future (as at Lucr. 5.1246), I have been visited with the reflection that Catullus might have used the postposition ambiguously, hinting that Nepos was *not* conferring immortality on Catullus, but rather the reverse. However, Niall Rudd (as I write this *collega tertium*) has persuaded me that such a *double entendre* ruins the lucidity of the poem; besides, the irony already detected suggests that the normal relationship of poet and patron exists after all. The tone of the poem is simply one of playful irony, much as if we should paraphrase the poem: "Cornelius, to you I dedicate the book as a token of gratitude, I being *tanto pessimus omnium poeta quanto tu optimus omnium patronus.*"

Much whimsical cerebration has been provoked by the forty-ninth poem. Schwabe deeming it a poetic return for Cicero's defence of Caelius, Westphal an expression of gratitude for the introduction to Clodia, and Kroll a thank-you note for a copy of the *In Vatinium* clash in violent disharmony like the members of a mutinous orchestra. Why on earth should the author omit all reference to the benefit received? And what is the point of his confession of lyric inadequacy, which we are asked to believe is as irrelevant as a love-story in a proposition of Euclid? What has Catullus's stature as a poet to do with the *Pro Caelio*, or admission to Clodia's salon, or Cicero's invective against Vatinius? Nothing. And the explanation must lie elsewhere. That the word *poeta* is the clue to the occasion of the poem has been realized by D. F. S. Thomson, who believes that "Cicero has written a poem" (*CW* 60, 1967, p. 227), and by McKay and Shepherd, who speculate that "the poem may be suggesting that as a poet Cicero is a very good lawyer" (*Roman Lyric Poetry*, London, 1969, p. 227). Yet this is no light, nor even darkness visible: in poem 49 Cicero receives not criticism, but thanks; and the person cast in the role of poet is not Cicero, but Catullus. For light we must go to Friedrich's commentary, though actually the matter is ludicrously simple. When a man who represents himself as a poet sends thanks to someone he describes as the most eloquent of patrons, we are told all we need to know: Marcus Tullius has paid some compliment to Catullus's poetry, and this was the poet's acknowledgement. Lacking the bearings for precise navigation, we should not try to land on the head of a pin. We cannot know, and perhaps we are not meant to know, Cicero's exact words of commendation: reality is the great spoiler of art and can never match the infinite demands of the imagination. We must also recognize that, whilst *gratias tibi maximas Catullus/ agit* sends thanks, it does not make up a poem: ornament is necessary. Catullus therefore has decided to thank Cicero with a friendly jest; he has drawn, as it were, a cartoon: himself absurdly small, his admirer absurdly large. The humour of the situation vanishes unless the thanks are real. Thus we may confidently reject the view that Cicero's was no compliment, but a harsh criticism, and Catullus's no thanks, but a stinging retort: if composed as vituperation, the poem hardly packs the punch one would have expected from the author of *Nil nimium studeo*, whereas it is quite effective as friendly banter like *Risi nescioquem*.

As with Cicero, so with Cornelius Nepos. We are not to infer that Catullus despised his friend's writings, but that he considered them as attesting more the author's hard work and learning than his artistic talent and originality. The irony of his dedication poem, like that of his thanks to Cicero, is transparent, and yet it is difficult not to feel in either case that the verses, which hit the mark so effectively, carry more affection than sting. Certainly in his Life of Atticus (12) Nepos was to confer on his protégé the highest tribute in his power. And certainly, my dear Togo, the poet's wit has raised a smile on the face of destiny, for in a lasting irony the *tres chartae* of the *Chronica* have perished and are now remembered among men chiefly because of the dedication poem of Gaius Valerius Catullus.

> quare habe tibi quidquid hoc libelli,
> qualecumque quidem patroni ut ergo
> plus uno maneat perenne saeclo.

> Wherefore, for better or for worse,
> Accept this little book of verse,
> That, though so slight, with patron's name
> It yet may win undying fame.

University of London   *G. P. Goold*

The Ethnography of the Celts and of the Algonkian-Iroquoian Tribes: A Comparison of Two Historical Traditions[1]

In 1953 excavations at Vix, on the Seine, just over 100 miles south-east of Paris, revealed a spectacular burial: a tumulus containing the remains of a bronze-fitted wagon and other rich grave-goods that included a superb Greek bronze crater, or mixing-bowl for wine, standing nearly 5 1/2 feet high, the finest yet known anywhere.[2] The ornaments and jewellery included a gold diadem or necklace, and among other vases and cups was one from Athens datable to around 520 B.C. This cemetery at Vix served the hill-fort on Mont Lassois, which lies just at the point where the Seine ceases to be navigable. Goods coming upriver from the Channel must be portaged from here across to the upper Saône, whence they can travel southwards down the Saône and the Rhône to the Mediterranean coast, and more particularly to Marseilles, founded by Greeks around 600 B.C., though finds show that Greeks had traded with the area around the mouth of the Rhône from a century earlier, even if they had not yet settled there.[3]

The Vix tomb appears to be that of a woman (romantic archaeologists usually call her a princess) of around the end of the sixth century B.C., whose people had grown rich as middlemen commanding the vital portage between Seine and Saône. Archaeology reveals an intense concentration of imported luxuries in this area at this period, some acquired in trade, others, no doubt, through "the interchange of rich gifts between civilized authorities and barbarian potentates to obtain concessions and of course (as in the *keimelion* of the early Greek world) the interchange of presents between the Celtic rulers themselves."[4] The importance of the Rhône-Saône-Seine route lay in the fact that it was one of the tin-routes to Britain, and, as such, particularly important to the Greeks, since by 600 the alternative route through the Straits of Gibraltar and up through the Bay of Biscay had come altogether under Phoenician control. The route maintained its importance throughout antiquity,[5] as it still does today. So too the St. Lawrence; the basic geographic factors of history do not change.

For the Greeks and for the natives alike, the foundation of Marseilles around 600 B.C. was the crucial event, "an important landmark," as Boardman calls it.[6] The archaeologist traces its influence, not only in imported Greek manufactured goods, but in the changes it wrought in native styles, for instance in pottery and belt-fastenings. The best indication of the extent of Massaliote trade is the distribution of the typical micaceous Massaliote wine amphorae.[7] We see how trade up the Rhône went not only northwards, but northeastwards as well, via Geneva and on to the Upper Danube, following prehistoric routes which the Roman armies were to use in their conquests some six centuries later. Massaliote amphorae, Greek bronzes and Greek pottery are also known in considerable concentration in this area, and here too, overlooking the Upper Danube, is another fortress, the Heuneburg, with ramparts in Greek style and technique:[8] is this a form of "technical aid to underdeveloped countries"? More striking still, in a sense, is the presence in a grave near the Heuneburg of scraps of clothing embroidered with Chinese silk, a reminder of the vast ramifications of the trade networks of the period.[9] The silk will of course have passed from hand to hand in barter; so too the Greek bronze cauldron of this period found near Stockholm in the far north, of the same pattern as one found at Ste. Colombe only a couple of miles from Vix.[10] The Stockholm cauldron suggests, however, how highly valued such Greek imports were by the natives. And what start as luxury imports end as necessities; nor should we undervalue the role of alcohol, in barbarian Europe as among the Indians. "If you indulge their intemperance by supplying as much as they crave, they will be conquered as easily by their vices as by arms" — it is Tacitus on the Germans,[11] but it might have been a Jesuit on the Indians.

Perhaps the parallel between the Greeks in Gaul in the seventh and sixth centuries B.C., and the French in Canada in the sixteenth and seventeenth centuries of our era is becoming clear. Newcomers with a relatively high level of material culture settle on or near a great river which offers easy access to an interior inhabited by savages of whom they know little.[12] They trade, offering the luxuries of civilization and their help in the interminable intertribal warfare of the natives, in return for raw materials (tin or furs, as the case may be). They are in competition with other civilized powers (the Phoenicians and Etruscans, the Dutch and the English), who control other access-routes to the source of raw materials. And in both cases, though we must not push the analogy too far, the rivals were to triumph; we all know what happened in Canada, while in Europe, from about 500 B.C. onwards, the centre of barbarian wealth and power moves east and north, out of Burgundy and South Germany into the middle Rhine and Marne regions. Mont Lassois is abandoned, Marseilles rapidly declines in prosperity, and the new routes from the Mediterranean to the interior go through Etruscan territory over the Alps.[13]

The situations may be parallel, but for the historian, there is one enormous difference. Although the archaeological evidence from Europe is relatively abundant, contemporary accounts are totally lacking. For North America, the archaeological evidence is perhaps somewhat slighter; it is the relative abundance of contemporary documentation that makes the historian of pre- or protohistoric Europe jealous. What should we not give for the writings of a seventh century Jacques Cartier, a Massaliote Samuel de Champlain? The standard edition of *The Jesuit Relations and Allied Documents* alone runs to seventy-three volumes. What does our knowledge of Gaul and Germany amount to from written sources before Caesar? Six hundred years of Greek contacts have left a few fragments only: borrowings from a sixth century Greek sailing-manual in the *Ora Maritima* of Avienus some eight hundred years later, and from the fourth century account of Pytheas in Strabo; fragments, passing references, quotations in later writers from historians and geographers such as Hecataeus, Herodotus, Ephorus, Eratosthenes; the relevant parts of Polybius and Posidonius. It is a pathetic selection, and only slightly improved when we get information coming in from the accounts of Roman military operations in Gaul from the end of the second century onwards.

But if it is less copious than our evidence for, say, the Huron, it is evidence of the same kind: "Our ethnographic information does not come from the Huron, who were nonliterate, but from Europeans who visited Huronia . . . and wrote accounts of what they saw there. The historical anthropologist is at an obvious disadvantage because he is unable to observe first-hand the people he is studying. Nevertheless, when the written sources are abundant (and, we may add, even when they are not, if there is no alternative), he can treat them in much the same way that the ethnologist does his informants. Different statements can be cross-checked against one another and compared with what is known about the closely related Iroquois and Wyandot cultures at a later period. Finally, additional clues about Huron culture may be sought in the related fields of archaeology and linguistics."[14]

It is this precise combination of literary, archaeological and linguistic evidence that we rely on for European history and ethnography in the period we are discussing. Greek writers, such as Herodotus, give us the name "Celts"; archaeology reveals a material culture, named for Hallstatt, a site in Austria, which has its centre, its most prosperous area, perhaps its origin, in the areas where we find wagon-burials like the one at Vix.[15] Finally, by comparing archaeological evidence with that of place-names, and observing that the boundaries of the Hallstatt culture are also more or less those of the occurrence of place-names with the Celtic terminations -briga, -dunum and -magus, we conclude that the Hallstatt culture was apparently developed and disseminated by Celtic-speaking peoples.[16]

The Hallstatt culture develops into that which archaeologists know as the La Tène culture, and the situation becomes more complicated. From about 500 onwards there appears in the Rhineland a new and distinctive art style. New types of weapons are found, new customs introduced. Wagon-burials become chariot-burials. The La Tène peoples expand: Rome is sacked around 390, Delphi in the next century, the Celtic-speaking kingdom of Galatia is established in Asia Minor, Celtic mercenaries serve in Sicily and Egypt. The old Hallstatt hill-forts get bigger and more complex, until they are real towns. Indeed the archaeologist borrows Caesar's terminology and calls them *oppida*. The *oppida* Caesar knew in Gaul, like Bibracte (Mont Beuvray), Alesia (Alise Ste-Reine) or Avaricum (Bourges), have their counterparts throughout the La Tène culture area, in Switzerland, in the Black Forest, in Bavaria, Bohemia, Austria, as far east as the Sava valley in Yugoslavia, and as far north as the Babilonie in the Wiehengebirge, near Lübbecke. The material culture characteristic of these *oppida* is remarkably homogeneous, and it has been suggested that in the late La Tène period the *oppida* may be taken as representing the area of Celtic settlement, although there is some reason to doubt whether the inhabitants of the most northerly *oppida* between Main and Lippe and beyond were truly Celts in the strict linguistic sense; they may rather have adopted the Celtic language along with the La Tène culture. Further north still were the tribes of the North German plain, Jutland and the Baltic coasts, at a far more primitive stage of development.[17]

Thus far, once again, the archaeological evidence. But we have now reached a period where the documentary evidence becomes much fuller. Caesar's commentary on his Gallic Wars contains first-hand evidence on the state of Gaul in his day, and his account was to become for his successors a standard ethnological work — which is unfortunate, since Caesar was not an ethnologist, not even a disinterested traveller, but a soldier, and a politician with an axe to grind. Wishing to justify his decision to extend Roman control to the Rhine and no further, he defines the Rhine as the boundary between the Celts, whom the Romans call Gauls, and the Germans, who, he says, are something quite different, a more savage, nomadic group of tribes. And yet, as we have seen, archaeology knows nothing of the Rhine as a boundary between different cultures, until the Romans make it one by making it also a clearly defined and defended political frontier, within which Gaul is Romanized, and beyond which develop the "German" cultures of the first centuries of our era, whose archaeological antecedents lie, however, further north and further east, along the Elbe and in the Baltic region.

Earlier writers moreover, like modern archaeologists, know nothing of the Rhine as a frontier between Celts and Germans. These men, Greeks, whose knowledge derives from Greek sources, traders and the like, not from military expeditions, place Celts on both sides of the Rhine, and their name for what the Romans, following Caesar, were to call Germany, is *Keltiké*. This is so in Herodotus, in the fifth century B.C., and it is still so in Posidonius, just before Caesar's time; but the Greek Strabo a generation after Caesar has adopted the Latin "Germania," and uses *Keltiké* for Gaul only. What has shifted? The population? or the terminology? Probably the original Germans, "Germani" in Latin, were a group of Celtic or Celticized tribes, originally settled east of the Rhine, some of whom had crossed to the west bank, others who in Caesar's time were trying to do so, as they were pushed westwards by pressure of the non-Celtic migratory tribes, such as the Suebi, to whom Caesar from ignorance or for reasons of his own transfers their name, and who subsequently come to monopolise it, as if *they* were the real Germans.[18]

We find in North America evidence for this same pattern of migration, or else for a similar confusion of terminology.[19] When Jacques Cartier made his first contact with the Indians in 1534, he relates that they informed him that they called the St. Lawrence the Hochelaga, which was also the name of a powerful kingdom somewhere upstream. Below Hochelaga there lay the kingdom of Canada, with Stadacona its main centre. There was also a kingdom of Saguenay, on the river of that name. Cartier himself, exploring the river in subsequent years, adds the names of other villages to our knowledge. The people of the St. Lawrence appear to have been Iroquois-speaking, to judge from two vocabularies prepared by Cartier, and from the names of the villages recorded. As for their culture, Cartier declares of the people of Hochelaga: "Tout ce dit peuple ne s'adonne qu'à labourage et pêcherie pour vivre ... et aussi qu'ils ne bougent de leur pays, et ne sont ambulatoires, comme ceux du Canada et du Saguenay; nonobstant lesdit Canadiens leur soient sujets, avec huit ou neuf autres peuples qui sont sur le dit fleuve."[20] The distinction Cartier makes between farmers and migratory tribes is crucial. As we have seen, it is the distinction between the original Celtic Germani on the one hand, and Suebi on the other. In time of danger, the former retire into their *oppida*, which were doubtless well fortified, like those which Caesar describes and archaeology reveals in the interior of Gaul, or like Hochelaga, as described by Cartier; the Suebi however, typical of nomads, abandon their settlements and flee into the forests.[21]

After the abandonment in 1545 of the French colony established by Cartier at Cap Rouge, we hear little of the St. Lawrence for sixty years, although it continued to be visited for fishing and trade. Then comes Champlain, and immediately on his first visit he meets Algonkian-speakers where Cartier had apparently met Iroquois; there is already a proposal afoot for a French-Algonkian alliance against the Iroquois, and the Algonkian chief, according to Cartier, declares "qu'il était fort aise que sadite Majesté peuplât leur terre et fit la guerre à leurs ennemis."[22] Going upstream,

Champlain finds the valley depopulated.[23] The Iroquois have gone. Thirty years later, in 1634, Père Le Jeune records that between Québec and Trois-Rivières, "Les sauvages m'ont montré quelques endroits où les Iroquois ont autrefois cultivé la terre."[24] The Jesuit Relation ten years later again says as much. The Iroquois are however trying to get back; in 1603 they are halted at the mouth of the Richelieu by the Algonkians, and Champlain contemplates establishing a fort near Trois-Rivières to ensure free passage of the river, obviously because of the importance to the French of the fur-trade along it. Already the Hurons, "les bons Iroquois," speaking an Iroquoian language, inhabiting the region east of Georgian Bay, but allied to the Algonquins and Montagnais, and perpetually at war with the Iroquois of New York State, are coming down to the region of Quebec City to trade. The Jesuit Relations of 1639 will record that they began doing this some forty years earlier. The St. Lawrence is the great artery, as was, 2000-odd years earlier, the Rhône, and the Iroquois must not be allowed to block it. The trade is as important for the Indians as for the French. The Indians are developing a liking for European goods, and will eventually forget how to supply their own wants.[25] The middlemen will get rich on the trade, as did the people of Mont Lassois. Hence the Huron-Iroquois rivalry for control of the trade. We even have the date when hostilities began: rather more than fifty years before 1621, according to a tradition reported by Champlain, if such second-hand oral traditions are to be trusted.[26] It reminds us of Caesar's reporting of such Gallic traditions as the supposed German origin of the Belgae.[27]

The expulsion of the Iroquois from the St. Lawrence valley seems then well established. Parallels from Celtic Europe are not hard to find: the occupation of Mattium by the Chatti, of Bohemia by the Marcomanni come to mind.[28] But where did the Iroquoian tribes come from originally? The old view that they came from the south and then divided in the Great Lakes region, the Hurons going further north and the Iroquois proper east, now seems to be "no longer supported by archaeological and linguistic evidence. It is clear that, rather than being intrusive, the northern Iroquoian cultures developed out of the indigenous woodland cultures of an earlier period."[29] The different Iroquoian groups were already linguistically distinct at an early date; Huron, for instance, appears to have separated off before A.D. 800, although it is not until around 1400 that the different groups become archaeologically distinguishable. At this time, and for nearly two centuries longer, the different Huron tribes had each a distinct tribal area, as did the "five nations" of the Iroquois right into historic times (i.e. into the seventeenth century). The grouping of all Huron tribes into Huronia, a closely-settled area between Georgian Bay and Lake Simcoe, took place late in the sixteenth century, just in time for them to be found there by Champlain when he wintered in Huronia in 1615/16. We see the migrations still going on in the historical period. For instance the Wenro, a small tribe south of Lake Ontario who were being attacked by the Iroquois, migrated to Huronia. We remember the "German" tribes along the Rhine in Caesar's time who sought refuge in Gaul under pressure from the Suebi, just as the discussion of Iroquois origins reminds us of the equally inconclusive discussion of the origins of the La Tène art style, and of such problems, so long discussed, so uncertain still, as who the Cimbri and Teutones really were, and where they came from.[30]

Now it is interesting to note that Champlain did not apparently realise that the Hurons were themselves divided into different tribes.[31] He refers to them collectively as the Attignawantan, which is the name of one particular Huron tribe. Some twenty years later Frère Sagard recognized three tribes; the Jesuits added a fourth, as well as referring to a fifth group, the Ataronchronon, who may however not formally have constituted a tribe. Champlain, Sagard and the Jesuits differ in their estimates of the number of Huron villages, and modern scholars have found it difficult to determine in every instance the tribal affiliation of a village. Some villages were unfortified, and their inhabitants took refuge in the larger fortified villages in time of danger, a practice we also find in the Celtic world.

The Hurons maintained peaceful relations with their neighbours, except for the Iroquois. They traded freely with the Algonkian-speaking peoples to the north, who were of different culture also, largely nomadic, non-agricultural hunters. We see that difference of language and culture is no barrier to alliance, where common interests exists, and similarity of language and culture, as between the Huron and the Iroquois, no guarantee of alliance. The internecine feuds of the Gauls too were notorious. Even within one tribe, they could not combine: they fight separately, but are joined in defeat, said Tacitus. Conversely, however, we are reminded that, where we find tribes in alliance against the Romans, as for instance the Suebi and Sugambri in the period of Drusus's campaigns (12-9 B.C.), we are not thereby justified in inferring a common language or culture; the Sugambri may be Celts, the Suebi Germans.

Champlain's failure to grasp the complex nature and nomenclature of Huron tribal society also has its parallels in Greek and Roman accounts of Celts and Germans.[32] Peoples and tribes moreover often come down to us under names given them by their neighbours, not what they called themselves. Thus the name "Huron" comes from the old French word "hure," meaning a savage. They called themselves Wendat, a name that has survived only in Wyandot, who are descendants of the remnants of the Huron, and especially of one tribe who moved west under Iroquois pressure. Similarly, "Iroquois" is said to be an Algonkian or Montagnais word.[33] Huron and Iroquois alike have therefore come down to us in history labelled with names that foreigners fixed upon them. The so-called Neutrals were so called by the French; the Montagnais likewise. The etymology of "Algonkian" seems uncertain. Similarly, "Gauls" was the name the Romans gave the Celts, "Celts" what they called themselves.[34] The etymology of "German" is totally obscure, but the word is not German, in the later sense, and has never become acclimatised in the German language, which prefers the word "Deutsch," originally meaning "vernacular," as opposed to Latin; as a collective name for all German speakers, it does not appear to go back beyond the eleventh century.[35] "Teutonic" may also now be used of Germans in general, but originally it applied to one particular German tribe, just as the first Hellenes too were only one tribe among many. Strangest metamorphosis of all, "Welsh" derives from the Volcae, whom the Germans knew as being at one time, for them, the nearest of the Celtic tribes, and whose name they subsequently applied to all Celts, even when they met them in remote Britain.

Similar comparisons might be made in other areas, particularly those of non-material culture, as for instance in trying to reconstruct Celtic and Indian, especially Huron, religion, where modern researchers must use the same methods in both cases, although the documentary evidence is very much fuller for the Huron. It is not however possible to go further within the limits of this present and necessarily brief article, which does not in any case pretend to be more than a somewhat hazardous venture into an unknown field. If it stimulates reflection, it will have served its purpose.

University of Ottawa   *C. M. Wells*

NOTES

1. An earlier version of this paper was originally given to a joint session of the Classical Association of Canada and the Canadian Historical Association at McGill University in June 1972. I am grateful to those Canadian historians who took part in the subsequent discussion, and to those colleagues in the Department of History at the University of Ottawa who helped me in that half of my subject on which I am an utter novice.

2. R. Joffroy, *L'oppidum de Vix et la civilisation hallstattienne finale dans l'est de la France*, Paris, 1960, with refs. to earlier articles.

3. On trade contacts and tin-routes, see F. Villard, *La céramique grecque de Marseilles, VIe-IVe siècle: essai d'histoire économique*, Paris, 1960; further, J. Boardman, *The Greeks Overseas*, Harmondsworth, 1964, pp. 216-30.

4. S. Piggott, *Ancient Europe from the beginnings of agriculture*

to classical antiquity: a survey, Edinburgh, 1965, p. 195, pp. 204-5, with map, p. 188, fig. 105, and refs. to earlier publications.

    5. Cf. Strabo 4.177.

    6. Boardman (supra n. 3), p. 226.

    7. Cf. map in Piggott (supra n. 4).

    8. W. Dehn in W. Krämer (ed.), *Neue Ausgrabungen in Deutschland*, Berlin, 1958, pp. 127-45.

    9. G. Riek and H. J. Hundt, *Der Hohmichele: ein Fürstengrabhügel der späten Hallstattzeit bei der Heuneburg*, Berlin, 1962.

    10. Piggott (supra n. 4) pp. 193-4, with refs. to earlier publications.

    11. Tac. *Germ.* 23.

    12. G. T. Hunt, *The wars of the Iroquois: a study in intertribal trade relations*, Madison, 1940, pp. 3-4, points out that "in most aspects the circumstances of the contact between white men and native in North America are unique in the history of such relationships," which is true over the past few centuries; but Hunt does not go back far enough into history for his parallels.

    13. Piggott (supra n. 4) pp. 195-6.

    14. B. G. Trigger, *The Huron: farmers of the North*, New York, 1969, p. 3.

    15. A useful map in Piggott (supra n. 4) p. 180, fig. 100.

    16. H. Rix, "Zur Verbreitung und Chronologie einiger keltischer Ortsnamentypen," in *Festschrift für Peter Goessler, Tübinger Beiträge zur Vor- und Frühgeschichte*, Stuttgart, 1954, pp. 99-107.

    17. The views expressed in this paragraph and in the two which follow are argued in greater detail, with full refs. to sources and earlier literature, in C. M. Wells, *The German Policy of Augustus: an examination of the archaeological evidence*, Oxford, 1972, pp. 14-31.

    18. The original Celtic or Celticized "Germani" will have included, among others, the so-called Germani Cisrhenani (Caesar *BG* 2.4; 6.32), the Usipetes and Tencteri, agriculturalists driven out by the nomadic Suebi, who are "new" Germans (Caesar *BG* 4.1-19), and the Ubii, also noted farmers (Pliny *NH* 17.42).

    19. Review of sources in E. Tooker, *An Ethnography of the Huron Indians 1615-49*, Midland, 1967, pp. 3-9; discussion in L. P. Desrosiers, *Iroquoisie I*, 1534-1646, Les études de l'Institut d'histoire de l'Amérique française, 1947; also Hunt (supra n. 12) pp. 13-22, whose reference, p. 13, to "that slow flux of native population, that advance and recession of tribes and cultures, which is always found in and is perhaps an inevitable characteristic of aboriginal life on a large and

thinly populated continent" applies equally well to pre- and proto-historic Europe.

20. Quoted in Desrosiers (supra n. 19) p. 15.

21. Cf. R. von Uslar, *Studien zu Frühgeschichtlichen Befestigungen zwischen Nordsee und Alpen*, *Bonner Jahrbücher*, Beiheft 11, Cologne and Graz, 1964, p. 10, n. 42, cf. Caesar *BG* 6.10, and 5.19.

22. Desrosiers (supra n. 19) p. 24.

23. B. G. Trigger, "Cartier's Hochelaga and the Dawson site," in E. Tooker (ed.), *Iroquois culture, history and prehistory: proceedings of the 1965 conference on Iroquois research*, Albany, 1967, pp. 63-66; cf. also n. 19 above.

24. Desrosiers (supra n. 19) p. 19.

25. R. M. Goldstein, *French-Iroquois diplomatic and military relations 1609-1701*, The Hague and Paris, 1969, p. 24.

26. Desrosiers (supra n. 19) p. 27.

27. Caesar *BG* 2.4.

28. On Mattium, Tac. *Ann.* 1.56, as discussed by Wells (supra n. 17) pp. 20-21.

29. Trigger (supra n. 14) p. 21; cf. Goldstein (supra n. 25) p. 30.

30. Refs. in Wells (supra n. 17) p. 16, n. 3.

31. Tooker (supra n. 19) pp. 9-12.

32. Cf. what has been said above, and for a particularly complex example see also Wells (supra n. 17) p. 61.

33. G. M. Day, "Iroquois: an etymology," in Tooker (supra n. 23) pp. 57-61.

34. Caesar *BG* 1.1.

35. Wells (supra n. 17) p. 31.

36. Volcae Tectosages in Caesar *BG* 6.24.

Addenda

Two of the above notes now require amplification, as follows:

n. 5. E. G. Bowen, *Britain and the Western Seaways*, London, 1972, pp. 58-60, gives fresh prominence to the theory of a tin-route from Britain to Corbilo at the mouth of the Loire, thence by sea to the mouth of the Garonne, and up the Garonne to Narbonne. I remain sceptical, especially for the sixth century, cf. Villard (supra n. 3) pp. 154-57. Arguments for the Corbilo route in H. O'N. Hencken, *The Archaeology of Cornwall and Scilly*, London, 1932, pp. 170-86.

n. 9. Mr. M. G. Raschke (Harvard University) has drawn to my attention an article by W. T. M. Forbes, *CPh* 25 (1930), pp. 22-26, conclusive against Piggott's suggestion that the silk may have come via Cos. J. P. Wild, *Textile Manufacture in the Northern Roman Provinces*, Cambridge, 1970, pp. 10-13, records another find of Chinese silk from the same period at Rheingönheim. I am grateful to Mr. Raschke for pointing out that this silk may have reached Central Europe via Central Asian and Scythian tribes rather than through the Mediterranean; and that the exchange of gifts and tribute may have played a bigger role than trade.

"Res Publica Restituta"* A Modern Illusion?

There is no evidence that Augustus ever claimed to have "restored the Republic," nor is it clear that such a phrase was commonly used by anyone else in antiquity in the sense now associated with it. Yet it is the general, if not universal, assumption of modern studies that this was the slogan under which the Augustan government liked to parade itself.[1] According to the "façade" theory, Augustus pretended to be going back to an older form of government (the "Republic"), when in fact he was surreptitiously establishing another (the "Principate"). Although everyone knows that Dio's picture of the conference of 29 B.C. (52.1-41), at which such a

* Offered in honour of Professor E. T. Salmon's contribution to the study of Augustus (he is one who has recognised that the phrase "res publica restituta" calls for explanation). This is based upon a paper read to the Conference of the Australian Society for Classical Studies in Sydney in August, 1967. I am grateful to members, particularly Sir Ronald Syme, for criticism on the occasion, and to Dr. E. J. Jory and Professor R. D. Milns for sending me references since. My conclusions then, published in résumé in the *Proceedings of the XIth Congress of the Australasian Universities Language and Literature Association*, are now partly modified. The opportunity of reworking the subject has been afforded by a period of study at the F. J. Dölger-Institut, Bonn, where I have been supported by the Alexander von Humboldt-Stiftung while on leave from Macquarie University.

279

policy was supposedly settled, is dramatised and anachronistic, the rhetorical attractions of the façade theory seem to have drawn attention away from the lack of evidence for it, not to speak of the unlikelihood that so realistic a devotee of self-display as Augustus would have wanted or needed to lurk behind anything, or that the Roman people would have expected him to do so, or would have been taken in if he had.

It is especially remarkable that not only general works, but even those specifically devoted to the analysis of the Augustan government and its political ideology, habitually return to the phrase "res publica restituta" as a kind of datum, which does not itself apparently call for investigation.[2] The assumption that such a slogan existed has even attracted its own "evidence," through the restoration and interpretation of two broken inscriptions.[3] It has no doubt been fortified and may even have been prompted by the unexamined impact of the inscription which has always displayed these words from the arch of Septimius Severus.[4] It would be an ironical example of the frailty of historical reconstruction if modern scholarship, through the habit of representing Augustus as deceiving the Roman people by a spurious "restoration of the republic," should have contrived to deceive itself by a false restoration of the evidence.

In order to appreciate the difficulties of the key texts, it is necessary to draw some important distinctions in the Roman usage of the two terms, res publica and restituere. We should observe for our purposes four different ways in which res publica is used, set off by the various renderings the term required in Greek.[5]

1. Its traditional, basic and commonest reference, and probably the only one in legal or official documents, is to "the common property" (of the Roman people). While we may find it convenient to use such terms as "state" or "commonwealth" in this connection, the standard Greek translation was simply τὰ κοινὰ πράγματα or τὰ δημόσια πράγματα, preserving both the Roman consciousness of the objectivity of the res publica and its lack of more precise

definition. All interests of the Roman people, institutional and material, might be embraced by the term, which can certainly not be taken simply as the name for the Roman system of government. It is notable that in official language the *res publica* itself does nothing, but is always rather the object of action, whether by its owners (the Roman people), its custodians (the magistrates), or those who might wish to attack it or remove it (when the "state" itself takes action that is of course a matter for the *senatus populusque Romanus*). Controversy about the *res publica* is regularly centred upon the question of who is to have charge of it, and so on. The formula, "res publica ne quid detrimenti caperet" (*RG* 1.3), and the terms of the triumviral commission, "rei publicae constituendae" (*RG* 1.4), together with the statement, "rem publicam ex mea potestate . . . transtuli" (*RG* 34.1), all fall squarely within this definition. In the last case it is noteworthy that the term is covered in advance by "potitus rerum omnium," and that this completely general phrase alone passes into the Greek version (πάντων τῶν πραγμάτων); so insignificant apparently to the translator was the barely more specific term *res publica*, upon which such a weight of special meaning has been placed in this instance by the conventional interpretation. A contemporary observer, Vitruvius (*De arch.*, pref.), could speak of Octavian's being concerned with "publicae rei constitutione" as a facet (or equivalent?) of the "vita communi omnium." This refers, I suggest, as in the similar language of the triumviral commission, to nothing more specific than "setting public affairs in order." The establishing of a "constitution" in any technical sense, given the Roman attitude to their state, can hardly have been in anyone's mind. In Augustus' final recommendations he advised entrusting τὰ κοινά (sc. *rem publicam*) to all who were capable of managing it (Dio 56.33.4), and the subsequent debate in the senate centred upon the question of partition of control over the *res publica* − "quam partem rei publicae mandari tibi velis?" (Tac. *Ann.* 1.12). Ateius Capito, in the next decade, could speak of what had always happened with Augustus "rem publicam obtinente" (Aul. Gell. *NA*

12.12.1,2). Hadrian used to say that he would manage the *res publica* in the consciousness that it was the people's property, not his own (*SHA Had.* 8.3; cf. Tac. *Ann.* 13.4). It was the importance of properly managing the *res publica* that led to the use of the term for that activity itself, "public life" as we might say, as when Augustus is said to have sought retirement from it ("vacationem a re publica," Sen. *De brev. vit.* 5.1).

2. By a kind of personification, arising easily from controversies over the control of the *res publica*, the term is used where we should say "the public good" or "the country." In such cases it may be translated into Greek by τὸ δημόσιον. This typically occurs in rhetorical or familiar speech, where some show of emotion was appropriate. But apart from dramatising the question of control, we cannot say that anything more specific is at stake than in the common, formal usage of *res publica*. It comes no closer to being a reference to the "constitution," let alone any particular type of constitution. The distinction between the "personified" and the normal use is therefore not crucial for our purpose, and is often somewhat difficult to determine. In the case of the edict of Octavian to the Rhodians,[6] for example, Seleucus is said to have shown πίστιν (sc. "fidem") to the δημοσίοις πράγμασιν, where the original *res publica* must surely be thought of as having had the "personified" force. It might have more naturally been rendered by τῇ πατρίδι (as was done in *RG* 2, though not in *RG* 1.1 – while in *RG* 25.1 *res publica* was simply omitted in the translation). The slogans after Actium, "rem publicam tristissimo periculo liberat" (sic, *Fasti Amit.* 1 Aug.) and "republica conservata" (*CIL* VI, 873), are most easily brought under this heading. So is the coin legend of 16 B.C., "quod per eu(m) r(es) p(ublica) in amp(liore) at(que) tran(quilliore) s(tatu) e(st)" (*BMC* no. 91, "because it is through him that the country is enjoying more peaceful and prosperous conditions"). Here, too, belong some famous sayings of Augustus: at the trial of Primus, where he said in reply to Murena's challenge that τὸ δημόσιον had summoned him (Dio 54.3.2);

in 2 B.C. (the last year in which he put up with Julia and the first in which he was *pater patriae*), when he said that he had two spoiled daughters, whom he had to put up with, "rem publicam et Iuliam" (Mac. *Sat.* 2.5.4); on 23 Sept., A.D. 1, when he wrote to Gaius of his desire to see out his days "in statu rei publicae felicissimo" (Aul. Gell. *NA* 15.7.3, "in good times for our country"); in A.D. 4, when he said of the adoption of Tiberius, "hoc . . . rei publicae causa facio" (Vell. 2.104.1); and in the final instructions, when he spoke of the danger that τὸ δημόσιον might come to grief if there were only a sole custodian of τὰ κοινά and he were to perish. (Dio 56.33.4, where both terms no doubt represent *res publica* and illustrate the two senses we have distinguished so far. For other examples of the "personified" use see Vell. 2.90, 93, 111; Val. Max. 4.3.3; Sen. *De clem.* 1.4.2,3.)

3. In a much more specialised sense, *res publica* may be used as the equivalent of πολιτεία, the "order" or "constitution" of the community, as in the title of Cicero's *De re publica*. This usage belongs to historical or political study, and it is hardly surprising that it does not occur at all in the surviving works or statements of Augustus. Velleius Paterculus has it in a striking passage on the unrest in Tiberius' legions, who "wanted a new leader (*dux*), new conditions (*status*), a new order (*res publica*)" (2.125). Similarly, perhaps, Tacitus can speak of Tiberius acting as though he still lived "under the old order" (*Ann.* 1.7). But the use of *res publica* on its own to carry this sense is very unusual in relation to the Augustan era. There were more specific ways of making the point: Vell. 2.89, "prisca illa et antiqua rei publicae forma"; Tac. *Ann.* 1.9, "principis nomine constitutam rem publicam"; 4.33, "delecta ex iis et consociata rei publicae forma." Again, the idea could be conveyed without the words *res publica* at all: Sen. *De ben.* 2.20.1,2, "optimus civitatis status," "civitatem in priorem formam posse revocari"; Tac. *Ann.* 1.4, "verso civitatis statu." So Augustus himself, in a notable phrase, speaks of the good citizen as one who does not seek to change "praesentem statum civitatis" (Mac. *Sat.* 2.4.18, "the existing order" or "conditions"). We

shall return later to the question of what Augustus could have said had he wanted to say what he is supposed to have meant by his alleged slogan "res publica restituta."

4. By a further refinement still, *res publica* may occasionally be used, in passages of political comment, to refer to the particular type of "constitution" or public order which prevailed at an earlier stage of Roman history. The Greek equivalent here is δημοκρατία. Cicero's way of referring to the *res publica* as dying, or, alternatively, being revived, in relation to events of Caesar's dictatorship is best brought under this heading, and it is no doubt the origin of our own habit of using "the Republic" as the name of a certain period of Roman history and the relevant type of government. That this is a highly tendentious and retrospective use of a term which normally had no such limited reference must be obvious, but it should also be noted that there is no adequate evidence at all that it found any place in the Augustan publicity. Apart from the two restored inscriptions, to be discussed below, the only support for such a possibility comes from Dio's version of what Octavian said on 13 January, 27 B.C. (53.5.4). He is supposed to have called upon the Romans to take back their "freedom and democracy." It does not help us, however, to recognise that these words should represent "libertatem et rem publicam." It is not in doubt that both terms featured on the occasion. But that they should have been coupled in this way, and carry the sense of political liberty and constitutional restoration, is ruled out by a close study of the direct evidence. Dio's version merely canonises the anachronistic schematism that has persisted to our own day. The earliest example of this retrospective use of *res publica* with reference to the Caesarian regime from a Latin writer may be Valerius Maximus 8.15.5 (Kempf). But here again, as with the inscriptions, we are dependent upon a reconstructed text, which must be disallowed, as begging the question, unless we could be certain that the editor himself was not influenced by the theory of the "restored republic." We must then wait until Tacitus before finding the word in Dio's sense. Even

here it is only brought out for occasional dramatic effect. At the death of Augustus, "who was left who had known democracy?" (*rem publicam, Ann.* 1.3). Such a statement depends upon the perspective of a hundred years, and implies a judgement, not dissimilar from our own, on the changed character of government under Augustus. It could only have occurred at the time in the rhetoric of political opponents. In two other passages Tacitus develops this device, as we also habitually do, by insinuating that the Julio-Claudians pretended that "democracy" still existed. Tiberius summoned the senate to attend to the case of Silius (*Ann.* 4.19), "as though they were living under a democracy (quasi . . . illud res publica esset) and he was going to be dealt with according to the laws." During the quinquennium Neronis Tacitus says that "there still remained the appearance of democracy" (*Ann.* 13.28, "manebat . . . quaedam imago rei publicae").

Insofar as it occurs in the ancient tradition itself, therefore, our familiar way of using "republic" in connection with the Augustan style of government is loaded, and alien to Augustus. It would be a great aid to historical accuracy if we were to abandon the term, together with the pseudo-Latin cliché which appears to lend it authority, and adopt a variety of renderings, as the Greeks did. For the four senses outlined above we might then say, 1) "commonwealth" or "public interests," 2) "country," 3) "order" or "constitution," 4) "democracy." Of these it can be seen that only the first two occur in the vocabulary of the Augustan government.

The term *restituere*, like its English counterpart "restore," covers two types of situation which may usefully be distinguished: a) that where one gives something back to its rightful owner (as with lost property); b) that where one puts something back into its former condition (as with a ruined building). In Livy the former sense is overwhelmingly more frequent, and the commonest form in which the latter sense seems to occur is in the general phrase, "rem restituere." The former sense is also normal with the commoner word *reddere*; if one wished to specify the latter sense one had available the term *reficere*, or might use a more specific phrase still. Given the sense in which Augustus can be shown to have regularly used *res publica*, and supposing he had in fact spoken of "restoring the republic," he should only have meant by this a transaction in the former sense of "restore" (as is clear from *RG* 34.1), whereas the modern cliché requires the latter sense.[7] If the political issue of the day was not in fact conceived by Augustus or anyone else in terms of constitutional theory (which will usually be readily admitted), it greatly handicaps our understanding of the position to saddle Augustus with a manufactured slogan that encourages us to think that he pretended it was. "Res publica restituta," as used in modern writing on Augustus, invokes the least likely sense of *res publica* and couples it with the less probable sense of *restituta*, and all of this in the face of a serious lack of evidence that it was ever used by Augustus. That it would have meant something quite different if it had been used is confirmed by its occasional appearance (though not, of course, in the slogan form) in Cicero and Livy.

The phrase occurs seven times in Cicero. In *Cat.* 3.1 it joins the second sense of *res publica* with the first of *restituere*: the people have seen their "country" restored to them practically from the jaws of fate. *Cato de sen.* 20 joins the second sense of *res publica* with the second of *restituere*: there have been very great states shaken by the younger generation but sustained and restored by the older. In neither of these cases is there any question of a constitutional sense, and it is noteworthy that the phrase occurs in the context of civil disruption, the restoration being the point at which the state is rescued *from those who had endangered it*. This is very different from the situation Augustus celebrated when he transferred the *res publica* from *his own* "potestas," into which it had been entrusted (*RG* 34.1). It would have been against Augustus' interest for such an act to be described as a "restitutio rei publicae," with the clear implication of such words in Ciceronian usage that the *res publica* had hitherto been in the *wrong* hands. The other five Cicero passages (*Post red. in sen.* 36, *Post red. ad Quir.* 14, *De domo* 145 and 146, *Phil.* 13.9) all use the phrase in connection with the restoration of exiles. By a kind of play upon words, it seems, the state is said to be restored to itself in the restoration of the exile, or restored to the exile in his own restoration to it. In three of the cases Cicero speaks as though one might consciously adopt this as a point of view, and his use of the verb "putare" suggests that it is a deliberate artifice of speech, distinct from normal usage. In view of this I suggest that it is best taken as coupling the second sense of *res publica* with the first of *restituere*, though one might have thought from some of the passages individually that the second sense of *restituere* was the more appropriate. This is certainly the case with the single passage in Livy where the phrase occurs, 3.20.1, where it is used essentially in the same way as in Cic. *Cato de sen.* 20.[8] Another passage of interest is Liv. 7.1, where Cicero's exile cases find a parallel in Camillus, who "by his restoration restored his own country (*patriam*) along with himself."

It was therefore possible, in certain limited contexts, that one might speak of "restoring one's country." But that the words "res publica restituta" could have been adopted as a regular formula with specific constitutional reference is another matter altogether. Had Augustus wished to develop it in connection with his own management of the *res publica*, in whatever sense, he would at least have had to break the phrase from its limiting associations with usurpation or exile. And this surely means that it is very unlikely that it could have suggested itself to him at all as an appropriate slogan for his regime. But beyond that lies a much larger doubt. The whole assumption that Augustus would have wanted a constitutional name or definition for his position implies a conception of politics and history thoroughly alien to the Roman mind. Political power at Rome was normally both understood and represented in personal terms, and the whole of the Augustan publicity, as one should have expected, was in fact devoted to securing for the *princeps* a place of honour within the succession of great leaders. It was these who had always marked, and in Augustus' view would continue to mark, such ages and intervals as Roman history required. The idea of a "restored republic" belongs to a fashion of thought which sees history as a series of constitutionally defined periods. This is no doubt appropriate in some ages, and to states which have precise constitutions that can be changed in a formal and systematic way. But it is a most misleading approach to the question of how political power was seen in Augustan Rome. Against this background of serious improbability we must now look more sceptically at the two inscriptions which have been used to support the belief that Augustus did try to characterise his policy in such terms.

The *fasti Praenestini* for 13 January, as edited by Mommsen (*CIL* I², p. 231), are taken to read as follows:—

corona quern[a uti super ianuam domus imp. Caesaris]
Augusti poner[etur senatus decrevit quod rem publicam]
p. R. rest[i]tui[t]

p(opulo) R(omano) *Mommsen* p. 307

Before discussing this restoration, we may consider what authority the entry in the calendar should be allowed, however it be reconstructed. Could it have incorporated the actual words of the *senatus consultum* or otherwise represent an official version of what was said on that occasion? Internal evidence shows that the *fasti Praenestini* were composed between A.D. 4 and 10; in our case the calendar is thus one generation removed from the event. This would make little difference if we could be confident that it was the rule for compilers of *fasti* to record public events by direct citation of official documents. That they were indeed capable of doing so can be demonstrated. The *fasti Amiternini* for 1 August record "feriae ex s.c. q(uod) e(o) d(ie) imp. Caesar divi f. rem public(am) tristissimo periculo liberat." That this preserves the phraseology of the *senatus consultum* itself is shown both by the allusiveness of the phrase referring to the capture of Alexandria, and by the fact that the nomenclature has not been updated to include "Augustus."[9] But in the case of the *fasti Praenestini* this very adjustment has in fact been made by the author, for the act he is recording for 13 January also antedated (even if only by three days) the conferring of the name "Augustus," which he himself correctly records for 16 January. A generation later such a discrepancy was of no consequence, as can be seen from Ovid's running the two events together under 13 January (*Fasti* 1.587-90), as well as from Augustus' own non-chronological arrangement of the several honours (*RG* 34.2). That this detail implies that the author of the *Praenestini* was also stating the point of substance more freely, we cannot positively assert; but the possibility exists, to say the least. We cannot therefore assume that what we have lost was the actual formula adopted in the senate on 13 January, 27 B.C.

The *fasti Praenestini* are peculiar amongst the "fasti anni Juliani" in having a known author: Verrius Flaccus, the famous grammarian, and tutor to Gaius and Lucius Caesar. He presumably composed the *fasti* in retirement at Praeneste after their deaths.[10] The *fasti* themselves show him to have been a man greatly interested in antiquarian detail. All this may seem to put him in a position where he is likely both to have cared about the correct formula and to have been able to get it right. Yet the possibility also clearly exists that such a person — a freedman-scholar, and conspicuous idiosyncratic, removed now also in time and place from any link with people in politics — may have felt free (for example, out of admiration for the family he had served, or in response to a popular mannerism) to state the matter otherwise than could have been officially done. And this is indeed what we should be obliged to say had happened if it could in fact be shown that the *fasti Praenestini* had read "rem publicam populo Romano restituit." For the possibility that the *senatus consultum* of 13 January, 27 B.C., used such a formula in connection with the oak crown is ruled out by other considerations. But, as will readily be seen, these are of such a kind as would be likely in any case to have guided Verrius Flaccus, so that in calculating the terms in which the senate most probably dealt with the matter, we are also assembling the material from which he would have composed his entry for the *fasti*. It is not therefore a futile exercise to attempt a reconstruction of the text on this basis.

The *corona civica* had traditionally been awarded for saving the life of a fellow-citizen in battle. There were precise conditions which had to be met. It was essential, moreover, that the rescued man himself present the crown to his deliverer, so personal was the matter.[11] Augustus could obviously not be represented as having won the crown in the prescribed way. What was needed, therefore, in the *senatus consultum*, was a formula which would show convincingly how what he had done was related to the familiar and inescapable meaning of the crown. The rescuing of "the public property," however precious that might be, would have been a most flat and awkward substitute for the personal deliverance which the crown stood for. Nor is it possible for us to allow that *res publica* (if it had been used here) could have carried its "personified" sense. Rescuing one's country might certainly have been represented as appropriate grounds for a civic crown.[12] But that sense would be ruled out decisively for our text by the surviving reference to the *populus Romanus* itself. The "personified" *res publica* is an alternative to this (in less formal speech); the two cannot stand together in the one phrase. It had to be shown, then, that the Roman people as such (or, if one wishes, the *res publica* in the sense of "the country") had been rescued, and not merely something belonging to them (and therefore not the *res publica* in its usual "property" sense, let alone the "constitution" or "democracy," even if it were to be thought possible, in spite of the arguments above, that the senate in a formal statement could have employed the term in either of those ways).[13]

I propose therefore that "res publica" be eliminated from the text, and also that Mommsen's supplement "p(opulo) R(omano)" be disregarded, to open the way for taking the *populus Romanus* itself as the direct object (or, for that matter, grammatical subject) of what is being said to have been achieved by Augustus. We must next take stock of the various points which it may have been necessary or highly desirable for the senate to make in justifying the award of the civic crown to him.

1) The proper name of the crown ("civica") must surely have featured. Oak crowns could be used for other purposes, and it is inconceivable that the senate would not have used the correct technical term — and Verrius Flaccus must surely have done so too (provided his space was not forcing him to extreme abbreviation) — since the ideological point of the crown depended upon its formal identity.[14] It is not, however, necessary to suppose that the senate would have needed to specify an "oak" crown, since that is what the *civica* by definition was: Augustus himself did not find the detail necessary, in contrast with the "laurels" associated with them, for which there was no corresponding technical term (*RG* 34.2). To start with the point that it was an "oak" crown is surely the mark of an observer already somewhat removed from the occasion, writing as an antiquarian (as Verrius Flaccus is), or as an interpreter of Roman technicalities to foreigners (as with Dio 53.16.4, or the Greek translator of the *RG*, both of whom, in contrast to Augustus, find it necessary to define and explain the crown instead of naming it).

2) The traditional citation, "ob cives servatos," must also come into consideration. It was not only regularly featured as a coin legend in association with the crown from 23 B.C. onwards, but must have been inscribed with the original emblem above the door of Augustus' house (Ov. *Trist.* 3. 1.47.8; Val. Max. 2. 8.7). Yet it could hardly have been built into the senate's formula as the direct statement of the grounds for the award, when the whole object of the exercise was to show that the crown was justified by something which could not simply be defined in the traditional terms. We possess, moreover, in the fragments of the *fasti* a causal statement which, as was to be expected, apparently excludes the use of the words "ob cives servatos" in that grammatical form. On the other hand, the remarkable aureus of the year 27 B.C. itself, clearly designed to celebrate this very occasion, carries the legend "civibus servateis" (*BMC* no. 656). The

292   E. A. JUDGE

conjecture lies ready to hand that this (unique?) form of the phrase arises from the syntax of the *senatus consultum* itself. The use of the ablative absolute would have enabled the senate to allude conveniently to the traditional citation as a preliminary step to the new definition. Once this point of protocol had been negotiated at the time with suitable propriety, the tribute could be briefly summed up thereafter in the time-honoured words, without further ado. But what then could have been the senate's explanation on the actual occasion? We must try to make something out of the other notions that are linked with the *corona civica* in subsequent references to it. Even the propaganda of a later age is more likely to guide us back to the senate's formula than is an extraneous slogan inspired by modern historical schematism.

3) In Pliny's day the crown was not only "the glorious emblem of a soldier's valour," but also stood for the clemency of an "imperator," since civil wars had long since made it seem a "meritum" not to take the life of a citizen (*NH* 16. 3.7). That the association with clemency did not first arise in the civil wars after Nero is shown by Seneca (*De clem.* 1. 26.5), who appeals to him to earn the "civica" by clemency (in judicial matters), and, although the actual word is not used in this case, the invocation of the oak crown above Augustus' door by a citizen in need of personal clemency (Ov. *Trist.* 3. 47-58) suggests that the idea was at least available by the end of Augustus' life. If, however, Pliny is right in linking it with civil wars, we can safely say that the theme of clemency played its part in the interpretation of the crown in 27 B.C. itself. All we lack indeed is a specific statement making the link at this point, for the elements are all individually present in the complex of ideas assembled by Augustus in *RG* 34.1, 2: the civil wars setting the context for the "meritum," which earns him the *civica*, together with the shield bearing (with the associated virtues) the word "clementia." Nor need we suppose that the conjunction would have seemed novel in 27 B.C. Civic crowns had been voted to the triumvirs to celebrate the fact that the number of victims in the proscription was not greater (Dio 47. 13.3), and the

assumption seems safe that Caesar's use of the *civica* had already established it as the symbol of clemency after civil war.[15] All that happened in 27 B.C. then may have been that the senate adapted a recognised sense of the crown to the particular occasion. The puzzle would then be why it had not been produced at an earlier stage. However, for whatever reason it had not been wanted sooner, why was it called for now? Surely because of the remarkable spirit of compromise in which Octavian and Crassus had resolved their impending collision of 28 B.C.[16] The fact that Augustus later found it convenient to link the tributes of January, 27 B.C., with the transfer of public affairs from his full control (*RG* 34. 2, "quo pro merito meo") need not define what they meant at the time. The term "meritum" and the formula of *RG* 34.3 show how the administrative adjustment was later given theoretical significance. But the transfer of 13 January must have been seen at the time not as any sort of programme for the future, but simply as the formal end to the emergency (as *RG* 34.1 makes clear enough). It is the sense of deliverance from the crisis, and popular relief that they were not after all to be plunged once more into civil war, that will have shaped people's response when the news was first announced. The "clemency," then, that had saved the lives of citizens by not carrying the emergency measures through to their intended conclusion is another likely candidate for a place in the lost formula.

4) A similar trail back may be opened up from the coin of A.D. 71 which represents the senate and people of Rome as offering the oak crown to Vespasian as the "assertor of public liberty" (*BMC* no. 572). This brings together the themes of "saving the citizens" and "liberty restored" which appear by turn (though not otherwise linked on a single coin?) in several forms in the coinage after the revolt against Nero, especially in that of Galba. The "liberty" types sometimes explicitly pick up those of Brutus (who also put the oak crown on his coins), but the display of the *civica* "ob cives servatos" is no doubt chiefly meant as a link with Augustus, which Galba needed to stress for the sake of

legitimacy.[17] We may then ask whether the juxtaposition of "liberty restored" with the oak crown is not itself a clue to the formula of 27 B.C. Is this the "restoration" to which our text refers? The senate had already in 30 B.C. pronounced the fall of Alexandria to be a liberation of the country from terrible danger (*Fast. Amit.*, 1 Aug.), and only in the previous year (28 B.C.) a tetradrachm from Ephesus (*BMC* no. 691) had hailed Octavian as "libertatis p. R. vindex." This legend no doubt also picks up the language of a senatorial resolution (though we know the phrase was conventional enough, and the opening gambit of the *Res Gestae* confirms that). The laureate head, and the image and legend of "Pax" on the reverse, confirm that liberty is won by military victory, and that the shadow of military crisis still lay across this year in particular. If we consider "liberty" for a place in our text, then, it should not be taken as an alternative way of expressing the supposed theme of the "restored republic." Certainly Drusus at a later stage, writing privately to his brother (Suet. *Tib.* 50), could speak, in something very like that sense, of "making Augustus restore liberty." But if such a phrase was to be used with Octavian's approval in 27 B.C. in the public definition of what was meant by the civic crown, it could only refer to the liberation of the people from military peril. I should, however, prefer not to propose (as when this paper was first read) "[libertatem] p(opulo) R(omano) rest[i]tui[t]," because that places the Roman people themselves in too passive a position. Much better would be a form of words in which the people directly acknowledge that they are "restored to liberty." This preserves the correct situation, required for the civic crown, in which the rescued themselves recognise their deliverer. But we do not need any actual thing for them to be restored to. It would be quite within the Ciceronian manner of using the phrase for them to profess that they were "restored to themselves."

5) A further possibility which should be mentioned, in spite of its apparent unlikelihood, arises from Pliny's remark (*NH* 16. 8) that Augustus accepted the civic crown "a genere

humano." In its own context this may be no more than a rhetorical flourish to enable Pliny to pass on neatly to his next point: it is certainly superfluous to his subject as he has been developing it. But it may also reflect the universalising of the responsibility of the ruler, a theme clearly related to that of clemency in Augustus' thought (*RG* 3.1). The Vienna cameo of A.D. 12 shows a woman, usually interpreted as Oikoumene, presenting an oak crown to Augustus. She must certainly be someone other than Roma herself, who is shown seated beside him as his consort. It is clearly possible, as the civil wars faded from view, and Augustus began deliberately to play down the traditional Roman pride in conquest in favour of a less nationalistic concern for the security of the civilised world as a whole, that the civic crown also took on a larger sense. But in the civil-war context of 27 B.C., and in the face of the "p. R." of our text, it seems impossible to allow that the original formula could have found room for more than the citizens of Rome in the strict sense.

6) This may be the place to mention a detail which must have been specified in the *senatus consultum*, though it need hardly have been considered for inclusion by Verrius Flaccus. Actual oak leaves are presumably not available on 13 January. Some provision must therefore have been made for the practicalities of the matter. In the case of the laurels at the doors of *flamines*, there was an annual replacement with fresh ones on 1 March (Ov. *Fast*. 3. 137-8). Ovid speaks elsewhere (*Trist*. 3. 1.39-40) as though both laurels and oak had their natural shade; this does not at first sight suggest a representation in stone or metal. On the other hand, the reference to the laurels as evergreen because one does not need to pick off the withered leaves (*Trist*. 3. 45-6) may imply just that; in which case we should rather say that Ovid was imagining the colours, or that they were painted on. One way or another the point must have been regulated in the decree.[18]

7) Finally we must note some considerations which arise from the form and spacing of the inscription. The three lines in question happen to fall opposite the symbol for 14

January, the proper entry for which has had to be dropped well down into the lower part of the space appropriate to it, and is marked off from our entry by an introductory dash. We ought then to assume that some such phrase as "eodem die" would have been added to our entry to warn readers that it still applied to 13 January. But the exact form of such a link depends upon what we think was contained in the five lines above, which occupy all the space available opposite the symbol for 13 January. The lack of a convincing reconstruction does not abolish the issue.

$$\text{[. . . . .]}$$
$$\text{puta[. . . . .]}$$
$$\text{id est[. . . . .]}$$
$$\text{non[. . . . .]}$$
$$\text{al[. . . . .]}$$

The received text of our three lines, which follow immediately upon this, ignores the possibility of a link. In *CIL* I^2 Mommsen simply repeated the statement of the first edition that the content of what went before is unknown. But in fact he had altered the text of the second line to allow a reference to "Luta[tius? . . .]," and in his note on 23 March (*CIL* I^2, p. 313), where Verrius Flaccus cites a Lutatius as an antiquarian authority, he makes it clear that in his view both passages refer to a work (*Communes historiae?*) of Q. Lutatius Catulus, consul of 102.[19] In 1883, moreover, Mommsen had made the point (implicit in the conjunction of the two symbols) that a single *senatus consultum* of 13 January would have provided both for the laurels and the civic crown (*RGDA* ^{2}, p. 149). He also assumed that Dio 53. 16.4 preserved the content of the *s.c.* (but see below), as well as recognising the inappropriateness of his restoration "[rem publicam] p(opulo) R(omano) rest[i]tui[t]" (see n. 3).

It is very curious (and has no doubt much to do with the strength of modern confidence in the reconstruction) that no hint of these developments in Mommsen's understanding of the matter was given in *CIL* I^2 (1893) with either the text of or notes on the *fasti Praenestini* for 13 January.[20] The consequences for the reconstruction of the text are in fact serious. Quite apart from the need to replace "[rem publicam]," the whole syntactical character of our three lines must be different from what Mommsen printed if they are linked with or part of a similar statement (concerning the laurels) contained in the preceding five lines. Not all of them, however, need be linked with our three. We should perhaps leave about half the space for a note on the Ides, occurring here for the first time in the calendar, or on the rites appropriate to 13 January (Jupiter Stator?).[21] Since the five lines are shorter than our three, there would not be much space left for the laurels. But a statement of the scale of "laureis postes aedium imp. Caesaris Augusti publice vincti sunt" would fit easily, and give all that was needed for clarity.[22] Neither Verrius Flaccus nor the senate (*pace* Mommsen) would have needed Dio's interpretative formula as well – laurels hardly call for an explanation in Rome, especially when their familiar sense fitted the facts so well (in contrast with the oak crown, which had to be shown to be appropriate). If there were in fact a link between the two parts of the entry for 13 January, and it were of some such grammatical form and content as this, several consequences would follow for our three lines. It would be natural to expect the change of subject to be marked (I suggest "autem" to call attention to the fact that the oak crown is to be given special treatment). The names of Augustus would become otiose (indeed it may count slightly against the case I am putting that "Augusti" is preserved – "eius" would have been strictly sufficient). The word "domus" is also superfluous, as in the *RG*. "Senatus decrevit" should give place to a form of words that would pick up its counterpart of the preceding lines. This would also enable us to assume a form of words that does not confine the initiative to the senate. While it was certainly proper that the senate should award the laurels, the crown should be seen to have come from the people, who had been rescued (though the senate would naturally need to specify the arrangements for it in such a peculiar case). For "sanctum est" see Tac. *Ann.* 1.6.3.

The exact length of the lines to be supplied is not clear.[23] But the considerations I have advanced could be adapted to a variety of lengths. What I suggest below is kept within the limits of space Mommsen set himself. I envisage that Verrius Flaccus was working from the text of a *senatus consultum* that ran along the following lines:[24]

> Quod M. Vipsanius Agrippa cos. v.f. de ornamentis imp. Caesari divi f. pro merito eius decernendis, q.d.e.r.f.p. d.e.r.i.c. uti laureis postes aedium imp. Caesaris divi f. publice vincirentur utique corona civica super ianuam eius figeretur, quod civibus per clementiam eius servatis ipse populus Romanus restitui in libertatem sibi videbatur.

Such a formula Verrius might then have adapted for the *fasti* as follows:

> corona querc[ea autem id est civica uti super ianuam]
> Augusti poner[etur quod civibus ab eo servatis ipse]
> p. R. rest[it]u[i sibi videbatur eodem s.c. sanctum est]

> *or* ipsum] p. R. rest[it]u[isse videbatur

I have illustrated my argument with a fresh reconstruction of the text, partly in order to pull together its various threads, and partly because only such a drastic confrontation is likely to make clear the weakness of the received reading. My object will have been fully achieved if this can now be "restored" to the limbo of doubt, or indeed improbability, to which I believe Mommsen had in the end himself consigned it. For my own version I wish to claim only this negative force; insofar as it may be less improbable than the other, it will serve as a warning against jumping to conclusions; I am very well aware of its own inconclusiveness.

The second inscription can be more briefly dealt with. In the so-called "Laudatio Turiae," lines 22-26 of the parallel fragments (*d*) and (*e*) are commonly read as follows:[25]

> (22) Sed quid plura? parcamu[s] orationi, quae debet et potest e[xire, ne viliter maxi-] (23)ma opera tractando pa[r]um digne

peragamus, quom pr[o documento] (24) meritorum tuorum oc[ulis] omnium praeferam titulum [vitae servatae]. (25) Pacato orbe terrarum, res[titut]a re publica, quieta deinde n[obis et felicia] (26) tempora contigerunt.

For the restoration "res[titut]a" in line 25 Mommsen followed Marini (1785) against Fabretti (1699), who had read "re[ddit]a." The latter had a slight advantage in brevity, for this is the longest gap in a run of 69 lines, in which the saw-cut has typically destroyed only one or two letters (as in lines 22 and 23 above, and again in line 26 [not shown]). There is however no doubt at all that the "s" is now present on the stone, and that the gap is sufficient for Marini's "res[titut]a."[26] Nor does it seem to me that any other word can plausibly be substituted for it. We face then the plain question of what the author of the *laudatio* must have meant by "restituta re publica."

The author has not been convincingly identified, but his position in relation to Augustus is clear. As a young man he had joined Pompey when Caesar invaded Italy, leaving his fiancée to cope with the assassination of her own parents and an attack on his mother by Milo, who hoped to recover the house their family had bought after the confiscation of Milo's property in 52 B.C. They were rescued, thanks to her efforts, by the intervention of Caesar. But in 43 the author, now married, found himself on the list of the proscribed. During his flight he was protected and secretly supported by his wife. In spite of a pardon issued by Octavian, she was rebuffed, and subjected to physical brutality, when she applied to Lepidus to have it implemented. The restoration was not secured until Octavian's return to Rome in 41. From then until the wife's death between 8 and 2 B.C. the couple seem to have remained completely withdrawn from public life. The phrases "pacato orbe terrarum, restituta re publica" introduce this change in their life's pattern. Apart from the apparent coincidence with themes that have come to be associated with the year 27 B.C., there is nothing that would have led us to think of that year; their quiet life began much earlier. But the author is in fact a perfect example of the type of person whom Augustus' propaganda postulated: he acknowledges gladly and without the slightest suggestion of constraint that he owed his life to Octavian's clemency in victory, clearly enjoyed his release from the hazards of politics, and continued to the end in undiminished admiration of Augustus. It is certainly possible that the phrase "restituta re publica" came into use amongst such people as a convenient way of referring to the settlement of 27 B.C. But if so we must recognise (a) that its lack of attestation elsewhere confirms its unofficial character (since virtually all our other evidence is "official" in the broad sense); (b) that this strengthens rather than weakens the arguments above against the possibility of an official theory of the "restored republic" (in the modern sense), since one would have expected the regime to take up such a gratuitous compliment for official use if it had been politically viable; and (c) that it refers to the time when "the country was put back into proper order" without specifically touching the supposed "constitutional" question — it is a date, not a definition: "the restoration of our country," not "the restored republic"; "restituta re publica," not "res publica restituta."

But there is a different way altogether of interpreting the phrase. It takes up the idea most commonly associated with such words in Cicero and Livy: our author, like them, is discussing the restoration of an exile. In the preceding twenty-four lines he speaks four times of being rescued ("servare" or "conservare" used in several forms), and four times of being restored (twice using the phrase "redditus patriae" and twice referring to "restitutio mea"). Were it not for "pacato orbe terrarum," we might have said without hesitation that "restituta re publica" is to be understood with the following "nobis." It would simply then have been a case of the husband's saying that in his restoration their country was, as it were, restored to them: "the restoration of our country" would be a rhetorical inversion of "my restoration to it." But if the incompatibility of "pacato orbe terrarum" with this means that we cannot go so far, surely we may say that the language of restoration, even though it may be used to allude to the wider political situation, arises in this author, as in Cicero and Livy, from the theme of personal restoration from exile. It need not therefore be evidence of a common usage at all and its lack of attestation otherwise would support this, except insofar as other exiles may have liked to talk that way.

Yet there is in the *laudatio* another emphasis that may lead us back to Augustus and official themes after all. The author three times refers to the clemency that secured his two restorations. While his point is to stress the wife's *merita* as a counterpart to official clemency, there is not the slightest trace of reserve towards the latter. The man had had every opportunity to appreciate the hypocrisy with which it is inescapably contaminated in our eyes, and he had long since passed beyond any need to conceal his true feelings. To say the least, no one could have taken it amiss if he had paid tribute to his wife alone in her memorial, and ignored Augustus. But his admiration goes deeper than the open tributes. Surely lines 23 and 24, immediately preceding our phrase, are an invocation of the theme of the civic crown, transposed to his wife. We are now not far from coming full circle in the argument, for it would be tempting in this light to say that "res publica restituta" is just the sort of slogan Augustus should have adopted to sum up the theme of the oak crown. But if he had done so, it would have had nothing to do with questions of constitutional theory. It would have meant, as our unknown author wished to put it, that in the saved lives of citizens the country itself is restored. And our main point remains: there simply is no evidence that Augustus did encourage such a formula, in any sense.

But how then did Augustus express his relation to the state? Three different ways in which he talked about it should be distinguished. The first and by far the commonest in the surviving evidence is the simple claim that the safety and well-being of the country depended upon him personally. This is the time-honoured theme of the Roman nobleman, rooted deep in such basic institutions as patronage and the tradition of self-display, understood and approved by all

Romans, whatever their place in society. Octavian's first recorded political utterance employs the idea, for Cicero's benefit (*Att.* 16. 11.6, in 44 B.C.); it was to enjoy a rich development in Augustan publicity, and its many aspects have been extensively studied. When the term "res publica" features in such a connection, as it frequently does, it means "the country" (my second sense, above, and examples there). The topic is at home on occasions of public display, and of some emotion; it is addressed to the Roman people at large, and has little directly to do with questions of formal power and theory of government. But its indirect effects in these fields were of course vast, and it could itself be elaborated into a statement of general policy, as in the notable edict preserved by Suetonius (*Aug.* 28.2). Although it has been claimed, that the edict was issued on 13 January, 27 B.C. itself, I do not find it compatible with the preoccupation with the immediate past which I think shaped that occasion. The edict is concerned with the future, and builds upon a clear assumption of lasting responsibility. Augustus speaks of laying foundations for the nation ("rem publicam"), of settling it safe and sound in its place, and of his winning a reputation as the founder of the best possible order ("optimi status auctor"). A more likely date than 27 is the period of consolidation after his return to Rome in 19 B.C. This marked the end of the major crises of control that had kept the future uncertain; from now on he sat between the consuls, and assumed more direct initiative in planning and legislation. There are many other suitable occasions for the edict: the renewal of his province in 18 or in 13; the *ludi saeculares* of 17; the vows for his health, reflected in the coins of 16; the return from Gaul in 13 and voting of the altar of Augustan peace. But no occasion is more appropriate than that of his return to Rome in 2 B.C., when on the insistence of the whole nation, as expressed by Valerius Messala in the senate he finally agreed to accept the title of "father of his country." The commitment has now passed beyond question.

The second way in which Augustus found it important to express his relation to the state was in terms of the formal division of power in the government. The debates and recriminations over the termination of the triumviral commission threw this topic into the forefront of political interest (Dio 50.7.1,2). The points at issue, however, are technical, and "res publica" in this connection bears its official sense of the public property. In spite of the overwhelming success of Augustus with the mass of the people, he faced an undertow of criticism amongst his former peers of the nobility. The *Res gestae* shows both the extent to which Augustus to the last remained sensitive to this, and the solution by which he hoped to silence criticism after his death. The various technical adjustments that had had to be made to his formal powers are not analysed in terms of constitutional theory, as our manner of looking at the matter would require. But neither are they suppressed altogether from close inspection. Instead, they are carefully built into the pattern of exceptional desert and the unprecedented honour it attracts that the *Res gestae* constructs. Thus legal formulae are extracted from their technical context, in which they could perhaps have been disputed, and validated as features of this simpler political reality. The famous "transfer of the commonwealth" from Augustus' control is the prime case in point.

In the new forum which Augustus opened in 2 B.C. was expressed symbolically his conception of his place in Roman history. The edict which Suetonius records (*Aug.* 31.5) defines the matter. Roman history is a succession of great leaders, age by age. They constitute a model by which continuity is preserved, as the people insist upon conformity to the standards set. In the *elogia* beneath the statues of the great men of the past, ranged in the forum, Augustus for his part carefully instils the model into the minds of the people. It is in fact a model different, in its emphasis at least, from what might have been expected. Although the symbolism of the forum, and the way the ancient writers refer to the statues, leads one to think of the leaders of the past as military heroes, this is not the point that is drawn out in the *elogia*. Instead, for each man in turn, a single episode is briefly detailed; this is clearly his distinctive *exemplum*, winning him his place in the procession of the ages. Each one is naturally peculiar, and in the fragmentary state of the texts the cumulative effect is not easy to sense. But it is clear that though the *exemplum* is often set in a military context, it is not the military virtues which are being displayed at all. What makes a man the leader in his age is rather that, in a crisis of survival for Rome, he is the one who can manage his relations with others with such remarkable foresight that Rome is saved: they typically fail in the crisis, often by maintaining a laudable position; but he meets the exceptional demand, often by abandoning what might have seemed in ordinary circumstances to have been his right. It is in this spirit, I suggest, that Augustus was to single out the transfer of administrative control after the crisis of 28 B.C., and elevate it into his unique and supreme service to Rome, his *meritum*. Augustus is not advancing a constitutional theory, although he is dealing with a matter which has constitutional significance, which he himself draws out. But the matter is presented in the context of desert and its compensating honour. In this way, then, Augustus could lift technical questions of statecraft out of their strict context, and, while preserving accuracy of legal detail insofar as that is given, enshrine them in the public regard as his monument for the future.

But if Augustus was trying to remove far-reaching administrative questions and decisions into the safer atmosphere of popular admiration, that in itself implies that other people wanted to pull them in a different direction, into a debate on constitutional theory. Our "res publica restituta" is the legacy of this latter process, and even if I am right in arguing that it has been only gratuitously and incongruously attributed, as a public slogan, to Augustus himself, it is clear that he must have had to tackle the issue it represents, at least in private debate and consultation. This is the third way in which he must have discussed his relations with the state. That even his most ardent admirers might, out of very enthusiasm, force him along this risky path is clear from the untidy but revealing drift of thought in Velleius Paterculus. Although he sets out to describe the benefits Augustus conferred on Rome in the piece-meal, untheoretical fashion Augustus would have desired, and although, in summing it up (2.90), he employs a metaphor (as does the "laudatio Turiae") that has nothing to do with a constitutional definition ("the civil wars were laid to rest, and the limbs of the commonwealth grew together again"), he has already taken the wrong turning by claiming that "the ancient and venerable pattern of the commonwealth was recalled" (2.89). In itself this may seem to be, and is certainly intended as, a perfect compliment to Augustus, but the latter, for all his emphasis on continuity with the past, never allowed himself to reify the notion of a given constitution inherited from the past even to that slight extent. He knew too well, from critical comment which must often have been relayed to him, how easily the idea could be turned against him (Seneca was to describe the aspirations of Brutus in just these terms: *De ben.* 2.20.1,2). Augustus was prepared to go so far as to speak loosely of the "order of the state," "status civitatis," and even of the "existing" order (Mac. *Sat.* 2.4.18), or the "best" order (Suet. *Aug.* 28.2). But to attempt to define this, one way or the other, in relation to a supposed "past" order would be to put himself in an invidious position. He had openly sought and won supremacy in the state; but the satisfaction of having won was slowly drained away as the extraordinary degree and permanency of his success corroded the will of others to compete. To assert formally that the "old constitution" was restored would have been a needless provocation to those already reduced to cynicism; to profess a new one would have tarnished the prize he had won; he therefore retreated from the growing problem of defining what was happening to the Roman government, into the security of the popular acclaim on which his power really depended, and the simple, non-constitutional themes it afforded.

Others, however, need not, or would not, be so cautious. Drusus had written to Tiberius about "compelling Augustus to restore liberty" (Suet. *Tib.* 50). By the time of Tiberius' own regime, according to Tacitus (*Ann.* 4.9), the "giving back of the commonwealth (to the consuls, or someone else)" had long been a theme for mockery. The later authors seem to lose touch with the reality of the dilemma of interpretation which faced Augustus. Suetonius introduces Augustus' edict on the "best possible order" (*Aug.* 28.2) by saying that it arises from his decision, twice considered, not to "give back the commonwealth," and concludes by saying that he did his best to see that no one regretted "the new order." Thus his formulation of the issue cuts right across the definition he is citing from Augustus, presumably without his realising it. The "giving back" theme may or may not arise from the language used on 13 Jan., 27 B.C. Ovid certainly uses that term (*Fasti* 1.589), but correctly specifies that what was given back was "omnis provincia." Yet the term in itself was common enough. And Augustus must have decided, when he completed the final draft of the *Res gestae*, that its use in the damaging cliché form with reference to 27 B.C. was not yet sufficiently hardened that he could not shatter it by his own definition of what precisely it was he had done with the *res publica* on that occasion. That Augustus was wrong about this is of course the reason why we now have to struggle not to be caught in the straitjacket Suetonius and the rest have designed for us. Suetonius says that Augustus was believed to have recalled and poisoned Drusus because he never made any secret of the fact that he would "restore the ancient order of the commonwealth" as soon as he could (*Claud.* 1.4). The theory of the "restored republic" attributes to Augustus the ideas his critics used against him. But he tried to avoid constitutional slogans altogether.

Macquarie University, N.S.W.   *E. A. Judge*

NOTES

1. References to the matter do not often go beyond the conventional use of the cliché (not surprisingly, since it does not bear closer inspection). There is no point in criticising individuals for a common habit. But solely by way of example I refer to H. Bengtson, *Grundriss der Römischen Geschichte*, 1967, p. 254, and D. C. Earl, *The Age of Augustus*, 1968, Ch. 3 "The Republic Restored." They are in fact somewhat unusual in that Earl tries to explain the phrase, and Bengtson to devise evidence for it.

2. E.g. J. Béranger, *Recherches sur l'aspect idéologique du principat*, 1953, p. 280; U. von Lübtow, *Das Römische Volk, sein Staat und sein Recht*, 1955, p. 368; P. Grenade, *Essai sur les origines du principat*, 1961, p. 394.

3. The *fasti Praenestini* for 13 January (*CIL* I², p. 231) and the "laudatio Turiae" (*CIL* VI, 1527, *d&e* 25). In either case the definitive treatment was by Mommsen, and first published in 1863. This marks the point at which the "res publica restituta" was "restored" to modern scholarship, and has a much better claim than 13 January, 27 B.C. to be the birthday of that conception, as now applied to Augustus. Mommsen stressed both its novelty to scholarship ("von den Neueren nicht erkannt") and his conviction that the sources confirmed it ("Es ist . . . mit Bestimmtheit nachzuweisen") as the official formula of 13 January, 27 ("die Reihe von Verfügungen . . . officiell aufgefasst ward als . . . die Rückkehr zu dem Verfassungsmässigen althergebrachten republikanischen Regiment") (*Abh. Berlin*, 1863, p. 417 = *Ges. Schr.* I, 1905, p. 478). So convinced was Mommsen of the unity of the evidence that he took it as obvious that Ovid, *Fasti* 1, 589 should be emended to read "res publica" (*CIL* I¹, 1863, p. 384). In 1883 he retracted this (*RGDA*², p. 147), and also recognised the inappropriateness of the restoration of "rem publicam" to the *fasti Praenestini* (ibid., p. 151, "causam . . . si quidem vere significavit fuisse provinciarum restitutionem"). So far as I can see, moreover, he did not make a habit of using the cliché "res publica restituta" to short-circuit the actual evidence (even when restored to fit), in spite of his original conviction. The melancholy conclusion must be that while Mommsen himself retreated somewhat from his first position, most other people were happy to settle for it without further question. Mommsen omitted to mention his doubts at the right place in *CIL* I², 1893 (see further my discussion of the *fasti Praenestini* on p. 296).

4. CIL VI, 1033, erected in A.D. 203, but apparently incorporating a *s.c.* of 195 in honour of the defeat of Didius Julianus or Pescennius Niger. Modern discussions agree on this civil war allusion, but assume that "ob rem publicam restitutam" is an established slogan that requires no explanation. In fact this may be its first occurrence in official propaganda, and it deserves closer inspection by Severan specialists in any case. See A. Birley, *Septimius Severus, the African Emperor*, 1971, p. 223; P. Brilliant, *The Arch of Septimius Severus* (= *Mem. Am. Ac. Rome* 29), 1967, p. 95; H. U. Instinsky, *Klio* 35, 1942, p. 216.

5. This review of the evidence is concentrated on Augustan usage, and is designed simply to clarify the issues relating to the two inscriptions to be examined. I have made no attempt to relate my suggestions to the very extensive discussions of the meaning of *res publica*, for which a good guide exists in W. Suerbaum, *Vom Antiken zum Frühmittelalterlichen Staatsbegriff*, 1961. He notes (p. 85) the lack of a proper investigation of the phrase "rem publicam restituere," and draws attention to its surprising frequency in the later Empire. So far as I can see, its earliest regular use (in the modern sense) in historical work is in the SHA, which, in the present state of opinion on that august history, will no doubt do more to encourage scepticism than anything else I can say!

6. *Insc. Syr.* III 1, 1950, no. 718, II 15.

7. German is forced to choose between these senses, and speak either of a "Rückgabe" or of a "Wiederherstellung." But the distinction is still not taken seriously. F. Bömer, on Ov. *Fast.* 1.590, says it means both at once. Grenade, p. 150, denies the importance of the distinction. But Augustus himself is alleged to have been playing with words, and my contention is that a careful observance both of what he did say and of what he would have had to say to convey the meaning usually attributed to him puts his political stance in a very different light from that posited by the façade theory.

8. R. M. Ogilvie, in his commentary on Livy, thinks "restitutam credebant rem publicam" may be "a contemporary echo for Augustan readers," but if so it could only confirm the non-constitutional force of the supposed slogan.

9. Contrast the entry for 2 Sept., which has not only "Augustus" but "apud Actium vicit," the prosaic note of the chronographer for an event which must have been celebrated at the time in as colourful a formula as that for Alexandria.

10. For Verrius Flaccus see Mommsen's introduction to the *fasti Praenestini* in *CIL* I.

11. The distinctive character of the crown was not lost sight of in its use in the enlarged Caesarian sense. See Polybius 6.39.6, 7; Plin. *NH* 16. 2.7-5.14, 22. 4.6-6.13; Gell. *NA* 5.6. 11-15.

12. As was proposed in the senate by L. Gellius for Cicero (*In Pis.* 3.6). The coins of both Brutus and Sextus Pompeius also attest its use in a wider sense (cf. A. Alföldi, "Die Geburt der kaiserlichen Bildersymbolik," *Mus Helv.* 9, 1952, pp. 219f.). Octavian, however, had already (13 Sept., 30) received the grass crown, the proper one for saving a whole city. The use of the two crowns for Caesar on a related pair of statues (Dio 44, 4.5) shows that a distinction was preserved; for details see S. Weinstock, *Divus Julius*, 1971, pp. 148-52 (grass), 163-7 (oak). In Augustus' case, however, the oak crown was coupled with the laurels, not with the grass crown, though the latter reappears in 2 B.C. (Plin. *NH* 22. 6.13).

13. The phrase "quo pro merito meo" (*RG* 34.2) immediately following the reference to the transfer of the commonwealth from Octavian's control no more ties the sense of the oak crown to that formula than it does the name Augustus, the laurels and the shield. *RG* 34.1 covers much more ground than the transfer, and that act in any case is lifted out of its strict context, as will be explained below.

14. Ovid (*Trist.* 3. 1.35-6) pretends to mistake the crown for the emblem of Jupiter. See also *RE* s.v. "corona," and (mainly for post-Augustan developments) K. Baus, *Der Kranz in Antike und Christentum*, 1940, pp. 117, 126, 130, 132, 147, 150, 181.

15. App. 2. 106, Dio 44. 5, Val. Max. 2. 8.7. The last may even imply that this association goes back beyond Caesar. But in Cicero's case it was certainly not proposed in order to mark his clemency. I conjecture that Sulla may have adopted it as an alternative to the use of laurel after victory in civil war, and that Caesar was responsible for developing it as a symbol of clemency in particular.

16. I accept the arguments of F. E. Adcock, *CQ* 45, 1951, pp. 130 ff., who explains the double dating of *RG* 34.1 in terms of this crisis; "potitus rerum omnium" then refers to the acquiescence of the community in Octavian's use of his consulship to take full control in 28, while the transfer is simply the return to the normal limits of consular action in 27 B.C.

17. C. M. Kraay, "The coinage of Vindex and Galba, A.D. 68, and the continuity of the Augustan principate," *NC* 9, 1949, pp. 129-49, esp. p. 147. See also now H. W. Ritter, "Adlocutio und Corona Civica unter Caligula und Tiberius," *JNG* 21, 1971, pp. 81-96, esp. p. 85.

18. For further details see Mommsen, *RGDA*², p. 150, and F.

Bömer on Ov. *Fast.* 3.137.

19. Presumably Mommsen had in mind an antiquarian note, such as I suggest below. There is no known Lutatius who could have been linked with the honours of 27 B.C., though it is intriguing that Q. Lutatius Cerco, quaestor of 90 B.C., minted denarii in honour of C. Catulus' victory at the Aegates Insulae (in 241), showing a war-ship with oak crown. The only two Lutatii recorded in *PIR* come from Praeneste, which may explain Verrius' interest in the historian. But Mommsen was misled. The change was one of two false improvements to these fragments offered in *CIL* I^2. The text I print above is that of *CIL* I^1, as now confirmed by A. E. and J. S. Gordon, *Album of Dated Latin Inscriptions*, I, 1958, 36, and by A. Degrassi, *Insc. Italiae* XIII, 2, 1963, pp. 112-3. They are also responsible for the putative first line, omitted by Mommsen. In the version of our three lines offered below I have also adopted two changes from them: "querc[ea" instead of Mommsen's "quern[a," and "rest[it]u[i." instead of Mommsen's "rest[i]tui[." T. W. Hillard (n. 23 below) doubts even the first "t," and suggests "res[p]u[blica," but the Gordons' squeeze and Degrassi's drawing both show a little more space than this would have needed.

20. Although Degrassi notes the inappropriateness of "[rem publicam]" and the lack of a reference to the laurels (*II* XIII, 2, p. 397), neither he nor the Gordons question the correctness of Mommsen's reconstruction. Its power to attract its own evidence (n. 3 above) has not diminished. The text of Tac. *Ann.* 1.9.5 can now be cited as "non regno tamen neque dictatura, sed principis nomine *restitutam* rem publicam" (Géza Alföldy, "Die Ablehnung der Diktatur durch Augustus," *Gymnasium* 79, 1972, p. 1 [italics mine]), a gratuitous change for which no authority is given, and which simply destroys the point of what Tacitus is saying. A more prudent response to Mommsen's spell is that of R. Syme, *Tacitus*, 1958, p. 409, n. 7: "Tacitus deliberately refuses in this passage [*Ann.* 1.2.1] to mention the much vaunted "Restoration of the Republic" in 28 and 27." H. Bengtson, *Grundriss der Römischen Geschichte*, 1967, p. 254, apparently relies upon Vell. Pat. 2. 89.4 for the claim that the senate justified the oak crown with the words, "quod priscam illam et antiquam formam restituit," a formula which, stripped even of explicit reference to the "res publica," can hardly have any meaning at all apart from Mommsen's theory.

21. Degrassi, p. 396, for details on Jupiter Stator. If we assume "puta[nt" or "puta[tur" we can easily envisage a comment of the sort Verrius Flaccus frequently gives (e.g. under 24 March), with "id est" introducing the final remark. See 23 April for a change of subject in mid-line.

22. My formula is based upon *RG* 34.2, preferring Mommsen's "vincti" to the usual "vestiti." The word is not preserved (apart from the initial letter in the Latin text and the passive ending of the Greek text). Mommsen was not willing to press "vincti" against the opinions of others. I choose it simply because it enables us to read "al[." as part of the verb "alligare." Otherwise I have not attempted to fit a reconstruction to the surviving fragments (it should be noted that the second "n" of "non[." is obscure), my point being simply to raise the possibility of a link between the two parts of the entry for 13 January.

23. The slab which contained January is apparently nowhere complete to its full width (though the Gordons [p. 50] seem to assume this), and Mommsen appears to have allowed himself some latitude in fixing its margin. Mr. and Mrs. T. W. Hillard went to much trouble to check it for me, but due to current restoration work at the baths of Diocletian the inscription had to be examined through a dust-covered plastic sheet (they rightly declined the generous offer of Signorina Lissi of the Museo Nazionale Romano to have this removed).

24. For the form of words see Frontinus, *De aqu.* 2. 100 ff., esp. 125. The suggestion is based upon the material in the *RG* (for "figeretur," e.g., see *RG* 34.2) together with the considerations advanced above. The use of Agrippa's name is of course a sheer guess, but someone close to Octavian had to do it: Munatius Plancus was to move the name "Augustus" three days later.

25. Text as given by M. Durry, *Éloge funèbre d'une matrone romaine*, 1950, who substantially follows Mommsen.

26. I am grateful to the Prince Torlonia for allowing me to inspect the stone in the Villa Albani, and to Signorina Fazzari of the British School in Rome for helping both Mr. Hillard and me with enquiries. Durry had not been able to check the text to his satisfaction due to poor light.

Editor's Afterword

It need hardly be said that this volume would never have come into being without the support, and active assistance of a great number of Dr. Salmon's friends, colleagues and former students, who are too many to name. Some, however, deserve special mention. The first person I approached about this project was Dr. J. H. Trueman, Dean of Humanities Studies at McMaster University, and his response was immediately helpful and constructive. Professor Will Ready, McMaster University Librarian, to whom I turned next, promised all the support he could muster, and suggested that I should form a dyarchy with his assistant, Miss Jean Montgomery, to raise the funds necessary for this volume. It proved a brilliant idea. I must record here that, without Miss Montgomery's help, and her zeal and devotion, this *Festschrift* would have remained simply a worthy idea which never reached fruition.

Others, too, should be mentioned. Professor Ezio Cappadocia, chairman of the McMaster University history department, was generous with his help and encouragement. Dr. A. G. McKay, then Dean of Humanities, whom I approached to draw up Dr. Salmon's bibliography, responded enthusiastically. I owe greater thanks than I can express to Professor Alan Samuel of the University of Toronto, who has seen this volume through the press, and has been an understanding publisher who has supported this project from the beginning. Finally, I must acknowledge here that the initial idea of this *Festschrift* was not mine, but my wife's, and hence I can claim credit only for constructive plagiarism.

The donors who gave money to finance this volume are listed below. All funds came from private sources, and I am very grateful to those individuals who responded generously to my appeals.

†A. G. O. Bahr, *Personnel Services, McMaster University*

M. B. Bates, *Assistant to the President, McMaster University (ret.)*

G. H. Blumenauer, *Chairman of the Board, and President, Otis Elevator Company, Ltd., Hamilton*

Dr. A. N. Bourns, *President and Vice-Chancellor, McMaster University*

Mr. and Mrs. Alex Brown, *Dean of the Faculty, Conestoga College of Applied Arts and Technology*

Mrs. V. R. Burville, *Southmount Secondary School, Hamilton*

Dr. Ezio Cappadocia, *Chairman, Department of History, McMaster University*

H. G. Chappell, Esq., Q.C., *Chappell, Walsh and Davidson, Toronto*

R. W. Cooper, *President, Cooper Construction Company (Eastern) Ltd., Hamilton*

F. F. Dalley, *Ancaster, Ont.*

Dorothy Davidson, *Associate Librarian, Arts, McMaster University*

H. C. Dixon, *Clarkson, Gordon and Company, Hamilton*

Dr. J. A. S. Evans, *Professor of Classics, University of British Columbia*

Dr. J. R. Evans, *President, University of Toronto*

T. W. D. Farmer, *Director of Information and Development, McMaster University*

C. P. Fell, *Matthews and Company, Ltd., Toronto*

Dr. G. S. French, *President and Vice-Chancellor, Victoria University, University of Toronto, and Professor of History, McMaster University*

D. K. Frid, *President, Frid Construction Company, Ltd., Hamilton*

Dr. R. P. Graham, *Dean of Science Studies, Professor of Chemistry, McMaster University*

H. F. Guite, *Professor of Classics, McMaster University*

D. M. Hedden, *Vice-President (Administration), McMaster University*

Dr. W. F. Hellmuth, *Vice-President (Arts), and Professor of Economics, McMaster University*

Dr. C. M. Johnston, *Professor of History, McMaster University*

†R. C. Labarge, *(formerly) Deputy Minister of National Revenue, Ottawa*

Dr. J. F. Leddy, *President, University of Windsor*

Dr. A. A. Lee, *Vice-President (Academic), McMaster University*

H. H. Levy, *Hamilton*

Dr. Argue Martin, Q.C., *Martin and Martin, Hamilton*

W. J. McCallion, *Dean of the School of Adult Education, and Professor of Mathematics, McMaster University*

Dr. H. W. McCready, *Professor of History, McMaster University*

Dr. M. F. McGregor, *Professor, and Head, Department of Classics, University of British Columbia*

Dr. R. C. McIvor, *Professor of Economics, McMaster University*

Dr. A. G. McKay, *Professor of Classics, McMaster University*

J. A. McKeen, *Assistant to the Vice-President (Arts), McMaster University*

McMaster University Professional Librarians' Association

Marget Meikleham, *Canadian Baptist Archives, McMaster University (ret.)*

Jean Montgomery, *Assistant to the Librarian, McMaster University*

T. E. Nichols, *Dundas, Ont.*

Dr. A. W. Patrick, *Professor of Romance Languages, Mc-Master University*

Dr. G. M. Paul, *Professor of Classics, McMaster University*

Dr. H. E. Petch, *Vice-President (Academic), The University of Waterloo*

W. P. Pigott, *President, Pigott Construction Company, Ltd., Hamilton*

Dr. M. A. Preston, *Professor of Physics and Applied Mathematics, McMaster University; Executive Vice-Chairman, Advisory Committee on Academic Planning, Ontario Council of Graduate Studies, Council of Ontario Universities, Toronto*

W. B. Ready, *University Librarian and Professor of Bibliography, McMaster University*

W. J. W. Reid, *Burlington, Ont.*

V. W. Scully, *Chairman of the Executive Committee of the Board, The Steel Company of Canada, Ltd., Toronto*

Dr. D. M. Shepherd, *Professor of Classics, McMaster University*

F. H. Sherman, *President and Chief Executive Officer, Dominion Foundries and Steel, Hamilton*

Dr. N. Shrive, *Chairman, Department of English, McMaster University*

R. B. Taylor, *Vice-President and Treasurer, The Steel Company of Canada, Ltd., Toronto*

Dr. H. G. Thode, *President (ret.) and Professor of Chemistry, McMaster University*

Dr. and Mrs. H. L. Tracy, *Professor of Classics (ret.) University of Guelph*

Dr. J. H. Trueman, *Dean of Humanities Studies and Professor of History, McMaster University*

Mary White, *Professor, Graduate Department of Classical Studies, The University of Toronto*

W. P. Wilder, *Chairman and Chief Executive Officer, Gas Arctic – North West Project Study Group, Toronto*

Dr. R. M. Wiles, *Professor of English, McMaster University (ret.)*

Mr. and Mrs. A. V. Young, *Hamilton*
W. H. Young, *President and General Manager, The Hamilton Group, Hamilton*
Manuel Zack, *Assistant to the President, McMaster University*

Finally, Togo, though we are separated now by half a continent, I am happy to be able to present this volume to you, in memory of a decade as your colleague, when we shared some pleasures and vicissitudes together.

The University of British Columbia   *J. A. S. Evans*